MEDIA, FEMINISM, CULTURAL STUDIES

*Liv Tyler: Star In Ascendance*
by Thomas A. Christie

*John Hughes and Eighties Cinema*
by Thomas A. Christie

*The Cinema of Richard Linklater*
by Thomas A. Christie

*The Christmas Movie Book*
by Thomas A. Christie

*The Cinema of Hayao Miyazaki*
by Jeremy Mark Robinson

*The Sacred Cinema of Andrei Tarkovsky*
by Jeremy Mark Robinson

*Jean-Luc Godard: The Passion of Cinema / Le Passion de Cinéma*
by Jeremy Mark Robinson

*Julia Kristeva: Art, Love, Melancholy, Philosophy, Semiotics*
by Kelly Ives

*Luce Irigaray: Lips, Kissing, and the Politics of Sexual Difference*
by Kelly Ives

*Helene Cixous I Love You: The* Jouissance *of Writing*
by Kelly Ives

*Stepping Forward: Essays, Lectures and Interviews*
by Wolfgang Iser

*Andrea Dworkin*
by Jeremy Mark Robinson

*Wild Zones: Pornography, Art and Feminism*
by Kelly Ives

*'Cosmo Woman': The World of Women's Magazines*
by Oliver Whitehorne

*Cixous, Irigaray, Kristeva: The Jouissance of French Feminism*
by Kelly Ives

*Sex in Art: Pornography and Pleasure in Painting and Sculpture*
by Cassidy Hughes

*The Erotic Object: Sexuality in Sculpture*
*From Prehistory to the Present Day*
by Susan Quinnell

*Women in Pop Music*
by Helen Challis

*Feminism and Shakespeare*
by B.D. Barnacle


FORTHCOMING CINEMA BOOKS

*Akira: The Movie and the Manga*
*Ghost In the Shell*
*Legend of the Overfiend*
*Fullmetal Alchemist*
*The Pirates of the Caribbean Movies*
*The Twilight Saga*
*The Harry Potter Movies*

# MEL BROOKS
## GENIUS AND LOVING IT!

# MEL BROOKS
## GENIUS AND LOVING IT!

Freedom and Liberation
In the Cinema of Mel Brooks

*Thomas A. Christie*

CRESCENT MOON

First edition 2015.
© Thomas A. Christie 2015.

Printed and bound in the U.S.A.
Set in Book Antiqua 10 on 14pt and Gill Sans.
Designed by Radiance Graphics.

The right of Thomas A. Christie to be identified as the author of this book has been asserted generally in accordance with sections 77 and 78 of the Copyright, Designs and Patents Act 1988.

All rights reserved. No part of this book may be reprinted or reproduced, stored in a retrieval system, or transmitted, in any form or by any means, electronic, mechanical, photocopying, recording or otherwise, without permission from the publisher.

Every effort has been made to contact copyright owners of the illustrations. No copyright infringement is intended. We welcome enquiries about any copyright issues for future editions of this book.

*British Library Cataloguing in Publication data available for this title.*

*ISBN-13 9781861715104 (Pbk)*
*ISBN-13 9781861715203 (Hbk)*

*Crescent Moon Publishing*
*P.O. Box 1312*
*Maidstone, Kent*
*ME14 5XU, Great Britain*
*www.crmoon.com*

# CONTENTS

Acknowledgements ❖ 9
Introduction ❖ 17

1   *The Producers* (1968) ❖ 32
2   *The Twelve Chairs* (1970) ❖ 54
3   *Blazing Saddles* (1974) ❖ 81
4   *Young Frankenstein* (1974) ❖ 111
5   *Silent Movie* (1976) ❖ 150
6   *High Anxiety* (1977) ❖ 173
7   *History of the World: Part I* (1981) ❖ 198
8   *Spaceballs* (1987) ❖ 232
9   *Life Stinks* (1991) ❖ 261
10  *Robin Hood: Men in Tights* (1993) ❖ 297
11  *Dracula: Dead and Loving It* (1995) ❖ 319

Conclusion ❖ 345
Chronological Filmography ❖ 357
Statistical Data and Representative Critical Opinion ❖ 368
Recommended Further Reading ❖ 381
Select Bibliography ❖ 383

# ACKNOWLEDGEMENTS

I would like to thank each of the following people for their much-appreciated fellowship and support while I was researching and writing this book:

David M. Addison, Douglas J. Allen, Dr Colin M. Barron, Eddy and Dorothy Bryan, Julie Christie, Michael Donnelly, Sarah Fletcher, James Geekie, Denham and Stella Hardwick, Dr Elspeth King, Ivy Lannon, Rachael J. McClure, Michael McGinnes, Ian and Anne McNeish, Mary Melville, Alex and Kelley Tucker, and Professor Rory Watson.

Many thanks to Berwick-upon-Tweed Library and Morpeth Film Library for their kind assistance with sourcing many of the research materials for this book.

Also, a sincere word of gratitude to the owners of the *Brookslyn* website (*www.brookslyn.com*) for their expertly-curated, publicly-available library of Mel Brooks interviews from the mid-sixties up to the present day.

Special thanks to Jeremy Mark Robinson of Crescent Moon Publishing for his suggestions as well as his enthusiasm for the project.

This book is dedicated to my friends and mentors
Mr David Addison and Mr James Geekie
'A journey of a thousand miles begins with a single step.'

"Oh, I'm not a true genius. I'm a near genius.
I would say I'm a short genius.
I'd rather be tall and normal than a short genius."

Mel Brooks

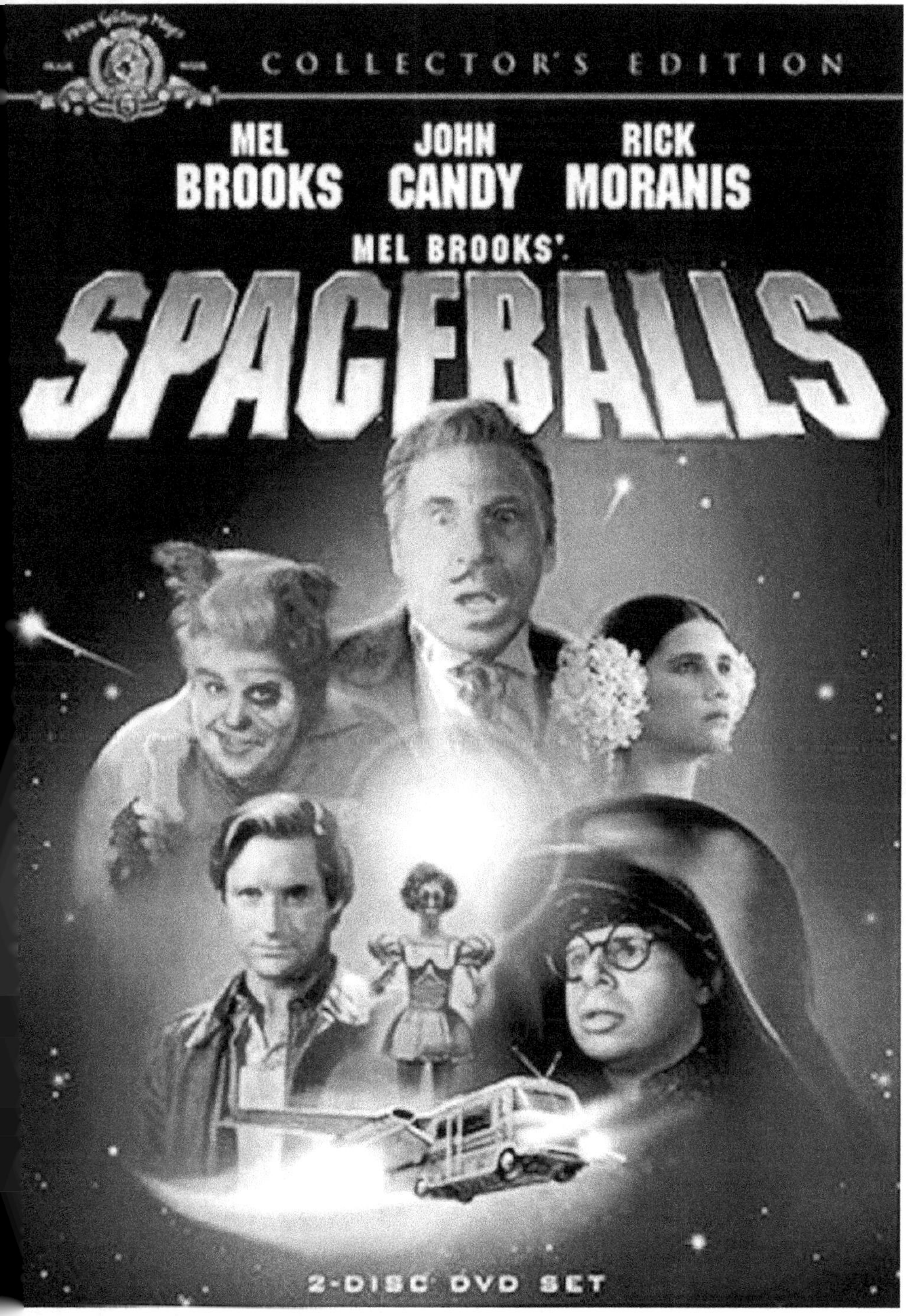
COLLECTOR'S EDITION
MEL BROOKS
JOHN CANDY
RICK MORANIS
MEL BROOKS'
SPACEBALLS
2-DISC DVD SET

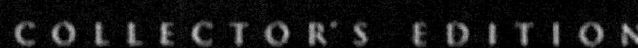

# INTRODUCTION

THERE ARE FEW things quite so subjective as comedy, and few directors whose work has proven to be as divisive over the years as that of Mel Brooks. Beloved by his fans and equally praised and derided by the critics at various points throughout his long career, Brooks is a creative polymath, a comic talent to be reckoned with – influential, fearless and totally unafraid of his detractors. Yet whether you admire his work or not, one thing remains absolutely certain: this larger-than-life character is a very difficult man to ignore.

Born Melvin James Kaminsky on 28 June 1926, the young Brooks's quick wit was readily apparent from an early age. He was studying psychology at Brooklyn College when he was drafted into the United States Army during the closing years of the Second World War. Serving as a Corporal from 1944, Brooks saw active service in Europe and witnessed first-hand the brutal atrocities of warfare – an experience which would later, often subtly, inform a number of motion pictures throughout his directorial career. After the conflict had ended, Brooks began performing to acclaim on the Borscht Belt, both as a stand-up comedian and as a musician (proving to be an accomplished pianist and drummer). However, from the late 1940s onwards he also became active as a comedy writer for television, working alongside new and established comic talent such as Sid Caesar, Neil Simon, Mel Tolkin, Larry Gelbart and Neil Simon. It was his work as part of the writing teams on shows such as *The Admiral Broadway Review* (1949), *Your Show of Shows* (1950-54) and *Caesar's Hour* (1954-57) which began to establish him as a major showbusiness talent.

The 1960s were to cement Brooks's reputation both as a writer and performer. The decade was to see the emergence of his now-famous '2000 Year Old Man' double-act with Carl Reiner, a routine which rapidly evolved from improvised sketches in the late fifties into well-received television sketches, eventually being adapted into full-length vinyl albums. Thanks to Brooks and Reiner's continual experimentation with the act, the concept endured in different formats (such as animated adaptations and reunion specials) for several decades. Brooks wrote the book for *All American*, a Tony-nominated Broadway musical with lyrics by Lee Adams which debuted in 1962, and provided the distinctive voice-over for Ernest Pintoff's *The Critic* (1963), a dryly satirical short film which lampooned the lofty pretensions of art criticism. Devised by Brooks and Pintoff, the feature would go on to win an Academy Award in the category of Short Animated Film.

Brooks's public profile continued to rise as the sixties progressed. In 1964 he married the actress and creative talent Anne Bancroft (Anna Maria Louisa Italiano) (1931-2005), beginning one of the best-known and longest-running of Hollywood marriages. Notably, he was also heavily involved in the concept and production of the pilot episode of Emmy Award-winning television series *Get Smart* (1965-70), spoofing the popular spy franchises of the time with great aplomb. However, it is for his career as a cinematic director that Brooks has become best remembered, and with the arrival of *The Producers* in 1968 – a film which would win him the Academy Award for Best Original Screenplay – he was to commence one of the most unique and contentious filmographies in twentieth century American comedy cinema.

Respected by many academics, commentators and movie buffs around the world, Brooks's thematically-layered films have been the subject of numerous studies over the years. These have included Maurice Yacowar's ground-breaking analysis of his comedic talents in *The Comic Art of Mel Brooks* (1982), Robert Alan Crick's comprehensive study of his directorial output in *The Big Screen Comedies of Mel Brooks* (2002), and Alex Symons's influential examination of the relevance and endurance of Brooks's career, *Mel Brooks in the Cultural Industries* (2012). In past decades there have been numerous papers and articles published on the subject of Brooks's status as the definitive maestro of big-screen bad taste, the influence of his Jewish cultural heritage on his film-making, his contribution to the history of the cinematic spoof, and a great many other aspects of his directorial career besides.

There is one aspect of Brooks's film-making which is often neglected, however: his ardent championship of liberty. Brooks is a man who earnestly and vigorously defends freedom in all of its forms, whether creative, personal, social, cultural or political. All of his films, in one way or another, bear witness to this passionate advocacy of independence and self-determination, from the dark satire of totalitarianism in *The Twelve Chairs* (1970) to his unyielding decimation of bigoted racist attitudes throughout *Blazing Saddles* (1974). Brooks's endorsement of individual liberty – his full-throated celebration of personal autonomy and unchecked artistic creativity – is a major factor in his lasting popularity with film audiences; his films may quite self-consciously be far removed from high art, but similarly they contain many subtle motifs which are often at their most effective when partially obscured by the chaotic action of his madcap narratives. As Neil Sinyard explains in *The Films of Mel Brooks* (1988), part of this film-maker's enduring recognition amongst audiences around the world lies precisely in his lack of pretence and affectation; his movies are accessible, but repeatedly make points which are as universal as they are optimistic:

> Basically Brooks has never been a dramatist: he has always been first and foremost a clown. He has never sought the pathos or the philo-sophizing of a Chaplin or a Woody Allen; has never attempted to emulate the balletic grace of a Keaton or the dazzling dexterity with words of a Groucho Marx. He rarely makes you smile; the response is either the groan or the guffaw. Yet his relentless gaiety comes from a passionate affirmation of life. The implicit message of some comed-ians is: Enjoy yourself – it's later than you think. Brooks' message is: Enjoy yourself – it's *better* than you think.[1]

Brooks is a director who displays genuine affection for his craft, and for the world of entertainment in general – film-making, music, literature and especially theatre are repeatedly referenced throughout his movies. Yet similarly he is not oblivious to the darker side of the industry, where clashing egos and profit motive obscures or subverts the clarity of the creative process; films such as *The Producers* (1968) and *Silent Movie* (1976) defend the need for creative liberty while also adeptly sending up the behind-the-scenes melange of deviousness and inventiveness which so often drives the trade. In their book *Mel Brooks and the Spoof Movie* (1982), Nick Smurthwaite and Paul Gelder emphasise the fact that although Brooks may have undeniable fondness for cinema in particular, he similarly proves that he considers no genre or artistic form to be beyond the reach of lampoonery: 'The Mel Brooks School of Spoof [...] is dedicated to the notion that no movie myth is too sacred to be spared a little parody – or in Mel Brooks's case, a lot of parody'.[2]

Brooks is one of the entertainment world's true survivors. Just as his creative career appeared to be nearing its conclusion, his triumphant return to Broadway with a musical stage adaptation of *The Producers* in 2001 saw him sweeping an armful of plaudits from distinguished bodies such as the Tony Awards, Grammy Awards and the Laurence Olivier Awards. It was a comeback so significant – and unexpected – that it rocked the entertainment world, and cemented his reputation as a giant of the industry; in 2010 he was awarded the supreme recognition of his peers in the form of a star on the Hollywood Walk of Fame, while he received the similarly-prestigious American Film Institute Lifetime Achievement Award in June 2013. Alex Symons has argued that Brooks has become 'a specialist in adaptation, [...] a long-term survivor in the cultural industries, and to some degree, a significant figure within the historical development of the multimedia strategies that are common with artists today',[3] and certainly it would be difficult to argue against this assertion when one considers Brooks's numerous Broadway productions, occasional forays into recording artistry, and more recently his experimentation with animation in the form of *Spaceballs: The Animated Series* (2008), the short-lived television cartoon spin-off based upon his 1980s parody of science fiction (a series which was itself to spoof various different nodes of entertainment such as popular video games).

With his wild, carnivalesque embrace of the outlandish and the unpredictable, Brooks's work has an irresistibly appealing quality that has continued to attract new generations of audiences across the world, and which has led to his films being reissued on successive formats of home entertainment system including DVD and Blu-Ray. There is a sense of unreserved emancipation about a Brooks screenplay which leaves viewers with the inescapable sense that just about anything may happen in the unfolding ninety minutes... and, true to form, in most cases just about anything does. As Maurice Yacowar has astutely observed, 'with his art of energy, openness and exuberance, Brooks values freedom more than discipline, outburst more than restraint, and emotion more than abstemious craft. Energy and present outweigh control and the future. Wild, even vulgar, valour is the better part of discretion'.4 But as we will see, Brooks aims higher than simply endeavouring to sweep his audience away into the realms of the eccentric and the ridiculous. Rather, he desires to make them value the potential of their lives, to embrace the possibilities which are all too often ignored, and to realise that there is no point in being a responsible adult if that means that we can't sometimes act the fool.

However, Brooks's cinematic output was not universally popular with the critical community, and many of even his most audience-pleasing features were pilloried by reviewers at their time of release. Especially in the case of his latter movies, the growing derision of commentators threatened to mar the critical reputation of a directorial career which had earned him industry awards alongside a dedicated army of fans, though the light of retrospective opinion – and the rise of the Internet, allowing new analytical voices to emerge – has certainly rehabilitated several of these works in the opinion of many. To this end, this study will examine the contemporary critical reception of Brooks's films as well as more recent examinations of his work by modern writers.

If Brooks's films throughout the eighties and nineties were generally received less favourably by commentators, it may be in large part due to the high expectations of those who had sampled his earlier, pioneering efforts in the field, when the originality of his early satires and (most especially) his ground-breaking spoofs were exhibiting a truly iconoclastic effect on audience expectations. Yet the later films had distinct thematic concerns of their own, and to disregard them is to ignore some compelling commentary on Brooks's part which informs greater understanding of his overall artistic intentions. Robert Alan Crick has explained that, as is the case with all comedy, presenting subjective critical opinion on Brooks's directorial canon can be an illusive proposition:

> [Brooks's films] defy analysis because, to Brooks lovers' never-ending frustration, they [...] have an unsettling tendency to turn out so much like the jokes that comprise them: peculiarly hit-and-miss endeavours, one minute shoot-the-moon brilliant, the next falling so far short of his own best work the disappointment as fans leave the theater hangs heavy in the popcorn-scented air.[5]

This book discusses all eleven of the films which Brooks helmed throughout the course of his long directorial career, from *The Producers* in 1968 through to *Dracula: Dead and Loving It* in 1995. It does not include discussion of films in which Brooks appeared as a performer but did not hold directorial duties (such as James Frawley's *The Muppet Movie*, 1979), or features which he produced but did not write or direct (for instance, Alan Johnson's *To Be or Not to Be*, 1983). His prolific career as a television performer is similarly not examined in detail. Tracing his career-long preoccupation with freedom and liberation, each chapter will explore the ways in which Brooks celebrates the autonomy and independence of his characters, advocates the need for free will and lack of restriction on individual expression, and attacks any force which stands in opposition to these aims – whatever its nature or composition. It is a critical journey which will involve visits to Revolutionary Paris and the Wild West, Transylvania by way of Sherwood Forest, and will move from the bright lights of Broadway to the darkest depths of outer space. But as we will see, while a Mel Brooks film may offer up any combination of flatulent cowboys, diminutive dark lords, song-and-dance Hitlers or even merry men in tights, one thing it will never do is conform to expectation.

REFERENCES

1. Neil Sinyard, *The Films of Mel Brooks* (New York: Exeter Books, 1988), p. 94.
2. Nick Smurthwaite and Paul Gelder, *Mel Brooks and the Spoof Movie* (London: Proteus Books, 1982), pp. 5-7.
3. Alex Symons, *Mel Brooks in the Cultural Industries: Survival and Prolonged Adaptation* (Edinburgh: Edinburgh University Press, 2012), p. 185.
4. Maurice Yacowar, *The Comic Art of Mel Brooks* (London: W.H. Allen, 1982), p. 199.
5. Robert Alan Crick, *The Big Screen Comedies of Mel Brooks* (Jefferson: McFarland and Company, 2009) [2002], p. 1.

With Hitch (above)
With Jerry Lewis (on The Ladies' Man, 1961)

With Sid Caesar in 1967 (above)
With Carl Reiner (below. Photo: William Claxton,
courtesy of Demont Photo Management LLC)

Mel Brooks in 1981, top (photo: Pam Barkentin Blackburn).
With Madeline Kahn in 1974, above (photo: Steven Schapiro).

Some of Mel Brooks's other films -
The Muppet Movie (above) and To Be Or
Not To Be (over).

Mel Brooks on set (this page and over)

Blazing Saddles and Spaceballs

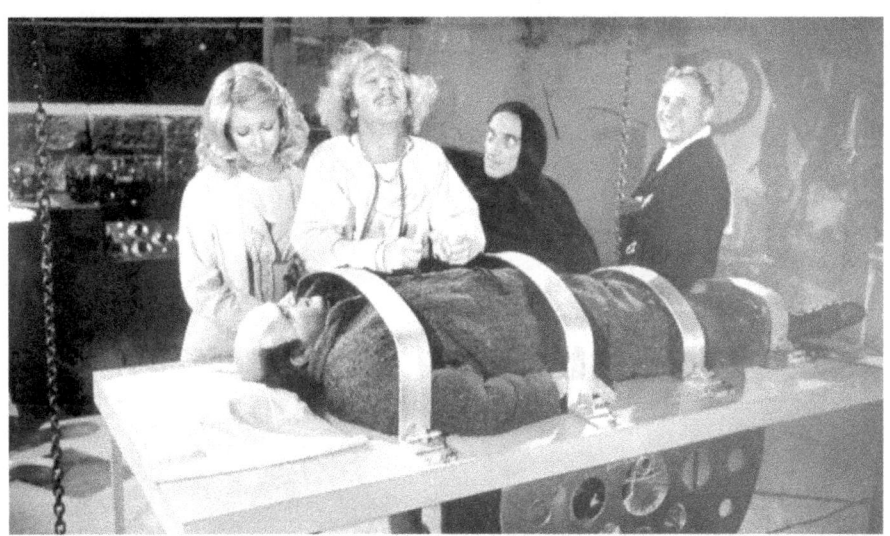

Young Frankenstein
(above from L.A. Times)

# 1

# THE PRODUCERS (1968)

IT SEEMS ALMOST ironic that in spite of his long-running career, it is Mel Brooks's directorial debut which has proven – in recent years at least – to have been his most enduring and instantly-recognisable cinematic success. In many ways this is a surprise, for *The Producers* was not a huge commercial triumph at the time of its release and seemed destined to become a cult feature even from day one, dividing critics at the same time as it won over a generation of fans who were immediately awed by Brooks's sheer creative audacity. However, the meteoric success of Brooks's later musical stage adaptation (and its subsequent remake for the big screen) has now firmly cemented this seminal film into popular culture in such a way that it may very well now have overtaken *Blazing Saddles* and *Young Frankenstein* as the definitive Mel Brooks film in the view of many filmgoers.

There is little doubt that *The Producers* has retained its ability to garner laughs in spite of its initial shock value having long since eroded over the course of passing decades. The endearingly daft but naggingly plausible central premise, the appealingly larger-than-life central performances and the oddly affecting morality tale played out by the main characters all combine to create a feature which demands (and endlessly rewards) repeated viewing. However, *The Producers* is also a film which conceals tangible anger beneath its surface. Brooks pursues clearly-demarcated objectives throughout the narrative regarding the ephemeral nature of fame, the creative compromises wrought by commercialism... and, above all else, he champions a universal need for individual freedom from the constraints of tyranny, however these personal limitations may manifest themselves.

Max Bialystock (Zero Mostel), a down-on-his-luck New York theatrical producer, has hit rock bottom. Barely able to pay the rent on his dilapidated offices, he has resorted to seducing elderly ladies in order to shamelessly con them into funding his increasingly unsuccessful stage productions. However, the arrival of a neurotic young accountant, Leo Bloom (Gene Wilder), brings the promise of a dramatic turnaround of fortune. Noticing a minor discrepancy in Bialystock's book-keeping, whereby he has raised more money to stage a play than was ultimately required (due to the play having failed before the funds were actually needed), Bloom casually remarks that if someone were to raise a large amount of money to produce a play which was guaranteed to close early, they could technically make more money with a flop than they could with a smash hit. And yet, if the play were to become a success then the fraud would immediately become obvious, as there would never be enough profits to pay off all the backers. The naïve Bloom is, of course, only positing a wild theory... but Bialystock immediately sees real potential in the plan. After all, if there's one area where Max has plenty of proven experience, it's the production of theatrical duds.

After successfully sweet-talking Bloom into helping him make the scheme a reality, Bialystock immediately sets to work overselling his new venture, racking up thousands of dollars in a charm offensive on every wealthy widow he can track down. Then, a mammoth search of the worst scripts the theatrical world has to offer eventually presents quite possibly the most distasteful play ever written: *Springtime for Hitler: A Gay Romp with Adolf and Eva at Berchtesgaden*. Bialystock and Bloom instantly track down the playwright, an unreformed and violently unstable former Nazi named Franz Liebkind (Kenneth Mars), who only agrees to his work appearing on Broadway when he has been assured that it will depict Adolf Hitler in a flattering light. The artistic team is then extended to include the most infamous theatrical director in town, Roger DeBris (Christopher Hewitt), a man totally convinced by his own creative genius but whose approach to drama is never knowingly burdened by good taste. Finally, Bialystock hits on the production's *coup de grace* when, after an open audition of woefully inept would-be Hitlers, he discovers Lorenzo St DuBois – better known to his friends as LSD (Dick Shawn) – a spaced-out hippy who is so stoned that he has managed to wander into the wrong audition. Bialystock immediately realises that he has found the perfect Hitler for his production, and gets LSD to sign up without delay.

The night of the premiere performance arrives, and Bialystock and Bloom are delighted when the audience is openly aghast at the show's opening song-and-dance number. Once they have triumphantly retired to the bar following the overture, however, LSD appears as Hitler and – having no memory of his lines – begins to improvise. The audience members immediately assume that the play is actually a farce, and begin to enjoy the depiction of a Third Reich populated by dazed, drug-addled lunatics. By the time *Springtime for Hitler* has concluded, the play is being hailed as a runaway success... much to the despair of Bialystock and Bloom, who must now desperately plan a way of avoiding prison. ('How could this happen?' bemoans Bialystock. 'I was so careful. I picked the wrong play, the wrong director, the wrong cast... where did I go right?')

A furious Liebkind arrives, incensed that Hitler has been treated as a figure of fun, and tries to murder the two producers... only for Bialystock to persuade him to blow up the theatre where the play is being held instead, reasoning that if the venue is destroyed then *Springtime for Hitler* will have to close irrespective of public opinion. However, Liebkind uses the wrong type of fuse, rapidly causing an explosion which brings the complicity of all three men to light. As the judge passes sentence after a court trial, Bialystock makes a heartfelt statement to the court that he has learned the hard way that his dishonest scheme was a mistake, and one which he has no intention of ever trying again. The film concludes with Bialystock, Bloom and Liebkind incarcerated in the state penitentiary... where they are already hard at work overselling a new play, *Prisoners of Love*, featuring their fellow inmates.

In the present day, it seems a fairly evident observation that when any production mocks Nazi Germany they are going after the safest of targets, precisely because they are assailing an historical entity that no reasonable person would ever defend. It is generally accepted that there is nothing good whatsoever to say about Nazism, a political movement which brought Europe to its knees, exposed countless innocents to unspeakable cruelty, and which led to the deaths of millions. For Brooks in the 1960s, however, a film which drew the main source of its levity from a concerted attack on the Nazis was a monumental creative risk, not least because the basis for that attack lay in a play-within-a-film which (superficially, at least) celebrated the kind of grotesque pageantry that typified fascist rallies of the 1930s. It raised the dangerous possibility of offending the sensibilities of audiences, many of whom would have remembered the war years all too vividly (and, like Brooks himself, may themselves have seen active military service during the conflict). Perhaps even worse, if Brooks's film had been perceived as trivialising the threat of Nazism as a result of its relentless barrage of ridicule, the response may have been even more hostile. As it was, however, his creative judgement proved to be entirely astute, and the result became movie history; as Jessica Hillman argues in her book *Echoes of the Holocaust on the American Musical Stage* (2012), the emergence of *The Producers* arrived at an opportune historical moment:

> Audiences generally accepted the film, despite its potentially shocking content. Brooks had his timing just right; many Americans were able to understand and then embrace the source of his humor. Public response to Brooks' movie mirrored the pivotal moment in the film where *Springtime for Hitler*'s first night audience initially reacts with open-mouthed shock and then hilarity.[1]

Perhaps unsurprisingly, Brooks faced an uphill struggle to get the film into production – not least given his own inexperience in a directorial role. He was openly discussing the project as early as 1966 when, in an feature which appeared in *Playboy* Magazine, he outlined a concept so audacious that the interviewers seemed unsure whether to take him seriously or not: 'It's going to be a play within a play, or a play within a film – I haven't decided yet. It's a romp with Adolf and Eva at Berchtesgaden. There was a whole nice side of Hitler. He was a good dancer – no one knows that. He loved a parakeet named Bob – no one knows that either. It's all brought out in the play.'[2] In truth, however, Brooks was entirely serious about the notion of parodying Hitler, and was determined to bring to life a narrative which would skewer

Nazism not through polemic, but via an unyielding onslaught of derision and outright contempt. It was his perceptible passion for the project which won over producer Sidney Glazier: 'Mel stood in front of my desk and did the movie. I was drinking coffee in a paper cup and I began to laugh. I began to choke. He did the movie from beginning to end. [...] And I said, I'll do it. I didn't know where the hell I was going to get the money, but I said I'll do it, I'll do it, and that's how it began'.3

Brooks employs within *The Producers* a parable for seeking our dreams and valuing our personal freedom. Nazism – indeed, totalitarianism of all kinds – stands diametrically opposed to the autonomy of individual expression, and therefore he shows that it must be opposed at all costs. No more is this evident than in the depiction of Franz Liebkind, a man trapped by his past who has become a self-made pariah in his present. Liebkind is so unhinged that he is in complete denial of the horrors wrought by Nazism, and repeatedly blames Allied propaganda for what he considers to be history's unfair depiction of Hitler: 'Churchill! With his cigars, with his brandy and his rotten painting. Rotten! Hitler... there was a painter. He could paint an entire apartment in one afternoon. Two coats!' In essence, Liebkind has detached himself not only from the unspeakable nature of Nazi war crimes (his own role in the conflict is never made clear), but largely from any kind of social reality – he seems unsure whether he wants to assimilate into American culture in any kind of meaningful way (he effortlessly alternates between singing 'Deutschland Über Alles' and 'I'm a Yankee Doodle Dandy' without a hint of irony), or retain the authentic trappings of his fascist tendencies; a wartime portait of Hitler hangs unabashedly on his apartment wall, and he is never apart from his battered military service helmet (now smeared with pigeon guano from his bird-keeping hobby) even at the gala premiere of the play. In a sense, he is a haunted man, though not by his actions during the war – rather, by the prospect of unanimous public repugnance towards Nazism, thus making him a prisoner of his own attitudes:

> BIALYSTOCK: Franz Liebkind?
> LIEBKIND: I was never a member of the Nazi Party! I'm not responsible! I only followed orders! Who are you? Why do you persecute me? My papers are in order. I love my adopted country! "O beautiful, for

spacious skies, for amber waves of..." WHAT DO YOU WANT?!

Liebkind's outsider status may explain part of his obsession with repairing Hitler's reputation in the public eye, a goal which any sane person would consider an impossibility but which Liebkind instead views as a challenge or even a kind of perverse moral purpose. Achieving such a goal would, from his own point of view at least, mollify the repulsion aimed towards his own unreconstructed ideology at the same time as 'clear[ing] the Führer's name'. He does, however, prove to be every bit as inept an assassin as he is a playwright, failing to execute Bialystock and Bloom at close range by proving that he couldn't hit a barn door at twenty paces with his Luger and thus throwing further doubt on his actual wartime function. (As Bialystock wearily proclaims – possibly in the grand tradition of many producers throughout history – 'The next time I produce a play – no author!')

Forming a kind of creative counterpoint to Liebkind is Roger DeBris, a director so thoroughly disconnected from everyday realities that even the basic historical facts of the war elude him entirely. ('Do you know, I never realised that the Third Reich meant Germany,' he exclaims breathlessly. 'I mean, it's drenched with historical goodies like that!') For DeBris, by contrast, his ignorance of the sheer malevolence perpetrated by the Nazis inoculates him from the audience's potential horror at the very concept of *Springtime for Hitler*, allowing his blatant bad taste to emerge unimpeded:

> DeBRIS: That whole third act has got to go. They're losing the war! It's too depressing! We shall have to put something in there. [...] I see it! A line of beautiful girls, dressed as storm troopers, black patent leather boots, S.M. All marching together! Two-three-kick-turn! Turn-turn-kick-turn! It will *work*!

DeBris is, of course, a completely hopeless director, but one who is absolutely confident in his abilities as a top theatrical talent in spite of the fact, as Bialystock notes with glee, 'he's perhaps the worst director that ever lived. He's the only director whose plays close on the first day of rehearsal.' With his exaggerated affectations and pretentious use of French, DeBris is exactly the sort of maladroit egotist that Bialystock can trust to sink *Springtime for Hitler* before it even leaves dry-dock. Both DeBris and Liebkind prize creative freedom, but in Liebkind's case this proves to be somewhat paradoxical as he is unwittingly cherishing a liberty of artistic expression that was rarely to be found in the censorious Nazi Germany (even when it glorified the regime to the extent that Liebkind's excessively flattering play does).

In *The Producers*, the director and playwright are seen to form two sides of the creative process; the confident extrovert, self-assured of his artistic intentions, and the suspicious introvert, riddled with insecurities and mistrustful of the effect of outside influences. However, DeBris and Liebkind provide contrast in other ways. DeBris is suave and assertive, whereas Liebkind is a paranoid recluse. DeBris enjoys a loving (if occasionally fractious) long-term relationship with his personal assistant Carmen Giya (Andreas Voutsinas), but Liebkind is reliant on his pigeons for company. And whereas Bialystock only has to appeal to DeBris's preening self-importance to convince him to join the production, he must lean more heavily on Liebkind for assent to his involvement, guaranteeing him a unique opportunity 'to show the world the true Hitler. The Hitler you loved. The Hitler you knew. The Hitler with a song in his heart!' In short, Bialystock promises Liebkind the chance to cast Hitler in a hagiographical light not because he shares the same objective (far from it), but rather because he is certain that the public will share his own view of the play as the repellent ravings of an extremist madman and thus immediately reject it. By that same token, he is all too aware that DeBris is incapable of providing any kind of competent theatrical direction, but knows that he is amply capable of directing the audience towards the exit – Bialystock's objective in a nutshell.

Ultimately the play's guaranteed failure is predicated on an undiluted portrayal of Liebkind's heartfelt defence of Nazism, which is why Bialystock goes to such lengths to give assurances that the play will stay true to Liebkind's thematic intentions. DeBris's absurdly outré choreography for the opening number is a cavalcade of bad taste, where chorus girls dressed in quasi-traditional German costumes (wearing hats bedecked with decorative pretzels and beer steins) are joined by tap-dancing uniformed members of the SS, goose-stepping and entering into a swastika formation to the sound of recorded gunshots.

Bialystock watches with palpable joy as the audience's slack-jawed horror becomes ever more tangible. The only person dim enough to applaud the overture is promptly swatted like a fly by the other patrons' theatre programmes as they march out of the theatre. However, just as in life, the approval of the audience proves to be fickle. When LSD's Hitler and Eva Braun (Renee Taylor) arrive, it quickly becomes apparent that Liebkind's creative objective has been derailed. When the audience sense that the narrative is being played for laughs, due to LSD's befuddled improvisation, they begin to accept it as satire instead. This infuriates and confuses Liebkind ('Why does he say this "baby"? The Führer never said "baby"!'), who tries to interrupt the play but is promptly foiled. Unaware of the playwright's deranged dramatic aims, the patrons have no difficulty in assuming that the intention has been to scoff at the excesses of Nazism all along. Whereas Brooks clearly intends the play's overture to betray some stylistic influence of the sinister pomp and ceremony of Nazi rallies in order to deliberately subvert it, thus ridiculing the excesses and iconography of fascism, the arrival of the rambling LSD and his cohort of similarly-befuddled cast-mates instantly casts a different light onto the production:

LSD: Hey, man. You're a German!
GÖRING: We are *all* Germans!
LSD: That's right! That means we *cannot* attack Germany. I mean, I got all my friends here, you know? And what about me? And then there's the country club and the laughs every night. We gotta do something. I got it! I got it, I got it, I got it!
GÖRING: What? What have you got?
LSD: A medal. It fell down my pants, man.

Brooks milks every ounce of comic potential from the addled LSD's interactions with the other characters in the play, all of whom are forced to improvise in order to accommodate his wild departures from Liebkind's script. Prominent Nazi characters – ranging from Barney Martin's perplexed Herman Göring to David Patch's cool-cat Joseph Goebbels ('That's my Joe. That's my little Joe. I *love* my little Joe!'), who refers to Hitler as 'Big Daddy' – provide a wildly dysfunctional view of the Third Reich that is as entertainingly comical as it is impossible to take even remotely seriously.

Ofer Ashkenazi has observed that in *The Producers*, 'Nazism appears so ridiculous that it can no longer be considered a threat.

In postwar American society, according to Brooks, Nazism is of interest only as a musical, not as an ideology.'[4] Indeed, Brooks's critique of the uncompromising ruthlessness of Nazism and its supporters extends beyond *Springtime for Hitler* itself to incisively interrogate the attitudes of the characters towards the play's content. Whereas Liebkind is lampooned as a mentally-disturbed buffoon, Brooks also seems to be making the point that we need no further persuasion to cherish our liberty than to look at the effect that fascism has had on its devotees; Liebkind proves so fundamentally unable to function in a free and egalitarian society such as the United States that he effectively invokes his own form of personal repression, isolating himself from the liberal values which surround him. As Chuck Bowen has perceptively noted, Brooks leaves no stone unturned in drawing the audience's attention to just how stark the contrast remains between freedom of creativity and the slavish conformity demanded by totalitarian state control:

> [There are] moments in the film that operate on a level of shockingly blunt political satire. *The Springtime for Hitler* number is a justifiably classic scene in American cinema, as angry and daring as anything in *The Great Dictator*, and it's all the more effective for how little Brooks prepares you for it; a contemporary audience member will suddenly feel as if they've flipped the channel from a rerun of *Your Show of Shows* to one of the darkest moments in *Cabaret*.[5]

This unrelenting effort to prick the pretensions of tyranny, as well as espousing the virtues of liberty (most especially creative freedom), has echoed throughout Brooks's entire filmography. He has summarised his aims succinctly, asserting that 'if you stand on a soapbox and trade rhetoric with a dictator you never win. [...] That's what they do so well; they seduce people. But if you ridicule them, bring them down with laughter – they can't win. You show how crazy they are.'[6] Indeed, his initial intention had been to entitle the film itself *Springtime for Hitler*, only to be advised that public sensibilities about the events of the Second World War remained so delicate at the time of production that – according to Brooks himself – producer Joseph E. Levine had cautioned that the film's commercial viability would almost certainly have been threatened: '[Levine] said, "You've got to change the title. Most of the people I know in distribution will never put *Springtime for Hitler* on their marquees – they just won't do it." So I went along with simply naming it *The Producers'*.7

Despite this level of moral sensitivity regarding the issues addressed by the film (and perhaps precisely because of them), it is particularly noteworthy that Brooks was determined to forge ahead with his artistic agenda rather than compromising the potential impact of *The Producers'* controversial narrative content. Kirsten Fermaglich, for instance, is one of a number of commentators who have drawn attention to the way in which Brooks uses the spectacle of the Nazi parade as a kind of dark mirror to reflect the contemporary entertainment industry in general:

> In the fantastic musical sequence, *Springtime for Hitler*, in *The Producers*, Brooks transgressed another convention of cold-war America by actually equating American society with Nazi Germany. A number of scholars and critics have noted that in his presentation of a Busby Berkeley swastika, jackbooting chorus girls, and elaborate costumes of German kitsch, in which young women wore pretzels and beer steins on their breasts and heads, Brooks made significant and pointed comparisons between Broadway showmanship and fascist pageantry. Brooks' portrait, moreover, of the uptight and tasteless middle-class audience uproariously embracing the play, *Springtime for Hitler*, presents the American bourgeoisie as insensitive, tasteless, and so amoral that they might be willing to embrace fascism itself if it were presented in a palatable or funny form, in much the same way that the real Hitler had initially seemed to many a harmless comic nobody in Weimar Germany.8

Is it in fact the case, then, that Brooks's artistic intentions reach beyond simply illuminating the savagery and moral bankruptcy presented by fascism, and extend to a more immediate warning that the underlying causes of such ideologies must be continually challenged lest they take hold once again? Or are his objectives even more nuanced than that? Bowen postulates that with *The Producers*, Brooks 'keeps threatening to veer off into a naked parable of how commercial impulses affect art for both the good and the bad, but he keeps pulling himself back to the overwritten zingers which the actors have been instructed to deliver with jolting, nagging loudness'.9 And certainly, we see in both DeBris and Liebkind a corruption of artistic intention for entirely different reasons. Rather than valuing art for art's sake, Liebkind desires to contort public opinion of fascism until it conforms with his own twisted logic – as far as he is concerned, the desire that the play actually have any artistic merit is clearly a secondary consideration. For DeBris, contrastingly, *Springtime for Hitler* offers him a golden opportunity to distort the content of Liebkind's script to suit his own outlandish creative tastes, allowing him to showcase his stylistic preferences irrespective of whether the play (as written) can actually sustain them. Both men are deluded enough to think that their work can achieve commercial success on its own merits; the producers, of course, are banking on the fact that just the opposite will be the case.

In Max Bialystock, Brooks presents the mastermind who lies behind this magnum opus of bad taste. Bialystock is, from the very outset, an enigma. With his down-at-heel trappings of one-time wealth, we first find him lurking around his dingy, ramshackle office as he falls foul of the (unintentionally violent) affections of one of his elderly conquests. Brooks repeatedly fills the screen with the features of Zero Mostel in extreme close-up, a colossus with a comb-over, as though consciously reminding the audience of the fact that Bialystock's personality dominates the film. And dominate it most certainly does. Like Bloom, though for radically different reasons, the arch-materialist Bialystock feels trapped by circumstance. He is acutely aware of the fact that his glory days are vanishing far into the distance, and that he is only holding on to his career by the skin of his teeth – and the good graces of some hoodwinked, white-haired backers. Brooks describes the genesis of Bialystock thus:

> I worked for a producer who wore a chicken fat-stained homburg and a black alpaca coat. He pounced on little old ladies and would make love to them. They gave him money for his plays, and they were so grateful for his attention. Later on there were a couple of guys who were doing flop after flop and living like kings. A press agent told me, 'God forbid they should ever get a hit, because they'd never be able to pay off the backers!' I coupled the producer with these two crooks and – BANG! – there was my story.[10]

Perhaps the most interesting thing about Bialystock is the fact that he is, from an ethical standpoint, completely reprehensible... and yet, for all that, he is so blatantly avaricious, so totally certain that he is entitled to live the high-life once more, that his sheer audacity makes him very difficult for the audience to dislike. With his ever-present homburg hat (which becomes increasingly dishevelled as his plans turn awry) and his inexhaustible supply of insincere schmooze which leaches throughout his every professional endeavour, Mostel plays Bialystock cranked to full throttle throughout the entire course of the film, and the sheer extent of the character's blustering, scheming persona ensures that his imprimatur is etched upon virtually every frame of the film. However, for all his iron projection of geniality Bialystock is deeply frustrated by his breadline status. Someone who has no difficulty in exclusively equating financial health with personal success, he is determined to do anything – quite literally – to guarantee a turnaround in his fortunes:

> BIALYSTOCK: How humiliating. Max Bialystock. Max Bialystock. Do you know who I used to be? Max Bialystock! King of Broadway! Six shows running at once. Lunch at Delmonico's. $200 suits. You see this? [*He indicates a decorative pin on his ascot.*] This once held a pearl as big as your eye. Look at me now. LOOK AT ME NOW! I'm wearing a cardboard belt! I used to have thousands of investors begging, pleading, to put their money in a Max Bialystock production. Look at my investors now. Voilà! Hundreds of little old ladies stopping off at Max Bialystock's office to grab a last thrill on the way to the cemetery. You have exactly ten seconds to change that look of disgusting pity into one of enormous respect.

Bialystock senses that the meek and unwitting Bloom holds the key to better times – even in a manner which runs contrary to all conventional wisdom (that is, rather than aiming for a hit and dreading a flop, their financial success hinges on ensuring commercial and critical failure at all costs). As Robert Alan Crick adroitly observes, the play is a direct – and slyly deliberate – subversion of countless old movies where characters spend the entire film preparing a song-and-dance show in order to save an orphanage, school or other similar establishment.[11] (Over the years, similar strategies have been scattered through films as diverse as Michael Curtiz's *White Christmas*, 1954, and John Landis's *The Blues Brothers*, 1980, amongst a great many others.) Thus Bialystock resolves to lure Bloom into his scheme like a spider with a web, his pitying glances speaking volumes about his distaste at having to win over someone who he considers entirely unworthy of his respect ('This man should be in a strait-jacket', he mutters directly to camera). Though he sets out to deceive the shy innocent into doing his will, Bialystock soon realises just how miserable Bloom's existence really is and eventually grows to be genuinely fond of the timid accountant, slowly ceasing to be his manipulator and eventually becoming a kind of mentor and surrogate father figure instead. Thus both men have a part to play in the liberation of the other; Bloom discovers that he is capable of more than the restrictive, repressed life that he has led up to this point, whereas the essentially isolated Bialystock gradually comes to appreciate the fact that genuine friendship – a true interpersonal meeting of minds – cannot be gained by confidence trickery any more than it can be quantified monetarily.

A fresh-faced Gene Wilder creates a memorably mild-mannered, eminently decent character in the often-childlike Leo Bloom, initially acting as a kind of moral counterweight to Bialystock's propensity towards brazen greed. (The fact that he shares his name with the worldly-wise protagonist of James Joyce's *Ulysses*, 1922, is not referred to.) However, once he – and his inseparable safety blanket – has been given a surreal afternoon out in New York, where Bialystock treats him to a helium balloon, a trip on a merry-go-round and a boat ride, he begins to question the purpose of his dull and joyless existence. Bialystock tempts Bloom with wild promises of the trappings of wealth, conjuring images of prosperity and influence at the top of the Empire State Building ('Money is honey!' he cajoles temptingly). This is followed by their attendance at the screening of a pornographic movie – an experience which is obviously new to Bloom, as it leaves him sucking his thumb and looking vaguely shell-shocked. Here Maurice Yacowar identifies a common motif in many of Brooks's films, namely that they often 'trace the maturing of childish adults. His central characters begin as self-seeking, narcissistic whimperers, but mature into responsible fraternal community. [...] In the later films this development extends beyond adolescent male cameraderie to embrace the challenges and rewards of heterosexual romance'.[12] Bloom's long, vaguely bizarre afternoon of self-examination culminates in his grand moment of realisation at the fountain of the Lincoln Center, where Bialystock's amoral seduction finally takes hold:

> BIALYSTOCK: Don't let me influence you. It's your decision.
> BLOOM: But if we get caught, we'll go to prison.
> BIALYSTOCK: You think you're not in prison now? Living in a grey little room? Going to a grey little job? Leading a grey little life?

BLOOM: That's right. I'm a nothing. I spend my life counting other people's money. People I'm smarter than. Better than. Where's my share? Where's Leo Bloom's share? I want... I want... I want everything I've ever seen in the movies!

There is great subtlety in Wilder's performance, even at the height of Bloom's histrionic mania, and the character's nervous tics and bizarre neurotic outbursts flare perfectly against Mostel's brand of slyly deliberate unctuousness. Although relatively little is said explicitly about Bloom's background and family life, Wilder conveys every uncomfortable aspect of the character's lack of self-esteem, his extreme social awkwardness, and the fact that his inability to find happiness stems from a deeply-ingrained failure to realise that he was even looking for it. Thus when the self-serving Bialystock attempts to open the accountant's eyes to a wider world, he succeeds not only in persuading him to question his job satisfaction, but the direction of his life too. Though Max's interest in Leo is primarily fuelled by his need to manipulate his financial talents, he soon begins to take joy in the blossoming of his new business partner's personal development. It comes as no surprise that this complex and unconventional cinematic pairing has become one of the most celebrated in the history of film comedies:

BIALYSTOCK: Having a good time?
BLOOM: I don't know. I feel so strange.
BIALYSTOCK: Maybe you're happy.
BLOOM: That's it. I'm happy. Well, what do you know about that? I'm happy!

Whereas Wilder's endearingly twitchy take on Bloom creates a beautifully rounded character, it is Mostel's dry comic timing which lingers in the memory longest. Whether shamelessly proffering courtesy tickets to a prominent theatre critic – wrapped unsubtly in a $100 bill – in the premeditated hope of outraging his professional sensibilities, or suffering his way though the montage of faux-romantic conquests with a seemingly endless procession of senior citizens (his deadpan expression as he pours the contents of an entire bottle of champagne down the lederhosen pocket of a 'romantic' tableside violinist being one particular highlight), Mostel's performance is never less than a *tour de force* of pokerfaced brilliance. The remarkable nature of the onscreen chemistry between Wilder and Mostel seemed all the more startling given their singular inability to replicate its elusive alchemy in Tom O'Horgan's *Rhinoceros*, an adaptation of the Eugène Ionesco play, which came along some years later in 1974.

Although the issue is not raised explicitly, Brooks demonstrates no small amount of amusement regarding the fact that Bialystock and Bloom both have a Jewish heritage, and yet are willing to stomach the deeply unedifying prospect of a play which celebrates Nazi Germany because they know that its failure will guarantee them a fortune at the expense of its bigoted creator's intolerant expectations. Roger Ebert observes that:

> It is obvious that Bialystock and Bloom are Jewish, but they never refer to that. As Franz Liebkind rants, they nod, because the more offensive he is, the more likely his play will fail. Brooks adds just one small moment to suggest their private thoughts. As the two men walk away from the playwright's apartment, Bloom covers the red-and-black Nazi armband Franz has given him. 'All right, take off the armband,' says Bialystock, taking off his own. They throw both armbands into a trash can. Leo spits into it, and then Max does.[13]

Bialystock and Bloom succeed in subverting the iconography and symbolism of Nazism to work against the redundant ideology of fascism – that is, they are not profiting from hatred, racism and murder, but rather are undermining those who did in order to make money from that ridicule. Likewise, Brooks's accomplishment is to show that this is not simply a case of two quick-thinking Jewish men outwitting the last vestiges of a regime which had subjected millions of innocent Jews (and countless other people from different ethnic backgrounds) to an agonising death; it also offers a more general allegory of the underdog emerging triumphant in the face of hostility. In *The Haunted Smile: The Story of Jewish Comedians* (2001), Lawrence J. Epstein makes the point that 'for Brooks, [*The Producers*] was a parable of Jewish life, a series of failures, but which, in America, becomes suddenly successful. Brooks also liked the fact that the script shocked audiences and attacked Germans; he liked mocking those who had attacked Jews.'[14]

While it is difficult to imagine the brash, little-old-lady-scamming Max Bialystock ever being mistaken for a paragon of virtue, there is no denying his quick wit or the fact that he knows exactly what he wants (and even how to get it). For Bloom, the transformation from timid accountant into criminal schemer is not so much cast in the light of the debasement of moral principle as it is instead an exploration of his growth as an individual – a celebration of risk, yes, but not a defence of swindling. Like Bialystock, Bloom is determined to pursue new-found ambitions in a way that his initial professional role could never have afforded him. If the system has failed him, he reasons, then why should he feel any need to respect that system? However, the established order gains the upper hand in the end. When the plan falls through, in spite of not being blind to Bialystock's faults, Bloom chooses not to apportion blame but rather to relish the fact that even as he heads for prison, in a sense he has already been set free:

> BLOOM: Your Honour, whom has Max Bialystock wronged? I mean, whom has he really hurt? Not me. Not me. I was... This man... No-one ever called me Leo before. I mean, I know it's not a big legal point, but... even in kindergarten they used to call me Bloom. I never sang a song before. I mean, with someone else. I never sang a song with someone else before. This man... This man... This is a wonderful man. He made me what I am today. He did. And what of the dear ladies? What would their lives have been without Max Bialystock? Max Bialystock, who made them feel young, and attractive, and wanted again.

With his statement to the court, Bloom proves that while he is fully aware of Bialystock's manipulation, underhandedness and scheming nature, his business partner's real crime ultimately boiled down to that of searching after a daring aspiration. And certainly, there is much to enjoy in Bialystock's wallowing in the fruits of his deception: the chauffeur-driven limousine, expensive cigars, sharp suits and upmarket new office. However, the ultimate proof of his new status of wealth is Ulla (Lee Meredith), a stunning Swedish personal assistant who – unable to speak much in the way of English – appears to have been hired by Bialystock for her dancing skills (along with other, even less secretarial activities which are heavily hinted at). Ulla is blissfully unaware of Bialystock and Bloom's scheme, and is so oblivious to what is really going on that she cheerfully interrupts the marauding, pistol-toting Liebkind (during his attack on the producers' office) to ask if he would like coffee. Ulla is just one amongst a handful of memorable supporting characters throughout the film who make an impact in spite of having a relatively small amount of screen time. Aside from Bialystock's endless little black book of cheque-waving elderly women ('I made it out just like you told me: to "cash". That's a funny name for a play'), others include an amiable but bewildered barfly (William Hickey) who helps Bialystock and Bloom celebrate their theatrical failure/ success, the wryly self-important concierge of Liebkind's apartment building (Madlyn Cates), and perhaps most entertainingly of all, a Central Park hot-dog vendor (Brutus Peck) with a very high opinion of his business:

> BIALYSTOCK: Mmm, excellent! Please tender our compliments to the chef.
> HOT-DOG VENDOR: Please tender half a buck.
> BIALYSTOCK: Of course. Here you are, my good man.
> HOT-DOG VENDOR: I'm not your good man. I happen to own this establishment.
> BIALYSTOCK: Gimme the change. Everybody's a big shot.

In spite of the engaging character development, the consistently witty dialogue and the brisk pace of the narrative, *The Producers* is likely to be remembered most for its unapologetic celebration of bad taste. Irv Slifkin notes sagely that 'before there was the phrase "politically incorrect," *The Producers* was politically incorrect. Hell, it may even have invented the concept'.[15] Yet, of course, throughout the film Brooks seeks to violate sensibilities not to offend general audiences, but rather to chip away at expectations regarding certain cultural shibboleths. Susan Gubar observes that 'the send-up of Nazism in *The Producers* [depends] upon alienating performances-within-the-movies that are meant to be in the worst possible taste, especially for those with a heightened conscience about death camps and the deadliness of ongoing racial prejudice,' adding that 'celebrating the Jews' escape from the German house of bondage, Brooks derides the tastes and definitions of the racists'.[16] And yet, of course, the inventive, high-camp satirising of fascist barbarity is only one part of *The Producers'* appeal. If shock factor alone had been key to the film's success, its influence would inevitably have waned over time as each new generation – progressively further removed from the atrocities of the war – became ever more familiar with the style and content of *Springtime for Hitler*'s big reveal. Instead, it is the way in which Brooks introduces us to wildly disparate characters who collaborate, under the unlikeliest of circumstances, to produce a veritable epic of bad taste – who revel in vulgarity and tackiness to achieve their ends, then amalgamate the worst excesses of the stage with the monstrous malice of Nazism to comic effect – which makes the film such an inventive and revolutionary achievement.

There are many other flourishes which help to make *The Producers* such a remarkable experience, from the famous Hitler casting call (a seemingly endless conveyor-belt of the hapless and bizarre) to LSD's rambling digressions ('One and one is two, two and two is four, I feel so bad 'cos I'm losing the war!'), by way of the script-reading sequence where a weary Bialystock – surrounded by endless mounds of slushpile plays, irritably discounts an adaptation of Franz Kafka's *The Metamorphosis* (1915) as being 'too good' (so tired that he doesn't even notice that he's holding his copy of the script upside-down). Even the conclusion of the film, where Bialystock and Bloom are condemned to prison for their fraudulent activities, seems perfectly pitched; the warden wants to get in on the act by investing in 50% of an in-house stage show that has already been oversold to the other inmates. Max's goals may have been humbled, but his sense of ambition certainly hasn't – previously he was reaching for the world, but now he'll settle for going on tour... to Leavenworth Penitentiary.

In the opinion of several commentators, *The Producers* marked a high water mark for Brooks's goal of challenging subjugation and tyranny, coming at an early point in his career where his work was solely behind the camera rather than being in front of it. As Nick Smurthwaite and Paul Gelder venture, 'Brooks talks of the serious import of his films, bursting the balloon of pomposity and ridiculing oppression, but he is inclined to undermine his own credibility as a film-maker worthy of serious consideration by doubling as the clown'.[17] In *The Producers*, Brooks's sole (uncredited) acting performance was to overdub a line of dialogue for one of the performing on-stage Nazis, and while his proficiency with serrated wit would last the entire duration of his directorial career, his focus as screenwriter and director was rarely quite so razor-sharp as it proved to be in this film – a fact which was recognised at the Academy Awards, when his work on the film saw him receiving the Oscar for Best Writing, Story and Screenplay

Written Directly for the Screen in 1969. (Gene Wilder was nominated for the Academy Award for Best Actor in a Supporting Role at the same ceremony.)

Though moderately successful at the box-office at the time of its release, *The Producers* initially met with a distinctly variable critical response, with Renata Adler of The *New York Times* being generally representative of the climate of opinion when voicing the view that 'there is nothing like having your make-believe audience catch on to a joke – and a joke that absolutely capsizes the plans of your leading characters – to make your real audience really hostile to you. [...] *The Producers*, leaves one alternately picking up one's coat to leave and sitting back to laugh'.[18] *Time* Magazine similarly bemoaned the fact that, in their opinion, '*Springtime* is supposed to be like *Valley of the Dolls* – so excessively bad that it's hilarious. Instead it is just excessive. *Producers* ends in a whimper of sentimentality out of keeping with the low jinks that went before'.[19] General opinion was not so easily dissuaded, however, and although the film had only a limited release across the United States it continued to garner fans for many years afterwards. Over time, the film's reputation was bolstered by its appearance in many published lists of the most amusing cinematic comedies and – in 1996 – the honour of its preservation in the United States National Film Registry. Considering its longevity at a point three and a half decades after its initial release, reviewer Nathan Rabin reflected that '*The Producers* is justly revered for the boundary-pushing shamelessness of its *Springtime For Hitler* production number, but the film's sweetness and craft stand out more than its shock value. Tightly structured, briskly paced, and loaded with one-liners worthy of Woody Allen at his best, *The Producers* has a sense of focus and narrative economy largely missing in Brooks' later work'.[20]

While its cult reputation meant that *The Producers* was never truly in danger of disappearing from public view over the decades following its production, its profile was boosted beyond all recognition when Brooks and Thomas Meehan adapted the film for the stage. Opening at the St James Theatre in April 2001, there was a certain irony in a film about a Broadway musical being adapted into an actual Broadway musical, but Brooks succeeded admirably – the stage adaptation of *The Producers* was a huge hit, running for many years and winning twelve Tony Awards amongst numerous other plaudits. Initially starring Nathan Lane and Matthew Broderick as Bialystock and Bloom, the play was written as a period piece (set in the late sixties, as the original film had been) and contained a number of impressive musical numbers including *Springtime for Hitler* itself – the infamous overture was retained and even expanded. The musical contained a number of deviations from the original source material, including the elimination of the LSD character (Liebkind now wins the Hitler part at the stage audition, only to be replaced by DeBris at the last minute) and a greatly expanded role for Ulla. The huge popularity of the production meant that it has been staged extensively around the world, including a tour of the US in 2002-03 and the UK in 2007-08.

In the light of the musical's monumental success, a remake of *The Producers* was commissioned by Brooksfilms and Relativity Media a few years later, being released in December 2005. Director and choreographer of the Broadway show, Susan Stroman, was to helm this adaptation of the stage musical, which retained most of the original theatrical cast. In a similar vein to the Broadway version, there are many sly allusions to Brooks's cinematic work (most especially *Blazing Saddles*) embedded in the dialogue, and additionally many subtle showbiz in-jokes are scattered throughout. However, the remake received a mixed range of reviews, many citing the fact that the film struggled to transcend its stage-based origins in a manner which, for obvious reasons, had never troubled the cinematic original. Over-familiarity with the events (and jokes) of the original film was also considered problematic from a critical point of view, given that moral sensibilities had gradually changed since the time of the Wilder/Mostel production to the point that the story's ability to either surprise or shock had been greatly diminished in the view of some commentators. However, as Fermaglich contends, the stage version of *The Producers* (and its cinematic adaptation) arguably proved to be a very different animal from its 1960s inspiration:

> The angry and chaotic 1967 version of *The Producers* reflected a country that was divided by generation and by politics, and a Jewish community that still perceived itself as being outside the mainstream of American culture, despite its middle-class white status. In 2001,

the tamer, nostalgic and triumphal interpretation of *The Producers* as a symbol of American Jewish success reflected a nation tired of culture wars, and an American Jewish community that felt much more comfortably integrated into the middle-class mainstream.[21]

There are many things which have been said and written about *The Producers* over the years, but perhaps the most obvious is that it is a film which is difficult to casually disregard. And that, more than anything, may have been Brooks's singular intention all along. His heartfelt attack – on Nazism, on creative oppression, on enforced conformity – had managed to weather the storm to inspire people of different generations and cultural backgrounds. This, perhaps more than any of his subsequent films, may stand as his crowning achievement, and the most potent of all his impassioned pleas to value and uphold individual liberty. As Alan Kennedy Shaffer observes, Brooks himself considered this one of his primary goals, and it is difficult to deny that he has succeeded convincingly in his objective:

> *The Producers* ranks among the best films ever produced with the goal of focusing attention on the Holocaust. Two decades after the Nazis systematically murdered millions of Jews, homosexuals, gypsies, and dissidents, Brooks effectively recast – through Jewish humor – Hitler as an object of ridicule at the mercy of Jewish producers and commercialization. Confronted with mixed reviews for the film, Brooks explained, 'More than anything, the great Holocaust by the Nazis is probably the great outrage of the Twentieth Century... if I get on the soapbox and wax eloquently, it'll be blown away in the wind, but if I do *Springtime for Hitler* it'll never be forgotten'.[22]

With *The Producers*, Mel Brooks had arrived with style – and with no small amount of industry recognition into the bargain. If his aim was to be noticed by mainstream audiences, he had certainly achieved this aspiration, and critical regard for *The Producers* – while mixed at the time of its release – has only grown as the film's vintage has matured. Like so many other enduring cult successes, its reputation has now become so firmly established amongst devotees that any impartial judgement towards it has long since been drowned out by its deafening ubiquity in popular culture. Though it may not have been immediately apparent in the late sixties, Mel Brooks had created a *bona fide* classic of cinematic comedy. The question became, with an Oscar to his name and growing interest in his directorial talents, how would he choose to build upon this accomplishment?

# REFERENCES

1. Jessica Hillman, *Echoes of the Holocaust on the American Musical Stage* (Jefferson: McFarland, 2012), p. 174.
2. Mel Brooks, in Larry Siegel, 'Interview: Mel Brooks', in *Playboy*, October 1966. <http://www.brookslyn.com/print/PlayboyOct1966/PlayboyOct1966.php>
3. Sidney Glazier, in Peter Hay, *Movie Anecdotes* (Oxford: Oxford University Press, 1990), p. 88.
4. Ofer Ashkenazi, 'Ridiculous Trauma: Comic Representations of the Nazi Past in Contemporary German Visual Culture', in *Cultural Critique*, No. 78, Spring 2011, 88-118, p. 100.
5. Chuck Bowen, '*The Producers*', in *Slant Magazine*, 28 June 2013. <http://www.slantmagazine.com/dvd/review/the-producers>
6. Brooks, in Nancy Shute, 'Mel Brooks: His Humor Brings Down Hitler and the House', in *U.S. News and World Report*, 20-27 August 2001, p. 71.
7. Brooks, in Timothy White, '*Producers* Producer: The Man Behind a Classic', in *Billboard*, 26 April 1997, 1; 86-88, p. 88.
8. Kirsten Fermaglich, 'Mel Brooks' *The Producers*: Tracing American Jewish Culture Through Comedy, 1967-2007', in *American Studies*, Vol. 48, No. 4, Winter 2007, 59-87, p. 62.
9. Bowen, 2013.
10. Brooks, in Damon Wise, 'The Making of *The Producers*', in *The Guardian*, 16 August 2008.
    <http://www.theguardian.com/film/2008/aug/16/comedy.theproducers>
11. Robert Alan Crick, *The Big Screen Comedies of Mel Brooks* (Jefferson: McFarland and Company, 2009) [2002], p. 26.
12. Maurice Yacowar, *The Comic Art of Mel Brooks* (London: W.H. Allen, 1982), pp. 196-97.
13. Roger Ebert, 'Great Movie: *The Producers*', in *The Chicago Sun-Times*, 23 July 2000.
    <http://www.rogerebert.com/reviews/great-movie-the-producers-1968>
14. Lawrence J. Epstein, *The Haunted Smile: The Story of Jewish Comedians* (Oxford: PublicAffairs, 2001), p. 209.
15. Irv Slifkin, '*The Producers*', in *VideoHound's Groovy Movies: Far-out Films of the Psychedelic Era*, ed. by Irv Slifkin (Canton: Invisible Ink Press, 2004), p. 379.
16. Susan Gubar, 'Racial Camp in *The Producers* and *Bamboozled*', in *Film Quarterly*, Vol. 60, No. 2, Winter 2006, 26-37, p. 26.
17. Nick Smurthwaite and Paul Gelder, *Mel Brooks and the Spoof Movie* (London: Proteus Books, 1982), p. 50.
18. Renata Adler, '*The Producers*', in *The New York Times*, 19 March 1968. <http://www.nytimes.com/movie/review?res=EE05E7DF173AE273BC4152DFB5668383679EDE>
19. Anon., 'Cinema: *The Producers*', in *Time Magazine*, 26 January 1968. <http://www.time.com/time/magazine/article/0,9171,837773-2,00.html>
20. Nathan Rabin, '*The Producers*', in *The Onion AV Club*, 13 December 2002. <http://www.avclub.com/review/the-producers-12196>
21. Fermaglich, p. 81.
22. Alan Kennedy Shaffer, '*The Producers*', in *Movies in American History: An Encyclopedia: Volume 1*, ed. by Philip C. DiMare (Santa Barbara: ABC-CLIO, 2011), 400-02, p. 401.

# 2
# THE TWELVE CHAIRS (1970)

IF THERE IS one entry in Mel Brooks's filmography that is worthy of the epithet 'hidden gem', *The Twelve Chairs* has no convincing rival. Largely ignored at the time of its release, of all Brooks's films this one has proven to be the most neglected over the years, and quite undeservedly so. Robert Alan Crick is not alone amongst commentators in naming the film one of Brooks's most accomplished as a director, praising its refined artistry, sophisticated characterisation and obvious attention to period detail,[1] and certainly the reissue of *The Twelve Chairs* on recent home entertainment platforms has gone some way towards reintroducing it to modern audiences who may otherwise have been oblivious to its very existence.

Whereas *The Producers* had hinted at the dark shadow of tyranny through its caustic satire of Nazism, *The Twelve Chairs* was to examine the social effects of a repressive regime from a different standpoint by setting the action against the totalitarian backdrop of 1920s Soviet Russia. Brooks was not the first to adapt Ilya Ilf and Yevgeny Petrov's novel for the big screen; over the years the story has been produced cinematically in countries as varied as Sweden, Germany and Iran, with some of the more prominent versions including *Keep Your Seats, Please* (Monty Banks, 1936), *It's in the Bag* (Richard Wallace, 1945) and *The Thirteen Chairs* (Nicolas Gessner and Luciano Lucignani, 1969). Unlike many of his predecessors, however, Brooks was determined to make certain that his adaptation of the text was not modernised or its action relocated, ensuring that it remained firmly rooted in the post-Revolutionary Russian era of the original, filming in various Yugoslavian locations to capture the authentic visual flavour and architecture of Eastern Europe. Although his screenplay differs from the novel in a number of ways (not least in circumventing its bleakly depressing conclusion), Brooks exerts obvious effort in retaining the moral complexity of Ilf and Petrov's eccentric *dramatis personae*, in addition to taking care that the savage satirical bite of the source text is never compromised.

The place is Stargorod, a small Russian village, and the time is around ten years after the Soviet Revolution of 1917. Ippolit Vorobyaninov (Ron Moody), a former aristocrat financially ruined by the toppling of the Czarist autocracy, is now forced to eke out a joyless existence as a minor provincial bureaucrat. Upon hearing that his mother-in-law Claudia Ivanova (Elaine Garreau) is gravely ill, he rushes to her deathbed only for the elderly woman to reveal an unexpected secret. Prior to the Revolution, she tells him, she had sewn a wealth of jewellery (50,000 roubles' worth, in pre-Soviet currency) into one of the family's dining chairs in order for the cache to evade detection by the incoming Communist authorities. However, there were twelve chairs in the set, and as she passes away it is clear that she has no idea of her jewellery's current whereabouts, having been forced to flee her home several years earlier. As Vorobyaninov anxiously resolves to recover the gems, seeing a way out of his straitened circumstances, he is unaware that the family's avaricious Russian Orthodox priest Father Fyodor (Dom DeLuise) – having heard Claudia's confession while administering the Last Rites – is now also in hot pursuit of the errant furniture.

Vorobyaninov visits his old family estate, now converted into a care home for the village's elderly residents, and accidentally runs into Tikon (Mel Brooks), his former manservant who is now responsible for janitorial duties in and around the building. Though his old employee is almost permanently inebriated, Vorobyaninov is able to persuade Tikon to explain what has happened to the dining room chairs – having been private property, all but one of them was appropriated by the authorities following the Revolution. However, Vorobyaninov's scheme is overheard by a young con artist, Ostap Bender (Frank Langella), who manages to inveigle his way into the recovery plan, offering his skills and resourcefulness in exchange for half of the loot. Fearing that Bender will report him to the authorities unless he complies, Vorobyaninov grudgingly acquiesces.

Bender suggests that Vorobyaninov should attempt to gain access to his old family home and persuade the building's supervisor to part with the single remaining chair on the premises, but Fyodor has beaten him to it – a frantic chase ensues, during which the chair is destroyed only to reveal nothing inside. Bender, meanwhile, has broken into the local Bureau of Housing and retrieves the paperwork relating to the location of the other eleven chairs after they were impounded by the authorities. He discovers that they have been collectively sold to a museum in Moscow. However, his departure is interrupted by the arrival of Fyodor, who has also sneaked into the office in search of the chairs' whereabouts. Spotting an opportunity, Bender impersonates a government official in charge of furniture and – finding records pertaining to another set of identical (but jewel-less) chairs – directs the covetous priest to an address in Siberia, thus temporarily throwing him many hundreds of miles off the scent.

Vorobyaninov and Bender arrive at the museum in Moscow, only to discover that seven of the chairs are in the process of being removed from the premises. They tear apart the remaining four (which are still forming part of an exhibition) before setting off in pursuit of the others, eventually tracking them down to a storage depot. Vorobyaninov spots one of the chairs being taken away by a railway worker, but his attempts to follow the man through a busy train yard are eventually thwarted. Bender, in the meantime, has been tracking the six other chairs, which are now the property of a theatre troupe. The company, led by pompous producer Nikolai Sestrin (Andreas Voutsinas), operates from a ship which is currently berthed in a dock at Yalta; the chairs have been purchased as props for a forthcoming play. Bender coerces Vorobyaninov into impersonating an actor so that he can take up a role in the company's current drama, thus gaining access to the chairs. But they only have time to examine a few of the seats in the production's storage area before Vorobyaninov's dire performance ability sees them ejected from the premises. Bender then hatches a plan to persuade Sevitsky (Vlada Petric), a light-fingered production assistant, to steal the remaining three chairs in exchange for a cash sum. However, even this scheme goes awry, as Sevitsky is only able to purloin two chairs – both of which prove to be empty. The other has been sold to a nearby circus, where it is being used as part of a tightrope walker's act.

In the intervening time, Fyodor has reached Siberia and insistently pesters prominent engineer Mr Bruns (David Lander) and his wife (Diana Coupland), whom he mistakenly believes to be in possession of the chairs. The couple are eventually relocated by the government to the Black Sea, unaware that Fyodor has followed them there. Eventually – after much badgering – Bruns gives in and sells the chairs to Fyodor, by now just desperate to get rid of the obsessive cleric. Elated, Fyodor assembles all eleven of the chairs at a scenic coastal locale and promptly tears them to pieces... only to discover that they, too, are devoid of jewellery.

Incensed at his repeatedly poor fortunes, Vorobyaninov storms the circus tent and wrestles the recently-purchased chair from a hapless acrobat in mid-performance. He speeds away into the distance, only to be intercepted by Fyodor – who by now has grasped the fact that he has been hoodwinked. Wrestling the chair from Vorobyaninov, he races off into the distance, his lust for riches literally managing to propel him up the side of a sheer cliff-face as he evades his pursuers. There, he breaks the chair apart only to find it empty. Unable to descend from the mountain he has scaled, Fyodor watches helplessly as Vorobyaninov and Bender – who now realise that the jewellery must be stashed in the one chair that remains unaccounted for – begin their long return journey to Moscow.

Back at the train yard, the pair discover that an opening ceremony is taking place for a new public building – the Railway Workers' Communal House of Recreation. Taking a careful look around the premises, the last surviving chair is spotted in an immaculate games room dedicated to chess; having located it, Bender surreptitiously leaves a window open so that he and Vorobyaninov can make an unauthorised return visit later on. This they do under cover of nightfall, but quickly discover that the final chair – just like all the others – contains nothing within. The duo's confusion is remedied by a kindly night watchman (Will Stampe), who explains that one of the railway workers had accidentally discovered the jewels – their presence only became known when he stumbled over the chair while hanging up a set of curtains. In the established Soviet tradition, the funds raised from the sale of the gems were used for the common good, as they had been spent on the construction of the communal house itself – built upon the site of the earlier building where the gems were found in the chair. His plans thwarted in spite of all his Herculean efforts, Vorobyaninov flies into a rage and attacks the night watchman along with a member of the police force, making a fugitive of Bender as well as himself. After a narrow escape, Bender tells him that it is now time they went on their separate ways, not least as this will make it easier for them to evade capture. However, when he sees first-hand that Vorobyaninov is now willing to put aside his pretensions of former glory in order to survive, Bender realises that his accomplice has changed for the better and decides to rejoin him.

Like Brooks's directorial debut, *The Twelve Chairs* is a film which operates on many different levels. *The Producers* had attacked fascism in all of its vainglorious brutality, but it had also slyly parodied the dark spectre of greed that can hover over the world of showbusiness. *The Twelve Chairs* was also to take greed as its primary theme, but in a broader sense it is a comedy which illuminates certain characteristics of human nature. Maurice Yacowar wisely notes the tendency of human beings towards self-destructiveness in the single-minded pursuit of their base desires, even in the face of unremitting sermonising by various organs of the state concerning the subject of noble ethical refinement.[2] We see this dichotomy abundantly articulated by Brooks through his exploration of the hypocrisy of both the ideological state apparatus and organised religion. The grandiosity of Soviet aims in creating a society free from inequality and prejudice is repeatedly lampooned in the harsh light of reality as Brooks introduces us to Russian citizens from all walks of life and emphasises the point – in the grand Orwellian tradition – that while all comrades should be considered equal, some are manifestly more equal than others.

While it is difficult to pinpoint the precise inception of the inspiration behind his decision to direct *The Twelve Chairs*, it is clear that it was a project that Brooks had long felt strongly about. Yacowar indicates the fact that Brooks had harboured ambitions to adapt the Ilf and Petrov novel even from an early age,[3] but the origins of the project may have had other formative stimulation. His old mentor Sid Caesar, for instance, has mentioned that 'Mel

Tolkin and I took Mel Brooks under our wing. [...] We also exposed Mel to classic literature, including Dostoevsky, Tolstoy, and Gogol, so we're probably indirectly responsible for his film version of *The Twelve Chairs*.[4] Yet whatever factors were ultimately responsible for his personal investment in the project, the film's central themes had much in common with those underlying *The Producers*, and his engagement with these core issues of human motivation and interaction would reverberate down throughout much of his later filmography. Brooks has described the film's primary concerns as those of 'eternal need and eternal greed',[5] and certainly his choice of Soviet Russia as the stage for this comedy of human nature was to prove particularly apt; set early in the life of the USSR, with the events of the Revolution still fresh in the memory of the characters, the potential for the satirical undermining of Communist ideals was never greater. David Desser and Lester D. Friedman have emphasised the fact that Brooks used the focal premise of the original novel to layer his film with a rather more universal social commentary:

> By emphasising the greed of the former nobleman and the priest, two representatives from the upper ranks of Russian life under the Czar, and then augmenting it with the figure of Bender, a man of the new order obsessed with the same overwhelming avarice, Brooks demonstrates that social systems may shift but essential human selfishness remains constant. This maniacal lust for riches also thematically ties *The Twelve Chairs* to *The Producers*, even though the film presents a darker, decidedly more pessimistic vision of humanity's essentially rapacious nature.[6]

Greed may well be the driving factor behind the motivation of all three of the main characters, but the way in which this is articulated varies considerably between each of them. The deviously calculating Bender, with his saturnine good looks and silver tongue, is almost always composed and self-assured, whereas his reluctant partner in crime Vorobyaninov spends much of the film looking twitchy and uncomfortable, when he isn't succumbing to full-blown mania. Yet easily outdoing both of them is Father Fyodor, who always seems to be in danger of pitching into all-out hysteria due to his sheer lust for riches. All three men are seeking a similar kind of freedom, hoping that access to the hidden stash of jewellery will offer a way out of the drudgery and utilitarianism of everyday life. Yet in the search of that liberation, they end up completely in thrall to their covetous desires, willing to risk everything for one last, desperate chance to escape the dejection of their current existence. This frenzied lust for material assets drives them to increasingly unhinged lengths as the film continues, causing Vorobyaninov to risk his life walking a tightrope without any formal training (without so much as a glimmer of self-consciousness towards the gasping crowd) whereas Fyodor – praising divine intervention – manages to scale a cliff in the manner of a Warner Brothers cartoon character, motivated solely by a desire to keep all of the wealth to himself.

At least part of the main characters' desperation for freedom, Brooks shows us so vividly throughout the film, lies in their reaction towards an essentially repressive society which aims to control every aspect of their lives. The absurd abundance of red tape and establishment formalities are beautifully conveyed by the Bureau of Housing sequence, leading Bender on a wild goose chase of official procedure (including a bureau dealing with bureaus) before culminating in his arrival at the 'Bureau of Furniture Not Listed in Other Bureaus'. Infighting within the Politburo is shrewdly alluded to with a sign which designates 'Marx, Engels, Lenin Street' with the word 'Trotsky' freshly eliminated. Vorobyaninov has become so wedded to his bureaucratic role that he accidentally imprints his dying mother-in-law on the cheek with an official 'cancelled' stamp as he embraces her while she draws her last breath. Even the Columbus Repertory Theatre proves that the dramatic arts are not impervious from limitations on freedom of expression when it presents '*Hamlet and the October Revolution* by William Shakespeare and Ivan Poppov'. But it is the frantic rush for the free buffet at the opening of the Railway Workers' Communal House of Recreation which speaks most clearly about the state's provision of even basic essentials such as food and shelter. It seems small wonder that commentator Nathan Rabin observed that, on the face of it, a narrative summary of the film can basically be reduced to that of 'a funny, manic, mean-spirited goof about a frantic race to find hidden treasure in a Soviet Union where much of the populace has gone half-mad from hunger and desperation'.[7]

And yet, on account of Brooks's satirical eye and insight into the human psyche, *The Twelve Chairs* becomes so much more than that. The only people who seem to have any kind of desire to uphold Communist principles with anything other than glib lip-service are those who are seen to benefit from it most, such as the well-to-do Mr and Madame Bruns. 'There will be no grovelling in this house!' Madame Bruns snaps indignantly in their comfortable home. 'This is a Soviet household – we don't allow grovelling!' For the majority of the characters, however, the stark reality of totalitarianism lends itself to a quite dissimilar way of life. Tikon, for instance (a brief but memorable role from Brooks himself), is embittered by his lot, preferring the serfdom of the past to an all-encompassing but ultimately hollow egalitarianism where everyone seems more or less equally miserable in one way or another. 'Comrade. Comrade!' he spits bitterly. 'Everybody calls me comrade. Everybody in the new Soviet Union is a comrade! People you don't know, strangers... everybody says "comrade". Oh, I miss Russia.' However, in spite of his disdain for the status quo Tikon still knows that he has to grudgingly play his part in the state-sanctioned game of comradely obeisance; hanging in his basement quarters is a portrait of Vladimir Lenin, a visage omnipresent throughout the USSR, mirroring the propaganda photo of Hitler in Franz Liebkind's apartment but with not a hint of the deranged playwright's impassioned zealotry. Such is Tikon's contempt for the recent direction of his country that he spends most of his leisure time staring at the bottom of a bottle, leading to an intoxicated, rose-tinted view of a brutally inequitable past. Thus he remembers Vorobyaninov with great fondness, even though the older man is seen casually beating his servant during their every encounter, while his disapproval towards Revolutionary fervour has been blunted to the point that it now forms a sort of vague, melancholic annoyance:

BENDER: Whatever became of your lovable master?
TIKON: One night, about ten years ago, was a fearful noise. It was bombs and cannons and soldiers shooting. It was terrible, terrible.
BENDER: Oh yes. I think it was called the Revolution.
TIKON: That was it! The revolution.

Just as the majority of the characters seem thoroughly ground down by the harshness of Soviet life, some nonetheless find ways to subvert the cultural mores of the new social order to their advantage. When we first meet Bender he is pretending to be an injured veteran of the storming of the Winter Palace in 1917 (an event which was depicted so memorably in Sergei Eisenstein's 1927 film *October*), and is holding a placard which proudly proclaims 'I left an eye and a leg at the Winter Palace. Won't you leave something with me?' In other words, he is happy to capitalise on nostalgic and/ or nationalistic fervour to serve his purposes. Then there is the hypocrisy of Father Fyodor, who almost immediately discards the trappings of his religious order as he races headlong after the hidden jewellery. Not only does he flagrantly disregard the sanctity of confession to use Ivanova's information for his own ends (never considering her own family's claim to their property), but when leaving her house he consoles a grieving neighbour with brief but vaguely comforting theological platitudes before roughly shoving her out of the way, such is his fixation on his new goal. Dispensing with his pastoral role as he begins his chaotic hunt for the wayward riches (almost taking the garden gate with him as he goes), the priest unwittingly calls attention to his dereliction of spiritual duty. It is manifestly obvious that Fyodor has no interest in using the gems for any kind of Christian practice, such as aiding the poor or supporting the church, and is thus every bit as driven by naked acquisitiveness as his rivals – a fact that Brooks ridicules in the way that the burly cleric's appearance is usually heralded by a burst of Gregorian Chant, emphasising the depth of his hypocrisy in being driven by mammon rather than a sense of spiritual responsibility. Such is the Fyodor's sheer duplicity and the potency of his base motivation, he sees (or allows himself to see) no irony in the fact that his greed runs diametrically opposed to the traditionally-stated Christian values of altruism and non-materialism:

> VOROBYANINOV: Why are you after my chair?
> FYODOR: It's not yours!
> VOROBYANINOV: Then whose is it?
> FYODOR: It's nationalised property. It belongs to the workers!
> VOROBYANINOV: Did you say the *workers*?
> FYODOR: Yes, the workers.
> VOROBYANINOV: Maybe the Holy Father is a member of the Communist Party?
> FYODOR: Maybe.
> VOROBYANINOV: But the Party is for atheists! How can a priest join the Party?

FYODOR: The Church must keep up with the times!

Because of the cleric's strange ambivalence towards his religious faith – just when he seems to have abandoned spirituality completely, he calls upon some aspect of it or another in moments of desperation – Fyodor's headlong rush into wanton cupidity becomes all the more fascinating and enigmatic, not least given Dom DeLuise's bravura display of out-of-control histrionics in more or less every scene he appears in. 'O thou who knowest all... You know,' he prays, entirely superficially, assuming that this glib cliché will justify his actions in the eyes of the Almighty. Later, the despair surrounding his thwarted ambitions override any pretence towards a spiritual mindset: 'Foolish, foolish man that I am. I must not weep. I must count my blessings. My blessings. [*Laughs hysterically.*] I DON'T WANT TO LIVE!' His eventual destiny, left to an uncertain fate at the pinnacle of a craggy mountain as the others desert him, may well be Brooks's idea of divine retribution for the priest's total abandonment of his moral principles; 'You're so strict!' he calls out to God, who appears no longer to be listening.

The relationship between Vorobyaninov and Bender is similarly complicated, though for different reasons. The two men constantly attempt to outmanoeuvre and manipulate one another, and though both grudgingly seem to acknowledge that their chances of success are greater when they work in concert, similarly there is rarely any sign of fraternal affection between them until the film's closing scene. Both Ron Moody and Frank Langella were experienced stage veterans, and they present a memorably testy double-act which is distantly removed from the surrogate father-and-son pairing of Bialystock and Bloom. The youthful Bender is clearly a man of the times, able to outwit even the most bellicose of foes with an unctuous word and sleight of hand, and Langella's dark, brooding looks are the perfect contrast to Moody's edgy expressions and deliberately erratic physicality. Bender rages at Vorobyaninov's haughty condescension when the older man refuses to beg because it offends his dignity; for the impoverished Bender, relying on his wits and the resources of others (whether they have been hoodwinked or freely offered) has always been a way of life, and he has never been allowed the comfort of even the straitened circumstances that the former aristocrat now occupies in his current role as a low-ranking office worker. Bender never tries to disguise the fact that he is quite plainly out for what he can get – this *raison d'être* has, through circumstance, simply become routine. Likewise, Vorobyaninov's selfishness is established from his very first appearance, even before he becomes aware of the lost jewels: 'That poor woman! That poor woman!' he laments upon hearing that his mother-in-law is dying, before promptly getting to the crux of it: 'Who is going to take care of me?' His concern for others is illuminated solely by the effects that they have on his own life. Even as his mother-in-law lies dying, he offers her words which bring not comfort but accusation: 'Stuffed in a ch... How could you do such a thing? Why didn't you give them to me? [...] Fifty thousand roubles' worth of jewellery, stuffed in a chair?' Yet by the use of a brief flashback, Brooks fleetingly shows us the former nobleman in all of his pre-Revolution finery, emphasising the man's acute sense of stolen position and lost worth. But even here, not everything is as it seems. As Ivanova makes abundantly clear, even her son-in-law's vaunted status and material prosperity were only made possible thanks to the fruits of a strategically-considered marriage; it was ultimately his wife's resources, not his own, which assured him a life of luxury. And the fact that Vorobyaninov spends the film lamenting the opulence of the past without ever expressing a word of sorrow for the death of his late spouse, or remorse over her absence from his life, is a further indicator of his shallow motivation and palpable lack of empathy.

Recognising that Vorobyaninov's sheer desperation to recover some aspect of his bygone comforts has rendered him susceptible to being outfoxed, Bender curtly reminds him that 'there is no personal property in the Soviet Union. Everything belongs to the people.' Or, to put it another way, he feels that he has just as much claim to the chair's hidden bounty as the older man does. Yet while neither can truly allege to be the owner of the jewels, it is of course equally true that in the Soviet Union the very same could be said of Ivanova herself. As Lenora P. Ledwon has observed, 'after the revolution, private property (such as the jewels and even the chairs) belongs to the State. In fact, the State has already nationalized the family estate. In hiding the jewels, the mother-in-law has potentially committed a crime against the State. No wonder she feels guilt at her actions, both from a personal/ family dynamics perspective, and from a societal/ juridical perspective'.[8] Thus Ivanova too has, of course, transgressed the law of the land, proving that – as Crick so judiciously notes – the rise of Communism and its state-enforced parity has done nothing to blunt the characters' innate human greed; neither politics, society nor even organised religion appear to have the ability to do so.[9]

It seems obvious, then, that while the proceeds of Ivanova's jewels may have improved living conditions for whomever may have discovered them, they could not have offered escape from the social repression of Soviet Russia itself, and thus offer only a partial and partisan respite from what is an essentially oppressive culture. Thus there is much irony in the fact that they are ultimately used to fund the construction of a communal house of recreation intended for the use of workers – the harnessing of once-private riches for a collective benefit, very much in the spirit of Communist economic practice. If there is any ideological virtue in this, it is unsurprisingly not recognised by the main characters. In Fyodor's failure, he finds only dejection and a sense of spiritual vacuum. For Vorobyaninov and Bender, by contrast, their disappointment brings a kind of closure – after all, the jewels cannot be stolen back as they have already been sold for a particular purpose, so the two men are forced to deal with the outcome that faces them in the here and now. Their dreams may have been shattered, but in their loss they find that they have gained something – namely, a bond of friendship which transcends the tetchy business partnership that drove their common effort throughout the film. Brooks has argued that, even more than a criticism of an innately human tendency towards greed, the film's real focus is that of the individual's need – and search – for love,[10] and certainly this is articulated in a number of ways throughout the film. Vorobyaninov shows an inability to reciprocate his mother-in-law's affection as she lies dying, but eventually grows to form a sincere fraternal companionship with his one-time competitor and reluctant ally. Bender likewise shows some degree of genuine affection for Vorobyaninov in the way that he continues to include him in the plan to retrieve the chairs (despite many threats to the contrary) even when he has ample opportunity to sideline him and strike out on his own. Cast in contrast to his fleeting promiscuous dalliances (where he leaves a married woman with no illusions by telling her that he is 'very much in lust' with her, before making a hasty retreat as soon as her husband arrives), the solidification of his personal association with Vorobyaninov over the course of the film seems all the more heartfelt. No such development is possible for Fyodor, who is willing to shed every aspect of his religious, professional and personal identity – his beard, his ecclesiastical robes, and even his concern for his parishioners – in order to embark on his own search for Ivanova's jewellery. For Fyodor – quite literally – nothing is sacred, and his dereliction of his responsibilities (to say nothing of the abandonment of his self-professed moral duties) ultimately leads to him being left alone and isolated just as his competitors are realising the potential of collective endeavour in addition to the personal benefits of shared camaraderie. As Richard Schickel commented, one of Brooks's key achievements with the film was to examine familiar qualities of character within a relatively unfamiliar milieu in order to present a commentary on the universality of human nature:

> Mr Brooks remains the only domestic maker of screen comedy who derives his effects not from situations but from bitterly truthful morality. Massively invaded by one or more of the seven deadlies, his people become caricatures of our worst selves. Yet they are never less than human. If anything, they are more than human, and from that fact our shocked, delighted laughter of recognition derives. All power to the Mel Brookses of the world.[11]

Although *The Twelve Chairs* continued Brooks's exploration of certain key themes that were in evidence throughout his first film, it did prove to be a distinctive artistic endeavour which demonstrated, even at an early stage, his ability as a director who had both range and ambition. As Brooks was subsequently to explain, his experience in directing *The Twelve Chairs* was to prove a formative one, offering fundamental knowledge of the film-making process which built confidently upon his professional cinematic debut.[12] Yet although it was released to a distinctly muted reaction from the public, Lawrence J. Epstein has observed that the film succeeded in bringing Brooks's talents to the attention of a wider audience: '*The Twelve Chairs* is technically much more sophisticated than *The Producers*, and many critics who didn't like the earlier film liked this one. Yet, *The Twelve Chairs* [...] was not a commercial success, though it did make money because it had cost so little to produce'.[13]

In subsequent years, Brooks's emotional attachment to the project has been made ever clearer. In 1975 he stated that 'I can never let a picture go, I think I could work on *Twelve Chairs* for the rest of my life. I spent a year of my life making that picture, I thought it was going to be my masterpiece'.[14] And yet, for all his grand thematic intentions, *The Twelve Chairs* remains, at heart, more comedy than drama. Dorde Nikolic's beautiful, sweeping cinematography, most notably during Vorobyaninov and Bender's concluding trek from Yalta back to Moscow, never seems to jar too gratingly with the sped-up chase sequences (complete with high-pitched dialogue) which accompany the Keystone Kops-style slapstick. Thus, as Nick Smurthwaite and Paul Gelder have noted, 'for all his literary pretensions, Brooks is primarily concerned with entertaining his audience by whatever means are most easily assimilated by the largest number of people',[15] and to this end the satirical aims – no matter how towering or how worthy – are never allowed to overwhelm the film's prevailing accessibility. There are also numerous instances of what would become staples in Brooks's film-making; references to the theatre and theatricality (in this case typified by the troupe led by the humorously pretentious Nikolai Sestrin, a return appearance by Andreas Voutsinas following his role as the waspish Carmen Ghia in *The Producers*), the simultaneous glorification and depreciation of con-artistry, and of course the obligatory in-joke which cunningly undermines the fourth wall: the rail worker who accidentally discovers the hidden jewels while putting up a pair of curtains is none other than Kaminsky – Brooks's own real surname.

Ken Hanke has argued that *The Twelve Chairs* 'is probably the closest Brooks ever came to making a "normal" film. That may also be why it's largely ignored today – sandwiched between the classic *The Producers* and the brazenly outrageous *Blazing Saddles*'.[16] Certainly there may be no small amount of truth in this statement, for *The Twelve Chairs* marks a rare occasion where the dramatic element of a Brooks movie comes close to (but is never quite allowed to exceed) its comedic content. John J. Puccio similarly makes the point that '*The Twelve Chairs* is not a typical Brooks film, not a parody of any other art form, and not a satire, unless you count its constant pokes at Mankind's greed. Certainly, it uses a string of gags like most Brooks films, but the gags are mostly visual this time, not verbal. Slapstick is the order of the day, some of it broad, a little of it subtle'.[17] Throughout all of his films, of course, Brooks has rarely been accused of delicate sensitivity... and this is exactly why he excels at making his point through indirect or even subversive means. He seems to take great delight, for instance, in setting a film in a drearily repressive totalitarian state and then using this largely cheerless environment as a backdrop for an exploration of common humanity, of basic human needs, and of a conscious and unconscious desire to be set free – aspects of life which affect everyone, irrespective of social class or nationality. All of these themes would be variously explored by Brooks later in his career, but rarely did their employment feel quite so heartfelt; Clark Douglas, for instance, notes that the film 'is actually a good deal more focused on its plot than many Brooks films. While Brooks' films grew increasingly episodic as his career progressed, *The Twelve Chairs* offers a story that rarely goes off on aimless tangents',[18] and certainly the desire to stay true to the spirit of the Ilf and Petrov source text (even when deviating from its incidents) seemed to encourage Brooks to explore the boundaries of the adaptation with care in order to make the most of its cinematic retelling, thus divesting the film of the kind of off-the-wall, frenetic reconfiguration of genre expectations which would be all too apparent in the likes of *Blazing Saddles* and *Young Frankenstein*.

Brooks also seems keen to treat the period and its denizens with genuine respect. Brutality, scarcity and state interference are highlighted, but so is the kindness of ordinary people trying to make the best of their lives in rarefied circumstances. Desser and Friedman have observed that '*The Twelve Chairs* demonstrates how Brooks draws on his cultural past and love of Russian literature, but he never forgets that such times, for Jews in particular, were both harsh and cruel',[19] and indeed Brooks himself has made no secret of his high regard for Russian prose fiction in general, explaining in no uncertain terms the admiration, even reverence, that he has developed for the form. Stephen J. Whitfield notes that:

> [Brooks] is on record as admiring not only Gogol but also the supreme diagnostician of crime and punishment. 'My God, I'd love to smash into the casket of Dostoevsky,' Brooks has announced with

characteristic nuance and scruple and self-restraint, 'grab that bony hand and scream at the remains, "Well done, you goddam genius"'.[20]

As had been the case with *The Producers* before it, *The Twelve Chairs* was to meet with a decidedly mixed response from the critical community at the time of its release. Some commentators, such as Judith Crist – writing in *New York* Magazine – praised the sincerity of Brooks's creative aims, remarking that 'it's the characters, the craziness and the lovability of fools that count in Mel Brooks' approach to comedy and that make his second feature, *The Twelve Chairs*, a complete joy,' adding that 'it's the creation of a man steeped in social comedy, and saturated with a kindliness of spirit that in no way dims his eye for satire'.[21] On the other side of the debate, the *New York Times*'s Vincent Canby seemed considerably less convinced of the film's merits:

> Most of the things that happen [...] are almost as joyless, and as joyless as the Soviet Union the film purposefully depicts. This is, I think, because Mr Brooks's sense of humor is expressed almost entirely in varying degrees of rudeness and cruelty, unrelieved by any comic vision of mankind, of the Soviet Union, or even of his characters. There is an innocence about *The Twelve Chairs*, but it is the kind of innocence in which one character will say to another 'You aren't worth spitting on.' To which the second replies: 'Well you are!' and then spits on the first. For some reason, this sort of comedy of physical insult seemed much funnier to me in the Broadway world of *The Producers*, which really is aggressive and nasty and cheap, than in a Russia that is not too far removed from the world of Sholem Aleichem.[22]

In spite of this lack of critical consensus, *The Twelve Chairs* was not forgotten at the awards ceremonies, with Frank Langella winning a National Board of Review Award for Best Supporting Actor in 1971, and Brooks himself being nominated for a Writers Guild of America Award in the category of Best Comedy Adapted from Another Medium the same year. Although the film was subsequently to depart the public consciousness into a state of near-obscurity, denied the blockbuster success of *Blazing Saddles* or the cult sustainability of *The Producers*, it nonetheless formed an important transitional landmark in Brooks's career, demarcating various new areas of thematic concern while reinforcing previously established ones. Today the film remains quite different from any other entry in Brooks's oeuvre, and is testament to the directorial scope of a film-maker for whom comedy was never a blunt instrument but rather a scalpel, hacking away at duplicity and pretence while making social, cultural and even moral points with deft precision. Though his later films would rarely delve too deeply into such self-consciously 'serious' comedy, *The Twelve Chairs* proved to be significant in the way that it emphasised Brooks's interest in interpersonal relationships, in social dynamics, and in the way that fundamental human nature adapts to – and remains largely unchanged by – the world around us. While the juxtaposition of liberty and tyranny would be revisited later in Brooks's films, rarely did the search for freedom seem quite so starkly drawn than in the desperate avarice of Vorobyaninov, his accomplice and his adversary.

# REFERENCES

1. Robert Alan Crick, *The Big Screen Comedies of Mel Brooks* (Jefferson: McFarland and Company, 2009) [2002], pp. 34-35.
2. Maurice Yacowar, *The Comic Art of Mel Brooks* (London: W.H. Allen, 1982), pp. 112-13.
3. ibid., p. 120.
4. Sid Caesar, in Sid Caesar with Eddy Friedfeld, *Caesar's Hours: My Life in Comedy, with Love and Laughter* (New York: Perseus, 2003), p. 137.
5. Mel Brooks, in Bill Adler and Jeffrey Feinman, *Mel Brooks: The Irreverent Funnyman* (Chicago: Playboy Press, 1976), p. 91.
6. David Desser and Lester D. Friedman, *American Jewish Filmmakers*, 2nd edn (Chicago: University of Illinois Press, 2004), p. 131.
7. Nathan Rabin, 'The Mel Brooks Collection', in *The Onion AV Club*, 11 April 2006.
   <http://www.avclub.com/review/the-mel-brooks-collection-9121>
8. Lenora P. Ledwon, 'Guilt, Greed, and Furniture: Using Mel Brooks' *The Twelve Chairs* to Teach Dying Declarations', in *California Law Review Circuit*, Vol. 3, No. 1, January 2012, 72-79, p. 78.
9. Crick, p. 37.
10. Brooks, in Fred Robbins, 'What Makes Mel Brooks Run?' in *Show*, 17 September 1970, pp. 12-15.
11. Richard Schickel, 'Critic's Roundup', in *Life*, 18 December 1970, pp. 6-7.
12. Brooks, 'My Movies: The Collusion of Art and Money', in *The Movie Business Book*, 3rd edn, ed. by Jason E. Squire (Maidenhead: Open University Press, 2006), 39-48, p. 42.
13. Lawrence J. Epstein, *The Haunted Smile: The Story of Jewish Comedians* (Oxford: PublicAffairs, 2001), pp. 210-11.
14. Brooks, in Jacoba Atlas, 'New Hollywood: Mel Brooks Interview', in *Film Comment*, March-April 1975.
    <http://www.brookslyn.com/print/FilmComment1975/FilmComment1975.php>
15. Nick Smurthwaite and Paul Gelder, *Mel Brooks and the Spoof Movie* (London: Proteus Books, 1982), p. 39.
16. Ken Hanke, '*The Twelve Chairs*', in *Mountain Xpress*, 26 July 2006.
    <http://mountainx.com/movies/reviews/twelvechairs-php/>
17. John J. Puccio, '*The Twelve Chairs*', in *Movie Metropolis*, 1 January 2000.
    <http://moviemet.com/review/twelve-chairs-dvd-review>
18. Clark Douglas, '*The Mel Brooks Collection*', in *DVD Verdict*, 21 December 2009.
    <http://www.dvdverdict.com/reviews/melbrooksbluray.php>
19. Desser and Friedman, p. 132.
20. Stephen J. Whitfield, 'The Distinctiveness of American Jewish Humor', in *Modern Judaism*, Vol. 6, No. 3, October 1986, 245-60, p. 254.
21. Judith Crist, 'Vintage Brando', in *New York Magazine*, 2 November 1970, p. 61.
22. Vincent Canby, 'Screen: Mel Brooks on Prowl in Soviet *12 Chairs*, a Comedy, at Tower East', in *The New York Times*, 29 October 1970.
    <http://www.nytimes.com/movie/review?res=9D04E4DC173BEE34BC4151DFB667838B669EDE>

The Producers (1967), this page and over.

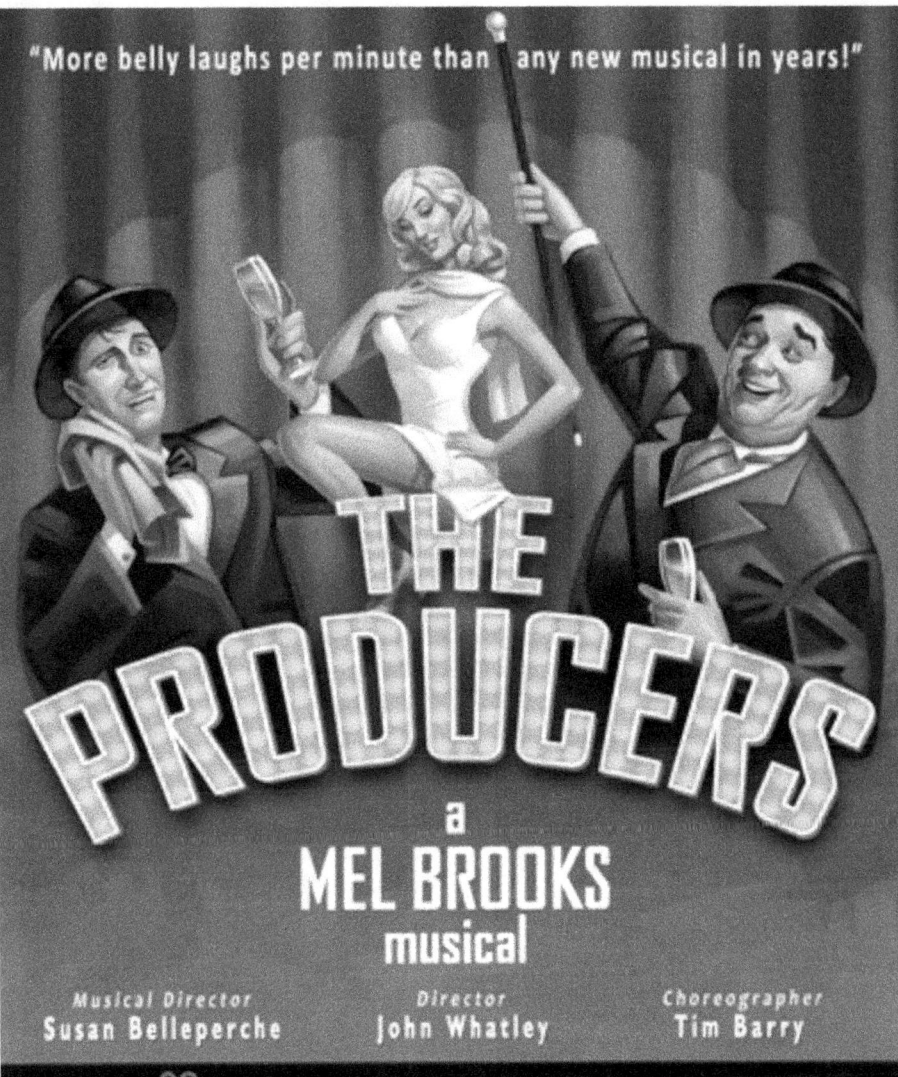

The Producers musical

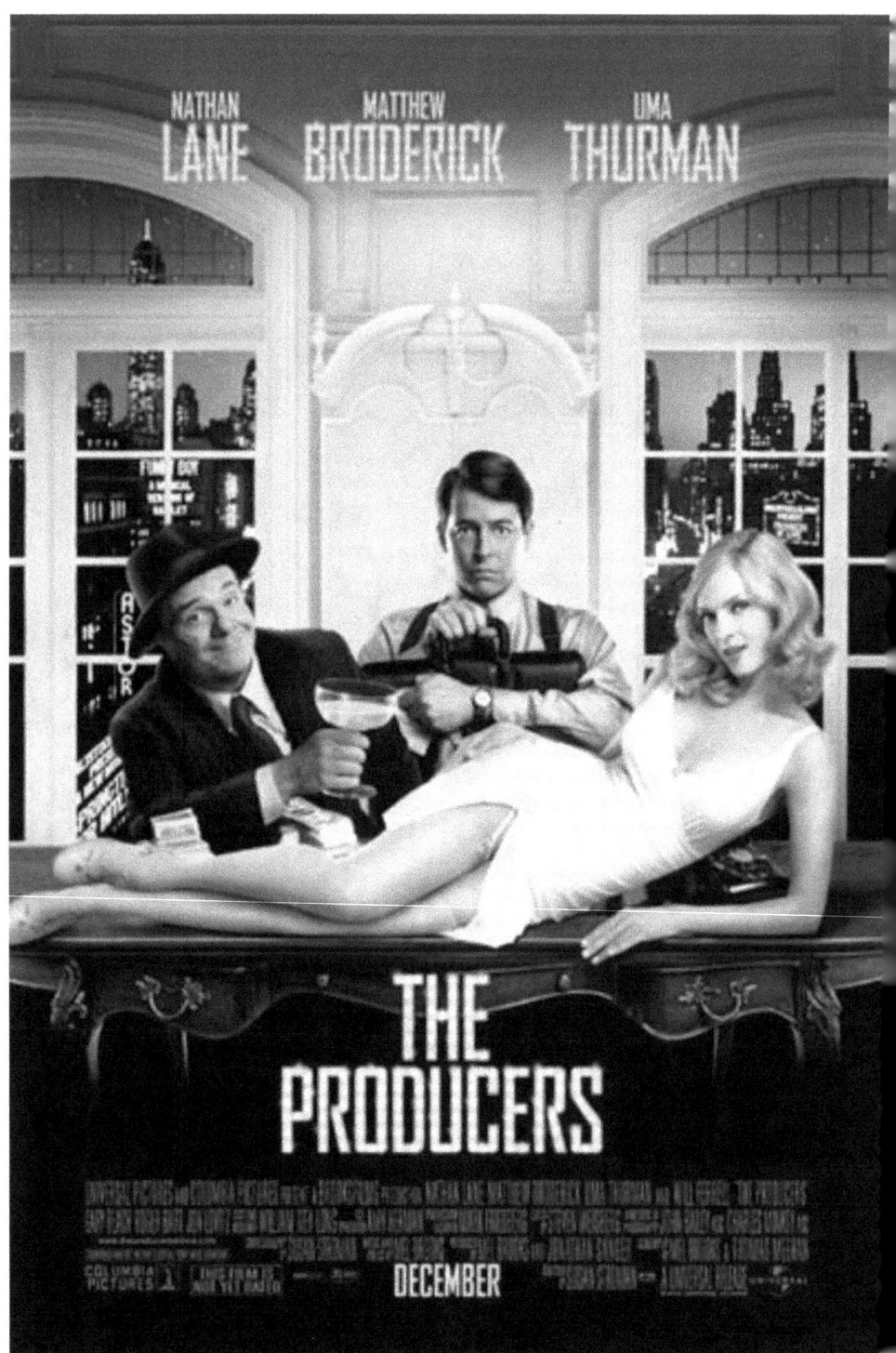

The Producers (2001)

12 Chairs (1970), this page and over.

A Mel Brooks Film
the Twelve Chairs

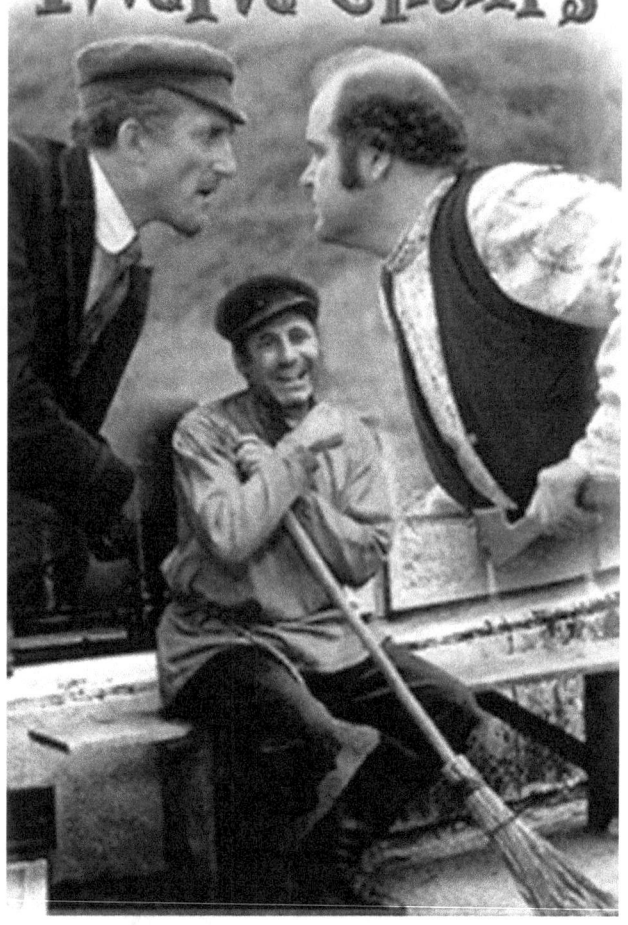

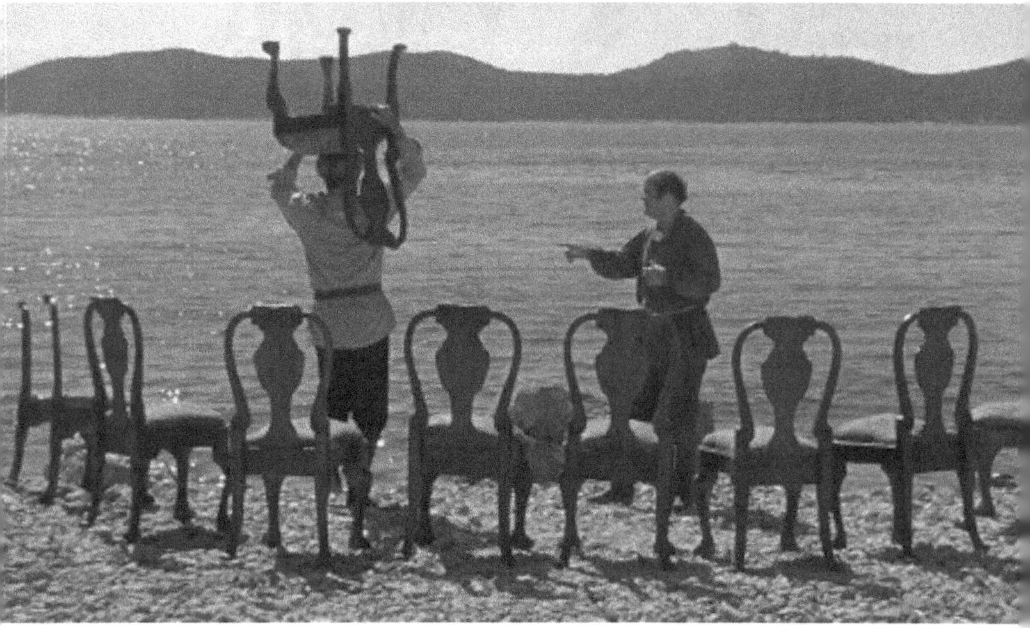

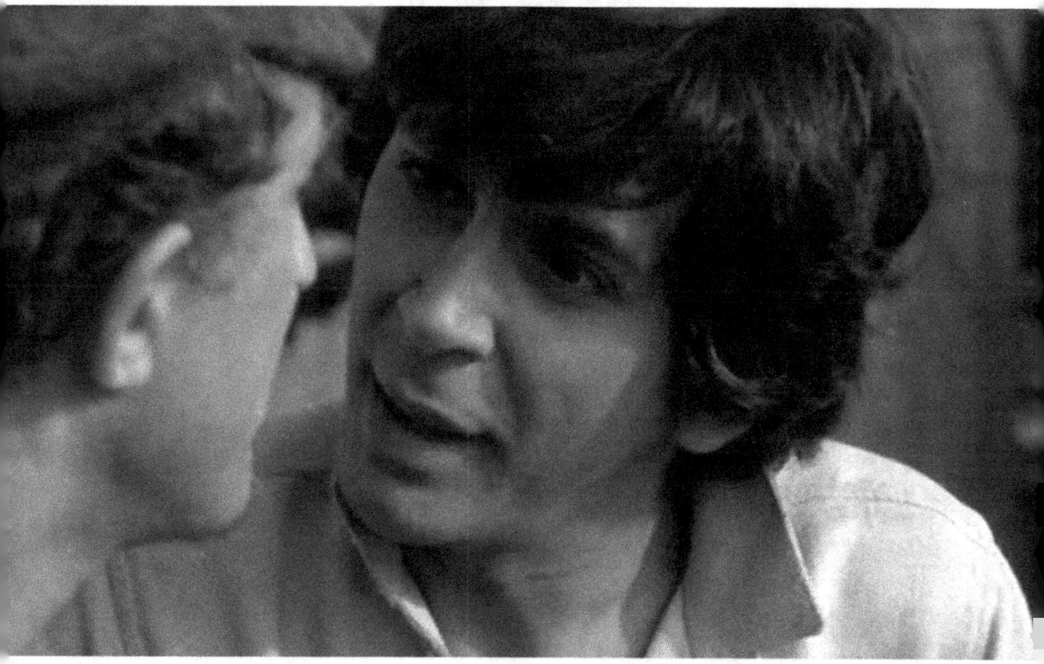

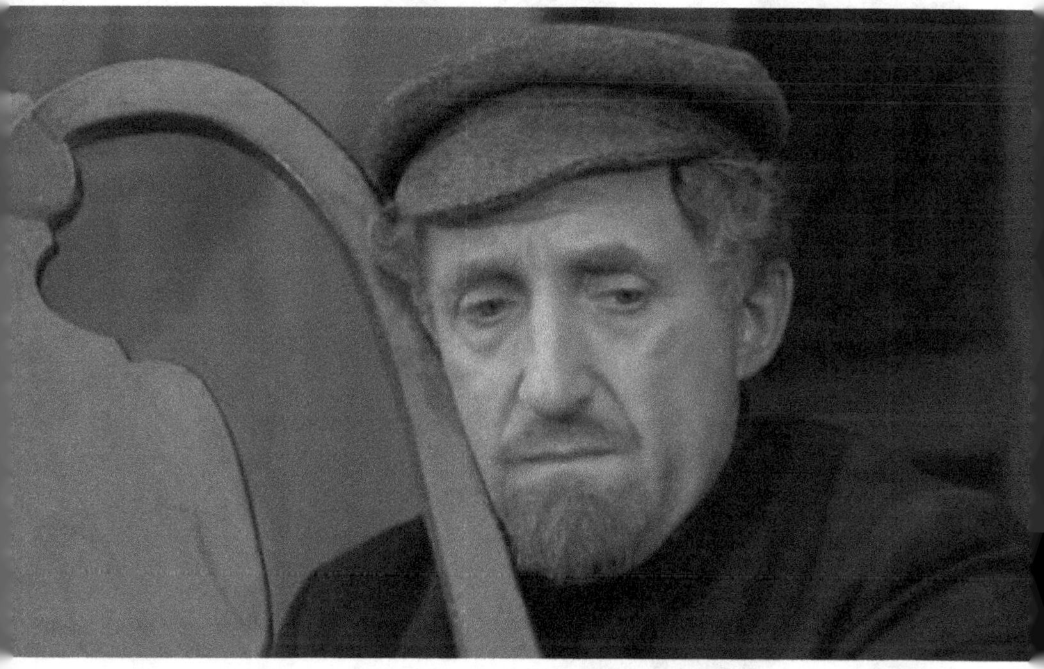

# 3

# BLAZING SADDLES (1974)

*BLAZING SADDLES* PROVED to be, in a number of ways, a watershed feature for Mel Brooks. No other film he has directed was to have quite as much critical attention lavished upon it by commentators and film scholars, and indeed its razor-sharp cultural critique has won it almost as many fans over the years as its iconoclastic humour. The film was a huge commercial success, grossing $119,500,000 at the American box-office,[1] and certainly its prominence was instrumental in establishing Brooks as a major talent in comedy cinema with broad audience appeal. However, its enormous profitability notwithstanding, the lasting prominence of *Blazing Saddles* in Brooks's filmography has been assured by the originality of its central concept, its vast influence on the spoof comedy subgenre in the years which followed, and the multiply-layered exploration of social justice and interpersonal equality which is skilfully (and often ingeniously) employed throughout the movie.

*Blazing Saddles* was to be a significant entry in the Brooks canon for several other reasons. For one, it marked an early instance in his career where Brooks was directing a film with a screenplay that had not been solely written by himself, but rather in collaboration with a number of co-writers including Richard Pryor (then a rapidly rising star in comedy) and the author of the initial draft of the film's script, Andrew Bergman. As Brooks himself has noted:

It was written very much like the old *Show of Shows*. I didn't have time to write it myself, so I asked Warner Bros. if I could hire a black writer, two Jews, and the original writer. And they said, why do you want the original writer when we have his script? And I said I'm sure there's more in his head since we liked his idea so much. So we got the original writer, Andrew Bergman; two Jews, Norman Steinberg and Alan Unger; and a black writer, Richard Pryor. And we all wailed. We sat in a room and wrote it like the *Show of Shows*. Everybody fighting to make the best joke. There was a secretary in with us on every session going crazy trying to take everything down. We didn't use a tape recorder because it inhibits writers, they start editing and playing to the recorder.[2]

Although *Blazing Saddles* had a hugely significant effect on the audiences of the time, and definitely pushed the boundaries of acceptability in ways which clearly laid the stylistic groundwork for later filmmakers such as the David Zucker-Jim Abrahams-Jerry Zucker parodies of the eighties and Peter and Bobby Farrelly in the nineties, the film was a fascinating amalgamation of the traditional and the revolutionary. Certainly the Western comedy was by no means a new Hollywood development, with prominent artists such as the Marx Brothers in *Go West* (Edward Buzzell, 1940) and Abbott and Costello in *Ride 'Em Cowboy* (Arthur Lubin, 1942) employing the stalwart genre as a backdrop for comedic situations, whereas John Sturges's wry mockumentary *The Hallelujah Trail* (1965) wittily considered the tropes of the Western as well as exploring (and satirising) some of the cultural characteristics inherent in the westward expansionism of nineteenth century American history. However, Brooks was not content to simply use the Old West as a mere period setting for his film; instead, he seemed intent on reducing the whitewashed truisms of Hollywood's invented historical conventions to their individual component parts, ridiculing an overused formula by casting it in the stark light of modern day anxieties. The result, as Matthew R. Turner has stated, was a breath of fresh air which informed almost as much as it entertained: 'The Western parody that is widely considered the magnum opus of the genre is Mel Brooks's *Blazing Saddles*, a film that systematically dissects nearly all the clichés and the very premises of the form'.[3]

On the American Frontier in the year 1874, a railroad work team are in the process of laying the rails of a new track when a quicksand swamp is discovered in the path of their intended route. One of the African American rail workers, Bart (Cleavon

Little), is sent to investigate, but inadvertently becomes trapped in the swamp himself. The team's Caucasian supervisors, Taggart (Slim Pickens) and Lyle (Burton Gilliam) arrive on the scene, but are so prejudiced that they elect to save a rapidly-submerging hand-cart while leaving Bart to his fate. Incensed at this injustice, Bart manages to trace his way along a sunken length of rail and thus escapes death, subsequently knocking out the callous Taggart in an angry (if entirely justifiable) fit of resentment.

The presence of quicksand means that the new railroad must be diverted, but it is rapidly discovered that this will force the construction to run straight through Rock Ridge, a nearby town. The state's corrupt Attorney General, Hedley Lamarr (Harvey Korman), instructs Taggart to round up some men and conduct a reign of terror upon Rock Ridge with the intention of forcing the town's inhabitants to abandon their homes and flee. This will pave the way for the land to be purchased cheaply, thus allowing the railroad construction to carry on unimpeded. Though daunted by the relentless violence that is being perpetrated against them, the townsfolk of Rock Ridge eventually resolve to make a stand and defend their properties rather than abandon them to the marauders. To this end, they write to the state Governor, William J. Le Petomane (Mel Brooks), requesting that he dispatch a new sheriff in the hope of restoring order.

Lamarr is initially frustrated by this turn of events until he notices Bart heading for the gallows, having been sentenced to execution for his earlier assault on Taggart. Immediately seizing on an idea, he recommends to Le Petomane that Bart be exonerated on the condition that he be appointed as the state-sanctioned sheriff of Rock Ridge. The Governor is initially sceptical, reasoning that the blatantly racist townsfolk will never accept an African American lawman and are likely to murder him out of sheer bigotry. However, Lamarr manages to talk the vain Le Petomane into the scheme by assuring him that his actions will cement his reputation as a pioneer of racial equality. Little does the Governor suspect that Lamarr actually intends to demoralise the citizens of Rock Ridge with the appointment of the new sheriff, expecting them to reject (or possibly even kill) Bart and thus speeding the Attorney General's own plans to destroy the town through force and underhanded coercion.

Bart arrives in Rock Ridge and immediately meets with a

wave of livid intolerance; only his quick thinking saves him from being shot dead by the outraged townsfolk during a hastily-abandoned welcoming committee. Retreating into the sheriff's office, he meets Jim (Gene Wilder), an alcoholic sharp-shooter who was formerly known as the Waco Kid due to his legendary gun-slinging skills. However, Jim is now a washed-up shadow of his former self, found napping in the drunk tank. The pair quickly become friends, as the easy-going Jim is free from racial prejudice (unlike his fellow townspeople) and is happy to accept the newcomer as an equal.

Bart attempts to fit in with the inhabitants of Rock Ridge, but is undermined and insulted at every turn. The town's council decides to write a letter of protest to Le Petomane, demanding that Bart be recalled from his post, but they are left with no choice but to call on the new sheriff's talents when the town is invaded by Mongo (Alex Karras), a simple-minded strongman in Taggart's employ who has been sent to spread hysteria throughout Rock Ridge. Mongo leaves a trail of destruction, managing to all but wreck the interior of the town's saloon (to say nothing of its patrons), but by employing some inspired chicanery Bart is able to subdue him, winning some grudging respect from the townsfolk in the process.

Exasperated by his inability to dispose of Bart, Lamarr calls on the beautiful German chanteuse Lili von Shtupp (Madeline Kahn) to seduce the sheriff and then crush his feelings by cruelly rejecting him, thus neutralising his nemesis by emotional rather than physical means. However, following a hastily-organised musical show at the town saloon, the super-cool Bart ends up sweeping Lili off her feet instead, leaving her besotted and thus foiling Lamarr's plans once again. Now desperate, the villainous Attorney General is left with no choice but to launch one final scheme to drive everyone out of Rock Ridge. He sets about recruiting every criminal and desperado in the West to lay siege to the town, seeking to leave the area deserted at all costs.

Getting wind of Lamarr's plans, Bart brings together the townsfolk and his one-time workmates from the railroad as he presents a potential counter-strategy. If they work together, they will have just enough time to construct an exact replica of Rock Ridge three miles east of the actual town. This will distract the invaders from attacking the real settlement, giving the inhabitants at least a fighting chance. In return for their efforts, the rail workers will be granted land of their own. At first the townsfolk are reluctant, unable to overcome their prejudice against the multi-racial workforce, but they eventually see that they have little choice in the matter and thus grudgingly agree to Bart's terms.

The next morning, with the facsimile town now complete, the denizens of Rock Ridge are populating the empty streets with life-sized replicas of themselves while Bart manages to successfully slow the approach of the criminals by erecting a tollbooth on the road leading towards the town. (Believing that the thruway is a state initiative to raise revenue, Taggart refuses to ignore the toll fee and sends a bandit back to camp for small change so that the mob can continue on their way.) Once they do eventually reach the fake Rock Ridge, the bandits only just manage to discern that they have been hoodwinked when Jim sets off a series of rigged dynamite charges, throwing them into complete disarray.

As the townsfolk sweep into the remnants of the replica Rock Ridge in order to finish off the invaders, the camera pans away from the scene to reveal that the action is situated not in the Old West, but in a modern-day studio back-lot. Soon after, the chaotic fight escapes into another set entirely, where indignant director Buddy Bizarre (Dom DeLuise) is choreographing an elaborate song-and-dance number. As the dancers involuntarily become embroiled in the running battle between the Rock Ridge townspeople and the criminals, the brawl spills into the Warner Brothers commissary where it abruptly degenerates into a wild custard pie fight. Sensing that the action has now slipped completely out of his control, Lamarr surreptitiously hails a taxi while the other characters pour out of the studios into the streets of Burbank.

Lamarr eventually winds up at the famous Grauman's Chinese Theatre, where he buys a ticket for the premiere screening of *Blazing Saddles*. As soon as he gets into the auditorium, however, he discovers that Bart and Jim are being projected onto the cinema screen... and furthermore. that they are being shown arriving at the same theatre in hot pursuit. Racing away from the scene, Lamarr is confronted by Bart and tries to trick his way out of being apprehended, only to be shot dead in retaliation for one last attempt on Bart's life. Back in Rock Ridge, the villain now vanquished and the townsfolk living in apparent harmony with the one-time railroad workers, Bart realises that his work is now done. Saying their goodbyes to the denizens of the town, Bart and Jim ride off into the sunset... though once they are out of the townsfolk's line of sight, an animal-handler takes safe custody of their horses as the crime-fighting pair are ushered away in the comfort of a chauffeur-driven limousine.

In spite of its gleeful embrace of unashamed lunacy, much of it wilfully surreal, *Blazing Saddles* highlighted two of Brooks's enduring thematic concerns: his abiding affection for the film industry and its heritage, and an overwhelming disdain towards bigotry and inequality of all kinds. While he is committing a wholesale demolition of the idealised frontier and ultra-noble lawmen of the golden age of the Western, he is also celebrating Hollywood's capacity for liberation through invention; the same apparatus which constructed this romanticised history in the first place was now equally offering him the power to deconstruct and reconfigure it for comic purposes. Yet it is the genuine sense of ire and indignation in the way that Brooks addresses race hate which seems most immediate. Maurice Yacowar, for instance, has observed that '*Blazing Saddles* is a critique of the Western genre. Specifically, Brooks charges the Western with racism, with projecting false ideals about masculinity, and with lying, i.e. with presenting as history an essentially fictitious fantasy. Brooks's Western is an anti-Western'.[4] The employment of many deliberate anachronisms throughout the film certainly succeeds in establishing the fact that Brooks does not intend his audience to take the action too seriously, but when it comes to engaging with racial discrimination it is equally clear that he considers the issue too important to treat in anything other than an earnest and meaningful way. As had been the case in *The Producers'* approach to Nazism, probing the tyranny of fascism through scorn and palpable contempt, Brooks examines the phenomenon of racism (both casual and deliberate) through a lens of constant mockery, subjecting it to an endless barrage of ridicule and derision to expose just how cruel, unnecessary and essentially meaningless such bigotry really is.

Robert Alan Crick sagely notes that 'much as *The Producers* equates Nazism as madness (particularly through Hitler-loving loony Franz Liebkind), Brooks here links racism with gullibility, narrow-mindedness and naïveté',[5] and indeed Brooks and his fellow scriptwriters expend every effort to make this distinction clear by rendering the overwhelming majority of the film's white characters in the unflattering light of the casually discriminatory attitudes they hold, while the characters with an ethnic minority heritage are largely portrayed as being open-minded, forward-thinking and tolerant. There is, additionally, a notable dissimilarity between them in that whereas characters such as the transparently racist townsfolk of Rock Ridge are largely hidebound by the conventions of the Western (such as their wide-eyed devotion to Randolph Scott and endless other clichés), Bart in particular transcends these kind of hackneyed, genre-based restrictions on his character and actions. To put it mildly, *The Lone Ranger* he is not. Articulated impeccably through Cleavon Little's warmly captivating performance, Bart constantly employs (then-) modern parlance such as 'I'm hip' and 'groovy', wears immaculate designer clothes in a manner far removed from an actual frontier sheriff of the nineteenth century, and to further underscore his coolness he regularly addresses the camera directly – usually to deliver an ironic commentary on the sheer idiocy of the Rock Ridge inhabitants' attitudes. As Beth E. Bonnstetter observes, the purposely current nature of Bart's character – in sharp contrast to the film's pseudo-historical setting – actively aided in Brooks's intended strategic undermining of the accepted conventions of the Western:

> The audience is especially invited to identify with Bart. Of all the characters in the film, it is African American Bart who is presented as smartest, bravest, most noble, and so on. Bart is not a placid, flawless, white bread 'hero' as is found in many Westerns. He displays aspects of African American culture characteristic of 1974, such as the use of contemporary vernacular (e.g., 'They in trouble' and multiple uses of the word 'baby'). Moreover, he exhibits behaviors common to the human condition. He smokes; he has sex with Lilly [sic]. Despite this, he is not a clod, a clown, or a stereotype; his actions are consistent with those of a reasonable person. In other words, Bart is a 'real person,' or as real as a movie character gets. In contrast, most of the white people of the film are in some way 'comic'.[6]

Because the audience is encouraged to sympathise with Bart's plight – first considered more expendable than a railroad handcart, then only saved from execution when he is assigned to a post where he is not expected to survive a full day in the job –

his grossly unfair treatment becomes all the more affecting. Even after only narrowly avoiding a hail of bullets following his oath as incoming sheriff, he is still visibly hurt by the racist insults of even the most seemingly-genteel townsfolk. It takes Jim, the Waco Kid – who, along with Lili, does not ascribe to racially bigoted attitudes – to restore Bart's spirits by illuminating the backward nature of the discrimination: 'What did you expect? "Welcome, sonny?" "Make yourself at home?" "Marry my daughter?" You've got to remember these are just simple farmers. These are people of the land. The common clay of the new West. You know. Morons.' By contrast, the people of Rock Ridge are defined by their slavish conformity to both social and generic expectations. The town's inward-looking nature is hinted at when it becomes clear that absolutely everyone has the surname Johnson, hinting at incestuous inbreeding as well as a general sense of insularity. (An elderly lady brings over an apple pie to thank Bart for defeating Mongo and to apologise for directing racial insults towards him earlier, only to undermine her apparently-good intentions by adding 'of course, you'll have the good taste not to mention that I spoke to you'.) Even the dialogue of the Rock Ridge inhabitants is largely limited by the kind of hoary old rhetorical chestnuts which are *de rigueur* to so many entries in the Western genre:

| REV. JOHNSON: | Well, I don't have to tell you good folks what has been happening here in our beloved town. Sheriff murdered, crops burned, stores looted, people stampeded, and cattle raped. Now the time has come to act, and act fast! I'm leaving. |
|---|---|
| GABBY JOHNSON: | You get back here, you old pious, candy-ass sidewinder! There ain't no way that nobody is going to leave this town! Hell, I was born here, and I was raised here, and goldarnit I'm going to die here! And no sidewinding, bush-whacking, hornswaggling cracker-croaker is going to ruin my biscuit-cutter! |
| OLSON JOHNSON: | Now who can argue with that? I think we're all indebted to Gabby Johnson for clearly stating what needed to be said. I'm particularly glad that these lovely children were here today to hear that speech. Not only was it authentic frontier gibberish; it expressed a courage little seen in this day and age. |

It seems clear, therefore, that although Bart's personal freedom is greatly curtailed by the way that he is virtually indentured by the railroad company, and then by his inability to function with any real degree of equality in Rock Ridge, when it comes to independence of thought and progressive social attitudes he is almost certainly the most liberated character in the film. This sense of individual emancipation in the face of unrelenting discrimination is mirrored in Brooks's own Yiddish-speaking Native American Chief, the character's warm-heartedness proving to be the converse of his other performance in the film, the callous Governor Le Petomane. As his tribe attack the white pioneers' wagon circle, the Chief notices that Bart and his family have been left to fend for themselves and thus elects to let them go free because of the fact that he recognises a kindred spirit: others who are being unfairly suppressed by the prevailing social attitudes of the incoming settlers. In the fact that the Chief's Yiddish dialogue is left untranslated, Brooks also appears to be stressing the character's 'otherness', making a restrained but nonetheless heartfelt statement about anti-Semitic discrimination. Because there are no subtitles, the audience must draw their own conclusions with regard to the Chief's intentions even if they can't discern the exact meaning of his words: '*Loz im geyn!* [Let them go!] Cop a walk, it's alright. *Abi gezint!* [As long as we're all healthy!] Take off!' As Werner Sollors suggests, this character and his surreal incongruity aids Brooks's intentions of drawing attention to inequality through strategies both familiar and unconventional: 'The Indian chieftain, played by Brooks himself, is quite unaristocratic, speaks Yiddish, and releases black captives with the nonchalance of a Brooklynite. By going back to John Brougham's burlesque mix of Indian, black, and immigrant lore and to the Indian motifs from the Yiddish stage, Brooks inverted and exploded some fixtures of perception'.[7]

Like Bart and his workmates, Native Americans are similarly being ill-treated by the state; in their case, because a wide-scale incursion onto large tracts of their land is being planned in exchange for a box of children's toys. Attorney General Lamarr's patronisingly paternalistic notion that this expansionism is necessary for the Native Americans' own good, and that it will have some kind of civilising effect, is made all the more reprehensible by Governor Le Petomane's complete apathy towards the issue. The (unnamed) state's politics are specifically defined by their dysfunction. Nowhere is this made more obvious than in the behaviour of Le Petomane himself. The cross-eyed Governor, his name an allusion to infamous French entertainer Joseph Pujol (1857–1945) (a performing flatulist whose stage name – Le Pétomane – can be roughly translated into 'The Farting Maniac'), has no interest in the duties of his elected office and is content to simply sign anything that Lamarr puts onto his desk. His lack of concern has reached a point where the Attorney General occasionally has to physically guide his superior's hand in order to persuade him even to mark his signature. Though always eager to launch into empty but grandiose political rhetoric, Le Petomane's professional ennui is partly motivated by the fact that his office is frequented by a seemingly-endless line of beautiful secretaries, leading him to declare that 'affairs of state must take precedence over the affairs of state'. The single issue which appears to motivate him lies in securing his continued electability, a fact which Lamarr realises and plays to his advantage when recommending Bart as sheriff. By appealing to the Governor's desire to be seen as a pioneer in the eyes of voters, he exposes the fact that both of them have no real interest in challenging racial inequality – merely in advancing their own respective aims. 'We've got to protect our phony baloney jobs!' Le Petomane cries, sensing the overarching need to keep his constituents satisfied... even as Lamarr talks him into converting a hospital into a casino. As had been the case in *The Producers* and *The Twelve Chairs*, Brooks's ire is directed not at the excesses of capitalistic commoditisation as such (how could it be, in a film where the hero owns a Gucci designer saddlebag?), but rather on the exclusivity and repressiveness of sheer greed. In this sense, though he is *de facto* the most powerful individual in the state Le Petomane actually reveals himself to be so restricted by public opinion and his own professional incompetence that his actions and attitudes seem profoundly constrained, in direct comparison to the collaborative and progressive mindset of those who are being oppressed by the avaricious dark side of westward expansionism.

Lamarr's intentions are, of course, even more malign than the Governor's, for he is only too aware of the extent and ramifications of his scheming; by his own admission he is 'on a great crusade to stamp out runaway decency in the West'. Whereas Le Petomane could at least lay claim to sexual distractions and general ineptitude as reasons for his amorality, Lamarr is affected by no such diversions; unbridled greed proves to be his primary motivation, with vanity a close second (he claims, in his personal opinion, to be 'risking an almost-certain Academy Award nomination for Best Supporting Actor'). Played to moustache-twirling perfection by Harvey Korman, the weaselly Lamarr is a character who revels in self-satisfaction and devious plotting, and yet at every turn he finds himself compared unfavourably with Bart. Whereas the suave sheriff effortlessly seduces the voracious man-eater Lili, Lamarr's advances are firmly rebuffed, rendering him so sexually ineffective that he is reduced to unconsciously fondling a statue of justice (an action which is somewhat paradoxical, given his total disregard of the values that the sculpture represents). Likewise, while Bart is ably supported by the encouraging and compassionate Jim ('What's a dazzling urbanite like you doing in a rustic setting like this?'), Lamarr is forced to rely on the dim-witted Taggart to act as his sidekick – a professional relationship which perpetually strains his patience:

> LAMARR: My mind is a raging torrent flooded with rivulets of thought, cascading into a waterfall of creative alternatives.
> TAGGART: Godarnit, Mr Lamarr. You use your tongue prettier than a $20 whore!

Just as Lamarr and Le Petomane act as a double-edged metaphor for corrupt government – one indifferent to the point of apathy, the other actively covetous and thoroughly unconcerned about the common good – so too Brooks has a tendency to attack the ineffectiveness of organised religion to play a meaningful role in challenging the injustice of either racism or out-of-control criminality. As was the case in *The Twelve Chairs*, he does not condemn religious belief *per sé*, but rather he strikes out at those who are willing to hide behind a veneer of piety whilst ignoring (wilfully or inadvertently) the actual tenets of the faith that they claim to ascribe to. The opening 'Ballad of Rock Ridge', which eventually transpires to be a church hymn, underscores a congregation which is more invested in their own self-interest than in spiritual matters; the fact that the church-based song ends in profanity underscores the hypocrisy of a so-called God-fearing congregation which disregards respect for their faith and deity by openly subordinating both to blatant self-centredness. Their hypocrisy is further reinforced when the skin-deep convictions of the town preacher (Reverend Johnson, naturally) are brutally exposed: imploring the townsfolk to respect the Gospels and recognise Bart as an equal in the eyes of God, he immediately abandons his conciliations when his copy of the Bible is shot out of his hand. In so doing, the Rock Ridge citizens reject the doctrine of mutual understanding upon which their faith is based, revealing the shallowness of their beliefs – a matter which is similarly highlighted when Rev. Johnson, faced with the unexpected arrival of a bomb through one of the church windows, directs his congregation not to prayer but rather to 'the Gospel of Matthew, Mark, Luke and... duck!' In Rock Ridge, faith cannot truly be a force to set individuals free because it has been degraded by those who preach it into a mere affectation to be discarded at will, and thus it ultimately becomes as impotent as the town's bungling elected representatives.

Ultimately all of the characters in *Blazing Saddles* are in search of liberty, though their individual needs are often very different. While the characters with an ethnic minority heritage seek freedom from the violence and unfairness of racial discrimination, the white characters require emancipation from their narrow, entrenched social attitudes. As Crick notes, however, Brooks proves very clearly that he does not seek to constrict the focus of his analysis too specifically, for just about everyone finds themselves the victim of his satirical eye at one point or another:

> African-Americans in particular are surely well within their rights to bristle at the racial cruelty the movie's white oppressors fling about, but no way in the world could anyone watch the film seriously believing he alone has been singled out. Almost to a man *Blazing Saddles*' whites are depicted as ditzy, dishonest, or just plain mean, and if we had just a nickel for everything likely to offend *somebody* – women, politicians, clergymen, whites, blacks, Native Americans, Germans, Mexicans, Chinese, Arabs, Irishmen, Christians, Jews, homosexuals, Klansmen, bikers, recovering alcoholics, struggling drug addicts, the speech impaired, families of the mentally challenged – well, we'd have a lot of nickels, that's what.[8]

In line with Brooks's frank treatment of race inequality, the screenplay for *Blazing Saddles* contains an eye-watering number of racial insults, and yet not once are these offensive slurs employed for gratuitous ends. Because they are spoken by people from every walk of society – brutish work-team supervisors, holders of high office and even supposedly-well-mannered elderly ladies – they emphasise the universality of racist attitudes which predominated throughout the society of the time, and are so blatant in their usage that they cannot help but call attention to the sheer ugliness of their sentiment. The deliberately ubiquitous nature of racially-offensive terms throughout the film, along with other aspects of its content, certainly alarmed the sensibilities of the studio at the time preceding its release, memorably leading Brooks into conflict with executives following a test screening:

> Right from the first scene, they never stopped laughing. Me as the Jewish Indian, they went nuts. People were running up and down the aisles. Ted Ashley, who ran Warner Bros. at the time, took me into the manager's office, and he had a legal pad with notes, and he said, 'Cut out the farting! That's out. Can't punch a horse. Can't hit an old lady! No sir! Can't use the N-word. Verboten! It's all out.' He had 22 notes. And when he left, John Calley was with me, and I crumpled up the notes and threw them into the waste paper basket. We just went with the audience's reaction, which was stu-PEN-dous! The manager of the theater said he thought there was an earthquake, he'd never heard the place rock so much. And it went on to do exceedingly well.[9]

Undoubtedly the film's conclusion makes a strong correlation between the victory of the townsfolk and their freshly-forged, seemingly-genuine collaboration with the newly-settled railroad work crew, their harmony suggesting that they have triumphed not only against Lamarr's scheming but also their own backward attitudes. The contrast between the affected pomposity of the white townsfolk and the genuine warmth and camaraderie demonstrated by Bart and his former railroad workmates could not be more marked – even when desperate for anyone to defend them against the chaos raging against Rock Ridge, the townsfolk still reject the new sheriff based upon their irrational prejudice towards him. (With every gun in town trained on Bart, he has to hold himself hostage in order to withdraw in one piece; the bizarre nature of the incident works only because he is so effortlessly able to confuse the mob's sense of convention and procedure.) However, when finally forced to overcome their narrow-minded bigotry they come to realise that a united front is infinitely stronger and more adaptable than a divided one, hence the definite thaw in interracial relations by the time of the film's conclusion. Bonnstetter has argued that *Blazing Saddles* is 'parodic-satiric [in that] it uses the comic frame of acceptance to correct and welcome back into society the majority of the "fools" that are racist',[10] and it is true that Brooks casts the townsfolk's change of heart in a redemptive light. However, his film managed to accomplish something just as significant in the way that it succeeded so thoroughly in situating Bart, an African American, as a hero who is just as effective and as gallant as any Caucasian protagonist – a central figure which had become more familiar in established Western lore. As Michael K. Johnson has stated:

> Like the citizens of Brooks's fictional town, Rock Ridge, we as film viewers don't expect to see a black man as the hero of a western, and *Blazing Saddles* plays for comic effect on the expectations established by the Hollywood western. Although black people have been part of every migration to every American frontier and have always been involved in the history of the settling of the American West, that participation has been mostly invisible to Hollywood, to literary criticism, and, more generally, to the writing of the history of the American West.[11]

Bart is not simply a successor to the square-jawed, sharp-shooting frontiersman of the genre's golden age, however; he is a thoroughly progressive individual, repeatedly shown to be as sophisticated as his detractors are foolish. Yet the oddity of situating a trend-setting, culturally relevant symbol of modernity such as Bart in the lead role of a supposedly-historical feature film is only the tip of the iceberg when it comes to Brooks's endless procession of deliberate anachronisms, each one systematically challenging expectations and subverting the apparatus of the Western genre. For instance, in being a free-thinking, sexually active, wisecracking protagonist who is despised by the very townsfolk he has been assigned to protect, Bart is the diametric opposite of the kind of figure audiences might have anticipated as being the principal figure in a Western. Janice Hocker Rushing makes the perceptive point that:

As is generally true of archetypal heroes, the hero of the classic Western originated from beyond the town. Even if he was the town marshal, he was not thoroughly identified with the townspeople. He practiced an ascetic lifestyle, refused to give in to temptations associated with community (drinking, gambling, sex, avarice), and jolted himself out of his normal state of 'contrived indolence' only when the villain threatened the town. Avoiding violence for as long as possible, he eventually deduced that 'a man's gotta do what a man's gotta do,' and rid the town of its evil, demonstrating masculine courage, consummate gunmanship, and gentlemanly grace in the act.[12]

Unexpected, off-kilter qualities can be observed in all of the various characters at one point or another, not least Jim – the erstwhile Waco Kid – who functions both as Bart's confidante and associate. With Jim, beautifully played with bleary-eyed languor by Gene Wilder, Brooks clearly parodies the figure of the washed-up sharp-shooter whose skills have eroded as a result of alcoholism, perhaps most notably evidenced in Dean Martin's character Dude in *Rio Bravo* (Howard Hawks, 1959). In spite of his straitened current circumstances, Jim claims to have once been a legend of the West ('I must have killed more men than Cecil B. De Mille,' he confides to Bart). Here too, however, not all is as it seems. Jim has become such a seasoned alcoholic that food makes him nauseous, and he explains that he has turned to drink not because of personal tragedy, but due to his legendary status as a gunslinger being undermined following an unfortunate encounter with a six-year-old sharp-shooter. Rather than the time-worn cliché of being forced to rediscover his dead-eye skills to save the day, the nature of his continuing proficiency with firearms is rendered early on and in typically absurd fashion. To prove his identity, Jim instigates what seems to be a pinhead-precision demonstration of gunmanship by shooting a chess piece before Bart can grab it, but appears to carry out this feat so quickly that rather than blowing the figure out of Bart's hand he produces it from his holster instead, thus making the entire feat seem more like some sort of magic illusion than the display of an expert marksman. Along with Lili, Jim is distinct from the other white characters as he considers himself a voluntary outcast, thus not only separate from their social concerns but their moral and even cultural anxieties too. This leaves him in a rare position in that he is able to provide support and friendship to the new sheriff without being hidebound by the prevailing discriminatory attitudes of the other townsfolk.

The character of Mongo is slightly different in that he is initially cast in the role of the villain's stooge, only to become gradually more sympathetic following his capture by Bart. Portrayed by professional wrestler and Detroit Lions American footballer Alex Karras, Mongo proves to be perfectly in line with Brooks's never-ending assembly of pop-culture puns; Yacowar explains that 'the hulk was named Mongo solely to set up the frightened citizen's cry "Mongo! Santa Maria!" in playful homage to the great bongo player Mongo Santamaria'.[13] Here, too, the screenplay derives amusement from undermining traditional expectations of the slow-witted strongman archetype. Mongo may have difficulty understanding his part in Lamarr's schemes, but he has enough *savoir-faire* to ally himself with Bart who he considers a more sympathetic associate. He also has the capacity to be perceptively ruminative about the very nature of his role in proceedings:

> JIM: Listen, Mongo; maybe you know... why's a high-roller like Hedley Lamarr interested in Rock Ridge?
> MONGO: Don't know. Got to do with where choo-choo go.
> BART: Mongo, why would Hedley Lamarr care about where the choo-choo goes?
> MONGO: Don't know. Mongo only pawn in game of life.

Mongo, who is so massive that he causes earth tremors when he rides his horse, proves to be so strong that he can fell a steed with a single punch. (His own mount bears the words "YES" and "NO" on its rear, in tribute to the vehicle overtaking instructions on American school buses.) Bart's circumvention of this man-mountain – by persuading him to open a box of chocolates rigged with explosives – is so transparently inspired by classic cartoons that the Looney Tunes theme can be heard playing as the interloper discovers that more than soft centres lie within the volatile container. Mongo has an intriguing impact upon the townsfolk; the threat he poses is so severe (as witnessed in his single-handed near-demolition of the saloon interior) that he causes the denizens of Rock Ridge to break character and drop the pretence of stale nineteenth century civility so common to Westerns of the type that Brooks is lampooning:

> HOWARD JOHNSON: And they say that now in Paris, France,

| | even as we speak, Louis Pasteur has devised a new vaccine that will obliterate anthrax once and for all. Think of it, gentlemen. Hoof-and-mouth disease a thing of the past! |
|---|---|
| OLSON JOHNSON: | Never mind that shit! Here comes Mongo! |

Lili, the self-styled 'Teutonic Titwillow', also has a wide-reaching effect upon Rock Ridge, though one which is considerably less violent. Madeline Kahn's magnificently arch performance saw her nominated for Best Actress in a Supporting Role at the 1974 Academy Awards, and deservedly so – she manages to balance perfectly her character's anachronistic absurdity and plain-speaking pragmatism, even bringing an occasional touch of vulnerability to the apparently-jaded *femme fatale*. Lili's legendary charms are shown to be in full effect during her stage performance, presaging her later tryst with Bart, though her sultry seductiveness (which bears more than a little resemblance to that of Marlene Dietrich) is offset by her linguistic rhotacism – a verbal idiosyncrasy which is used repeatedly throughout her dialogue, not least during her set-piece song at the saloon. What is perhaps more interesting is the way that Brooks uses the character's heritage to highlight and ridicule historical German imperialism. The dancing Prussian soldiers on stage are an obvious homage to *The Producers*'s 'Springtime for Hitler', while Lili is seen serenading a platoon of World War II-era German troops – part of Lamarr's gang of villains – near the film's conclusion. (Just for good measure, during the commissary sequence Brooks also drops in an actor with a toothbrush moustache – in full Hitler costume – lamenting that he will soon be out of work because 'they lose me right after the bunker scene'.)

Whereas the main villains such as Lamarr are shown to be socially inept or behaviourally peculiar (the Attorney General seems immune to the charms of Le Petomane's many voluptuous female companions, but is at the point of hysteria when he believes that he has lost his bath-time rubber duck), the supporting 'bad guys' are delineated in a way which filters their malignity through ignorance and sheer stupidity. Following a request by the Caucasian supervisors for a work song, Bart immediately launches into a classy rendition of Cole Porter's 'I Get a Kick Out of You' (1936), given able vocal support from his fellow rail workers. This confuses the thuggish overseers, who are unfamiliar with Bart's sophisticated musical tastes and instead try to encourage the team to perform a spiritual like 'Swing Low, Sweet Chariot' (c.1862)... only to discover that the workers have never heard of it. This then leads the supervisors themselves to launch into 'The Camptown Races' (1850), a song contemporary to the era which reinforces trite and distasteful racial stereotypes. The white work-team bosses accompany their singing with raucous dancing, which baffles the labour force into confounded laughter. The workers thus show that they are free from the cultural expectations of their suppressors; the supervisors are so puzzled by the autonomy and non-conformity of the characters with an ethnic minority background that they decide to play out the workers' anticipated roles themselves, in order to reinforce their perceived sense of customariness. (Bart ends up singing 'The Camptown Races' to himself – with much intentional irony – at various points throughout the remainder of the film.) Yet perhaps the ultimate humiliation for the work supervisors lies in the infamous camp-fire sequence, where a traditional cowboy diet of beans and coffee leads to an inevitable biological outcome. As Turner has explained:

> The campfire scene becomes humorous because the Western convention of the campfire is serene, often accompanied by the lonely sound of a harmonica. In Brooks' film, however, he recognizes that the even-ing meal would have probably consisted of beans and exaggerates the effect of those beans on the characters' digestive systems. Because viewers expect the typical camp scene, but are greeted with the sound of flatulence, the situation becomes comic. The humor from the reversal is, no doubt, augmented by the uncomfortable laughter that flatulence jokes traditionally receive.[14]

*Blazing Saddles* is a film steeped in Hollywood lore and its celebration, though its roots are often explored in wildly unexpected ways. The central land-grab storyline has its basis in innumerable westerns, not least Sergio Leone's *Once Upon a Time in the West* (1968). The Buddy Bizarre character (a brief appearance by Dom DeLuise in fine form) is an evident riff on Busby Berkeley, as is the character's meticulously-choreographed routine 'The French Mistake'. The Rock Ridge welcoming committee offer Bart a 'laurel and a hearty handshake', an obvious allusion to Stan Laurel and Oliver Hardy, the reference to these legends of slapstick foreshadowing the chaotic custard pie fight later in the film. The rambling Gabby Johnson is an apparent parody of famous character actor Gabby Hayes, while the casting of Western stalwarts like Slim Pickens and David Huddleston – both playing their roles (fairly) straight for the most part – lends the film just as much additional genre authenticity as its thundering Frankie Laine title song. As in many Westerns, gunshots – even directed at major organs – appear to have strangely bloodless results, which is especially apparent at the Grauman's Chinese Theatre shoot-out. And the running gag surrounding Hedley Lamarr's name – which is repeatedly mistaken for that of veteran actress Hedy Lamarr, much to his annoyance – leads the Governor to wryly comment: 'What the hell are you worried about? This is 1874! *You'll* be able to sue *her!*' As Brooks has explained, although this metacinematic approach may have seemed scattershot in places, in actuality the unremitting ridicule doled out by his material was carefully planned out for maximum effect:

> I was satirizing the non-story-line Western, where if they ended up with their horse it was a big story. When you make fun of the typical Western you make fun of the plot. When you satirize you have to be careful to know what the clichés are, and use them. As a matter of fact there is a moment when Harvey Korman looks at the camera and says, 'Why am I telling you this? You already know it.' It was satirizing the whole thing.[15]

Beyond the visual tributes and plentiful in-jokes, Brooks also sets in motion many premeditated, out-of-left field anachronisms which are often so wantonly surreal that they encourage the audience to laugh and scratch their heads at the same time. The state executioner, for instance, is dressed in medieval style, complete with chainmail garments and a hunchback. (He is a man so dedicated to his work that he hangs not only the criminal, but their horse too.) Bart's parents are forced to form their own, somewhat redundant wagon circle – consisting of only one wagon – while the white settlers purposely leave them out of their own, thus undermining one of the most iconic Western images by showing that the collective unity of the circle is in this case allowed to go only so far. 'Have you ever seen such cruelty?' an elderly lady asks with calm indignation, directing her question straight to camera as two hoodlums punch her repeatedly in the stomach. A Mexican bandito proudly proclaims 'Badges? We don't need no stinkin' badges!', a reference to John Huston's *The*

*Treasure of the Sierra Madre* (1948), while (in one of the film's most-quoted lines) Taggart demands to know 'what in the wide, *Wide World of Sports* is going on here?', calling to mind the famous ABC television series (1961-98).

Perhaps most perplexingly of all, cattle can often be seen wandering freely around Rock Ridge, including the interior of the saloon and filing through a meeting of the town council. As no-one seems to consider their presence even remotely odd, this may seem at face value to be a commentary on the provincial attitudes of the townsfolk... but then, the cattle can also be seen at the conclusion queuing up in Grauman's Chinese Theatre as they wait to see the film itself. Even the film's poster subtitle, 'Never give a saga an even break', recalls W.C. Fields's earlier motion picture and famous catchphrase *Never Give a Sucker an Even Break* (Edward F. Cline, 1941). There are many, many other references to popular culture and classic cinema as well as the history of the Western genre – not least Lamarr's 'Head them off at the pass? I hate that cliche!' or the very obvious painted backdrop framing the saloon door – which highlight Brooks's mimicry (and subsequent outright demolition) of the recognised tropes of the form. Turner observes that:

> Although *Blazing Saddles* is specifically a parody of the Western, it is also a product of its time. The film's deconstructionist techniques reflect the widespread turmoil of a nation dealing with Vietnam and Watergate. Just as people were questioning the things they once thought were fixed, Brooks questions and undermines every established convention of the Western. Borders become thin and even nonexistent, as previously separate genres such as the Western and the top-hat musical literally collide in a violent encounter. The film foregrounds the racial tensions that are still prevalent in society and shows the world as a nonsensical place where nothing, not even the myth of the Western, which society has created for itself, has any real meaning.[16]

Even more striking than the sight of Count Basie's orchestra playing 'April in Paris' in the middle of the wilderness, the film's fourth-wall-breaking conclusion has proven to be one of *Blazing Saddles*'s most famous – and contentious – sequences. Here, Brooks's focus switches from Bart's search for individual freedom and acceptance to a raucous carnival of creative liberation... and then some. Electing to launch a full-scale attack on the citizens of Rock Ridge in a final attempt to scatter them, destroying the town and moving his plans ahead, Lamarr hatches a plan to gather every criminal in the West in order to achieve his scheme:

> LAMARR: I've decided to launch an attack that will reduce Rock Ridge to ashes!
> TAGGART: What do you want me to do, sir?
> LAMARR: I want you to round up every vicious criminal and gunslinger in the West. Take this down. I want rustlers, cutthroats, murderers, bounty hunters, desperados, mugs, pugs, thugs, nitwits, halfwits, dimwits, vipers, snipers, con-men, Indian agents, Mexican bandits, muggers, buggerers, bushwhackers, hornswagglers, horse thieves, bull dykes, train robbers, bank robbers, ass-kickers, shit-kickers and Methodists!
> TAGGART: [*Finding his notepad and pen*] Could you repeat that, sir?

Lamarr and Taggart subsequently assemble a rag-tag collection of ne'er-do-wells, including Ku Klux Klansmen (complete with "Have a Nice Day" emblazoned on the back of their robes) and a gang of belligerent Hell's Angels, each grasping handlebars which have no attachment to an actual motorbike but which later appear fitted to the necks of their horses. Yet for all Brooks's unrestrained revelry in the unbridled weirdness of Lamarr's final masterplan – the brazen anachronism of the scheme sees him pulling together 'bad guys' ranging from Mexican banditos to Nazis – the dated humour of some parts of this sequence perhaps best typifies why *Blazing Saddles* (in its existing form, at least) could not have been produced in the modern day due to perceptible changes in the cultural climate. Terms such as 'buggerer' and 'bull dyke', as offensive to the LGBT community then as they are now, in present times have the potential to be every bit as distasteful to mainstream audiences. Anyone who finds themselves in agreement with Brooks's strident defence of equality with regard to race, for instance, would understandably take major exception to the sheer incongruity of using homophobia as a basis for humour, but sadly this was by no means uncommon in film narratives of the time. Lamarr including homophobic terminology within what is, in effect, a muster list of moral transgression seems especially objectionable to modern sensibilities, but newly enlightened, egalitarian attitudes towards the expression and depiction of individual sexual characteristics have since rendered such a casually provocative approach unacceptable in the present day. (This is in particularly marked contrast to the film's employment of racial insults, which are almost always used specifically to shame the characters who are using them rather than simply for comic effect.) Similarly, the outlaw who mentions rape twice in his inventory of crimes – solely because he considers it a personal favourite – is perhaps the most egregious incidence in the film of a joke which is bluntly suggestive of misogynistic overtones; a strain of humour which, in its forthright implication of both male chauvinism and insensitivity towards sexual abuse, could mercifully have no place in a major studio production today.

Lamarr's panoply of lawbreakers, drawn from across history (and framed by the odd logic of his supremely ironic claim that he is an 'equal opportunities employer'), race headlong towards Bart's ersatz Rock Ridge, the faux town now looking suspiciously like a film set. With wooden props holding up painstakingly-detailed facades, the scene is eerily reminiscent of *Star Trek*'s famous 'Spectre of the Gun' episode (1968), right down to its intentional artificiality and the initially-deserted streets. But Brooks, of course, is merely preparing the audience for the ultimate shattering of the fourth wall when the riotous fight between Lamarr's criminals and the Rock Ridge townsfolk tips over from a Warner Brothers backlot into the heart of the studio itself. Brooks appears to take much satisfaction in the unexpected invasion of his Western into the ultra-regimented choreography of waspish director Buddy Bizarre, and has an unapologetic riposte for any critics of this distinctly postmodern approach:

> BUDDY BIZARRE: *Cut!* What in the hell do you think you're doing here? This is a closed set!
> TAGGART: Piss on you! I'm workin' for Mel Brooks!

Brooks adopts a shamelessly no-holds-barred approach throughout the chaotic closing sequences of the film, cranking up the anarchic disarray until it eventually degenerates (in the grand tradition of the early cinematic comedy) into a custard pie fight which takes no prisoners – heroes, villains, dancers, studio staff, random bystanders... no-one is safe from the general sense of pandemonium. More than any other section of the film, these climactic scenes have divided commentators into those who believe that Brooks employed this genre-oscillating frenzy in lieu of a logical ending, and others who came to the conclusion that it formed a reasonable end-point to his intention to transcend and reconfigure the convention of the Western for comic ends. Chip Rhodes has argued that the film's conclusion 'reveals the basic theme of Hollywood-on-Hollywood movies: movies are not true-to-life; instead they conform to strict genre formulas to create their own "reality"',[17] and in merrily juxtaposing two of the great traditional Hollywood staples in a manner that could hardly be called seamless, Brooks shifts his annihilation of genre expectations into a still-higher gear. As Barry Langford notes:

> Brooks's stereotypically epicene dancers, campily fleeing across their never-never-land set from this sudden intrusion from a definitively 'masculine' generic universe and shrilly defending if not their honour then their looks [...] reflect dominant perceptions of the musical as organised around tropes of narcissistic display and artificiality as opposed to the Western's rugged veracity. As ever, the parodic thrust cuts both ways: while the streamlined, pristine musical set bespeaks an 'artifice' in contrast to the rough, workmanlike surfaces of the Western, at the same time the latter's incorporation into the generic space of the musical both undermines the Westerner's monolithic masculinity and also reminds us that their ostensibly more 'historical' milieu is, as a construction of genre, in its way as stylised and out-of-time as that of the musical. In fact, the Western and the musical are two halves of a whole: the cowboy and the song-and-dance man together are strong and universal metonymic signifiers of Hollywood, and Hollywood genre, as a whole.[18]

Balancing such weighty thematic concerns with the need to provide qualitative continuity of the film's comic content is by no means an easy proposition, and certainly some reviewers were left cold by this everything-but-the-kitchen-sink methodology – especially given the determined challenge to expectation which comes from the self-conscious fiction-versus-reality conceit. *The New York Times*'s Vincent Canby, for instance, berated the film, claiming that '*Blazing Saddles* has no dominant personality, and it looks as if it includes every gag thought up in every story conference. Whether good, bad, or mild, nothing was thrown out'.[19] At the time, adopting such an *avant-garde* technique in a mainstream comedy seemed certain to be a risky gamble, not least as it considerably blurs an often delicate line which lies between fictional characters, actors portraying fictional characters, and actors portraying actors. Yacowar reminds us of the sheer audacity of this strategy, observing that Brooks 'obeyed the single most revolutionary tenet of modern art – escape from the limitations of a single, fixed perspective – and of modern social philosophy – humanist relativism. *Blazing Saddles* reminds us of the arbitrary and wilful nature of any set of conventions by which we choose to live or to perceive, whether in art or in life'.[20] Nor can there be any doubt that in exploiting this particular approach, Brooks also succeeded in broadening the scope of his film, relating its themes not just to the characters but, by implication, to the world at large. Bonnstetter suggests that:

> Read through the comic frame, by [the] end of this sequence, *Blazing Saddles* no longer has villains or heroes. Everyone is being hurled down to earth via participation in the pie fight (including Bart). 'Everyone' means not just characters in the film, but everyone – society itself. Combatants include workers in the studio, tourists, actors in the commissary, and even people on the street. Symbolically and as synecdoche, then, this fight can be read as *Blazing Saddles'* implication of all of society. Everyone is involved in the fight because everyone – Hollywood and society itself – is responsible for perpetuating that which the film critiques: bigotry, racism, and the racist discursive structures of Old West mythology.[21]

Brooks's film exudes an air of jubilation with regard to its sheer, unfettered willingness to explore the outer edges of genre boundaries, only to then – in an act of unbridled creative freedom – smash through them with great gusto. As Turner states, 'Brooks systematically dissects all the clichés of the Western in a deconstructionist attack on its very premises,' adding that 'there are no conventions that are sacred and no joke too easy or too obscure for him to use in his satire. The last extended sequence of the film, in particular, is notable for its deconstruction of the Western and its use of metafilmic inversions'.[22] Yet alongside Brooks's emasculation of the rigid genre conventions at work in Hollywood productions, a palpable desire to rejoice in the creative potential of the film industry is also regularly on display. Roman James has drawn attention to the way in which the film 'ends as a movie within a movie as Hedley hails a taxi and is driven to Grauman's Chinese Theatre, settling into a seat only to leave when he sees that the movie is *Blazing Saddles*. Once outside, he is shot in the groin by Bart and then falls into wet cement, writing his name followed by a dollar sign'.[23] The most prominent subversion here derives from the nature of Lamarr's dying actions; when marking out his name for the last time, he firmly underscores 'Hedley' (in response to the running gag of his forename constantly being mispronounced), and in doing so is attempting to insinuate himself into Hollywood legend. His dreams of Oscar glory now gone forever, Lamarr collapses onto the cement footprints of Douglas Fairbanks as he utters his famous last words: 'How did he do such fantastic stunts with such little feet?' Brooks's attempts to commemorate the history of the American film industry, to revel in its triumphs while also deriding its occasional pretension and vanity, can be summed up in microcosm through the Grauman's sequence; Brooks has himself described the fact that Lamarr 'actually says to those people who are looking at the square sidewalk outside the Chinese Theater on Hollywood Boulevard... and they say, "Oh, look, darling, Heddy Lamarr." [sic] And he walks by and says, "Hedley! Hedley!" I love how that connects 1874 and 1974 in one frame of film, one hundred years of cinema. It's amazing'.24

As the custard pie fight sees its participants ejected out of the studio and into the 'real world', Brooks clearly realises that the genie will no longer fit back into the bottle and thus wisely chooses to tie the film up soon afterwards. Once the action returns to Rock Ridge, it is obvious that the audience are now all too aware of the town's existence as a detailed exterior set in the Warner Brothers' back-lot, and thus he is able to toy dexterously with this realisation in surprisingly fulfilling ways. (Jim, for instance, is very clearly still holding the box of popcorn he had purchased at the theatre earlier.) In so doing, he reaches the conclusion of an approach which widens his attack on genre expectation from the specific to the general, as Erica Stein has observed:

> Brooks' climactic sequence – and the basis for analysis of the film as a revisionist Western – depends on a strategy of exposure. In order for more equitable living situations to occur, the iconographic conventions of the genre must be revealed as flimsy alibis for conventional narrative structure and exceptionalist ideology, their representation structured not by reference to a material historical reality but by the demands of a capitalist production system. The acknowledgement of such truth is tantamount to demolishing the structures built to conceal it and, the mythic function of the Western now visible and intelligible, a corrected, corrective narrative can emerge.
> Although *Blazing Saddles* is a parody or burlesque of the Western, its understanding of the politics of the classical Western and its articu-

lation of a genre critique is both paradigmatic of the Hollywood Renaissance cycle of revisionist Westerns and consonant with the genre's theorization by the discipline of film studies during the same period.[25]

Perhaps because of Brooks's shibboleth-shattering intentions, *Blazing Saddles* split critical opinion dramatically. On one hand, reviewers such as Roger Ebert delighted in 'a crazed grabbag of a movie that does everything to keep us laughing except hit us over the head with a rubber chicken. Mostly, it succeeds. It's an audience picture; it doesn't have a lot of classy polish and its structure is a total mess. But of course! What does that matter while Alex Karris is knocking a horse cold with a right cross to the jaw?'[26] On the other end of the critical spectrum, Pauline Kael's withering reception of the film saw her bluntly stating her opinion that 'as a director, [Brooks] doesn't have enough style to make the unfunny funny. In *Blazing Saddles* he makes the unfunny desperate'.[27] This polarisation of critical appraisal was widespread amongst commentators, but in spite of such divergence in opinion the film itself proved difficult to ignore. Its enormous success at the box-office could not have failed to be a relief for Brooks, who had fought to retain his distinctive creative vision for the film, and it validated his chosen artistic direction. Paul D. Zimmerman has observed that '*Blazing Saddles* played to stony silence before studio executives, an emotional catastrophe for Brooks, who is so anxious for immediate confirmation of his work that he invites large numbers of people to view rough-cuts of his movies months before they're ready. But the public loved *Blazing Saddles* and the kind of insanity that had Count Basie's band wailing in the middle of the Palmdale Desert'.[28]

The commercial achievement of *Blazing Saddles* was to have an enormous impact on the future of Brooks's directorial career. While his cleverly structured, thought-provoking earlier films had made an impact with many in the critical community, if not necessarily with the viewing public at large at the time of their release, *Blazing Saddles* was to catapult his work into the spotlight as never before. Brooks has since been somewhat philosophical about this breakthrough, going so far as to note – in an article by Scott Hettrick – that in some ways he 'regrets the release of *Blazing Saddles* because it moved him to a level at which he became thereafter compelled to try to make major movies to fill theater seats, instead of small films such as *The Producers* and *The Twelve Chairs*, which he says he enjoyed more. "*Blazing Saddles* was a hit, and that was the making and the breaking of me," he says'.[29]

Undoubtedly the timing of *Blazing Saddles* was advantageous, both for Brooks's career and for the evolution of cinematic comedy. It is certainly difficult to imagine the pull-out-all-the-stops genre-mangling of later film parodies, such as David Zucker, Jim Abrahams and Jerry Zucker's influential *Airplane!* (1980), without Brooks having set the ball rolling with such confident panache. But providing solid proof that there was commercial mileage in such an approach was only part of the story. As Lawrence J. Epstein has stated, the arrival of *Blazing Saddles* heralded the point where Brooks discovered a narrative format which naturally lent itself to his comedic talents: '*Blazing Saddles* is Brooks's first clear spoof. Finding this form was crucial. A spoof pokes fun at social, artistic, and other conventions. It is not, and does not wish to be, as serious as its conceptual relative, satire. Nor does it follow the original as closely as does its other relative, the parody'.[30]

Because of its conscious engagement with racism and social justice, *Blazing Saddles* remains one of Brooks's most thematically sophisticated features, and this is perhaps part of the reason why it has remained such a popular focus for scholarly discourse. Although his earlier films had handled heavyweight subject matter with deceptively blithe sleight of hand, and he would continue to approach challenging socio-cultural topics within many later entries in his filmography, there was both indignation and immediacy within *Blazing Saddles* which arrested audiences and captured their imagination. Wes Gehring remarks that 'this movie is unique in Brooks' spoofing career for its satirical underpinnings, such as references to Western racism and violence. The use of verbal obscenities, however, brings up a popular buzz phrase later applied to the blue language of stand-up comic Richard Pryor and a co-scriptor of *Blazing Saddles* – "the theatre of real life"'.[31] No later Brooks film would employ such racially-offensive terms, or even general profanity on quite the same scale. But then, no later Brooks film would convey quite such acute moral outrage towards prejudice or inequality. Even Brooks himself has admitted, during the celebrations of the film's fortieth anniversary, that it would be highly unlikely that *Blazing Saddles* could ever have been produced in the current cultural environment, due to a conspicuous shift in sensibilities; Matt Wilstein notes that when the director was asked 'if he really believed the film could not be made today because of "political correctness," he said he does believe that to be true. "Political correctness restricts and restrains humor," he said. "Humor has to be very crazy and very free and very liberated. And dangerous!"' [32]

*Blazing Saddles* is, in the view of many cineastes, the archetypal Mel Brooks film. With its uncontainable irreverence, recurring pop-culture references and the way in which it plays fast and loose with established conventions, it laid down the format for many future entries in his filmography and – its huge commercial accomplishment at the box-office guaranteeing wide circulation amongst viewers in many countries – the movie informed audience expectation regarding his later work in very particular ways. Yet in its spirited appeal for social justice and the blatant elation with which it celebrates creative freedom and the challenging of the rules which govern genre, *Blazing Saddles* also built upon the narrative themes of Brooks's earlier films, underscoring his commitment to promoting equality and advocating the potential for personal development by confronting and overcoming any factors or attitudes which render society less free – or less just – than it ideally should be.

# REFERENCES

1. Box-office data drawn from *BoxOfficeMojo.com*.
   <http://www.boxofficemojo.com/movies/?id=blazingsaddles.htm>
2. Mel Brooks, in Jacoba Atlas, 'New Hollywood: Mel Brooks Interview', in *Film Comment*, March-April 1975.
   <http://www.brookslyn.com/print/FilmComment1975/FilmComment1975.php>
3. Matthew R. Turner, 'Cowboys and Comedy: The Simultaneous Deconstruction and Reinforcement of Generic Conventions in the Western Parody', in *Hollywood's West: The American Frontier in Film, Television and History*, ed. by Peter C. Rollins and John E. O'Connor (Lexington: The University Press of Kentucky, 2005), 218-38, p. 223.
4. Maurice Yacowar, *The Comic Art of Mel Brooks* (London: W.H. Allen, 1982), p. 124.
5. Robert Alan Crick, *The Big Screen Comedies of Mel Brooks* (Jefferson: McFarland and Company, 2009) [2002], p. 59.
6. Beth E. Bonnstetter, 'Mel Brooks Meets Kenneth Burke (and Mikhail Bakhtin): Comedy and Burlesque in Satiric Film', in *Journal of Film and Video*, Vol. 63, No. 1, Spring 2011, 18-31, p. 21.
7. Werner Sollors, *Beyond Ethnicity: Consent and Descent in American Culture* (Oxford: Oxford University Press, 1986), p. 141.
8. Crick, p. 53.
9. Brooks, in Gary Susman, 'Mel Brooks on *Blazing Saddles* at 40, Richard Pryor's Genius, and Keeping His Edge at 87', in *Moviefone*, 20 May 2014.
   <http://news.moviefone.com/2014/05/20/mel-brooks-blazing-saddles-richard-pryor/>
10. Bonnstetter, 'An Analytical Framework of Parody and Satire: Mel Brooks and His World' (unpublished doctoral thesis, The University of Minnesota, June 2008), p. 102.
11. Michael K. Johnson, 'Migration, Masculinity, and Racial Identity in Taylor Gordon's *Born to Be*', in *Moving Stories: Migration and the American West 1850-2000*, ed. by Scott E. Casper and Lucinda M. Long (Reno: University of Nevada Press, 2001), 119-42, p. 119.
12. Janice Hocker Rushing, 'The Rhetoric of the American Western Myth', in *Communication Monographs*, Issue 50, 1983, 14-32, pp.19-20.
13. Yacowar, p. 135.
14. Turner, 'Cowboys and Comedy: The Simultaneous Deconstruction and Reinforcement of Generic Conventions in the Western Parody', in *Film & History: An Interdisciplinary Journal of Film and Television Studies*, Vol. 33, No. 2, 2003, 48-54, pp. 51-52.
15. Brooks, in Jacoba Atlas, 'New Hollywood: Mel Brooks Interview', in *Film Comment*, March-April 1975.
    <http://www.brookslyn.com/print/FilmComment1975/FilmComment1975.php>
16. Turner, 2005, p. 224.
17. Chip Rhodes, 'Hollywood Fictions', in *The Cambridge Companion to the Literature of Los Angeles*, ed. by Kevin R. McNamara (Cambridge: Cambridge University Press, 2010), 135-44, p. 135.
18. Barry Langford, *Film Genre: Hollywood and Beyond* (Edinburgh: Edinburgh University Press, 2005), p. 82.
19. Vincent Canby, '*Blazing Saddles*', in *The New York Times*, 8 February 1974.
    <http://www.nytimes.com/movie/review?res=EE05E7DF1730E261BC4053DFB466838F669EDE>

20. Yacowar, p. 138.
21. Bonnstetter, 2001, pp. 23-24.
22. Turner, 2003, pp. 49-50.
23. Roman James, *Bigger Than Blockbusters: Movies That Defined America* (Westport: Greenwood Press, 2009), p. 206.
24. Brooks, in Drew McWeeny, 'If You Didn't Already Love Mel Brooks, This May Change Your Mind', in *HitFix*, 12 May 2014.
<http://www.hitfix.com/motion-captured/mel-brooks-discusses-blazing-saddles-brooksfilms-and-the-best-screening-ever/single-page>
25. Erica Stein, '"A Hell of a Place": The Everyday as Revisionist Content in Contemporary Westerns', in *Mediascape: UCLA's Journal of Cinema and Media Studies*, No. 3, Fall 2009.
<http://www.tft.ucla.edu/mediascape/fall09_western.html>
26. Roger Ebert, '*Blazing Saddles*', in *The Chicago Sun-Times*, 7 February 1974.
<http://www.rogerebert.com/reviews/blazing-saddles-1974>
27. Pauline Kael, '*Blazing Saddles*', in *The New Yorker*, 18 February 1974, p. 100.
28. Paul D. Zimmerman, 'The Mad Mad Mel Brooks', in *Newsweek*, 17 February 1975.
<http://www.brookslyn.com/print/Newsweek02-15-1975/Newsweek02-17-1975.php>
29. Brooks, in Scott Hettrick, '*Spaceballs* Laserdisc Adds Little To Film', in *The Sun Sentinel*, 24 May 1996.
<http://articles.sun-sentinel.com/1996-05-24/entertainment/9605220414_1_brooks-spaceballs-young-frankenstein>
30. Lawrence J. Epstein, *The Haunted Smile: The Story of Jewish Comedians* (Oxford: PublicAffairs, 2001), p. 211.
31. Wes Gehring, *Parody as Film Genre: Never Give a Saga an Even Break* (Westport: Greenwood Press, 1999), p. 141.
32. Matt Wilstein, 'Mel Brooks: I Would Never Get Away with Using "N-Word" on Screen Today', in *Mediaite*, 14 May 2014.
<http://www.mediaite.com/tv/mel-brooks-i-would-never-get-away-with-using-n-word-on-screen-today/>

# 4

# YOUNG FRANKENSTEIN (1974)

WITH *BLAZING SADDLES*, Mel Brooks had championed the right of – and need for – personal liberty in the face of prejudice and discrimination, whilst simultaneously celebrating the emancipative qualities of unfettered creative freedom. He would continue to stress the essential nature of free will in his next film, *Young Frankenstein*, but through an exploration of self-determination that was much more specific and intimate – perhaps surprisingly so, given the exuberantly implausible central premise. Many critics have come to consider *Young Frankenstein* to be Brooks's most accomplished mainstream cinematic feature, in part because of the film's scrupulous respect for its source material but largely due to its narrative sophistication and droll characterisation. There is an understated emotional profundity to the film's action which would rarely be seen again to quite the same degree in Brooks's later features; an emotional insightfulness that he never squanders or undermines, even when the film reaches the apex of its mock-Gothic hysterics.

    *Young Frankenstein* came about from a script treatment written by actor Gene Wilder, who had worked with Brooks to no small acclaim in *The Producers* and *Blazing Saddles*. Wilder was to flesh out his idea into a full-length screenplay, which was later developed in collaboration with Brooks into the film that eventually reached cinemas in the December of 1974. As Michael V. Tueth notes, 'Although Brooks was reluctant to work on a film that was not based on his own material, he agreed that he and Wilder would work on a rewritten version of the screenplay, and, if a studio agreed to film it, Brooks would direct. [...] After Twentieth Century Fox agreed to produce the film, Brooks managed to shoot the entire film in less than two months, in March and April of 1974'.[1] Following the success of *Blazing Saddles*, the earlier feature's box-office triumph having come only a few months earlier, expectations were high for *Young Frankenstein*, though audiences and critics were soon to discover that Brooks was presenting them with a very different kind of comedy in comparison to the unrestrained comedic mayhem of his earlier assault on the mythos of the cinematic Western. The result was to be a career highlight for both Brooks and Wilder, as Joe Garner has observed:

> *Young Frankenstein* is more than just funny; it's a beautifully filmed, impeccably acted, and carefully scripted movie. Much of the humor derives from the plotting, watching everything go awry for Gene Wilder's descendant of Dr Frankenstein – 'that's Frahnk-en-shteen!' – as he tries denying, then extolling, his heritage. The monster was born in Gene Wilder's head when he was suddenly struck with the notion of a tale of 'Young Frankenstein'. He fleshed out a story and, after his agent suggested that Wilder work with fellow clients Marty Feldman and Peter Boyle, penned a script spoofing the whole horror genre, but especially *Bride of Frankenstein*. Wilder then handed the script off to Brooks, his director in *Blazing Saddles* and *The Producers*. Brooks reworked the screenplay, but even while directing he maintained a constant give-and-take with Wilder, who once said 'My job was to make Mel more subtle. His job was to make me more broad. I would say, "I don't want this to be *Blazing Frankenstein*", and he'd answer "I don't want an art film that only fourteen people see"'.[2]

Dr Frederick Frankenstein (Gene Wilder) is a successful American neurosurgeon with a highly respectable professional reputation, who is determined to put the infamy of his family name far behind him. (To this end, he repeatedly insists that everyone addresses him as 'Fronckensteen' in order to distance himself from the actions of his corpse-reanimating relative.) Following a routine lecture – where he firmly dismisses his ancestor's research as crackpot nonsense – he is informed that he has been bequeathed the Frankenstein estate in the Will of his great-grandfather, the late Baron Beaufort von Frankenstein. Thus he travels from the United States to the darkest reaches of

Transylvania, leaving behind his upper-crust fiancée Elizabeth (Madeline Kahn), in order to view the family's iconic castle for the first time. Waiting for him at the rural train station is Igor (Marty Feldman), the hunchbacked descendant of his grandfather Victor's manservant, and the beautiful Inga (Teri Garr), a laboratory assistant.

Upon reaching the predictably sinister Frankenstein residence, the doctor is puzzled when he discovers only a modest library of general medical books, expecting the departed Victor (son of Beaufort) to have a rather more specific range of texts in his collection given his all-too-well-known research interests. The castle's formidable housekeeper, Frau Blücher (Cloris Leachman), professes no knowledge of a larger private library on the premises. But the elderly woman's enigmatic nature intrigues Frankenstein, not least when he spots her tenderly kissing a portrait of his grandfather (who bears a striking resemblance to the doctor himself).

Frankenstein wakes from a vivid nightmare ('Destiny! Destiny! No escaping that for me!') to hear the sound of a solo violin. Following the music, he discovers a hidden passageway behind one of the bookcases in his grandfather's bedchamber, which leads him to the secret laboratory where the famous Frankenstein reanimation experiments had taken place many years beforehand. Further into the depths of the concealed chambers, he unearths Victor's extensive personal library; a recently-abandoned violin is found nearby, but with no trace of its mysterious player. Upon reading through his grandfather's consolidated laboratory notes, Frankenstein soon becomes convinced of the scientific foundation of Victor's work. This causes him to completely reassess everything he thought he had known about the experiments, considering them now as being legitimate, pioneering scientific research rather than the necromantic ambitions of a deranged lunatic.

Working from Victor's findings, Frankenstein determines that he must replicate his grandfather's experiments if he is to redeem his ancestor's reputation and etch his own name in the history books. However, he will need a subject who is of larger than average stature in order to accommodate the delicate surgical techniques which will be necessary to achieve the reanimation. To this end, he and Igor retrieve the corpse of a recently-hanged criminal from a shallow grave in a nearby cemetery. Next, Frankenstein instructs Igor to break into the village's local brain depository (!) and retrieve the brain of the late Hans Delbrück ('Scientist and Saint'). Everything seems to be going to plan until a random bolt of lightning illuminates Igor's reflection in a mirror, startling him into accidentally dropping the jar and shattering it. The brain within is destroyed on impact. Keen not to disappoint, Igor collects another specimen for Frankenstein's experiment instead, seemingly unaware that it is an abnormal sample.

Oblivious to Igor's blunder, Frankenstein transplants the malformed brain into the recovered body and subjects it to a lightning-powered reanimation process in his grandfather's old laboratory. The creature (Peter Boyle) remains steadfastly unmoved by the doctor's best efforts, however, leading Frankenstein to erupt into a frustrated tantrum. Meanwhile, the village residents meet to discuss the arrival of the latest Frankenstein to take up residence in the castle. They are concerned that he will attempt to carry on his grandfather's work, but are divided over the issue of what action to take; some believe that his intentions should not be prejudged, whereas others are deeply suspicious of his intentions given his family's well-established track record (the village having been attacked several times by reanimated monsters in decades past). The automaton-like Inspector Kemp (Kenneth Mars), the community's most senior investigator, resolves to meet with Frankenstein and ascertain his motives before any firm plans are made.

Inga and Igor commiserate with the sulking Frankenstein over the apparent failure of the experiment, until the muffled sound of groaning alerts them to the fact that the creature's revival had not been unsuccessful at all; upon returning to the laboratory, they find that the body has been successfully reanimated via a delayed reaction from the earlier lightning strike. Frankenstein is delighted by the dazed creature's response to simple verbal commands once he is released from his restraints, but when Igor strikes a match the revived corpse is startled by the tiny flame and suddenly becomes violently agitated; Inga has to sedate him in order to free a half-strangled Frankenstein. The doctor becomes suspicious of the creature's anomalous behaviour and manages to extract a confession from Igor regarding the true origin of the transplanted brain. Much to Igor's relief, a knock at the castle door interrupts Frankenstein's frenzied retribution; Inspector Kemp has decided to make an unplanned evening visit. Over a drink and a game of darts, the doctor denies any intention of revisiting his grandfather's work, but Kemp does not seem entirely convinced of the American's spirited protestations.

Meanwhile, Frau Blücher is in the process of setting the creature free from his restraints. She is interrupted by Frankenstein who, horrified, demands to know the reason for her actions. Blücher explains that she was the one responsible for playing the violin music that led the doctor to his grandfather's laboratory, and had deliberately left the correct notes for him to find. As Blücher was Victor's lover ('Say it! He was my *boyfriend!*'), she intended to keep the Frankenstein legacy alive by persuading Frederick to follow the path of his ancestor's research. And now she is determined to set the experiment free. Frankenstein is appalled when the creature appears to be gearing up for another rampage, but Blücher reveals that violin music has the ability to soothe him, calming his violent behaviour. However, when the monster accidentally shocks himself on a piece of electrical laboratory equipment he becomes uncontrollable once more and storms out of the castle, taking the front door with him. Frankenstein looks on helplessly, resolving to get his creation back at all costs.

The next day, word has circulated that the creature is on the loose, causing panic amongst the villagers (who are barricading themselves into their homes as a precautionary measure). The shambling monster encounters a little girl (Anne Beesley) innocently dropping flower petals into a well. Because of the innocence of youth, the child sees not a grotesque threat but rather a new playmate. As her parents panic over the young girl's whereabouts, the creature discovers that his immense strength presents a disadvantage as he plays games with the child; when attempting to join her on a see-saw, he accidentally propels her through the air, where she flies through her bedroom window and lands unconscious on her bed. This is no small relief to her parents, who – upon discovering her – come to the conclusion that she must never have been missing from home in the first place.

The monster's wandering later brings him to a secluded

cottage in a forest. There, he meets Harold (Gene Hackman), a blind monk whose remotely-situated home has become a kind of hermitage. Having prayed diligently for company, the lonely cleric is delighted when the creature arrives; as he is unable to see the newcomer's monstrous form, he has no prejudice towards him based upon his appearance, and reasons from his grunting discourse that the creature is actually a mute traveller. However, the kindness he shows towards his guest proves to have painful consequences due to his impaired vision. After ladling copious amounts of scalding soup into the creature's lap, then smashing his guest's ceramic mug of wine with a metal beer stein during a toast, Harold eventually sends his visitor running after he sets light to the creature's thumb, accidentally believing it to be a cigar.

Back in the village in the dead of night, Frankenstein succeeds in using violin music to lure the creature into a trap. Once he has been sedated, the errant experiment is finally returned to the castle, where the doctor chains him up to prevent any further unintended excursions. Frankenstein determines that the only way to turn the creature's behaviour around is to persuade him that he is valued and has a place in society. With this in mind, he eventually convinces his creation of his innate self-worth, promising to coach him in all the necessary life skills he will need to operate effectively in modern life. Together, he pledges, they will make scientific history. At last, he freely admits that he is not a 'Fronckensteen' but a Frankenstein.

Some time later, Dr Frankenstein has arranged to make a presentation of his research at the Bucharest Academy of Science. Delivering his lecture to a packed auditorium, watched over by Inspector Kemp and his men, the doctor's assertions of successful bodily reanimation are met at first by hostility and then by open derision. The audience are shocked when Frankenstein brings the creature onto the stage, but become impressed when he encourages his experiment into demonstrating evidence of sophisticated motor function. The doctor then launches into an elaborate song-and-dance act, the creature's participation beguiling the assembled scientists until one of the stage footlights bursts into flame, sending the monster into a blind panic. The jeers of the audience, accompanied by the throwing of rotten vegetables, cause the creature to push Frankenstein aside and launch off the stage into an attack, where he is eventually subdued by the officers of Kemp's constabulary.

With the monster chained in a police cell, tortured by his captors and taunted by the villagers, Frankenstein determines that only by correcting the balance of his creation's cerebrospinal fluid will the creature be able to operate like an ordinary human being. While the doctor and Inga embark on a relationship together, his conscience still tortured by the question of how he can improve the creature's mental function, Frau Blücher brings news that Frankenstein's fiancée Elizabeth has sent word that she will be making a surprise visit to the castle later that day. However, just as the upmarket socialite is arriving from the United States the creature is breaking free from his shackles, spurred into violent action when a sadistic jailer goads him with lit matches.

The villagers form an angry mob, stereotypically armed with flaming torches and pitchforks, and under Kemp's leadership they set off in pursuit of the wayward monster. Unknown to any of them, the creature has kidnapped Elizabeth from her guest room in the castle, spiriting her away to a cave near the village. There, he makes clear his romantic interest in Elizabeth; at first she is resistant to his advances, but soon reciprocates the attraction. After repeatedly demonstrating his affections, the creature is again enticed away by the sound of violin music; Frederick is playing the instrument through amplification equipment atop the castle, eventually luring his creation back 'home'.

Safely returned to the laboratory, the creature is hooked up to an elaborate apparatus through which Frankenstein plans to transfer some of his own cerebral fluid to his creation, thus correcting the imbalance that is causing the monster's abnormal behaviour. Just before the procedure can be completed, however, the angry mob of villagers arrive at the castle and break through the barricaded main doorway (using Kemp as a battering ram). Storming the laboratory mere seconds before the process has run its course, the invaders begin smashing up the equipment and accosting Frankenstein and his colleagues... until the creature suddenly speaks up in his creator's defence. Now perfectly civil and urbane in his delivery, the monster gives a heartfelt justification of Frankenstein's altruistic actions, so moving the villagers that even Kemp feels compelled to offer the hand of friendship.

As the film concludes, Frankenstein marries Inga and remains at his family castle, while the creature returns to America with Elizabeth and quickly integrates himself into high society life. Yet just as the Wall Street Journal-perusing monster finds that he has benefited from a portion of Frankenstein's vast intellect as a result of the transference procedure, the melody of Frau Blücher's violin solo (when hummed by Inga on her wedding night) leads to the realisation that some of the creature's prodigious physical talents have also been unexpectedly transferred to his creator. And thus – unlike the repeated tragedy of the original *Frankenstein* tale – there is a happy ending for all concerned.

If any film in Brooks's oeuvre comes close to a labour of love, it surely must be *Young Frankenstein*. As Robert Alan Crick so perceptively states, the feature exhibits so much affectionate respect towards its source material that it almost ceases to be a spoof at all,[3] and certainly Brooks appeared determined to recreate every nuance of the golden age of horror cinema that he sought to simultaneously emulate and then cheerfully chip away at with characteristic good humour. Donald F. Glut observes that:

> Mel Brooks had always harbored a love for the 'old style' horror movies of the 1930s – the early *Frankenstein*s and *Dracula*s produced at Universal Pictures, films that relied upon story, characterization, fine acting and Gothic atmosphere rather than gratuitous violence and gore. Consequently, in *Young Frankenstein*, Brooks took the most extreme care to recreate the look, mood and 'feel' of those much-revered classics. It was the director's goal to ensure that *Young Frankenstein*, although poking fun at those old Universal movies, would be made with integrity, affection and care. For the sakes of authenticity and tradition, Brooks wisely chose to have his film shot in black and white (as were the old Universal movies).[4]

It is immediately obvious that Brooks's choice of monochrome over colour benefits the atmosphere of the film enormously, even from the remarkably realised Universal-style opening credits, as does the scrupulous attention to detail evident in Bob de Vestel's immaculate set decoration. No stone is left unturned in Brooks's attempt to conjure up a faithful re-enactment of the shadowy Gothic milieu of countless horror films past. Yet his efforts reached much further than simply presenting an authentic recreation of the stylistic techniques, tone and ambience of the celebrated bygone days of the genre. Brooks's many allusions and visual tributes to the golden age of horror have already been exhaustively documented by others, not least Maurice Yacowar who notes the similarities between Madeline Kahn's Elizabeth and Elsa Lanchester in *The Bride of Frankenstein* (James Whale, 1935), Gene Wilder's Dr Frederick Frankenstein emulating the visual appearance of Basil Rathbone's dashing Baron Wolf von Frankenstein in *Son of Frankenstein* (Rowland V. Lee, 1939), and even the film's climactic surgical transplantation of brain function which mirrors the plot device in *The Ghost of Frankenstein* (Erle C. Kenton, 1942).5 Indeed, the screenplay makes explicit the debt owed to past horror cinema by the Transylvanian village leader's weary assertion that 'We still have nightmares from five times before!', in a scene analogous to *Blazing Saddles*'s wittily-observed town council sequence. In other words, these characters know what to expect every bit as much as the audience does. The movie is positively brimming with *homage* to various different aspects of the Universal horror films, as Albert J. Lavalley has explained:

> Mel Brooks's film *Young Frankenstein* is an unpretentious spoof which lovingly recreates the texture and images of the early *Frank-enstein* films in black and white. Its strength is in the wit with which it sends up familiar images. There is no real attempt at reinterpret-ation, though a viewer is free to do this if he wants. For instances, are we to make anything out of Frankenstein's real bride ending up with the Monster in bed? And Frankenstein in bed with his buxom blonde assistant? The real pleasure is in seeing the old images in a new context: Madeline Kahn with frizzed 'Elsa Lanchester' hair, replete with lightning bolt, hissing at Peter Boyle the Monster. Image after image is saluted, then undermined.6

With typical Brooksian zeal, creating a set in the style of the old Frankenstein laboratory simply wasn't enough; with a perfectionist's eye for even the smallest detail, he decided to track down the real thing in order to add further authenticity to his production. Yacowar recounts that 'in a stroke of rare fortune, he was able to use the same laboratory set that Dr Frankenstein used in the original James Whale *Frankenstein* (1931). Designer Kenneth Strickfaden, now seventy-eight years old, had the original set in his garage'.7 Brooks's collaboration with the celebrated Strickfaden, so warmly remembered for his unforgettable contribution to cinema throughout the earlier *Frankenstein* movies, paved the way for some excellent sight gags – not least Igor irritatedly bashing the sparking equipment when it fails to shut down, in a manner far removed from the awed reverence of the original. Yet as Harry Goldman has noted, Brooks's determination to acknowledge Strickfaden's input clearly showed the value that he placed in the veteran designer's involvement in the production:

> *Young Frankenstein* marked the last *Frankenstein* picture show in which the original 1931 laboratory machines appeared collectively. And it is a sad fact that the film was the last (major) *Frankenstein* picture show for [set designer and electrical effects creator] Ken Strickfaden. Although the film industry has thoroughly documented Mel Brooks' comedic side, it has given less attention to the man's compassionate nature. An example of the latter endowment was revealed in *Young Frankenstein* when Brooks honored Strickfaden with a screen credit.[8]

For all Brooks's scrupulous attention to production detail, central to the success of the film is Gene Wilder's all-guns-blazing performance as the eponymous scientist, first fiercely denying his heritage and then wholeheartedly embracing it. The versatile Wilder, here a mile away from the self-effacing Leopold Bloom or zen-like drunkard The Waco Kid, was only rarely so dashing and debonair as he appeared here. There is an uncommon touch of finesse in his transformation from arrogantly staid, *Lancet*-reading surgeon to mad scientist, for he is equally credible as an aloof intellectual as he is when portraying the epitome of necromantic obsession. Here, unusually for a spoof, the audience witnesses a fidelity to the sentiment of the source text quite far removed from other comedies of this type; Crick notes the way that Brooks' and Wilder's screenplay effectively harnesses something of the 'human yearning, desperation [and] longing' of Mary Shelley's novel.[9] Yet of course, the film quite consciously deviates from the plotline of both the nineteenth century text and the James Whale adaptation, embracing a far broader interpretation of the *Frankenstein* mythology which had been repeatedly revisited and reconfigured over the decades. As Vijay Mishra explains:

> *Frankenstein* cannot be read as a single, unified text. Like the paradigmatic precursor text (*The Castle of Otranto*), which underwent a process of expansion and rewriting, *Frankenstein* (and the Gothic generally) must be read as a 'process' inextricably linked to other, not

necessarily novelistic, semiotic systems. Mel Brooks' film spoof *Young Frankenstein* (1974) may be taken as an example of this process of expansion and rewriting, since its target texts (for purposes of parody) are the multiplicity of texts inspired by the original.[10]

By bargaining upon audience familiarity with both the central premise of bodily reanimation and certain key scenes from the Universal horror movies which had become embedded within popular culture, Brooks is able to rely upon certain reactions which are triggered by particular sequences and situations presented within the film. The blind man who shows the creature kindness, and the drowning (or not, in this case) of the innocent little girl are both simultaneously tributes and subversions of well-known scenes in earlier *Frankenstein* movies. Because the girl's death in the original, caused by a tragic accident, was in a sense the demise of an innocent at the hands of an innocent, the scene has enormous emotional potency; thus in *Young Frankenstein* when the child wonders aloud what they should throw in the well, the monster's knowingly mischievous look to camera seems all the funnier because the audience knows what to expect. The ultimate security of the girl, catapulted to the safety of her room and into the arms of her parents, removes any ambiguity regarding her fate. Likewise, Gene Hackman's hilarious cameo as Harold, the lonely but well-meaning monk ('Where are you going? I was going to make espresso!'), undermines the premise of the original scenario to uproarious effect. Being unable to see the creature's gruesome, lumbering form, Harold is not repelled by his presence but rather treats him with compassion and friendship. (The monster's arrival is, in effect, an instantaneous response to the monk's faithful prayer – just as had been the case with Father Fyodor's rather less benign requests for divine intervention in *The Twelve Chairs*.) Yet while his inability to see makes it possible for him to strike up genuine camaraderie with the creature without preconception, at the same time it proves to be the downfall of their relationship; Harold unwittingly subjects his hapless guest to a succession of painful encounters including scalding, soaking and eventually setting him alight, cumulatively sending the uninvited visitor running for the hills.

In a sense, Frederick Frankenstein's story demonstrates a search for two kinds of liberation – freedom from societal expectation, and freedom from generic convention. Yacowar argues that the central premise is essentially one of Frankenstein's 'maturing from naive young man to self-aware adult',[11] and certainly much is made of the character's evolution from coldly clinical paragon of scientific orthodoxy into a compassionate, hot-blooded individual who is able and willing to embrace his family's infamous heritage. As was the case with *Blazing Saddles*, though more subtly employed, *Young Frankenstein* exhibits a philosophy that is deeply sceptical of the establishment: an underlying but fervent plea by Brooks to remain constantly aware of when cultural mores are beneficial and when they have a constrictive effect on individual liberty. Frankenstein's spirited discourse with the pushily impertinent medical student concerning his grandfather's work ('We *all* know what he did!') – at first defensive and then gradually turning almost histrionic – is so impassioned that it causes him to inadvertently pierce his own leg with a scalpel while making a rhetorical point. (He is, of course, too proud to acknowledge this *faux-pas*, no matter how painful the result obviously is.) Yet even when espousing the rational materialism of scientific convention – 'I am not interested in death! The only thing that concerns me is the preservation of *life!*' – Frankenstein still foreshadows the theatricality of his later scientific approach; his public medical examination almost takes on the tone of an illusionist's stage show ('Mr Hilltop, with whom I have never worked, or given any prior instructions to...'), presaging the showiness of his later song-and-dance act alongside the creature, while his demonstration of voluntary and reflex nerve impulses proves to be particularly over-dramatic – as can be witnessed in his openly callous treatment of his ill-fated clinical volunteer/ victim (an excellently tongue-in-cheek turn from Liam Dunn). It is this journey of self-realisation, highlighting Frankenstein's dawning comprehension that intellect and wisdom are far from the same thing, which makes Wilder's thoughtfully-considered performance all the more noteworthy.

Though he has battled constantly throughout his medical career to break free of the notoriety of his family name, going so far as to intentionally mispronounce his name as 'Fronckensteen', the doctor eventually realises that he has been equally as inhibited by the conformist expectations of his scientific peers and by social convention. His relationship with his chaste, image-conscious fiancée Elizabeth, though shot through with flashes of genuine affection, seems so dispassionate in general that they are reduced to placidly rubbing elbows upon parting due to her displeasure at him touching her perfectly-conditioned fingernails, lips, hair, etc. This is contrasted with the instant attraction shown towards him by Inga, the practical and supportive laboratory assistant... though he is so preoccupied with his work that he spends most of the film inattentive of the need to recognise (and then reciprocate) her feelings. His eventual response to Inga's loving warmth, underscoring his rejection of the orthodoxy that Elizabeth and her high status represents, leads to their marriage and his ultimate acceptance of his Frankenstein heritage.

Concurrently, his relationship with his creature also grows and develops over time. Initially viewing the reanimated corpse primarily in terms of a scientific experiment, he eventually assumes an almost parental role, taking responsibility for his actions in a way that the Victor Frankenstein of Shelley's text could never bring himself to. Thus Frederick transcends the expectations of the mainstream Frankenstein mythos, proving to be a more benevolent and emotionally articulate creator than his mad scientist forebears, just as his creature is a more expressive and self-aware being than many such cinematic monsters of years gone by. As Yacowar notes, these dual catalysts of growth spur Frankenstein into becoming a rounder individual, shaking off the dogmatism of his scientific peers as well as the audience's expectations surrounding his likely actions and attitudes as a member of the Frankenstein family: 'Through the joint emotional expansions by the monster and by Inga, Brooks's Frankenstein matures into a creature who is both fuller and healthier. So there is a psychoanalytic aspect to Frankenstein's intellectual exchange with his monster [...] and the blithering doctor learns passion'.[12]

If Wilder's Frankenstein challenges expectation with his conduct and overall character arc, Marty Feldman's Igor quite happily tears up the rule book and throws it out of the window. In the tradition of the genre-conscious Sheriff Bart, Igor knows all too well the role that he is envisaged to fulfil and thus seems determined to dispute and undercut audience anticipation at every turn:

IGOR: Dr Frankenstein?
FRANKENSTEIN: Fronckensteen.
IGOR: You're putting me on.

| | |
|---|---|
| FRANKENSTEIN: | No. It's pronounced Fronckensteen. |
| IGOR: | Do you also say 'Froderick'? |
| FRANKENSTEIN: | No. Frederick. |
| IGOR: | Well, why isn't it 'Froderick Fronckensteen'? |
| FRANKENSTEIN: | It isn't! It's *Frederick* Fronckensteen. |
| IGOR: | I see. |
| FRANKENSTEIN: | You must be Igor. |
| IGOR: | No, it's pronounced I-gor. |
| FRANKENSTEIN: | But they told me it was Igor! |
| IGOR: | Well, they were wrong then, weren't they? |

It is left entirely to the viewer to make their own minds up regarding whether Igor's name really is pronounced in the way he indicates, or whether he has simply improvised the assertion in response to Frankenstein's blatant affectation in altering the cadence of his own name. But then, Igor is a mass of contradictions in every sense; an affable hunchback with a constantly shifting hump ('Didn't you use to have that on your other side?') which randomly disappears altogether, the crazy-eyed Feldman comes close to stealing the show in a film that is packed with winning performances. Unforgettable even from his introductory scraping footsteps, we are soon made aware that this frivolous manservant is a direct descendant of the gargoyle-like assistants of *Frankenstein* movies past – though, as he is quick to point out, 'the rates have gone up' since then. The obvious fact that Frankenstein finds his company distinctly off-putting throughout the film only enhances Igor's ability to raise a smile; the awkward silence which lingers after the doctor offers to operate on Igor's hump, resulting in the mystified response 'What hump?', leaves the audience wondering whether his statement is sincere or ironic, but laughing either way. The many consciously corny jokes on the subject which follow, not least 'Call it a hunch!', firmly suggest that Igor is pulling his new employer's leg. Indeed, Igor seems perfectly happy to use his unusual physical characteristics as a facilitator for comic effect. By enunciating his name as 'Eye-Gore', he sets in motion a fusillade of jokes referencing Feldman's own strabismus-afflicted eyes as well as their prominence, the result of a real-life thyroid condition, leading to ironic exchanges such as the famous 'Damn your eyes!'/ 'Too late!' witticism. Igor's immortal 'Walk this way!' visual gag would be reprised several times in later Brooks features, while the character's one-liners are pure vaudeville drollness; when asked by Frankenstein to help him with some bags, his Marx Brothers-tinged response is 'Certainly! You take the blonde, and I'll take the one in the turban,' deeply perplexing the onlooking Inga and Elizabeth. Yet it is Feldman's copious, sardonic glances to camera and the sheer fascinating weirdness of Igor's behaviour – from impersonating a recently-decapitated head just for a lark, to spontaneously (and inexplicably) savaging Elizabeth's fur stole – which helps to make this appealingly odd character so memorable. And in his unabashed cack-handedness in carrying out Frankenstein's instructions regarding the recovery of a brain, Igor is inadvertently responsible for much of the film's subsequent action:

FRANKENSTEIN: Now, that brain that you gave me... was it Hans Delbrück's?
IGOR: No.
FRANKENSTEIN: Ah! Good. Uh... would you mind telling me whose brain I *did* put in?
IGOR: And you won't be angry?
FRANKENSTEIN: I will *not* be angry.
IGOR: Abbie someone.
FRANKENSTEIN: Abbie someone? Abbie who?
IGOR: Abbie... Normal.
FRANKENSTEIN: Abbie Normal.
IGOR: I'm almost sure that was the name.
FRANKENSTEIN: Are you saying that I put an abnormal brain into a seven-and-a-half-foot long, fifty-four inch wide gorilla? Is that what you're telling me?!

As the creature, Peter Boyle demonstrates a masterclass in expressive talent. Given that the reanimated corpse is a huge, unwieldy grotesque who is unable to verbally communicate beyond a narrow range of grunts and groans, Boyle manages to flesh out the character into a sympathetic and self-aware individual with remarkable panache. Despite sporting a zipper along his throat in place of the traditional neck-mounted metal electrodes of Boris Karloff-style Frankenstein's monsters (a point which Elizabeth draws attention to when she affectionately calls him 'you little zipper-neck'), the creature is as authentic a reproduction of the classic Universal horror make-up and costume design as it is possible to imagine. Here too we see Brooks's mischievous wit at play: while the presence of the nuts-and-bolts electrodes in the original film was self-explanatory, here the scientific purpose of the neck-zipper remains cheerfully ignored for the duration of the film. Likewise, Boyle's creature is no inhuman fiend, nor a pitiful figure of tragedy, but rather someone who is firmly in on the joke (as his knowing expressions directed at the audience frequently make clear). And yet it is in exploring the character's complex and troubled relationship with his creator that the film is at its most thought-provoking. Caroline Joan S. Picart makes the point that:

> Brooks reveals a conscious manipulation of the Koestlerian conjunctions of normally separated planes or contexts, generating both humor and melodrama. To him, great comics, to generate humor, must root their emotions in the seriousness of 'reality and passion'. [...] Brooks is also one of the few directors (actor/ director Kenneth Branagh is another) who actually talks overtly about the parthenogenetic theme at the heart of the *Frankenstein* narrative [...]: 'I always thought... that the monster was born out of the scientist's ego and his rage at not being able to do what any woman can do, and that is to give birth'.[13]

Because Frankenstein's development hinges upon the role that he plays in his creature's journey from (re-)birth to fully functioning member of polite society, it is interesting to note the way that both characters evolve in tandem, culminating in the brain-fluid transference sequence at the film's climax. Like his creator, the monster is seeking freedom – in his case, from prejudice and persecution. Yet as Frankenstein's sense of responsibility towards the creature grows, triggering a kind of parental duty which opens him to a wider range of emotional experience, he faces a particular challenge in envisioning his creation as more than a scientific curiosity – an experimental gambit proven through technical methodology – but rather as a living being and thus the rightful recipient of mutual respect and consideration. This dichotomy is perhaps most tellingly exposed following the monster's initial recapture, where Frankenstein makes plain his acknowledgement that he is responsible not only for the creature's reanimation, but also the quality of his life: 'Love is the only thing that can save this poor creature. And I am going to convince him that he is loved, even at the cost of my own life'. Following the doctor's desperate but heartfelt attempts to boost the monster's self-esteem ('Hey, handsome! [...] Do you want to talk about the Olympian ideal?'), assuring him that he will do everything in his power to assist in integrating him into mainstream society, comes the infamous 'Puttin' on the Ritz' sequence based at the Budapest Academy of Science. This sequence is so pivotal within the film, it is important to remember that it was very nearly absent from the final cut altogether; as Bruce G. Hallenbeck notes, Wilder recollected 'that he had to fight Brooks for what turned out to be one of the movie's signature scenes, the "Puttin' on the Ritz" routine. Originally, Brooks thought it would be too silly, but Wilder was so passionate in his defense of it that Brooks finally agreed it should stay in. The rest, as they say, is history'.[14]

Wilder's creative judgement was to reap dividends; in juxtaposing the clinical precision of an academic presentation with the razzmatazz of music hall song-and-dance routines, the inventive image of the monster-as-entertainer became one of the film's most readily-recognisable within the annals of popular culture. Yet there is significance to the employment of the creature within this presentational framework, and one which extends beyond the enjoyable absurdity of watching an audience of eminent scientists attending a lecture on neurobiology who just happen to have brought along rotten vegetables to throw at unsuccessful 'acts'. While Frankenstein had promised to tutor his creature in essential life skills, this sequence casts harsh light upon the conflict which exists between his own search for scientific glory and the requirements of moral responsibility. He may assert the nurturing of the monster into 'a cultured, sophisticated man about town', but by feeding his creation treats like a performing pet to encourage him through the routine and mouthing 'Love him!' theatrically to the audience, he demeans both the creature and himself, reducing the significance of his groundbreaking research to the level of a circus sideshow. Only when Frankenstein realises the extent of his folly and finds a way of dealing constructively with his guilt does he fully understand his moral duty to secure the wellbeing of his creation. The juxtaposition of high society glamour and the gruesome nature of a dancing reanimated corpse has its own surreal qualities, but ultimately it finds the unfortunate creature wanting – a fact which Frankenstein has denied until the last moment because of his personal pride and self-importance. Ian Conrich has made the insightful point that '"Puttin' on the Ritz', an Irving Berlin composition most associated with Fred Astaire [...] promotes sophistication and style, and conveys a public statement of an individual's affluent intentions. Furthermore, as a performer, Astaire is an iconic figure within the screen musical noted for his elegance and dance ability. In contrast, the figure of The Monster, who is revealed on stage wearing reinforced metal boots, and who initially struggles to execute even rudimentary walking movements, appears as a lumbering grotesque'.[15] Indeed, even the ostentatious choice of music proves to be significant, in sharp contrast to the simple but evocative violin melodies offered by Frau Blücher. As Raymond Knapp argues, '"Puttin' on the Ritz" is first of all about simple folk *pretending* to a sophistication they do not actually possess,' adding that 'the subtext [...] points both to the hubris of the creature in pretending to a sophistication he has learned by rote, and to the larger hubris of Frankenstein's aspiration to create life. But more important here is what we actually see in this number: the control exercised, through music, both *over* the creature and *by* the creature. This is the flip side of the creature's mesmerised response to music earlier in the film, where music seems to awaken his soul'.[16] Beyond the comic and thematic significance of the scene, of course, lies another very clear Brooksian contestation of genre expectations, which is the equal of any such narrative dexterity offered up in *Blazing Saddles*. Conrich has observed that:

> When Dr Frankenstein first reveals his creation to the startled audience the movie is operating within the conventions of the Gothic horror film. This dramatically alters, however, with a sudden musical number largely constructed around the incongruous performance of The Monster as an unlikely debonair figure who incredibly has the ability to dance and entertain. [...] The smartly-attired Monster reinforces the doctor's claim as he performs the number with some grace, dancing nimbly in his heavy boots, though he is unable to disguise his lack of a singing voice as he bellows out his solo line, 'Puttin' on the Ritz'. The classical Hollywood musical is subverted by this performance, in which even though the original number is respectfully referenced, the deliberate combining of the horror film and the musical – a song and dance moment celebrating refinement and class, together with a primordial Gothic creation, a monstrous body of stitched-together parts of corpses – functions as a direct challenge to genre boundaries.[17]

The film is full of cunningly-employed surrealistic humour which, though rarely as cheerfully unsubtle as the copious deliberate anachronisms of *Blazing Saddles*, never fails to dispute the audience's anticipation of accepted cinematic conventions. The fact that a small, rustic Transylvanian village should house a clinical 'brain depository', where brains are deposited in a door-mounted slot after-hours in a manner similar to a night-safe, and the absurdity of the darts game with Kemp – where Frankenstein manages to break glass even when he doesn't throw any darts – may seem oddly low-key by the standard set by the previous film, but are no less amusing for their relative restraint. The potentially lethal darts game is a particular highlight; the inspector's driver is shown with a dart lodged in his helmet as he leaves the castle, later revealing that the departing car's tyres are peppered with them, even though only a few handfuls of darts were ever shown being thrown in the earlier scene. The screeching cat which appears to fall foul of one of the doctor's misdirected darts was performed by Brooks himself; though he was not to appear as a performer in the film, he did add some uncredited vocal cameos including the voice-over which accompanies Victor Frankenstein's ethereal laboratory flashback. His meticulous attention to detail regarding even the smallest incidental sound effect was typical of the sheer depth of his perfectionism; as Brad Darrach has remarked, 'after *Young Frankenstein* was in the can, [Brooks] edited the picture frame by frame at least 12 times and in the last week of production spent several hours in a recording room, gleefully snorting, grunting, snarling, groaning, sighing and guffawing to fill tiny gaps in the talk track. "The man is a demon," says one of his editors. "Nothing less than greatness will satisfy him. He has the lonely passion for perfection"'.[18]

Even on occasions where *Young Frankenstein* engages directly with the recognised genre characteristics of classic horror cinema, Brooks's and Wilder's screenplay has a great deal of fun at the expense of the audience's presumptions. The clock at the beginning of the film strikes thirteen, a portent which encourages the audience to expect the unexpected and thus setting the scene for various convolutions in the horror format. The oft-imitated line 'It's alive!' is present and correct, originally uttered by Colin Clive in the James Whale original, but after Frankenstein has delivered his grandiloquent speech in defiance of the strictures of scientific orthodoxy ('Tonight, we shall hurl the gauntlet of science into the frightful face of death itself. Tonight we shall ascend into the heavens! We shall mock the earthquake! We shall command the thunders and penetrate into the very womb of impervious nature herself!'), Brooks immediately sets about deflating the character's hubris. Thus the doctor finds himself simultaneously being comically throttled by his own creation and then being forced into desperately acting out a series of charades in order to persuade his assistants that they need to subdue the rampaging creature ('Said-a-give?!'). There is ample evidence of Wilder's flawless comic timing, not least in the scene where he finds himself concealing a cart-bound corpse from a sociable village policeman by manipulating one of its dead hands as if it were his own, and the way that his starched collar pops open at precisely the moment he insists that he has to look normal at all costs. Naturally, given the sinister Transylvanian locale Brooks ensures that genre-based truisms abound: beyond the cobwebs and long shadows there are plentiful deafening thunderstorms, with lightning illuminating the action at key points such as Igor's unfortunate brain-smashing accident and the doctor's discovery of his grandfather's bound notes (entitled, perhaps inevitably, *How I Did It* by Victor Frankenstein). For every horror cliché which is invoked, such as the seemingly-inescapable hidden passageway discovered behind a revolving bookcase, there is a counter-intuitive development such as Inga's heartfelt cries of 'You'll kill him!' when Frankenstein repeatedly thumps the still-dead corpse that will eventually become the creature. In a manner similar to *Blazing Saddles*'s stylistic free-for-all, cribbing from the modern and the historical at will, there is a degree of uncertainty cast over the exact period when *Young Frankenstein* is supposed to be situated. Frankenstein's American students, glimpsed briefly in the introductory scenes, are dressed neutrally enough to defy expectation about their decade of origin, and little can be discerned from the departing train in the United States before we reach the even more ambiguous surroundings of rural Transylvania ('Pardon me, boy? Is this the Transylvania Station?'). Likewise, Brooks gives us no reason to assume that the shenanigans surrounding the freshly-removed brain of Hans Delbrück – which Frankenstein initially intends to use for transplantation into his creature – is meant to imply any connection to the celebrated real-life German military historian Hans Delbrück (1848-1929). Thus the audience must derive their own assumptions as regards the temporal placement of this Gothic Never-Neverland. It is, in many respects, an environment frozen in time: a nostalgic tribute to the bygone cinematic horror features of Brooks's and Wilder's respective childhoods. Esther Schor makes the point that:

> The title evokes as well Mel Brooks's own young *Frankenstein*, an impressionable boy's mesmerized, anxious, and jokey encounter with both of James Whale's classic films. In the black and white *Young Frankenstein*, Brooks exquisitely captures the gloomy luminosity of Whale's films, aping both [Kenneth] Strickfaden's sets and Jack Pierce's makeup (minus the precipitous brow). For transitions between sequences, Brooks uses nostalgic iris-in shots (beginning with a point of light and expanding gradually to a large circle) and iris-out shots (a circular shot that gradually diminishes to a point); in some cases, he uses a campy heart shape in lieu of a circle. He also recalls the cinema of the 1930s with vertical wipes, gradually replacing one shot with another, as though wiping the previous shot away from right to left or left to right.[19]

Just as is the case with the film's central triptych of Frankenstein, Igor and the creature, the supporting cast proves to be universally excellent. Each performance, in its own way, reflects something of the shrewd self-awareness of the film as a whole, from Golden Globe-nominated Cloris Leachman's fearsome Frau Blücher (so alarming that she invariably causes the sound of horses rearing up and whinnying, even when there are no horses present) to Kenneth Mars's seemingly-clockwork Inspector Kemp, with his monocle placed daintily (and curiously) over his eyepatch and his strangely untraceable Eastern European accent which is so prominent that not even the other Transylvanians can fully understand what he is saying. With his oddly cartoonish movements and a comedic inflection which is far removed from that of Mars's earlier turn as the unbalanced Hitler aficionado Franz Liebkind in *The Producers*, Crick observes that Kemp is likely inspired by Lionel Atwill's performance as the ominous Inspector Keogh in *Son of Frankenstein*, even down to the character having lost an arm during an unfortunate encounter with a previous Frankenstein creation.[20] Madeline Kahn makes the most of a brief but well-crafted appearance as Elizabeth, Frankenstein's socialite wife-to-be who proves rather less prim than her initial depiction suggests (and, though markedly different from Mae Clarke's depiction of Elizabeth in the James Whale film, she ultimately enjoys a rather more harmonious finale than the character in Shelley's novel). For all the relative concision of her screen time, Kahn's performance impressed the critical community of the time; her success with the role was to see her placed third in the New York Film Critics Circle Awards for Best Supporting Actress in 1974, and nominated for a Golden Globe Award in 1975. Teri Garr is similarly excellent as Inga, the considerate laboratory assistant who understands the doctor's emotional needs far better than he ever could himself. Garr succeeds in generating much comic capital from Frankenstein's oblivious ignorance of Inga's romantic interest in him; his misunderstood command for her to 'elevate' him, referring to the pulley-operated platform in his laboratory, ironically proves to be somewhat prescient when the two sleep together on the same apparatus later in the film. These two supporting characters reflect different aspects of Frankenstein's character. In his relationship with Elizabeth, we see his desire to seek mainstream legitimacy, both with regard to his work and his social standing. Their emotional rapport may be somewhat anaemic, sterile even, but both can see that a marriage between them will ensure respectability and mutual societal decorum. His blossoming attraction to Inga, on the other hand, illuminates his growing maturity as an individual, making him able to look beyond the constriction of the expectation of his peers in a manner similar to the way that his pursuit of his grandfather's work allows him to outgrow the limitations imposed on him by recognised scientific convention. While marriage to Elizabeth may have brought him the approval expected of his professional background and social class, only the love of the warm-hearted, empathetic Inga has the potential to truly set him free.

At its best, *Young Frankenstein* succeeds in unifying themes from the three Brooks films which proceeded it; the affirmation of self-determination in *The Producers*, the call for greater interpersonal cooperation (and its potential for individual development) in *The Twelve Chairs*, and the aggressive defiance of genre boundaries and celebration of the outsider presented by *Blazing Saddles*. Certainly Brooks appeared keen to present a more profound degree of character development throughout the film, asserting in an interview with Jacoba Atlas that *Young Frankenstein* was his 'first attempt at fifty-fifty, laughs and story.

It's a love story, like *The Producers* it's an emotional give and take. When you leave *Young Frankenstein* I want you to feel emotionally satisfied and have a lot of affection for the characters and not want to leave the theater. I don't think I'll get as many laughs as in *Blazing Saddles*. Instead of ten thousand laughs, maybe only eight thousand'.[21] Yet for all the film's exploration of the outer edges of the genre, where Brooks playfully toys with areas of overlap between horror and comedy, *Young Frankenstein* has primarily been noted for its loving (and painstaking) recreation of the very type of film that Brooks and Wilder intended to send up, its innate geniality never savaging the genre quite so thoroughly as had been the case with his earlier full-scale onslaught on the Western. Picart notes that 'Brooks runs a fine line between homage and comic allusion in *Young Frankenstein*. Marty Feldman [...] saw the film as "a mad tribute to the early Hollywood versions... particularly the Boris Karloff hit of 1931". The *Los Angeles Times* Entertainment Editor, Charles Champlin, echoed a similar observation: "...the tribute is respectful, loaded with updating jokes but stopping well short of the tear-apart parody which leaves the object of the tribute in a crumpled heap"'.[22]

There is also much to enjoy in the technical aspects of the film, in no small part due to the qualities of loving pastiche evident in Gerald Hirschfeld's wonderfully evocative cinematography. Brooks's long-time collaborator John Morris, who had provided a rousingly kinetic original score for *Blazing Saddles*, excels here in recreating the edgy eeriness of the golden age of horror cinema. Morris's staggeringly faithful original score, replete with all the expected jarring chords, contains many moments of quiet – almost ingenious – subtlety, and in a film where music plays such a crucial role this is of vital importance. It is this obvious desire to construct a faithful facsimile of silver screen horror, prior to reconfiguring and subverting its precepts, which marks the film out from the many pale imitations which would follow. As Hallenbeck suggests:

> What makes this film such an affectionate homage to its source material is the fact that Brooks went to the trouble of recreating the monochrome look of the old Universal horrors. [...] It's this type of attention to detail that makes *Young Frankenstein* soar above most other horror parodies. While some parody filmmakers deride their

source material, Brooks and Wilder obviously love it. They've seen the films they're parodying hundreds of times and know their every nuance. Ultimately, *Young Frankenstein* is a movie for film buffs, but written, directed and performed in such a way that average Joes and Josephines can enjoy it just as much for its outrageous and wacky humor.[23]

Although *Young Frankenstein* has since become established as one of Brooks's most refined comedies, critical reception of the film was mixed at the time of its release. Katharine Lowry, writing for *Texas Monthly*, was particularly scathing when offering her opinion that that 'Brooks exhumes every moldy oldie he's ever created, commissioned, or plagiarized, and tosses in a handful of potty jokes and silly sex gags long in the public domain. Only rarely does he capitalize on the abundance of humor intrinsic to the *Frankenstein* story, maybe because it's difficult to make such melodrama more absurd than it already is'.[24] Pauline Kael, on the other hand, addressed the film with guarded compliments in *The New Yorker*: 'It isn't a dialogue comedy; it's visceral and lower. It's what used to be called a crazy comedy, and there hasn't been this kind of craziness on the screen in years. It's a film to go to when your rhythm is slowed down and you're too tired to think. [...] The style of the picture is controlled excess, and the whole thing is remarkably consistent in tone'.[25] At the other end of the spectrum, *The Chicago Sun-Times*'s Roger Ebert praised the evolution of Brooks's directorial talents, remarking that '*Young Frankenstein* is as funny as we expect a Mel Brooks comedy to be, but it's more than that: It shows artistic growth and a more sure-handed control of the material by a director who once seemed willing to do literally anything for a laugh. It's more confident and less breathless'.[26] The film even seemed to win over Vincent Canby of *The New York Times*, who echoed Ebert's sentiment that the film marked a new maturity in Brooks's filmmaking: 'Although it hasn't as many roof-raising boffs as *Blazing Saddles*, it is funnier over the long run because it is more disciplined. The anarchy is controlled. Mr Brooks sticks to the subject, recalling the clichés of horror films of the 1930s as lovingly as someone remembering the small sins of youth. Perhaps the nicest thing about *Young Frankenstein* is that one can laugh with it and never feel as if the target film, James Whale's 1931 classic that starred Boris Karloff, is being rudely used'.[27]

In spite of the division of opinion amongst media commentators, *Young Frankenstein* achieved significant box-office success, earning $86,273,333 from American cinemas – a figure which dwarfed the film's budget of $2.78 million.[28] The screenplay by Brooks and Wilder was nominated for the Academy Award for Writing (Adapted Screenplay) in 1975, but also went on to win major genre prizes such as the Hugo Award for Best Dramatic Presentation (1975) and the Nebula Award for Best Dramatic Writing (1976) as well as international plaudits including a Golden Screen Award in Germany. Becoming firmly ensconced in the public consciousness following many repeat showings on television and various releases on home entertainment formats, *Young Frankenstein* received the honour of being selected by the United States National Film Preservation Board to be conserved within the Library of Congress National Film Registry in 2003, almost thirty years after its first cinematic release. This mark of distinction was only to underscore the reputation of the film as being amongst Brooks's most fondly remembered productions; as *Young Frankenstein* reached its fortieth anniversary, its status remained positively glowing amongst modern critics. Glut posits that '*Young Frankenstein* – decades after its first-run release – has earned itself the deserved reputation of a modern-day classic. In this writer's subjective opinion, it is Mel Brooks' best motion picture and one that works on several levels. It is also one of the last great films of any genre to be shot in black and white, utilizing actual black and white (as opposed to color, later to be dropped out) film stock'.[29] Tueth mirrors this appraisal, observing that '*Young Frankenstein* ranks as a brilliant parody for several reasons. First, for a parody to succeed, the original work must be well enough known to its intended audience. It can be even more helpful if the original work is well respected or culturally significant. The original must be dense enough to offer sufficient material to be imitated, especially if the parody runs almost two hours, as does *Young Frankenstein*. The original novel and film versions of the *Frankenstein* story meet this criterion better than any of the works that inspired Brooks's other film parodies'.[30] However, perhaps the most representative view of all is offered by Robert C. Ring, who places the film within the wider pantheon of cinematic comedy:

> *Young Frankenstein* is hilarious, thanks to a combination of Brooks' wit and the actors' comedic timing. [The performers] devote themselves to their roles with an enthusiasm that is rarely equaled. Wilder's outbursts are as amusing as they are heaven-defying, Feldman's continual glances at the camera with his bulbous eyeballs are priceless, and Boyle plays the monster so believably that it is not difficult to imagine him taking the role in one of the original films. When these actors' sensibilities are applied to Brooks' humor, the result is comedy gold. [...] *Young Frankenstein* must be one of the greatest parodies of all time. You would be hard-pressed to find any such film so true to its source and so consistently funny. It stands as undeniable proof that Brooks is not only a funny director, he is a great one.[31]

As had been the case with *The Producers*, Brooks was to revisit *Young Frankenstein* many years later by developing the story into a stage musical in collaboration with writer Thomas Meehan. The musical offered an expanded version of events in comparison to the original film, including an enlarged role for Elizabeth and a considerably embellished finale. Opening on Broadway in the November of 2007, the show received a decidedly lukewarm critical reception, but nonetheless developed into what Stewart F. Lane termed 'a modest hit [which] ran for nearly 500 performances'.[32] It was also the recipient of numerous award nominations throughout the course of its run, winning Best Musical at the Outer Critics Circle Awards in 2008. Though the stage version of *Young Frankenstein* did not fare as well as the monumentally successful stage adaptation of *The Producers* had done, neither did it come even remotely close to mirroring the disappointment of *Black Bart*, CBS's ill-fated TV spin-off based on *Blazing Saddles* which failed to be developed beyond the pilot stage.

With its welcoming sense of nostalgia, genuine fondness for its source material and subtle emotional insight, *Young Frankenstein* denoted a high water-mark in Brooks's film-making. Though he would unleash his incisive wit on many other cinematic genres before returning to the horror movie years later with *Dracula: Dead and Loving It*, for many critics and moviegoers Brooks would never again reach quite the same precise balance of inspired absurdity and respectful reproduction of the stylistic conventions of his target subject. However, *Young Frankenstein* was also significant in the development of its multiply-layered characters, challenging genre expectations not simply through the surrealism of its visual and auditory gags but by way of exploring the unexpected reactions and behaviours of well-established archetypes; the simple-minded manservant turned witty sidekick, the gruntingly inarticulate creature with his knowing glances to the audience, and of course the mad scientist who discovers humility and wisdom through adversity. As in *Blazing Saddles*, the characters who work best are those who transcend their established function, and who show awareness of having done so. Once again, Brooks had upheld the need for freedom from established generic formulae, championing individual autonomy and the importance of avoiding the hidebound restraint of the Hollywood rulebook in the name of unfettered invention.

# REFERENCES

1. Michael V. Tueth, *Reeling with Laughter: American Film Comedies – From Anarchy to Mockumentary* (Plymouth: Scarecrow Press, 2012), p. 119.
2. Joe Garner, *Made You Laugh!: The Funniest Moments in Radio, Television, Stand-Up, and Movie Comedy* (Kansas City: Andrews McMeel Publishing, 2004), p. 178.
3. Robert Alan Crick, *The Big Screen Comedies of Mel Brooks* (Jefferson: McFarland and Company, 2009) [2002], p. 72.
4. Donald F. Glut, *The Frankenstein Archive: Essays on the Monster, the Myth, the Movies, and More* (Jefferson: McFarland, 2002), p. 69.
5. Maurice Yacowar, *The Comic Art of Mel Brooks* (London: W.H. Allen, 1982), pp. 145-46.
6. Albert J. Lavalley, 'The Stage and Film Children of *Frankenstein*: A Survey', in *The Endurance of Frankenstein: Essays on Mary Shelley's Novel*, ed. by George Levine and U.C. Knoepflmacher (Berkeley: University of California Press, 1979), 243-90, p. 282.
7. Yacowar, pp. 144-45.
8. Harry Goldman, *Kenneth Strickfaden: Dr Frankenstein's Electrician* (Jefferson: McFarland, 2005), p. 95.
9. Crick, p. 76.
10. Vijay Mishra, *The Gothic Sublime* (Albany: State University of New York Press, 1994), p. 210.
11. Yacowar, p. 148.
12. ibid., p. 159.
13. Caroline Joan S. Picart, *Remaking the Frankenstein Myth on Film: Between Laughter and Horror* (Albany: State University of New York Press, 2003), p. 43.
14. Bruce G. Hallenbeck, *Comedy-Horror Films: A Chronological History, 1914-2008* (Jefferson: McFarland, 2009), p. 107.
15. Ian Conrich, 'Musical Performance and the Cult Film Experience', in *Film's Musical Moments*, ed. by Ian Conrich and Estella Tincknell (Edinburgh: Edinburgh University Press, 2006), 115-31, p. 125.
16. Raymond Knapp, 'Music, Electricity, and the "Sweet Mystery of Life" in *Young Frankenstein*', in *Changing Tunes: The Use of Pre-Existing Music in Film*, ed. by Phil Powrie and Robynn Stilwell (Aldershot: Ashgate Publishing, 2006), 105-18, pp. 113-14.
17. Conrich, p. 125.
18. Brad Darrach, 'Mel Brooks', in *Playboy*, February 1975. <http://www.brookslyn.com/print/PlayboyFeb1975/PlayboyFeb1975_part1.php>
19. Esther Schor, 'Frankenstein and Film', in *The Cambridge Companion to Mary Shelley*, ed. by Esther Schor (Cambridge: Cambridge University Press, 2003), 63-83, p. 75.
20. Crick, p. 81.
21. Mel Brooks, in Jacoba Atlas, 'New Hollywood: Mel Brooks Interview', in *Film Comment*, March-April 1975. <http://www.brookslyn.com/print/FilmComment1975/FilmComment1975.php>
22. Picart, p. 42.
23. Bruce G. Hallenbeck, *Comedy-Horror Films: A Chronological History*, 1914-2008 (Jefferson: McFarland, 2009), p. 108.
24. Katharine Lowry, 'Film: Doin' the Monster Mashed', in *Texas Monthly*, March 1975, p. 40.
25. Pauline Kael, 'A Magnetic Blur', in *The New Yorker*, 30 December 1974.

&lt;http://www.newyorker.com/magazine/1974/12/30/a-magnetic-blur?currentPage=all&gt;
26. Roger Ebert, '*Young Frankenstein*', in *The Chicago Sun-Times*, 16 December 1974. &lt;http://www.rogerebert.com/reviews/young-frankenstein-1974&gt;
27. Vincent Canby, '*Young Frankenstein*', in *The New York Times*, 16 December 1974, &lt;http://www.nytimes.com/movie/review?res=EE05E7DF173EAF2CA5494CC2B779988C6896&gt;
28. Statistical data drawn from *BoxOfficeMojo.com*. &lt;http://www.boxofficemojo.com/movies/?id=youngfrankenstein.htm&gt;
29. Glut, p. 67.
30. Tueth, p. 119.
31. Robert C. Ring, *Sci-Fi Movie Freak* (Iola: Krause Publications, 2011), p. 35.
32. Stewart F. Lane, *Jews on Broadway: An Historical Survey of Performers, Playwrights, Composers, Lyricists and Producers* (Jefferson: McFarland, 2011), p. 180.

This page and over from Blazing Saddles (1974)

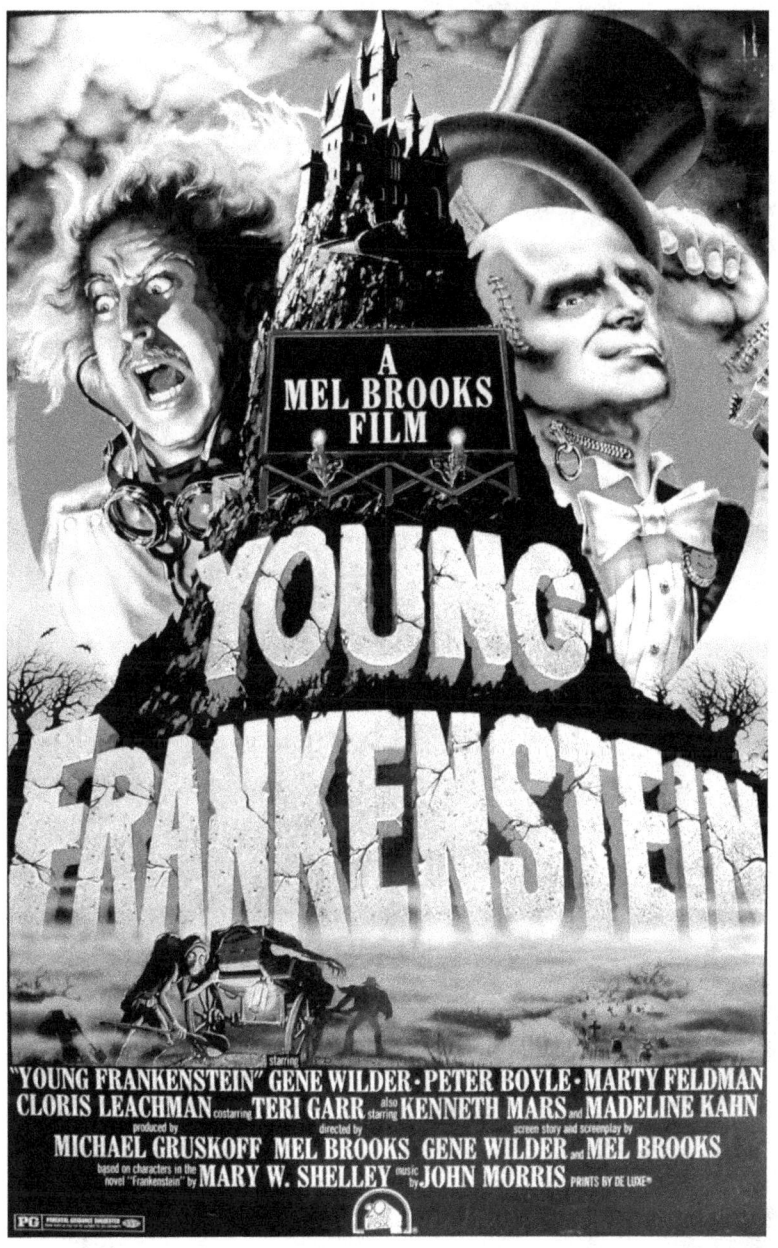

Young Frankenstein (1974),
this page and over.

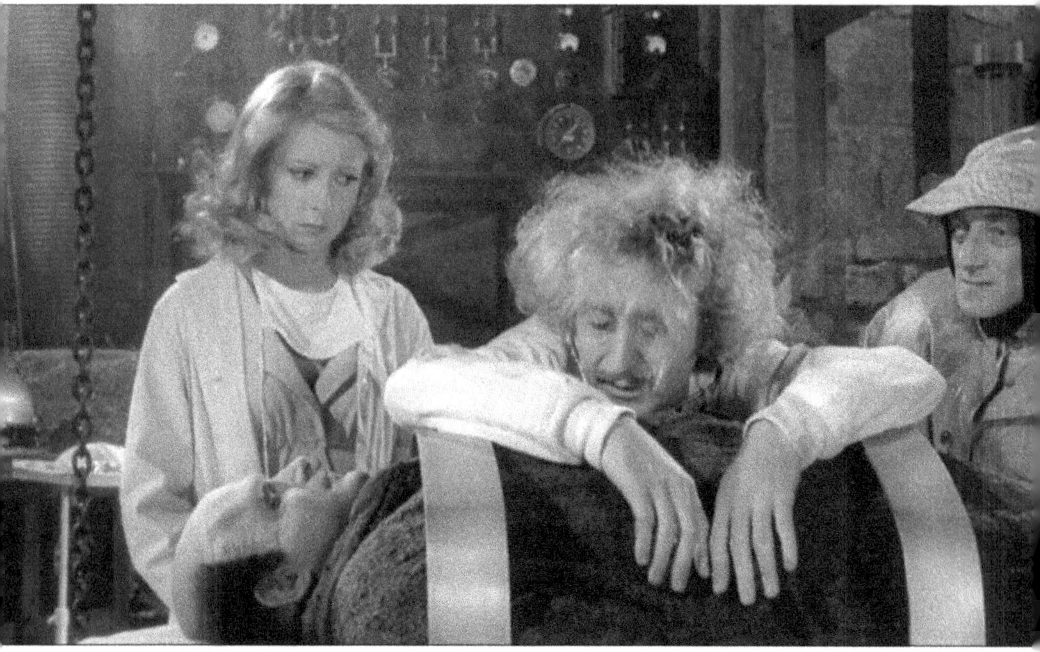

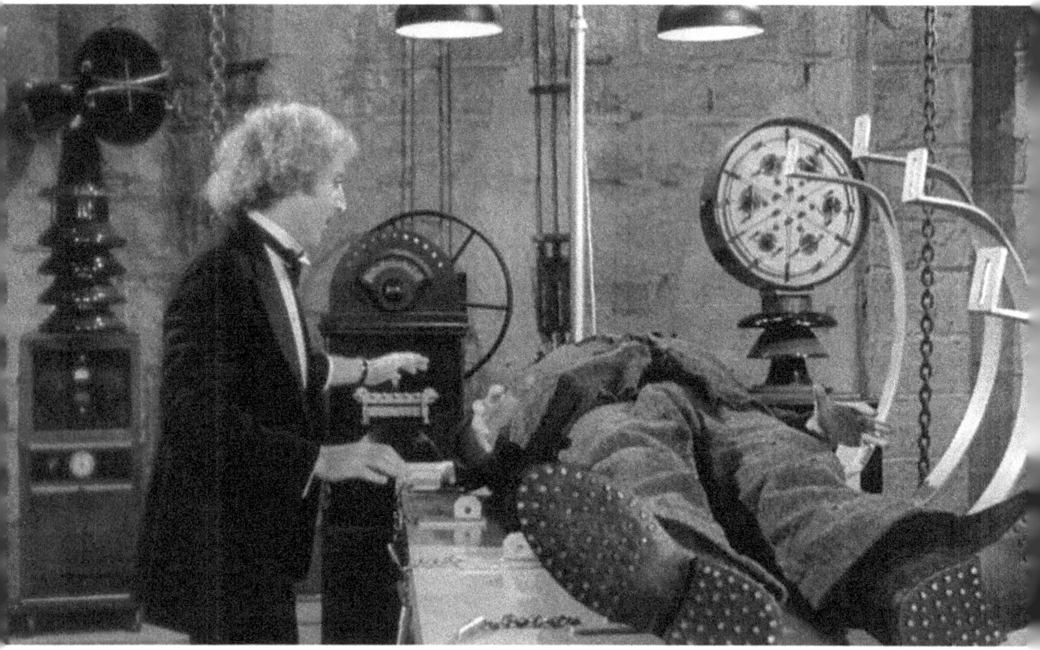

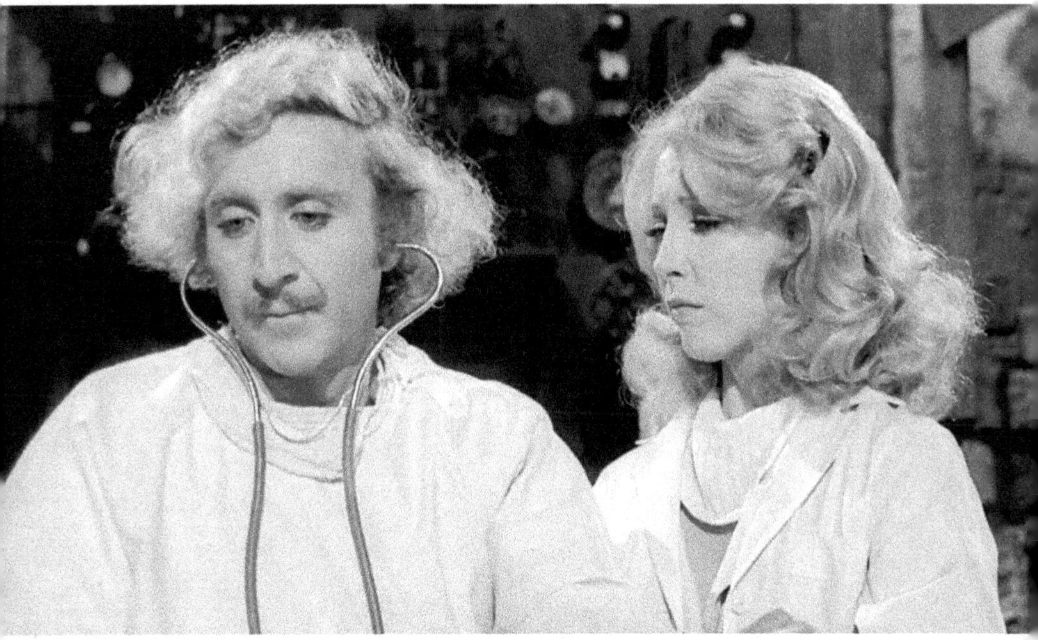

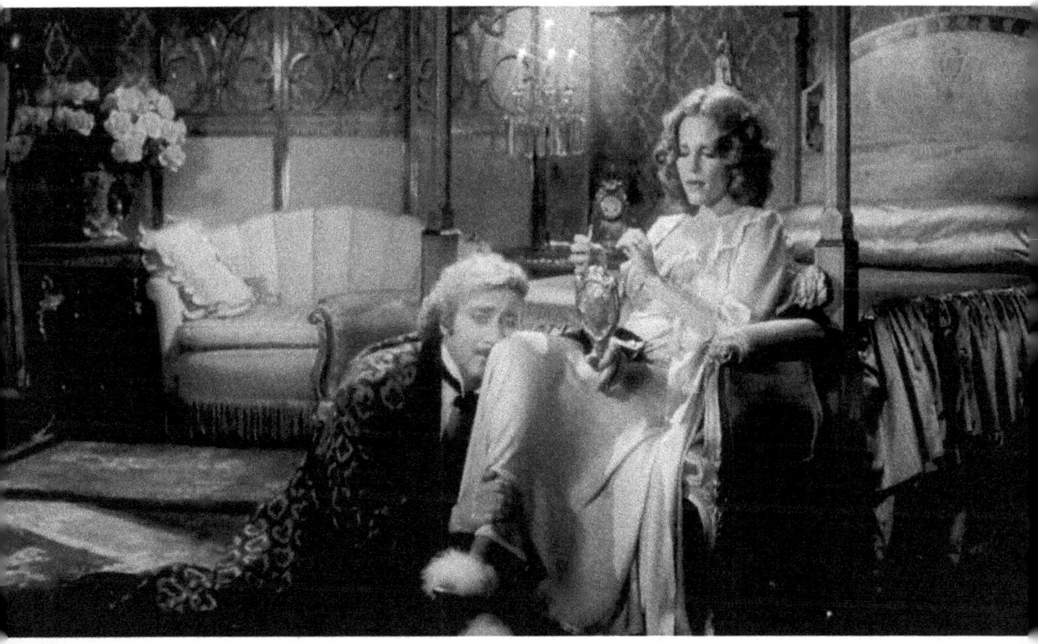

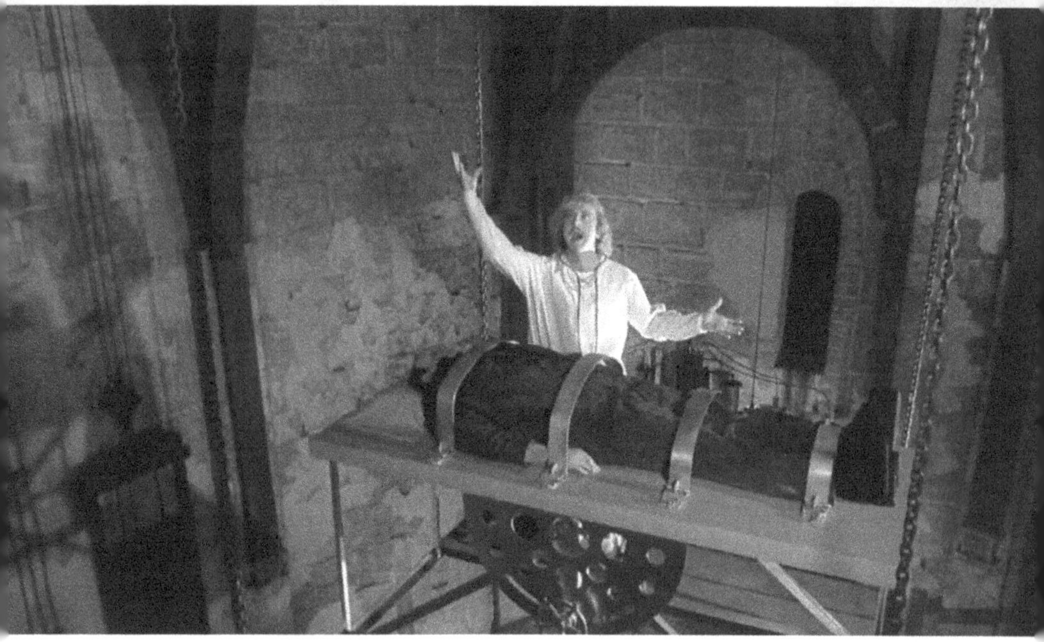

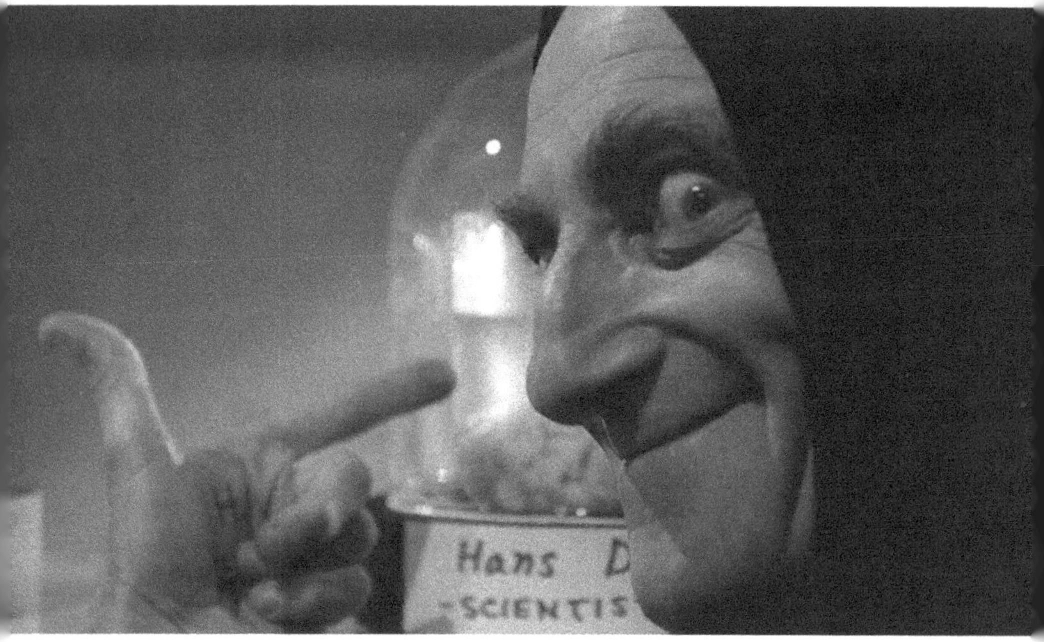
Hans D
-SCIENTIS

The Young Frankenstein musical

# 5

# SILENT MOVIE (1976)

BY THE MID-SEVENTIES, Mel Brooks had firmly proven that he had no reservations when it came to challenging audience expectations – indeed, more often than not he had shown it to be amongst the most prominent of his driving objectives when directing a film. With *Silent Movie*, however, he was to take a particularly profound creative risk. Following the twin successes of *Blazing Saddles* and *Young Frankenstein* in 1974, Brooks would make full use of his growing creative influence to bring about a highly unconventional development in his cinematic career: his first starring role as a film actor was to be in a silent movie.

While the notion of producing a film with no spoken dialogue may suggest the same kind of nostalgic reflex which was responsible for the passionate attention to historical production detail he had lavished upon *Young Frankenstein*, it was soon to transpire that *Silent Movie* would be a very different kind of feature altogether. For one, unlike its predecessor the film would be produced in full colour, and although the notion of a silent movie had been an antiquated one for several decades, the feature itself employs thoroughly modern fashions and sensibilities: in spite of using a convention more commonly associated with the very earliest days of cinema, *Silent Movie* could not be more firmly grounded in the mid-1970s. Likewise, while *Blazing Saddles* had at times moved beyond parodying the Western in order to poke fun at filmmaking in general – especially during its closing sequences – *Silent Movie* was to take this approach one step further by presenting a feature which more closely interrogated the production process. In this sense the movie is much more than simply a logical progression of the kind of silent-era cinema parodies which had featured throughout Brooks's early career in *Your Show of Shows*; although slapstick would feature extensively, the film also offered a wide-ranging satire of show-business by highlighting many factors that Brooks considered to be undermining or even threatening the industry at the time, as well as revelling in the various aspects of creative freedom offered and promoted by Hollywood which had enthused him right throughout his career. But as Brooks and his co-writers Ron Clark, Rudy DeLuca and Barry Levinson knew only too well, while the world of movies may often promise larger-than-life action and fairytale endings, the truth behind film production was often considerably less glamorous and regularly offered up challenges which were as intractable as anything presented in the fiction of film narratives. As Nathan Rabin has argued, *Silent Movie* clearly demonstrated a central contradiction that lay at the heart of much of Brooks's filmmaking; the paradox of presenting modern anxieties through an essentially timeless, even backward-looking comic framework, drawing upon the full range of expression that his craft has the ability to present:

> For much of his career, Mel Brooks has had the peculiar distinction of being simultaneously ahead of and behind the times. Brooks' singing Nazis and flatulent cowboys radically expanded the parameters of mainstream comedy. Yet when American films were addressing social turmoil like never before, Brooks used his clout to turn back the clock by combining silly sight gags, show-biz satire, silence, and celebrity cameos in 1976's aptly named, ingratiatingly goofy *Silent Movie*. Brooks' cheerfully crude oeuvre connects the dots between vaudeville and the gross-out gags of *American Pie*, between the brothers Marx and Farrelly. Brooks ranks as one of the preeminent architects of contemporary comedy, yet his heart remains stuck in Hollywood's Golden Age.[1]

Mel Funn (Mel Brooks), a once-legendary Hollywood director, is now a mere shadow of his former self. His career in tatters after a battle with alcoholism, he is given one last chance to rekindle the glory of his earlier cinematic triumphs when the Chief of Big Picture Studios (Sid Caesar) reluctantly agrees to fund Funn's revolutionary new scheme – a silent movie. This requires no small amount of persuasion, not least as the studio is deeply in the red and teeters on the brink of being bought over by multinational conglomerate Engulf and Devour. Funn only just manages to talk the Chief into making the production of his film possible; given that the silent movie has been a redundant format for decades, he can only convince the harried executive to back his plans by assuring him that it will feature the biggest stars in Hollywood. There's only one problem with his strategy: Funn has absolutely no idea how he's going to hire this kind of promised star power in order to make his movie a reality.

Working with his inseparable creative collaborators Marty Eggs (Marty Feldman) and Dom Bell (Dom DeLuise), Funn sets off to scour Los Angeles in search of top talent. Firstly, they attempt to contact Burt Reynolds (John Boorman's *Deliverance*, 1972; Richard C. Sarafian's *The Man Who Loved Cat Dancing*, 1973) by turning up unannounced at the front door of his opulent mansion. Funn's reputation precedes him, alas, and so the undaunted trio end up deciding to break into the residence instead. Accosting Reynolds while he is having a shower, Funn makes his casting pitch but only succeeds in alarming the megastar by his unexpected presence. Yet after some perseverance, and only after Reynolds narrowly escapes being flattened by a steamroller thanks to Funn's continued attempts at persuasion, the harassed actor finally agrees to sign up for a role in the movie.

Next, Funn decides to target James Caan (Francis Ford Coppola's *The Godfather*, 1972; Norman Jewison's *Rollerball*, 1975). Finding him training with a punchbag next to his film set trailer, the three collaborators discover Caan to be an affable character who seems receptive to the idea of Funn's movie. The star invites them to join him for lunch inside his trailer, but they soon discover that one of the springs has been damaged which makes the floor very unstable. Food is consumed very delicately by the visitors... until some spilt pepper causes Bell to sneeze, throwing the interior of the trailer into chaos. In spite of the bedlam which then unfolds, by some miracle Caan also decides to agree to appear in Funn's movie.

Meanwhile, in New York City, the board of Engulf and Devour is being chaired by the corporation's founders Engulf (Harold Gould) and Devour (Ron Carey). Meekly, the board members report that they have been unable to buy Big Picture

Studios as their purchase offer has been rebuffed. The chairman is particularly incensed when he learns of Funn's big-name signings for the silent movie, knowing that a blockbuster hit could revive the studio's fortunes and scupper his plans of a successful takeover bid. Aggrieved at Funn's sheer tenacity, it is decided that the entire board will fly to California in a bid to sabotage the director's casting attempts once and for all.

Back in L.A., word of Engulf and Devour's plans filter through to Funn and his colleagues via the Studio Chief. This only galvanises Funn into trying even harder to sign up major stars while he still can. At the studio commissary, the trio spots Liza Minnelli (Albert Finney's *Charlie Bubbles*, 1967; Bob Fosse's *Cabaret*, 1972) in costume during a break in a period historical production and decide to approach her about the movie. Quickly purloining three suits of medieval armour, they join Minnelli as she eats lunch – a task made almost impossible when they discover that sitting down while wearing chainmail and metal plating is not as easy as they had anticipated. After much effort, however, they eventually discover that the famous actress is not only aware of their movie (having read about it in *The Hollywood Reporter*), but that she actively wants to appear in it.

Word quickly spreads to Engulf and Devour's West Coast offices that Liza Minnelli has been signed for Funn's movie, and Anne Bancroft (Mike Nichols's *The Graduate*, 1967; Richard Attenborough's *Young Winston*, 1972) is to be next on their list of prospective talent. Enraged, both Engulf and Devour set off with the intention of thwarting Funn's latest recruitment plans. At the Rio Bomba Club, a chic L.A. nightclub, the three creative partners are impersonating Mariachi band The Flamencos (redubbed The 'New' Flamencos) in order to get close access to the famous actress when she visits the premises. Sure enough, the glamorous Bancroft soon arrives with a crowd of debonair male suitors in tow, and immediately sees right through Funn's ruse. Correctly suspecting that they want her to appear in their movie, she appears distinctly jaded by the prospect until Funn draws her into a romantic tango (later shared, improbably enough, with Eggs and Bell) from which she is fortunate to emerge with her life due to various near-injuries encountered along the way. Impressed by their resolve, Bancroft agrees to appear in the movie. Engulf and Devour arrive just as the trio are leaving the club's stage, livid that they have reached their destination too late to throw a spanner in the works.

Funn discovers that the pressure has finally proven too much for the Studio Chief, who has been admitted to the intensive care ward of an L.A. hospital ('I'm all right – apart from the constant pain'). Paying him a bedside visit, Funn tries to buoy the executive's spirits by telling him that he has had another plan; he intends to sign up Marcel Marceau, the most famous miming artist on the planet. The Chief insists that Funn telephones Marceau in Paris right there and then, but when he does so the mime brusquely refuses the offer. Keen not to dampen the Chief's optimism, Funn explains that he doesn't speak French and thus has no idea what Marceau's definitive 'Non!' actually meant.

From the window of the Chief's hospital room, Bell spots top actor Paul Newman (George Roy Hill's *The Sting*, 1973; Stuart Rosenberg's *Cool Hand Luke*, 1967) convalescing in a wheelchair, seated next to a wrecked racing car. Immediately resolving to add him to their cast list, Funn, Eggs and Bell sneak up on Newman in wheelchairs of their own, quickly leading to an implausibly high-octane chase in and out of the hospital where mayhem is promptly caused for anyone unfortunate enough to get in their way. Eventually making his escape in a death-defying leap from the building (still in his wheelchair), Newman salutes Funn's efforts and, now recognising the director, asks if he can feature in the silent movie too. Funn, unable to believe his luck, slyly tells Newman that he'll think about it and get back to him. Seconds later, a newspaper headline informs the audience that Newman, too, has been signed up.

At Engulf and Devour's West Coast boardroom, tempers are fraying as never before. Learning that Funn has now completed his starry cast and is planning to begin production, Engulf announces a new plan; he will employ legendary seductress Vilma Kaplan (Bernadette Peters) to entice Funn away from his directorial responsibilities and distract him from his duties, ultimately ensuring the silent movie's failure and the studio's eventual takeover. Sure enough, Funn is enjoying an evening with Bell and Eggs at the Rio Bomba Club when Kaplan appears onstage with a raunchy dance routine. The director is immediately smitten by the sultry performer ('I hope to God she's not a female impersonator!'), and thus is delighted when she suggests that they leave together after her act is over. Left behind, Bell and Eggs watch despondently as their friend races off into the night with his new acquaintance.

Funn and Kaplan enjoy a brief but intense romance which leads the director, after only a short period together with his new lover, to consider marriage. The pair appear genuinely besotted, until Eggs and Bell arrive at the nightclub following one of Kaplan's performances to confront Funn with the ugly truth – they have uncovered a company cheque signed by Engulf and Devour, made out in Kaplan's name to the tune of $50,000 'for pretending to be in love with Mel Funn'. Faced with such undeniable evidence, Funn is devastated and immediately hits the bottle. This causes no end of vexation for Bell and Eggs, partly because they are naturally concerned for their close friend's wellbeing but also due to the fact that the film is due to start shooting the next day.

Further complicating matters, Funn's colleagues overhear Kaplan on the phone to Engulf and Devour, resigning her services from their employ because she has discovered that she has now genuinely fallen in love with Funn. Bell explains to her that the director has descended back into alcoholism due to his broken heart, leading them all to race after the inebriated Funn in a last-ditch effort to resolve matters. Meanwhile, Funn is settling down for the night in a downmarket hotel, complete with a gargantuan bottle of booze. Following a rather extreme mishap with a pull-down bed, however, he takes to the streets once more, eventually winding up in a run-down alleyway where he is hailed as a kind of saint by a gang of homeless people when they catch sight of his awesomely outsized whisky bottle.

Eventually Kaplan, Eggs and Bell are able to track down their friend, but only after they discover that he has emptied the entire bottle (containing roughly his own body-weight in alcohol) and is thus in a state of catatonia. Returning him to the nightclub, they quickly provide Funn with dozens of cups of black coffee, sobering him up to the point where he is able to stride around unaided. Proudly proclaiming that 'If I can walk, I can direct!', he marches out of the building with total determination as he heads straight for the movie set.

Funn completes work on the film in record time, and a preview screening of the feature is hurriedly arranged. The

Studio Chief, now discharged from hospital, seems delighted by the public interest that the 'sneak' showing of the movie has attracted. His already-fragile nerves are once again tested, however, when it is discovered that the film reel has been stolen; Funn immediately suspects the involvement of the underhand Engulf and Devour. While the director and his companions race off to recover the film (of which, as luck would have it, there is only one copy), Kaplan stalls the audience with an enthusiastically-received dance performance.

Engulf and Devour are toasting their own ingenuity as the *Silent Movie* film reel is gleefully lowered onto their boardroom's roaring fireplace. Before their celebrations are fully underway, though, Eggs's hands can be seen reaching down from the chimney stack and plucking the reel away from incineration in the nick of time. Watching in horror, the board members race out of the building in pursuit of the already-departing Funn and friends. A frantic and protracted road chase ensues before Funn finally makes it back to the cinema; the film starts to screen at the very point that the audience are starting to leave. In spite of Eggs's very novel (if somewhat unintentional) method of re-winding the film, the audience response is rapturous. Amongst a carnival atmosphere, audience acrobatics and copious helium balloons bedecking the auditorium, Funn eventually exclaims – with much understatement – 'They seem to like it.' And thus the jubilant viewers parade out of the cinema, the jittery studio chief appears relieved at his organisation's apparent stay of execution, and Funn can at last make good on his proposal of marriage to Kaplan.

Two things are immediately apparent upon a viewing of *Silent Movie*: Mel Brooks's abiding love for the history and conventions of American studio-based movie-making, and the growing economic threat that he perceives to be challenging this creative tradition. Certainly he does not look back upon the film industry as exhibiting a kind of idealised past to which contemporary output must be judged unfavourably, but rather he suggests early cinema history to be a more innocent time that should be celebrated rather than cynically derided or even forgotten. The script demonstrates a keen awareness of the industry's shortcomings even before it deals with the threat of corporate encroachment. Big Picture Studios, which are ostensibly the heroes of the hour, are shown to be more concerned with the fiscal draw of big-name stars than with providing cinematic quality; their motto 'Ars Es Pecunia' translates to 'Art is Money', thus parodying both the words and the sentiment of Metro-Goldwyn-Mayer's famous 'Ars Gratia Artis' dictum. During a private screening of another film, the studio's top executive (described as the 'Current Studio Chief', thus emphasising the tenuous nature of his hold on the position) is shown to have no idea of how to critically gauge the standard of the films that are being produced on his watch – possibly a sly dig by Brooks towards his earlier experiences working on films such as *Blazing Saddles*, where his own creative vision was significantly at variance with the studio's top brass. While the plotline centres around Mel Funn's desperate attempts to shore up the studio by directing a smash hit, thus generating a huge revenue stream in order to confound the intended buyout, his efforts are driven at least as much by a need to restore his own tarnished reputation as they are by any sense of loyalty to the organisation itself. Nonetheless, because Brooks recognises the film industry as an arbiter of creative freedom – albeit an imperfect one – he clearly believes it to be worth defending from forces which are hostile to its artistic intent. With the film's many tips of the hat to bygone conventions of the silent era, there is clearly no disguising Brooks's genuine affection for Hollywood – even taking into account its various dysfunctions. Maurice Yacowar sagely observes that:

> Brooks claims the writing team pursued two objectives. One was nonverbal comedy that was also contemporary. 'We cannot go back to any old silent movie techniques; we must create our own with the given technology of the moment'. The second was to 'write a strong story and make a comment'. About what? Well, Brooks told one reviewer that the film deals with his strong feelings about multinationals and conglomerates 'moving into an art form and I hate them for it'.[2]

The ferocity of Brooks's assault on corporate greed mirrors the concerns he raised in *Blazing Saddles*, where Hedley Lamarr's intended land-grab exhibits many similarities to the planned hostile takeover of Big Picture Studios. Brooks makes clear the fact that the self-important executives' motives are stimulated entirely by profit, and laments the inability of conglomerates to either understand or identify with the culture of the creative arts industry that they are actively carving up for commercial gain – and with no concern for the cultural consequences. This examination of the corrupting influence of capital avarice would surface again in Brooks's work, not least in *Spaceballs* and *Life Stinks*, but rarely would he make his point quite so bluntly as in the depiction of the literally foaming-at-the-mouth chairman of Engulf and Devour, whose cartoonish demeanour is summed up by his enquiry to the boardroom 'Have we taken over Big Picture Studios yet, which I want more than anything else in my life?' (a proclamation which instantly configures his intentions as being more in the tradition of *The Wacky Races*'s cackling Dick Dastardly than that of *Wall Street*'s hard-nosed financier Gordon Gecko). The board members quite literally offer their collective worship to the almighty dollar, reciting a morning prayer to Mammon in order to emphasise their sheer material covetousness, whereas the comedy slapping routine doled out to the (essentially faceless and interchangeable) junior executives owes more than a little to the routines of *The Three Stooges*. Their opulent boardroom's lavatory pointedly bears the marble-etched slogan 'Our Toilets Are Nicer Than Most Peoples' Homes', while even their graffiti is determinedly upper-crust ('Yea for the rich!'). With a company maxim like 'Our Fingers Are In Everything', their materialistic function could not be made any starker by Brooks, and yet – as Roger Ebert notes – there is a clear contemporary edge to this satire of corporate dynamics beyond a traditional lampoonery of excessive greed: 'Big Pictures Studio ("If it's a big picture, we've made it") teeters on the edge of bankruptcy and a takeover from the giant Engulf and Devour conglomerate. [...] This is a situation that gives rise to a lot of inside jokes (I wonder whether executives at Gulf and Western, which took over Paramount, will notice any parallels), but the thing about Brooks's inside jokes is that their outsides are funny, too'.[3]

If the intended corporate takeover bid at the heart of *Silent Movie* exhibits similarity to the central premise of *Blazing Saddles*, so too is there familiarity in the Vilma Kaplan subplot which bears all the hallmarks of Hedley Lamarr's attempted (and foiled) manipulation of Sheriff Bart with the charms of Lili von Shtupp in the earlier film. Yet here, the blossoming relationship between Funn and Kaplan is employed not just to emphasise the power of true love to overcome misdirection fuelled by base financial influence, but also to highlight the central difference between the romantic ambitions of Funn (who seeks lasting happiness) and that of the would-be lothario Eggs, whose comic lechery offers up such eyebrow-raising chat-up lines as 'Would you mind dancing with a mild-mannered pervert?' Through the character of Eggs, Feldman evokes the same kind of off-kilter, edgy quality which made *Young Frankenstein*'s Igor both disconcerting and strangely likeable at the same time. Even the three collaborators' respective modes of dress are used to accentuate this contrast. Funn almost always wears a smart yachting outfit, suggestive of his previous fortunes as well as his expectations of future glory ('What's the matter with you? Don't you know who I used to be?' he irritably snaps at a security officer as his attempts to gain access to the studio are initially thwarted). His dapperness is juxtaposed with Eggs's puzzling aviation headgear and scarf (his jumpsuit later temporarily exchanged for a tuxedo-themed one-piece outfit) which – in line with its owner's eccentrically contradictory nature – is an ensemble which manages to be neither entirely formal nor informal, but always wholly incongruous. Rounding off the trio is Dom DeLuise's gluttonous Bell, a good-natured foodie who sometimes seems oblivious to the action taking place around him due to the distractive qualities of his primary concern – a ravenous appetite which is so often the source of the trio's mishaps. Startlingly outsized food is the foundation of several of the film's visual jokes, from the trash-can sized bucket of popcorn being served in the cinema (a commentary on the ever-increasing portions being demanded by consumers to accompany their movie-going) to Funn's comically exaggerated, gigantic bottle of booze – initially presented as an advertising prop, but later revealed to be the real deal – which symbolises his crashing descent back into alcoholism. (If this seems unsubtle, just consider by comparison the inevitable 'There's a fly in my soup!' gag, when a pest exterminator's massive promotional model accidentally falls into a nearby diner's meal.) Yet Bell is all too often the cause – as well as being on the receiving end – of the film's food-related gags, whether accidentally showering a traffic cop with blueberry pie to capsizing James Caan's damaged set trailer thanks to plucking too many lunchtime melon balls from a plate. (Admittedly his scene with the defective Coca-Cola vending machine does overstay its welcome somewhat, but later proves to be unexpectedly significant during the film's climactic chase sequence.) However, for all his perpetual hunger Bell is a pleasant and good-humoured companion, the perfect balance between the determined Funn and oddball Eggs, as is articulated through his own attire: a hat and coat which is possibly the closest that any of the three ever comes to normal everyday dress. Collectively they make a confusing but strangely compelling trio, whose presence would not have seemed entirely out of place in the early era of cinema that they are seeking to emulate. Henry Jenkins makes the point that:

> Of all of Brooks' films, *Silent Movie* may be the most clearly focused around a central team of disruptive comedians (Brooks, Feldman, DeLuise). When they court various Hollywood stars in the hopes of convincing them to appear in their movie, the stars may initially be read as figures of order against which we read their clownish disorder but the stars end up very much part of the physical comedy and very much enjoying the pleasures of comic performance. [...] The stars cannot resist trying their hands at slapstick comedy, and this is how they get suckered into joining the troubled film production. The decentring of the comic performers into a comic universe might link Brooks' films back to that vulgar modernist classic, *Hellzapoppin'* (1941), where any and every performer has the ability to freeze the frame, reverse the motion, or otherwise manipulate filmic convention.[4]

The mismatched friends somehow manage to remain unified in their central creative purpose despite their dissimilarity (as the perfectly-synchronised spring in their step suggests), not least in their continuing efforts to persuade distinguished acting talent to sign up for the film's production. Here, of course, Brooks has enormous fun showing the ways that art imitates life; the film closes by assuring the audience that 'This was a true story', and indeed the way that Funn must track down big name stars to make his film credible directly mirrors Brooks's own efforts in employing major star power to get *Silent Movie* off the ground in a fiercely competitive market. It helps, of course, that the stars in question are so obviously revelling in the movie's brazen mayhem. Whether watching the antics of Burt Reynolds, clearly enjoying the chance to portray a larger-than-life caricature of himself in the form of a flamboyant egomaniac, or James Caan accidentally walloping everyone while wearing boxing gloves, there is clearly a lot of merriment to be had here for star-spotters keen to see movie icons acting out of character. The always-classy Anne Bancroft causes the Rio Bomba Club's ageing maitre'd (Fritz Feld) to fall prostrate before her in awe of her very presence... and then break into push-ups in an attempt (though hopeless) to demonstrate physical prowess. Bancroft eventually tips him with her own jewellery, largely just to get rid of him – and perhaps because, being a gentleman of a certain age, he creaks noisily while bouncing on the spot in anticipation of this gratuity. (Bancroft's ennui in the presence of her smarmy suitors is very deliberately juxtaposed with the amusement she has with Funn and his partners in crime – the way that she apes the crazy movement of Feldman's crossed eyes is particularly well-judged.) Then there is the premeditated irony of Liza Minnelli, world-renowned for her singing and dancing skills, not being given the opportunity to showcase either of these famous talents at any point during her appearance. Taken collectively, as Yacowar has noted, Brooks makes the point that in art as in life, everything is rarely as it seems to the untrained eye: 'Through lover Reynolds, fighter Caan, gamin Minelli, and vamp Bancroft, Brooks surveys Hollywood's basic star types and their remoteness from the actors' real natures. [...] Marceau is the only star who refuses to participate in Funn's project; of course, he makes his appearance in the act of refusing to appear'.[5]

It seems almost superfluous to note that with legendary mime Marcel Marceau famously providing the film's one word of spoken dialogue when he had become globally celebrated for his silent performances, the audience may naturally find the presence of any audible statement emanating from him to be jarring. But the utterance of a single spoken word – especially when it takes place midway through the movie – also heightens awareness of Brooks's craft in having delivered all of the dialogue through visual rather than audible means up to this point (and then beyond), laying additionally emphasis on the achievement. For a film which features no spoken dialogue beyond Marceau's, Brooks exhibits great playfulness with regard to dialogic convention. Much of this centres around the use of onscreen dialogue captions ('intertitles') as a substitute for the spoken word in very inventive ways. When Eggs tries out his best chat-up lines on the voluptuous nurse at the maternity unit, only the obvious failure of his hopeless efforts at romance reflect the quality of his unheard dialogue; with no intertitle, the fine detail is left to the audience's imagination. Funn stares disparaging at his colleague, very perceptibly mouthing 'You dirty son of a bitch!' at him, only for the intertitle to articulate his actual dialogue as 'You bad boy'. There is no end to Brooks's inventiveness with this principle; Burt Reynolds speaks a silent but emphatic 'No way!' when asked to appear in the film, only for the intertitle to assert 'I'll do it' – the total contradiction between what we see him saying and what we are told he has said suggests that the director is intent on driving his way forward to the endgame irrespective of whatever the on-screen action may imply. In another impressively offbeat conceit, when Marcel Marceau's telephone rings in his Parisian apartment we are informed that is accompanied by the sound of 'sonnez sonnez' – roughly translated as the French expression for 'ring ring', as though somehow this incidental noise would sound different if heard in another country where English is not the predominant language.

Because Brooks himself appears in the film's starring role, his uncharacteristic silence seems all the more conspicuous when he had become so well-known to the public for his rapid-fire one-liners. As Vincent Canby explained, the incongruity makes for an unusual viewing experience when considering likely audience expectation: 'Mel Funn is polite, sweet and vulnerable, qualities one associates with some of the old silent film comedians and that fit Mr Brooks less well than a nun's habit. The lack of spoken dialogue doesn't disable the character. It's the concept. When you have a Mel Brooks who doesn't allow himself to be rude, testy and master of the low leer, you don't have a funny man. You have an affable floorwalker. He's a surprise and sort of pleasant but not what you were expecting. By being thus prepared, you should be able to appreciate the good things that Mr Brooks has brought off'.[6] Indeed, many of *Silent Movie*'s incidents appear to be an attempt by Brooks to subvert every cliché of early cinema, albeit within the confines of an undeniably modern milieu. Perhaps to underscore his point, the film begins in total silence, the opening sequence with Carol Arthur's cameo as a pregnant bystander being given a lift in Funn's sporty yellow roadster (which looks like it could have been lifted straight out of any number of silent era classics) taking place in its entirety before a single note of John Morris's score is played. In so doing, Brooks toys with preconceived anticipation, knowing that audiences would be aware of the film's novelty qualities but similarly would not be entirely sure how he would seek to employ them in stylistic terms. As Jenkins has stated:

> The opening of *Silent Movie* [...] plays upon audience expectations about the nature of silent film, continuing for several minutes in total silence, before adding music and sound effects. In another early sequence, a secretary tries to tell the studio chief that Funn has a drinking problem by pantomiming an uplifted bottle, but her boss remains confused, wondering if she's trying to say that he sucks his thumb, a joke that rests on the difference between the guessing games we play at charades and the expressive gestures of silent cinema.[7]

Brooks makes thorough use of the silent movie's propensity for visual humour, and his intentions are made crystal clear at the beginning of the film when Sid Caesar's Studio Chief stridently proclaims 'Don't you know that slapstick is DEAD?'... mere seconds before his chair collapses, tears through his desk, and ends up propelling him across his office in true Buster Keaton style. As had been the case in the early days of cinema, slapstick remains a highly subjective art-form, and some of the film's attempts to engage with it are more successful than others. A few of the jokes, such as the hospital's geriatric lounge and the scene featuring the patient emerging from an acupuncturist's clinic (Arnold Soboloff), are purposely obvious and groan-inducing. Others are more obviously calculated to accentuate the film's outlandish strain of non-realism. For instance, Bell, his foot slammed in the door of Burt Reynolds's mansion when he attempts to gain admission, finds his shoe to be painfully squashed in the manner of a Warner Brothers cartoon character. This kind of overstated visual humour is further underlined by the steamroller gag, the self-dividing driving school car in the final chase, and – in one of the film's best visual conceits – Funn's visibly beating heart actually transpiring to be a live frog he inexplicably discovers in one of the pockets in his suit jacket. The larger set-pieces likewise vary dramatically in quality; the impossibly high-speed wheelchair race around the hospital with Paul Newman (conveniently dressed in full Formula One gear) is in the best tradition of *The Keystone Kops*, riffing on the actor's well-publicised interest in the sport, while the commissary scene with Liza Minnelli – where Funn, Eggs and Bell seem to spend an eternity trying to sit down while wearing medieval suits of armour, causing chaos as they do so – eventually becomes laboured in the extreme.

Some of the film's best visual humour lies in its more subtle moments. Sid Caesar's Studio Chief, his nerves constantly on edge, is driven to smoking two cigars at once, while his secretary (Yvonne Wilder) vigilantly stands guard over the office's mini-bar as soon as Funn arrives – just as a precautionary measure. There is much enjoyment to be found in Funn and Kaplan's hilariously exaggerated romantic interlude, including an unforgettable moment on a merry-go-round where the behaviour of the model horses proves somewhat closer to real life than is the case with most fairground attractions. And, perhaps most unavoidably of all, Funn exclaims 'I've got a great idea!' just as a lightbulb (belonging to a conveniently-placed electric lamp-stand) illuminates right on cue above his head. However, although the film is devoid of spoken dialogue, it does contain a wide variety of sound effects – often chosen precisely for their inaptness – which are cleverly synchronised with the film's action to striking effect. The perfectly harmonised 'plinking' sound of Funn's attempts to cross his fingers for luck is soon transferred to the Studio Chief and later his secretary – a joke which would have fallen flat without the accompanying sound. Eggs comically pings around a hospital corridor from elevator to elevator, complemented by the sound of a pinball table. Likewise, when the Big Picture Studios logo appears, it displays an emblem similar to MGM's roaring lion... but with the legendary king of the jungle replaced by Sid Caesar as the Studio Chief who brays like a donkey instead, thus emphasising the character's comparative ineffectiveness (and, by extension, that of his studio).

If sound plays an important part in the presentation of the action, John Morris's highly inventive score proves to be an equally vital part of the film's success – all the more remarkable when Brooks's initial creative intent had been for the movie to feature no musical soundtrack at all. Morris's extensive compositional talents had already provided everything from the bombastic Broadway-esque themes of *The Producers* to the remarkably authentic vintage horror score of *Young Frankenstein*, but *Silent Movie* was to present him with a new and quite dissimilar challenge – and one that he rose to with characteristic enthusiasm. Given the film's obvious lack of audible speech, music becomes crucial to illustrating the action, and Morris never misses a beat (quite literally) whether providing the archetypal 'tipsy' music for Funn's drunken wanderings or the electronic theme (predating much early eighties synthesizer music) which accompanies the heart monitor in the Studio Chief's hospital room – eventually used by Bell and Eggs to play 'Pong', the classic bats-and-ball game so famous in the early years of video arcades. While for many the frenetic accompaniment to the Paul Newman wheelchair race may provide the closest evocation of the hyperactivity of early comedy cinema, one of the best jokes in the film occurs – as Yacowar has observed[8] – when the familiar sight of New York's iconic skyscrapers is initially accompanied by Bronislaw Kaper and Walter Jurmann's 'Theme from *San Francisco*' ('San Francisco, Open Your Golden Gate')... only to be hastily replaced by the more appropriate 'Manhattan' by Richard Rodgers ('I'll Take Manhattan') when the orchestra members realise their mistake.

Brooks's equation of the film industry's potential for creative freedom and the individual liberation of *Silent Movie*'s central characters is an important one, as it again underscores his intent to depict artistically motivated people as demonstrating a willingness and a potential to avoid the deadening effects of mainstream society, including its conventions and its restraints. Funn and the Studio Chief aim, through the box-office revenue to be generated by their movie's performance, to pull the organisation out of the clutches of corporate ownership and thus ensure greater creative autonomy for all, but Kaplan manages to accomplish a personal liberation which achieves the same goal: unwilling to act as an instrument of the conglomerate, thus tacitly endorsing its underhanded tactics, she ultimately elects to choose individual self-determination over commercial imbursement. Therefore Brooks endorses the benefits of one collective (well-meaning individuals willingly working together towards a positive goal) over another (the corporation, seeking its own self-interested ends at all costs).

Crick explains that in presenting a silent movie so long after this type of cinema had become obsolete, Brooks actually succeeded in appearing not only nostalgic but also innovative –

especially given that so many members of his audience would have had no first-hand awareness of the classic sound-free comedy film beyond the occasional repeat showing on late-night television.[9] And certainly, there is no lack of dexterity in Brooks's central conceit of making a film about the production of a silent movie which directly echoed his own challenges in getting the project in motion. Brooks has described his interaction with Twentieth Century-Fox at the time as being considerably more cordial than that of Mel Funn and Big Picture Studios, however:

> When I said '*Silent Movie*,' in 1976, they said, 'Sounds interesting'. I knew in their hearts they were saying, 'Oh, God! How can we say no without hurting his feelings, without losing him?' I explained later that there might be some great movie stars in it. [...] Fox was more amenable to the idea of *Silent Movie* when I told them there would be stars in it. 'No dialogue in 1976? That's a toughie.' They were very brave to make that picture. I wasn't frightened at all until the first dailies. I said, 'What the hell are we doing? I can't hear anybody! This is crazy. You've done it, Brooks, this is it. Sanity has finally caught up with you.' But it all worked out, and the picture was a huge success.[10]

The actual commercial achievement of the film was not quite as extensive as Brook's comment may initially suggest, however – at least in terms of its domestic gross. Although *Silent Movie* more than made its money back, it did not generate nearly the same impact at the box-office as Brooks's breakthrough successes of two years previously. As James Robert Parish has noted, '*Silent Movie* was made for about $4.5 million (with another $5 million devoted to release promotion) and generated $21.24 million in domestic theater rentals. While the picture was certainly profitable, it was not in the same league as *Young Frankenstein* (which owed so much to Gene Wilder's input) and thus not the anticipated financial bonanza Twentieth Century-Fox had counted on so heavily to rescue the studio during a particularly bad fiscal quarter'.[11]

Did Brooks's sheer originality in presenting a film without dialogue prove to be a step too far for audiences who had become so accustomed to his fast wit and readiness with brisk verbal put-downs? Certainly it is possible that *Silent Movie*'s stylistic ingenuity, while undoubtedly fascinating many due to its novelty value, was to alienate others who had felt that Brooks had finally taken his desire to topple established expectations of the format to a length that was too extreme. Paul Buhle asserts that the film was 'a true experiment with only music and sound effects to punctuate the action. It came fifty years too late to work either dramatically or commercially, but it was still a remarkable effort'.[12] And irrefutably, this acknowledgement of Brooks's unrestrained creativity (and audacity) can be found elsewhere, but crucially the target of his acid wit throughout the film has also not been forgotten. David A. Cook, for instance, observes that *Silent Movie* 'was less a parody than an attempt to resurrect silent slapstick comedy, although it also works as a satire on the Byzantine business practices of contemporary Hollywood (the plot revolves around the attempted takeover of a studio by a conglomerate named Engulf & Devour – clearly Gulf & Western)'.[13] Although the film has become best remembered for Brooks's determination to engage with the cinematic configurations (if not necessarily the filmic techniques) of comedy's yesteryear in a manner which was as challenging as it was unwaveringly modern, it is noteworthy that the resentment of his attack on the perceived moral bankruptcy of big business seemed so heartfelt that its antagonistic bite would rarely feel quite so serrated when he engaged with similar themes in later films. Crick has explored in detail Brooks's incisive satire on the dynamics of major Hollywood studios – the idiosyncratic behaviour of executives and their lackeys, the restriction of creative freedom by commercial concerns, and of course the instability caused by studios becoming subordinates of larger, multinational business corporations[14] – and although the exaggeratedly villainous Engulf and Devour are the very epitome of boardroom excess, their caricatural nature fits perfectly into the film's deliberately overstated environment and wild scenarios. Just as Funn and his companions typified the freewheeling heroes of the Laurel and Hardy era, so too did the disdainful corporate adversaries and their loftily contemptuous intent reflect the 'black hat' villainy of morality plays past. Thus, as critic John Simon observed, Brooks was not only aiming to make a satirical point in a way which confounded hidebound conventional opinion, but he was also seeking to celebrate the wellspring from which contemporary cinematic comedy had owed its genesis:

The rationale might be that silent comedy is believed by many to have been America's greatest contribution to the art of film, and that to emulate it even at this late date might prove beneficial – if only as a stimulant to that sense of visual comedy allegedly in abeyance since the heyday of Chaplin, Keaton, Lloyd, and the rest. Inspired slapstick, the argument might run, has no need of words, except perhaps for the occasional intertitle; and the nostalgia for 'comedy's greatest era', as James Agee dubbed it, might provide a source of emotions ready to be tapped. Against this, it can be claimed that nostalgia is one of the flimsier human sentiments, rather like crying over spilt milk; that Mel Brooks's comic gift, such as it is, is largely verbal and stands to lose too much in a silent movie; and that what was once done so well was done out of necessity, the need to overcome the limitations of a mute medium. Remove the necessity, which is the mother of invention, and you come up with test-tube babies of scant viability.[15]

Simon was certainly not alone in his scepticism regarding the efficacy of Brooks's artistic endeavours; perhaps even more so than his previous films, *Silent Movie* caused entrenched division amongst reviewers of the time. At one end of the scale, *Texas Monthly*'s Marie Brenner's response was withering: '"Laughter will be the sound track," Mel Brooks thought as he began work on *Silent Movie*, the film he hoped would be the family entertainment of the year. He didn't keep his promise. The sound track is filled with editorial comment in the form of music and effects, and laughter, unhappily, is the smallest of them'.[16] Counterbalancing this chilly reception was Roger Ebert's wholehearted praise for the film in *The Chicago Sun-Times*, who noted that '*Silent Movie* is not only funny, it's fun. It's clear at almost every moment that the filmmakers had a ball making it. [...] Everything's done amid an encyclopedia of sight gags, old and new, borrowed and with a fly in their soup. There are gags that don't work and stretches of up to a minute, I suppose, when we don't laugh – but even then we're smiling because of Brooks's manic desire to entertain'.[17] Perhaps more surprisingly, even Vincent Canby – who had proven to be far from Brooks's greatest critical proponent in years past – offered qualified approval of *Silent Movie* in the pages of *The New York Times*: 'You might suspect that Mel Brooks's decision to make a contemporary silent movie titled "*Silent Movie*," starring himself as a director trying to make a silent movie today, was not the wisest thing he'd ever done, and you'd be right. But having recognized that fact immediately, you can relax and enjoy *Silent Movie* as a virtually uninterrupted series of smiles'.[18]

*Silent Movie* was nominated for four Golden Globe Awards in 1977, including Best Motion Picture: Musical/ Comedy, and was also listed in the National Board of Review's Top Ten Films as well as seeing its screenplay nominated for a Writers' Guild of America Award. In spite of this industry recognition, the film has since become one of the less immediately recognisable of Brooks's canon, though it continues to remain popular amongst his loyal fan-base thanks to its release on home entertainment formats. In a more recent review of the film, commentator Ryan Keefer makes the point that '*Silent Movie* has the novelty of being a modern silent film going for it, but the thing that makes this film work is the story that it tells',[19] and in a film so packed with enjoyable performances and wry visual observations as this one it is hard to disagree. Sid Caesar, who had famously worked with Brooks during their time together on *Your Show of Shows*, provides a scene-stealing turn as the tense but domineering Studio Chief, a character who wielded his power with high-handed gusto while remaining painfully aware that his own position was far from secure. (Because his hopes of reviving his studio's fortunes lie entirely on the success of the silent movie, we see the Chief descending into ever greater anxiety – and eventually becoming hospitalised – due to his shattered nerves, his doubtfulness surrounding Funn's abilities giving Caesar a golden opportunity to use his legendary expressiveness to full effect in a film where such physical perspicuity was so vitally important.) Other notable performances include Carol Arthur, real-life spouse of Dom DeLuise, as the heavily pregnant bystander given a lift to the maternity hospital in Funn's car during the film's opening sequence (thus comically upending the car as they drive), and Liam Dunn – *Young Frankenstein*'s hapless medical guinea pig Mr Hilltop – appearing as an equally mishap-prone news vendor ('Newspaper vendor struck down by bundle of papers again', reads the headline on a pile of periodicals as it lands painfully on top of him). There is also much pleasure to be found in watching Brooks's manic tango with his wife Anne Bancroft, to say nothing of Marty Feldman's line in improbably acrobatic somersaulting and – of course – welcome cameo appearances by heroes of early American cinematic comedy such as Fritz Feld and Harry Ritz (of the Ritz Brothers). And this is merely scratching the surface in a film where Brooks throws in everything up to and including the kitchen sink, such is his determination to raise a smile.

The real *Silent Movie* may not have been the monumental blockbuster success that Funn's film-within-a-film turned out to be, but its release continued to cement Brooks into the framework of seventies popular culture as a pioneering and increasingly fearless creative force in comedy cinema. (As we can see from the careful placement of several film posters on its exterior, *Young Frankenstein* is still showing at the same cinema where the preview screening of Funn's movie is taking place, drawing attention to the then-recent feature's continued popularity in the public eye and suggesting that Brooks had every intention of building upon its success.) Jenkins correctly states that '*Silent Movie* is neither Brooks' best comedy nor his most popular, but it is the film where his awareness of his medium is most pronounced. In short, Brooks is not only a clown who works across media, but also someone who clowns with the properties of media'.[20] This characteristic had been suggested as early as *Blazing Saddles*, but his dexterity with bending and breaking filmic conventions would of course be revisited in several of his later features. Yet however successful Brooks had been in breathing new life into the silent movie format, his distinctive project stands apart from the other entries in his filmography not just because of its soundless nature, but also because of its desire to recreate the past within the present using modern techniques and sensibilities – a motivation quite different from that shown in the loving evocation of Universal's horror classics in *Young Frankenstein*, where film history was meticulously re-enacted for comic effect without an intention to truly revive or modernise it. Yacowar has thoughtfully explained: 'If we take the public satire and the personal nostalgia together, Brooks's two given motives make sense of the entire film. *Silent Movie* is a meditation on the remoteness of the past, the impossibility of returning to an antiquated rhetoric, art form, or state of innocence. Both personally and culturally, the film details the desire and the impossibility of retrieving a lost innocence and simplicity'.[21] This may go some way to explaining why the film's nostalgic objective exhibits a tinge of the melancholic even in spite of its end-to-end pandemonium and general sense of unruliness; not only does Brooks mourn the fact that the relative minimalism and essential guilelessness of the silent movie era has gone forever, but he also laments the upheaval taking place in the modern cinema industry which was actively subordinating creative risk to calculated commercial concerns. The emergence of an industry which was even more aggressively driven by financial viability, he made clear in an interview a few years after *Silent Movie*'s release, was a development in direct contradiction to his own free-thinking artistic intentions; when asked if he sought to follow in the creative tradition of Charlie Chaplin, Brooks replied that 'I don't want to create anything. I don't think in terms of results at all. I think: what next insanity can I shock the world with? What can I say to, for, my fellow citizens of the world? How crazy shall I be? And whether they're failures like *The Producers*, or successes like *Blazing Saddles*, it's not important'.[22] And this, perhaps more than any other statement, summed up both his hard-earned reputation for creative fearlessness and his determination not to be limited by either mainstream attitudes regarding genre, or a system which was to increasingly value the accountant's ledger over the artistic impulse. Mel Brooks may have been swimming against the tide, but in so doing he at least made no secret of cherishing the freedom involved in choosing his own direction.

# REFERENCES

1. Nathan Rabin, '*The Mel Brooks Collection*', in *The Onion AV Club*, 11 April 2006. <http://www.avclub.com/review/the-mel-brooks-collection-9121>
2. Maurice Yacowar, *The Comic Art of Mel Brooks* (London: W.H. Allen, 1982), p. 168.
3. Roger Ebert, '*Silent Movie*', in *The Chicago Sun-Times*, 30 June 1976. <http://www.rogerebert.com/reviews/silent-movie-1976>
4. Henry Jenkins, 'Mel Brooks, Vulgar Modernism, and Comic Remediation', in *A Companion to Film Comedy*, ed. by Andrew Horton and Joanna E. Rapf (Chichester: John Wiley and Sons, 2013), 151-74, p. 157.
5. Yacowar, p. 172.
6. Vincent Canby, '*Silent Movie* with Golden Subtitles', in *The New York Times*, 1 July 1976. <http://www.nytimes.com/movie/review?res=9E0CE6DA143FE334BC4953DFB166838D669EDE>
7. Jenkins, p. 166.
8. Yacowar, p. 169.
9. Robert Alan Crick, *The Big Screen Comedies of Mel Brooks* (Jefferson: McFarland and Company, 2009) [2002], p. 89.
10. Mel Brooks, 'My Movies: The Collusion of Art and Money', in *The Movie Business Book*, 3rd edn, ed. by Jason E. Squire (Maidenhead: Open University Press, 2006), 39-48, p. 45.
11. James Robert Parish, *It's Good to Be the King: The Seriously Funny Life of Mel Brooks* (Hoboken: John Wiley and Sons, 2007), p. 216.
12. Paul Buhle, *From the Lower East Side to Hollywood: Jews in American Popular Culture* (London: Verso, 2004), p. 233.
13. David A. Cook, *Lost Illusions: American Cinema in the Shadow of Watergate and Vietnam, 1970-1979* (Berkeley: University of California Press, 2002), p. 127.
14. Crick, p. 90.
15. John Simon, 'Movies: Unbabbling Brooks', in *New York Magazine*, 19 July 1976, 84-88, p. 84.
16. Marie Brenner, 'Film: Easy Outing', in *Texas Monthly*, September 1976, 60-64, p. 62.
17. Roger Ebert, '*Silent Movie*', in *The Chicago Sun-Times*, 30 June 1976. <http://www.rogerebert.com/reviews/silent-movie-1976>
18. Vincent Canby, '*Silent Movie* with Golden Subtitles', in *The New York Times*, 1 July 1976. <http://www.nytimes.com/movie/review?res=9E0CE6DA143FE334BC4953DFB166838D669EDE>
19. Ryan Keefer, '*The Mel Brooks Collection*', in *DVD Verdict*, 1 May 2006. <http://www.dvdverdict.com/reviews/melbrookscoll.php>
20. Jenkins, p. 152.
21. Yacowar, p. 168.
22. Mel Brooks, in Philip Fleishman, 'Interview with Mel Brooks', in *Maclean's Magazine*, 17 April 1978. <http://www.brookslyn.com/print/Maclean04-17-78/Maclean04-17-78.php>

# 6

# HIGH ANXIETY (1977)

OF ALL MEL BROOKS'S FILMS of the 1970s, *High Anxiety* is perhaps the most acutely concerned with the concept and nature of individual freedom. A clear break from the heartfelt observance of creative liberation which was celebrated throughout *Silent Movie*, or even the clamorous social criticism of *Blazing Saddles*, Brooks was to use *High Anxiety* to explore different aspects of what can emancipate us, to ask what it is to actually be free, and indeed to enquire whether any of us truly have full autonomy to forge and shape our individual identities. Whereas his previous spoofs had been intended to focus upon a particular cinematic genre – the Western, the classic horror film, or the silent movie – *High Anxiety* took a slightly different approach by concentrating (in the main) on the work of one particular director. And, in true Brooksian fashion, he was to set his sights sky-high by choosing as his subject one of the greatest and most heavily discussed film-makers ever to set foot on a film set.

As the movie's trailer made clear, *High Anxiety* was explicitly intended to be 'A Tribute to Alfred Hitchcock' – a fact which Brooks emphasises still further with a prominent opening dedication to the legendary 'Master of Suspense' in the film itself. An unabashed admirer of Hitchcock's (1899-1980) work, Brooks was all too aware of the celebrated director's towering reputation within the industry, and thus was very conscious of the high expectations which would accompany a spoof of his work. The film is replete with many allusions to the entire gamut of

Hitchcock's canon, some very obvious but many of them highly subtle. The choice of Hitchcock's films as *High Anxiety*'s subject meant that the movie was unusually focused for a Brooks spoof, its tight script never allowing it to become an all-out parody of the psychological thriller genre due to a determination by Brooks and his co-screenwriters Ron Clark, Rudy DeLuca and Barry Levinson (returning from their collaboration on *Silent Movie*, and indeed all making cameo appearances throughout the movie) to provide both a parody of – and homage to – Hitchcock's renowned filmography. In addition to providing Brooks with his first speaking lead role on the big screen, *High Anxiety* was also to prominently feature a variety of key Hitchcockian themes including the act of murder, the dynamics of human psychology, and the audience acting as voyeur.

Eminent Harvard University professor of psychiatry Dr Richard H. Thorndyke (Mel Brooks) has just been appointed the new director of California's prestigious Psycho-Neurotic Institute for the Very, <u>Very</u> Nervous. Following a nerve-shredding arrival at Los Angeles International Airport, during which he finds himself in situations of imagined peril as well as being accosted by a sex pest posing as an undercover policeman (Robert Manuel), Thorndyke meets his new 'driver and sidekick' Brophy (Ron Carey), a keen amateur photographer, who drives him to his new place of work. As they travel, Brophy regales his new boss with an hilariously expositional account of recent events at the Institute. He tells Thorndyke that his predecessor Dr Ashley had died under suspicious circumstances – a heart attack was the claimed cause of his demise, but Brophy doesn't believe a word of it given that the previous director was in peak physical condition. Furthermore, it seems that the Institute's deputy director, Dr Charles Montague (Harvey Korman) is highly resentful that an outsider has been appointed to head up the organisation when he had felt certain that he would have been promoted to the role himself following Ashley's death.

At the Institute Thorndyke is welcomed by Dr Philip Wentworth (Dick Van Patten), an amiable psychiatrist who is an admirer of the new director's academic research. Wentworth begins to tell Thorndyke of strange happenings at the Institute but is curtly interrupted by the unctuous Montague, whose smarmy greeting cannot disguise his umbrage at Thorndyke's arrival ('I was in charge here *until you showed up!*'). Montague also introduces the frighteningly austere but efficient Charlotte Diesel (Cloris Leachman), the Institute's Head Nurse, who has prepared patient files pending the director's arrival. It soon becomes clear that Diesel exerts her ruthless authority over everyone in the workplace, including Montague.

Thorndyke is unpacking his belongings when his old mentor, the elderly Professor Lilloman (Howard Morris), appears at his new quarters. Lilloman is delighted to see his former student again, not least given Thorndyke's starry academic career – one which has seen him become a Nobel Prizewinner, and now 'the head of the most prestigious psychiatric institute on the West Coast'. The mature psychiatrist explains that he was appointed as a consultant at the Institute by the departed Dr Ashley, and that he laments the late director's passing – not least given the fact that his death coincided with major administrative changes that he had planned to make, but never had the chance to see through. Lilloman is alarmed when, after suggesting that Thorndyke take a look at the view from his room's balcony, his old pupil rapidly descends into a state of panic. Determining that Thorndyke is still suffering from 'high anxiety' – an acute fear of heights – Lilloman suggests that he undergo a period of psychoanalysis starting the next day.

Over dinner with his new colleagues, Thorndyke attempts to ascertain the nature of his predecessor's planned changes to the Institute, but his enquiries are firmly rebuffed by the dictatorial Nurse Diesel. He does, however, grow more curious about the odd relationship which appears to exist between her and Montague. Thorndyke asks about the patient recovery rate at the Institute, only to be told by his deputy that the conditions of people who are admitted there only rarely improve. Diesel goads him that front-line psychiatry throws up many more practical challenges than may be apparent to someone who is more used to a lecture theatre. When asked if he will be attending the annual American Psychiatric Convention in San Francisco, which will be taking place in a week's time, Thorndyke replies in the affirmative; he feels it will be an honour to represent the Institute so early in his tenure.

As he prepares for bed, Thorndyke is alarmed when a rock smashes through his bathroom window – an attached message wishes him a 'welcome from the violent ward'. No sooner has he had time to process this strange occurrence when the sound of distant screaming can be heard. Joined by Brophy, who has been alerted by the earlier disturbance, Thorndyke races to the source of the commotion – which happens to be Nurse Diesel's room. In typically waspish style, Diesel tells the two men that there is no reason for alarm; they have presumably overheard her television set. Brusquely, she sends them packing, but it soon becomes apparent that their concerns were not entirely unfounded – returning to her quarters, it is revealed that Thorndyke had interrupted a sado-masochistic bondage session between Diesel and Montague, who is currently chained up in her wardrobe.

The next day, Thorndyke calls Montague to his office and confronts him with an unsettling fact; it has come to his attention, having reviewed the Institute's case histories, that several patients have been in the organisation's care for many months – at huge expense to their families – while exhibiting no abnormal psychological symptoms. Montague tries to alleviate his concerns by assuring him that case histories are often imprecise, and that a patient who appears to be well may actually retain volatile psychiatric characteristics. Thorndyke calls in one apparently-cured patient, Zachary Cartwright (Ron Clark), who was admitted two years previously with nervous exhaustion but is now perfectly lucid and healthy. When the patient explains that he has been free from intermittent pains for six months, however, Montague begins to pelt him with projectiles (though Thorndyke remains oblivious to the fact), making it appear as though Cartwright is having a relapse. As the man flies into hysteria, Thorndyke eventually has no choice but to have him returned to the safety of his room – though he remains puzzled by his sudden change in condition.

As Cartwright is removed from his office, Thorndyke notices someone signalling to him from another building of the Institute. Montague explains that the signal (light reflecting on a mirror) is coming from the room of Arthur Brisbane, a well-known industrialist. Thorndyke is confused by this, noting that there is no mention of Brisbane in the files, and arranges to meet the patient later that day. Montague seems alarmed by this prospect, but when it becomes clear that the director won't be deterred he telephones Nurse Diesel on an internal line and mysteriously informs her (in Pig Latin) that 'you know what to do'.

During a period of hypnotic regression, Lilloman discovers that Thorndyke's fear of heights appears to stem from his childhood. Before he can delve any deeper into the director's psyche, however, Thorndyke breaks into a pugilistic, hypnosis-induced delusion when Lilloman suggests that the only way he can overcome the phobia is to fight it. Overhearing the resulting tumult, Montague races into the room and asks for an explanation. Lilloman clarifies the situation to the deputy, who appears quietly ecstatic when he learns of the new director's debilitating problem. The elderly consultant swears Montague to secrecy, but -in spite of his protestations that he always respects professional confidentiality – the perfidious second-in-command immediately begins to spread gossip of Thorndyke's predicament to his colleagues.

At Thorndyke's insistence, Montague takes the director to the Violent Ward where he is introduced to Arthur Brisbane. The director is amazed that this apparent giant of the industrial world is now a barking, writhing, disturbed shadow of his former self (Charlie Callas), dressed in a one-piece suit, who believes himself to be a cocker spaniel. Montague seems pleased that Thorndyke accepts the situation at face value, but the Institute's new head is mystified by the puzzle of how a man convinced he is a dog would be physically able to signal towards his office with a mirror.

In Diesel's office, the mild-mannered Dr Wentworth begs the autocratic nurse to let him resign from his post. He has become uncomfortable with the situation that is unfolding at the Institute, and promises not to breathe a word of what he has seen to anyone (though in true Hitchcockian style he does not explain what it is that he has witnessed). In an uncharacteristic moment of mercy, Diesel appears to assent to his resignation. But that evening as he drives home from work, he turns on his car radio and inexplicably discovers that only one channel is playable – a repetitive, loud disco track. Eventually driving off the road as he struggles in vain to change the frequency, Wentworth is killed by the deafening music – blood dripping from his ruined eardrums – when he finds that it is impossible to escape from the car.

The next day, Thorndyke is stunned to hear the news of Wentworth's passing; Montague informs him that the cause of death was a cerebral haemorrhage, but the director is unconvinced by the coroner's report. Thorndyke considers cancelling his attendance at the forthcoming psychiatric convention, but Diesel and Montague both assure him that everything is under control and that he should not neglect the opportunity to represent the Institute amongst their professional peers. Eventually he acquiesces and departs with Brophy for San Franscisco (much to the unspoken relief of the deputy and head nurse).

Soon after, Thorndyke arrives at the hotel which is hosting the conference. He is alarmed to discover that he has been allocated a room on the top floor of the building; a mysterious caller had contacted the hotel ahead of time to countermand Thorndyke's request that he be assigned ground-floor accommodation. The luckless psychiatrist finds his nerves tested to the limit as he endures a glass elevator trip to the seventeenth floor, but this is nothing compared to his panic when he is attacked in his shower by a hysterical bellboy (Barry Levinson), driven to distraction by Thorndyke's continual requests for a newspaper so that he can check for details of Wentworth's recent demise. ('That kid gets no tip,' the director asserts after being reepeatedly walloped by the soggy periodical.)

Later, Thorndyke is visited in his hotel room by the enigmatic Victoria Brisbane (Madeline Kahn). The cautious woman tells him that she believes that her father Arthur is being incarcerated at the Institute against his will. Thorndyke explains that, having examined her parent only recently, he believes him to be deeply disturbed. Their conversation is interrupted when Thorndyke is called to give his keynote speech to the conference, but concerned for Victoria's state of mind – and keen to provide assurance about Arthur's wellbeing – he arranges to meet her after his presentation. Unseen by either of them, their movements are being closely watched by a shadowy figure (Rudy DeLuca).

While Thorndyke delivers his speech to wild acclaim from his fellow psychiatric professionals, the man who has been tracking him is speaking on a public payphone to an unseen collaborator. It becomes clear that this nameless figure is responsible for the deaths of both Ashley and Wentworth, and that he also intends to add Thorndyke and Victoria to his list of casualties. However, the person on the other end of the phone line warns him to wait for further instructions. Afterwards, Thorndyke meets Victoria at the hotel bar as promised, where he tells her he will personally make arrangements for the young woman to visit her father at the Institute as soon as he gets back from the conference. However, when she accidentally drops her purse Thorndyke spots a picture of a middle-aged man amongst her possessions who Victoria identifies as her father. Realising that the photo shows an entirely different man from the patient he examined at the Institute, Thorndyke smells a rat. As he airs his suspicions, neither he nor Victoria realise that the inscrutable hit-man has been listening in on their conversation.

Back at the Institute, Montague is starting to panic. In a private meeting with Diesel, he has just received a report that Thorndyke is aware that the patient with the cocker spaniel complex was not the real Arthur Brisbane and reflects that they will now have no choice but to order the new director's assassination. Diesel is unconvinced, however – with Ashley and now Wentworth both murdered after only a short period of time, another killing would be certain to raise suspicions. Instead, they resolve to have Thorndyke framed instead, believing that the police will never listen to the director's concerns if he becomes a crime suspect himself.

The next day, Brophy is making arrangements for Thorndyke's early departure from the hotel. As he takes some photos of the lobby for his collection prior to leaving, he spots Thorndyke arriving in the reception area. When a delegate from the conference enquires about his premature exit, Thorndyke abruptly pulls out a handgun and shoots him at point-blank range. As the lobby erupts into panicked horror, the assassin retreats to the elevators... where another Thorndyke is emerging from the upper floor of the hotel. The newly-arrived psychiatrist is stunned as his apparent doppelganger presses the murder weapon into his hand. Tearing off a rubber mask, it becomes apparent that the killer is the hit-man who has been tracking Thorndyke since his arrival in San Francisco. As the assassin disappears into the elevator, leaving the confused Thorndyke in his wake, the hapless Institute director is immediately assumed to be the murderer. Realising that he is being framed, Thorndyke races away with two hotel security guards hot on his tail. Totally perplexed, Brophy helplessly watches his employer's flight from the safety of the sidelines.

Some time later, Thorndyke is lying low in Golden Gate Park. He makes a call to an unheard ally on a nearby public phone, but a troubling attack by a flock of malevolent pigeons finds him abandoning his plans in favour of finding a nearby dry cleaners instead. Nonetheless, he is still able to make a rendezvous with the recipient of his earlier call, which turns out to be Victoria. She is confounded by recent developments, and has difficulty accepting Thorndyke's account of events at face value. Showing him a newspaper front page report about the murder, Thorndyke spots himself in the background of the illustrative photo – descending in a glass elevator – while the homicide is taking place. However, the picture has only very low resolution, meaning that his features are unidentifiable. As he recognises the photograph as one that Brophy had taken in the lobby, he asks Victoria to track down the driver and get him to blow up his original negative. This should provide the evidence Thorndyke needs to clear his name. He then suggests that they split up in an effort to make it more difficult to track them down.

Back at the Institute, Brophy succeeds in using the negative to create a vastly scaled-up copy of the hotel lobby photograph. Sure enough, it clearly shows Thorndyke in the elevator at the time that the murder was committed. However, before he can inform anyone of his discovery Diesel and Montague arrive in his darkroom and confiscate the original negative. Brophy is condemned to incarceration in the Institute's dreaded north wing, but Diesel is still dissatisfied – copies of the negative have already been circulated to every newspaper in San Francisco, meaning that there is every possibility that someone else could produce their own blow-up copy of the photo at any time. Instead, she resolves to order the hit-man to kill Thorndyke, thus neutralising any threat that he poses.

Unfortunately for Diesel, her plans don't quite work out as anticipated. When Thorndyke makes a call to Victoria from a public phone box near the Golden Gate Bridge, he is attacked by the hit-man and – fighting off an attempt at strangulation – accidentally kills the assassin by impaling him on a jagged shard of broken glass. Victoria explains that she has lost contact with Brophy, suggesting to Thorndyke that Montague and Diesel are now fully aware of his attempts to clear his name. To this end, they must return to the Institute so that he can confront his colleagues. Victoria points out the impossibility of this, given that every police officer in San Francisco is currently looking for them.

However, Thorndyke suggests that they obtain some second-hand clothing from the Salvation Army and – posing as an obnoxiously loud middle-aged married couple – they manage to bluff their way through the airport without being identified, effectively hiding in plain sight.

Finally back in Los Angeles, Thorndyke and Victoria break into the Institute by cover of darkness. Meeting with Professor Lilloman, they discover that Brophy is being held in a secure area and determine to release him. Sure enough, on his escape the driver reveals that Diesel and Montague plan to kill Arthur Brisbane – the real one – by drugging him and throwing him from the top of the Institute's observation tower, thus making his death look like a suicide. Together, they race to the tower and discover sadistic orderly Norton (Lee Delano) manhandling the semi-catatonic Brisbane (Arthur J. Whitlock) towards the summit. Thorndyke's acrophobia prevents him from making an ascent; even when he tries to overcome his apprehension he becomes paralysed by fear when a wooden stair breaks beneath his feet, leaving him dangling in midair. Fortunately Lilloman quickly manages to regress him to his infancy, where he reveals the childhood roots of Thorndyke's phobia; his endlessly quarrelling parents blamed his existence for their woes, and at the apex of their disagreement he fell from his high chair while still a baby, thus causing him to fear heights thereafter. Realising that he can now overcome this irrational terror, he scrambles back onto the stairs and races to the top of the tower.

Arriving just in time to overcome Norton and save Brisbane from plummeting to his death, Thorndyke only narrowly manages to avoid an attack by an enraged Diesel who, making a fatal misstep, topples from the tower onto the cliffs below. The spineless Montague, realising that the game is up, offers his unconditional surrender. At long last, Arthur Brisbane and the Institute's other patients are finally safe again. Elated at seeing her father again, Victoria proposes to Thorndyke, thus marking an end to the nightmare and the beginning of a new future together.

With its disciplined, cohesive storyline and purposeful pastiche of an instantly recognisable format popular with cineastes worldwide, *High Anxiety* marked a bold deviation from the broadstroke genre spoofs which had earned Brooks such acclaim during his earlier features throughout the seventies. A blatant love-letter to the work of Alfred Hitchcock, like *Young Frankenstein* and *Silent Movie* there is much affection shown by Brooks towards his chosen source material throughout the film. In the years which followed, he has made explicit the desire he had during the production of *High Anxiety* to ensure that Hitchcock was made aware of the project and even to seek his approval:

> I wrote a letter saying, basically, 'Dear Mr Hitchcock, I do genre parodies and in my estimation you are a genre. I don't mean that you're overweight. I mean that you've done every style and type of movie, and that you're just amazing, and I would like to do a movie dedicated to you based on your style and your work'. [...] He called me and he said, 'I loved *Blazing Saddles*. I think you're a very talented guy, and come to my office.' I came to his office at Universal, and he told me to come back every Friday at a quarter to 12, because at 12:30 we would eat. So 45 minutes of work. And he would work on my script – on *High Anxiety* – with me. And he said, 'Well, don't leave out this and don't leave out that...'[1]

A director with an acute interest in the output of the greats of many different genres, Brooks showed real commitment in his quest to salute Hitchcock's monumental contribution to cinema. Maurice Yacowar has exhaustively chronicled Brooks's many allusions to the work of Hitchcock throughout the film, not least the choice of setting and the nature of the central mystery which bears more than a little similarity to *Spellbound* (1945), and Thorndyke's acrophobia which has obvious correlation with *Vertigo* (1958).[2] Given Brooks's famously fastidious attention to detail, it is of little surprise that just about every entry in Hitchcock's extensive canon is acknowledged at one point or another during *High Anxiety*; some of the movie's most entertaining sequences parody famously iconic scenes in *Rear Window* (1954), *Psycho* (1960) and *The Birds* (1963). But as Robert Alan Crick has noted, there are also many subtle references to several of Hitchcock's lesser-known films too,[3] moving Brooks beyond the territory he had occupied with *Young Frankenstein* (that is, spoofing not just James Whale's *Frankenstein* adaptation of 1931 but the whole cinematic phenomenon which was to follow it) and into uncharted waters, where the work of a single filmmaker was to inform not just the tone and style but also the subject matter of the movie. However, to simply classify *High Anxiety* as a straightforward pastiche – a tongue-in-cheek compilation patched together from Hitchcock's wide-ranging back-catalogue – would be to do it a grave disservice. As Yacowar observes, '*High Anxiety* is something more than a collection of Hitchcock jokes. For one thing, it avoids the danger of bitsiness by possessing Brooks's most direct narrative and consistent characterisation since *The Twelve Chairs*. Brooks realised that "logic is everything. A film has to have a centre to hold it together". However impressive the individual gags in *High Anxiety* may be, "there are no space fillers. Every moment is significant because we were dealing with the elements found in every Hitchcock suspense thriller"'.[4]

Human psychology was crucial to most of Hitchcock's films, albeit that the subject was addressed in radically different ways through his career, and Brooks chose to make this theme central to *High Anxiety*; its protagonist is an eminent psychiatrist, many of the supporting characters have professional links to either psychology or psychiatry, and of course most of the action takes place on the premises of a psychiatric institute. Behind the fiction, however, lies a rather more personal *modus operandi*. Brooks has spoken in interviews about having undergone a beneficial period of psychotherapy in early adulthood, giving him first-hand insight into the subject of the film; as he revealed in an interview with Arthur Cooper: 'I went into analysis when I was twenty-two and had my first nervous breakdown. [...] I found a psychiatrist and I was with him for six years, five times a week. Initially, I was afraid analysis would make me "normal" and take away my talent. But what it did was to free me to be a more complete artist and a good writer'.[5] Yet in spite of the high regard for the science of psychiatry which he has voiced in interviews over the years, Brooks was far from unaware of the discipline's potential abuses and sought to explore this issue by satirical means throughout *High Anxiety*. As he explained in an interview with Jerry Bauer some years after the film's release:

> The axe I'm grinding this time is the misuse of psychiatry. It's become such a popular life style in America that people hop on the couch the way they regularly drop into their local supermarket. They only difference I can see is they're getting less value for their money from the neighborhood shrink. A bottle of Dom Perignon from Piffily Wiggily would do more to lift up their dejected spirits. Seriously, however, a few months of kinotherapy has wrought greater wonders than years of analysis. But why should a psychiatrist wise up a

patient when the patient is helping send the psychiatrist's kids through college and paying for his wife's latest mink coat?[6]

David Desser and Lester D. Friedman correctly discern that 'Brooks's personal debt to psychotherapy does little to deflect his humor from this eternally ripe sacred cow,'[7] and indeed there is no disguising his contempt for the exploitation of this branch of learning amongst certain professionals active in the field. Most obvious, of course, is the film's central premise, where Montague and Diesel are working in concert to ensure that patients at the institute will remain resident there indefinitely (the mental and physical wellbeing of those in their care is apparently of little interest to them). As this plot is being perpetrated by the two lead villains, naturally Brooks makes clear his disapproval for the nature of their plans. But then, even the ostensibly virtuous Thorndyke is not immune from Brooks's censure. His conversation with his mentor (the similarly-benign Professor Lilloman) illuminates the fact that in the world of *High Anxiety*, even honest psychiatrists are not entirely resistant to materialistic concerns:

| | |
|---|---|
| LILLOMAN: | A patient comes to you. He is suffering from Belden's Hysteria. He has a seizure right in your office. What do you give him? |
| THORNDYKE: | Two ccs of aqueous Thorazine, coupled with one cc of Somadiazine. |
| LILLOMAN: | Ah, good, good, good! And the most important thing? |
| THORNDYKE: | Never take a personal cheque! |

Beyond recognising the professional expense of psychiatric treatment, Brooks widens the target range of his satire by implicating the discipline at large; during his keynote speech at the psychiatric conference, Thorndyke's opening remarks further expound upon the connection between ensuring the wellbeing of patients and being adequately reimbursed for so doing: 'One hundred years ago, psychology was akin to witchcraft. But some of these great people, these giants behind me [Sigmund Freud, Carl Jung, etc.], gave us a nice living'. The obvious difference between Thorndyke and his antagonists, of course, lies in his empathy; unlike Diesel and Montague, his patients' mental health is of paramount concern... but upholding high standards of medical ethics is not mutually exclusive from seeking sufficient recompense for his professional efforts, as a telling discourse with Victoria makes clear:

> VICTORIA: Jeepers, Richard! That was terrific.
> THORNDYKE: Thank you.
> VICTORIA: I am so impressed. Have you ever thought of singing professionally?
> THORNDYKE: No, no, no. The big bucks are in psychiatry. I mean, it's so much more emotionally rewarding.
> VICTORIA: Exactly.
> THORNDYKE: To help people.
> VICTORIA: Exactly.

The cerebral Brooks gives a thoughtful and comparatively restrained performance as the renowned intellectual Thorndyke, a character who owes more than a little to the dashing, sophisticated protagonists of Hitchcock films past, and who proved to be a world away from his freewheeling debut starring role (to say nothing of his earlier supporting appearances). Mel Funn's freedom was articulated through his vigorous defence of creative liberty, but Dr Thorndyke instead must find his own emancipation – from personal demons, from the machinations of malign forces, and ultimately in setting the patients of his institute free from their (often entirely constructed) neuroses. Crick notes that 'Richard H. Thorndyke is a take-off on Cary Grant's Roger O. Thornhill in *North by Northwest*,[8] Hitchcock's famous 1959 spy thriller which similarly provides the inspiration for much of *High Anxiety*'s third-act fugitive storyline, and indeed Brooks's finely-attuned performance reproduces many of the qualities of Grant's famous everyman – his likeability, grace under fire, and cool refinement. Brooks has claimed that:

> I am the star, the Jewish star, the Mogan David of this film. I am the six-pointed beauty. It's basically a straight role because when you do a send-up of an Alfred Hitchcock film, it's incumbent upon you to play the central role like James Stewart or Cary Grant or any number of Hitchcock heroes. He usually has a very well dressed man in a vest and a Phi Beta Kappa key being chased by all kinds of villains and the police. He's on the run from everybody, and usually at his side is a girl named Tippy with blonde hair. Tippy or Doris... they always have blonde hair.[9]

Yet of course, in being forced to struggle against his own psychological fears the normally-unruffled Thorndyke is able to sympathise with his patients' predicaments more fully than his more antagonistic subordinates at the Institute. Beyond the acrophobia in which it primarily presents itself, the condition 'high anxiety' is, of course, ultimately revealed to have an obvious double meaning – not simply fretfulness on account of fear of heights, but also a heightened sense of anxiety due to the condition itself. The multifaceted nature of this phobic tendency – and the unease and apprehension that it generates – is crucial not only to understanding Thorndyke's character, but the nature of the threat that he grapples against throughout the film. Thorndyke has become a prisoner of an unresolved irrational fear, just as the patients of the Institute have quite literally become prisoners – not only of the ramifications deriving from mental health issues, but also from the machinations of Diesel and Montague. But by overcoming his phobia, which is ultimately revealed to be directly related to childhood trauma, he is able to extend this power of liberation from the specific to the general by defeating his adversaries and assuring the freedom of the people living in the Institute's care. It is the universal nature of this kind of anxiety – fear of personal entrapment by one means or another – which makes it so relatable to the audience at large. Richard Nelson-Jones, for instance, observes that:

> The ancient Roman poet Horace wrote, 'At the rider's back sits dark Anxiety'. The same topic is approached in a humorous way by comedian Mel Brooks, who claims to suffer from high anxiety. Anxiety is a part of our animal nature. Just as you cannot avoid choosing and thinking, you cannot avoid your potential for anxiety. Ultimately the fear of death, non-being or destruction is the underlying fear from which all other anxieties are derived. I prefer the term survival anxiety. Anxiety has a survival value in that it alerts you to realistic dangers to your existence. Unfortunately, all people suffer in varying degrees from what I, like Mel Brooks, term high anxiety. Sometimes anxiety can be high because of actual threats to your existence. However, the importance of high anxiety here is that it is higher than that required to cope efficiently with life's challenges, either general or specific. As such it is disproportionate and debilitating rather than facilitating.[10]

*High Anxiety*, in general, treats the issue of mental illness with a certain degree of respect – the 'keep in' notice on the Institute's gates notwithstanding. With the exception of the patient who is substituted for Arthur Brisbane (an exceptional display of physical comedy by Charlie Callas), whose vivid canine delusions are used for comic effect – witness the fire hydrant and other dog-related paraphernalia on display in his secure room – the film does not linger for long on the serious psychological maladies of the Institute's residents but instead spends the majority of its time reflecting upon the various dysfunctions of the staff. Chief among them is the petrifying Charlotte Diesel, played to malign perfection by Cloris Leachman. Nurse Diesel is an obvious parody of Louise Fletcher's Academy Award-winning role as the icily authoritarian Nurse Ratched in Milos Forman's *One Flew Over the Cuckoo's Nest* (1975) (though Crick also suggests similarity to the character of Mrs Danvers, as played by Judith Anderson, in Hitchcock's *Rebecca*, 1940).[11] Yet in Leachman's hands, strangulating her dialogue as though throttling every line on the way out of her mouth, the character becomes something even more sinister – and truly startling to behold. (Brooks makes the character's witchlike nature explicit when she appears, just prior to her death, cackling evilly in a black cape, broom in hand.) Georgette S. Fox has commented that 'Nurse Diesel is as terrifying as an image out of Lovecraft or Poe. A caricature, she stomps about mechanically, stiff-necked and tight-lipped, her starched uniform as unyielding as a suit of armor. She barks her words as fierce commands, her speech coarse and guttural. Most electrifying is the sight of her formidable pointed breasts, encased as in steel, rather than a softly feminine bosom. Nurse Diesel is the last person in the world one would want as a personal "caregiver"'.[12] Leachman was, of course, a Brooks alumnus, having appeared in *Young Frankenstein* as the similarly-intimidating Frau Blucher. Harvey Korman too had collaborated with Brooks earlier, in his case in *Blazing Saddles*, and the essentially spineless Dr Montague – in turns smarmy and cowardly – had much in common with Korman's earlier, well-received turn as the slimy Hedley Lamarr. Though inventively deceptive, Montague's life is spent cowering in the shadow of the dictatorial Diesel – not just in regard to their shared criminal plans, but also in their decidedly kinky love life (where Diesel makes his subordination all the more apparent – hence his obvious difficulty sitting down after a particularly rough session of sadomasochism). Like Leachman, Korman is clearly enjoying himself in the role of Montague, relishing the challenge of depicting a character who exhibits no redeeming features save for the amusement value of his sheer underhandedness. His professional corruption is perhaps best summed up by his malicious werewolf impersonation, complete with false fangs, in an attempt to terrify a patient with a morbid fear of lycanthropes – a wonderfully over-the-top instance of comic excess. Yet for all his attempts at outward sophistication, Montague is just about as inept a Hitchcock villain as it is possible to be, very noticeably plotting in plain sight when he collaborates over the phone with Diesel using Pig Latin and later tripping himself up with his own schemes: 'Yes, enjoy yourself, for God's sake. Get your mind off the Wentworth murder. Accident. *Accident!* Have a good time'. Thus whereas Thorndyke and Victoria are ensnared by circumstance and the scheming of others, Montague and Diesel are shown to be prisoners of their own essentially corrupt natures.

The film also benefits from an appealingly eccentric supporting cast of characters, led by the mesmerising Madeline Kahn as Victoria Brisbane. Victoria proves to be a more fully developed female supporting character than either *Blazing Saddles*'s Lili von Shtupp or *Silent Movie*'s Vilma Kaplan, and thus affords Kahn an even greater opportunity to showcase her comic talents than had been the case when portraying Elizabeth in *Young Frankenstein*. Right from her first appearance – complete with her hilariously overdramatic heavy breathing – Victoria makes for an interesting character, alternating between edgy paranoia and understatedly outré sexuality (her expression speaks volumes when Thorndyke lashes the cable of his microphone like a whip, for instance). Like Thorndyke, though for different reasons, Victoria is unable to find contentment as long as the mystery surrounding her estranged father remains; her hopes of freedom are unknowingly entwined with that of the unfortunate Institute director, whose liberty and safety are similarly reliant upon unfurling the ambiguous crime which has been orchestrated by his deadly colleagues. Yet the interplay between her and Thorndyke helps to emphasise not only Victoria's own resourcefulness and level-headedness in attempting to uncover the foul play taking place at the Institute, but also the psychiatrist's comparative emotional distance both as a social being and as a professional. Occasionally this detachment is used for light-hearted effect – all the more striking given that this was one of

Brooks's ostensibly more serious roles, as he is at pains to puncture the character's earnestness through an exploration of his shortcomings. Thorndyke's social awkwardness is highlighted when, delivering a lecture which touches on decidedly adult themes in psychiatry, he suddenly spots children in the audience and abruptly switches to a range of infantile euphemisms to protect their innocence. (The children themselves seem far from impressed by his efforts.) However, his less than ideal bedside manner is perhaps most clearly witnessed when he tries – and singularly fails – to articulate the mental condition of Victoria's father in anything approaching a sensitive way:

VICTORIA: Have you seen my father at the Institute? Is he all right?
THORNDYKE: He's fine, he's fine – he's coming along fine. He's very affectionate. He licked me.
VICTORIA: He what?
THORNDYKE: Well, he thinks he's a dog these days.
VICTORIA: A dog?!
THORNDYKE: A dog, yes.

Other noteworthy supporting performances include Howard Morris as Professor Lilloman, Thorndyke's father figure and (indeed, as Thorndyke initially misnames him) an archetypal 'little old man'. Portrayed as a jovial, affable take on Sigmund Freud-as-sidekick, his associate role at the Institute means that the whimsical Lilloman is untainted by the sinister goings-on of his workplace, though his insider status as a member of the staff gives Thorndyke the crucial opening he needs to enact his revenge at the film's conclusion. Lilloman is, of course, also the eventual arbiter of Thorndyke's liberation from the childhood distress which has blighted much of his adult life. Ron Carey gives a pleasing turn as Brophy, the sociable but highly suspicious Institute driver who doubles (as it turns out, very fortunately) as a keen amateur photographer. The character's name is likely a reference to character actor Edward Brophy, a recognised supporting performer and voice artist in many movies from the silent era onwards (where he often played typical 'sidekick' characters). With his prominent braces, Rudy DeLuca's hit-man is an evident play on Jaws, the metal-toothed nemesis of James Bond so memorably portrayed by Richard Kiel in *The Spy Who Loved Me* (Lewis Gilbert, 1977) and, later, *Moonraker* (Lewis Gilbert, 1979).

And Albert Whitlock, who cameos as (the real) Arthur Brisbane, was responsible for the special effects on many of Hitchcock's films, adding a further touch of authenticity to Brooks's creative intentions.

Brooks did, of course, set out with the intention of doing more than simply producing a film which presented a narrative redolent with Hitchcockian motifs; he also aimed to communicate his own commentary on Hitchcock's famed cinematic techniques, examining their effectiveness when employed within the confines of a comedy setting. Yacowar has explained that 'Brooks emphasises the process by which our perception alters our sense of what we see. In this respect, the film is about a key element in Hitchcock's art. Hitchcock frequently explored the moral issues in the act of intrusive viewing and the involving powers of subjective cinema'.[13] There are a number of occasions in the film where Brooks toys with the preconceptions of audience awareness, knowing that the framing of shots and motions of the camera can drastically affect the depiction of any given scene. Hitchcock's precision (and perfectionism) in creating such complex and deftly-composed shots had become legendary, meaning that Brooks had considerable scope when it came to sending them up. The camera 'accident' which takes place in the closing motel scene – a parody of Hitchcock's famous through-the-wall tracking shots – is just one such example of presenting a recognisable Hitchcockian filmic convention and then subverting it, as Desser and Friedman observe:

> Brooks concentrates more energy on direct parodies of famous Hitchcock moments. He includes the shower scene from *Psycho* (1960), the bird attack from *The Birds* (1963), the tower climbing from *Vertigo* (1958), the setting of *Spellbound* (1946), the picture taking from *Rear Window* (1954), and many other allusions. Such parodies also take the form of casual homages, although, as one might expect with Brooks, each contains a distinctively humorous moment of recognition. For example, a long tracking shot from the garden to the dining room ends abruptly when the camera crashes into the glass door and shatters a window pane. Later, the equally inept camera literally hits a brick wall as a technician mutters, 'Maybe no one will notice'. Such reflective moments draw attention to the artifice of filmmaking as well as to the often ignored artificiality of the entire production.[14]

Because Hitchcock was a director noted for his meticulousness and accuracy, Brooks takes great delight in turning these qualities on their head when offering the viewer cleverly unconventional shots which, for one reason or another, deliberately and amusingly don't quite work as planned. This is especially well realised during a scene where Diesel and Montague plot to keep their malevolent schemes afloat by removing Thorndyke from his post. Gloria Withalm makes the point that Brooks is able to advance the storyline while combining expository dialogue with a very self-conscious attempt to attract audience awareness of the camera: 'When Cloris Leachman (as Nurse Diesel) and one of the doctors have a conspiratorial talk while having coffee and cookies, we can watch them from underneath the glass table in a low-angle shot. Unfortunately, Leachman is constantly moving around every single item on the table – the cups, the sugar bowl, the plate with the cookies, the coffeepot – putting them right above the lenses, and thus, the camera also has to move around constantly in order to correct the framing'.[15]

Sound and music also play a vital part in Brooks's defiance of expectation; unusually for a Hitchcock film, the characters seem all too aware of incidental auditory phenomena, leading them to react in unexpected ways. For instance, when Brophy reveals what he has learned of the plans to murder Victoria's father, a jarring chord causes Thorndyke and his entourage to react by looking towards the ceiling (where the point of view has suddenly shifted) in perfect synchronisation. Likewise, convention is challenged when Thorndyke's secretary buzzes him over the intercom with a stereotypically nasal intonation; he asks her to repeat her statement without her hand squeezing her nose, and she then does so in a perfectly normal voice. And at the other end of the spectrum, a seemingly-innocuous disco track eventually transpires to be the means of Dr Wentworth's demise – his bizarre death, complete with bleeding ears, shrewdly reflecting Brooks's opinion of this type of music.

John Morris's original score once again proves to be intensely faithful to the source material – in this case, the eerie incidental music and tense compositions of the great Bernard Herrmann. (This is especially obvious during the shower scene, the bellboy's hysterical shrieking closely echoing the effect of the violin music from Herrmann's seminal *Psycho* score.) Even early in the film, the characters' perception of the score becomes significant;

accompanied by relentlessly dramatic music as he travels through Los Angeles International Airport, Thorndyke is so relieved to make it to the exit (when the music finally begins to tail off) that he nervously exclaims: 'What a dramatic airport!' But occasionally Brooks combines this awareness of accompanying music with sight gags to complex effect, as Keyvan Sarkhosh has described:

> In a striking scene, we see Thorndyke and his chauffeur Brophy (Ron Carey) sitting in a car when suddenly there is the sound of thrilling music. What first seems merely to supply the atmospheric background turns out to be audible to Thorndyke and Brophy, too, who are both obviously quite distressed by the uneasy music. This already being metaleptic, the twist is pushed further when, to the relief of the two characters, the source of the music becomes visible: a bus pulls over, in it sitting the members of the Los Angeles Symphony Orchestra playing their instruments. [...] In contrast to diegetic music within the story which the characters refer to or interact with, a film's score is not part of the diegesis. Referring to [Etienne] Souriau's terminology, the score in its materialisation is located on the filmophanic level, and in its effect on the audience on the spectatorial level. In the [above example] from Mel Brooks, the boundary to the diegetic world is breached, the score thus becomes diegetic and the characters can react to it.[16]

Many of Brooks's allusions to Hitchcock are considerably more understated, from Thorndyke arranging to meet Victoria at San Francisco's Golden Gate Park 'at the North by Northwest corner' to the rearrangement of hotel rooms by the unseen 'Mr MacGuffin', which of course recalls Hitchcock's name for an activator object responsible for setting a film's plot in motion (but which had little or no relevance to the storyline beyond that point). Suggestions of the dramatic tension of *Rear Window* in Brophy's obsessive photo-taking are comically undercut when he asks to take a photo of Thorndyke's departure from the Institute; although Diesel and Montague claim to be reluctant to appear in the shot, they all immediately jump into a photogenic pose for the snapshot with mirthful expressions and odd exactitude. Also well-judged is the brief presence of Bullets Durgom as the hapless man in the public phone booth who is assaulted by the dentally-augmented hit-man; with more than a passing visual resemblance to Alfred Hitchcock himself, Durgom's appearance seems to be a purposeful suggestion of Hitchcock's own famous in-movie cameos. Yet perhaps the most subtle allusion of all occurs when

Thorndyke, albeit somewhat unexpectedly, accepts an offer of serenading Victoria and various other patrons at the hotel where the psychiatric conference is taking place – a decision which, as Gerald Mast has explained, actually achieves a surprising duality of purpose:

> *High Anxiety* transcends its Hitchcock parody when, for no reason of plot or character, the distinguished psychiatrist croons the film's title tune, a la Tony Bennett or Frank Sinatra, in the bar of San Francisco's Hyatt Hotel. Although the song may be a sly allusion to Doris Day's 'Que Sera Sera' in Hitchcock's 1956 version of *The Man Who Knew Too Much*, it seems more a comment on Hollywood's general willingness to abandon the logic of plot and character if the star is one that the audience expects to sing (except we most certainly do not expect Mel Brooks to sing, either as Dr Thorndyke or in any other guise!).17

In this intriguing scene, Brooks (as Thorndyke) performs the 'High Anxiety' song in the style of Frank Sinatra, deliberately exaggerating the legendary crooner's well-known vocal mannerisms as he does so. (Brooks was also the song's composer and lyricist.) However, by making prominent mention of Harpo Marx ('Harpo' turns out to be Thorndyke's middle name) following the conclusion of the song, Brooks may also be parodying the Marx Brothers's tendency to include a musical interlude in many of their films. From a character point of view, though, the scene is puzzling. Why does Thorndyke sing about 'High Anxiety' when he is actively trying to conceal the fact that he has the condition? Certainly there is a possibility that in opening up about his phobia, he is acknowledging Lilloman's advice that he should consciously fight it, thus foreshadowing his later ability to overcome his acrophobia altogether. Yet the childhood origins of Thorndyke's 'High Anxiety' are also foregrounded in his obsessive teeth-cleaning practices – chanting a well-rehearsed routine, as though he has learnt it in childhood and is now unable to grow out of it. Yacowar has alluded to similarities with Brooks's own trauma over the early loss of his own father, which had an effect on much of his formative life: 'The adult's traumatic shaping by his childhood is the central theme of *High Anxiety*. It makes the film one of Brooks's most personal and revealing works, despite its form as a Hitchcock pastiche'.18 Any worries that Brooks was to lend too much dramatic weight to the issue of youthful emotional disturbance skewing normative adult experience are easily dispelled, however, by a flashback sequence which shows a middle-aged Brooks portraying Thorndyke as crying, bib-bedecked infant. Even when exploring such a personal and sensitive psychological subject, Brooks still seemed determined to make the point that one of the most profound ways of illuminating a serious concern can be by provoking laughter.

Critical reception of *High Anxiety* was largely lukewarm at the time of the film's release; while Brooks's accuracy in reproducing various aspects of Hitchcock's distinctive cinematic style was widely acknowledged, the effectiveness of its comedy was the subject of much debate amongst commentators. Molly Haskell of *New York* Magazine spoke for many when she observed that 'the Hitchcock quotations are just that – fond references rather than luxuriant gags. With one or two notable exceptions [...] the citations elicit the milder laughter of recognition without increasing our appreciation of Hitchcock, whose own precipices of terror and anxiety are not only terrifying, and not only funnier than the psychological foothills of Mel Brooks, but far crazier than anything in *High Anxiety*'.[19] Even *The Chicago Sun-Times*'s Roger Ebert, who had been one of the most vocal supporters of Brooks's earlier films, had to concede that 'maybe it wasn't such a hot idea for Brooks to spoof Hitchcock in the first place. What he's done, though, is to go ahead and take the Hitchcock material, and almost bury his own comic talent in the attempt to fit things into his satirical formula. [...] It's one thing to kid the self-conscious seriousness of a Western or a horror movie. It's another to take on a director of such sophistication that half the audience won't even get the in-jokes the other half is laughing at'.[20]

Interestingly, the passing years have done little to ameliorate popular opinion with regard to *High Anxiety*, with critical division persisting in more recent reviews of the film. In a retrospective of the film for *The Chicago Reader*, Jonathan Rosenbaum notes that the film is 'not everything one wants it to be, but Mel Brooks's parody of Hitchcock, in which he plays a psychiatrist, has enough high spirits to guide it over some of the rough and low spots; he does a particularly nice bit singing in a nightclub. If you can put up with his usual hit-or-miss attack, you might find yourself amused'.[21] *Movie Metropolis*'s James Plath opined that '*High Anxiety* comes closer in tone and approach to *Young Frankenstein*

(1974) than anything else of Brooks', though in truth there probably aren't as many classic, laugh-out-loud moments. Perhaps that's because while Brooks stayed pretty close to the *Frankenstein* plot, in this one he gets kind of caught up in his own fascination with all of the Hitchcock films to where the parody starts to get a little fuzzy in places. The allusions themselves can be dizzying'.[22] And commentator Tom Becker voiced an analytical viewpoint which has become largely representative of the modern critical community when he remarked that *'High Anxiety* lacks the freewheeling spirit of *Blazing Saddles* and spot-on inventiveness of *Young Frankenstein*. Part of the problem seems to be Brooks' efforts to make this a faithful and affectionate tribute. The Hitchcock-specific gags work to a point, but [...] the parodies rarely rise above the level of sit-com. It's like Brooks knows the words, but he can't hear the music, and we end up with lot of fairly obvious Hitchcock riffs that tend to go on too long and boast little in the way of style. *High Anxiety* is a funny idea that just never comes together as well as it should'.[23]

In spite of its generally tepid appraisal by reviewers, *High Anxiety* was nominated for two Golden Globe Awards in 1978 in the categories of Best Motion Picture: Musical/ Comedy and Best Motion Picture Actor: Musical/ Comedy for Brooks's headlining performance. Perhaps even more significantly for Brooks, the film also famously attracted the approval of Alfred Hitchcock himself. Brooks explains that:

> [Hitchcock] eventually saw a rough cut of *High Anxiety*. He enjoyed it. But he said nothing after it. He just left. I [thought he] wasn't happy. The next day, about 11 o'clock in the morning, I get this enormous, beautiful case of Chateau Haut-Brion 1961. That was almost 20 years old [at the time]. I mean, it was priceless. And there were magnums, six of them, in a wooden case. Haut-Brion. I mean, oh my God.[24]

If imitation is genuinely the sincerest form of flattery, it appeared that Hitchcock had taken *High Anxiety* in the manner in which it had been intended and thus was to judge Brooks's tribute fondly. The film had been a modest commercial success, and one which had kept Brooks in the public eye. Yet it had also been witness to his most explicit advocacy of personal liberty since the unvarnished encouragement of individual and social emancipation in *Blazing Saddles,* deploying some classic Hitchcockian themes – the threat of looming incarceration, paranoia surrounding personal harm or even death, and personal inability to combat inner demons – to emphasise the need for continual vigilance where freedom in all its manifold guises is concerned. Throughout the seventies, Brooks had returned again and again to the issue of liberty, warning against the dangers and unacceptability of avaricious obsession in *The Twelve Chairs*, bigotry and social segregation in *Blazing Saddles*, individual isolation in *Young Frankenstein*, and creative stagnation in *Silent Movie*. With *High Anxiety*'s clamorous defence of personal autonomy in the face of covetous scheming, latent peril and the wrongful social stigma related to mental health, Brooks had effectively bookended the decade by presenting themes which typified his stance on individual and collective liberation in an unambiguous and typically distinctive manner, whilst setting the scene for a rather more broadly encompassing exploration of freedom in his next feature.

# REFERENCES

1. Mel Brooks, in David Bianculli, 'Fresh Air: Mel Brooks – "I'm An EGOT; I Don't Need Any More"', on *National Public Radio*, 20 May 2013.
   <http://www.npr.org/2013/12/27/256597762/mel-brooks-im-an-egot-i-dont-need-any-more>
2. Maurice Yacowar, *The Comic Art of Mel Brooks* (W.H. Allen, 1982), pp. 176-78.
3. Robert Alan Crick, *The Big Screen Comedies of Mel Brooks* (Jefferson: McFarland and Company, 2009) [2002], pp. 110-12.
4. Yacowar, pp. 178-79.
5. Mel Brooks, in Arthur Cooper, 'Blazing Anxieties: Mel Brooks is Just a Little Bit Crazy', in *Mademoiselle*, August 1981.
   <http://www.brookslyn.com/print/Mademoiselle-8-1981/Mademoiselle-8-1981.php>
6. Mel Brooks, in Jerry Bauer, 'Mel Brooks: A Revealing Dialogue with the World's Funniest Man', in *Adelina Magazine*, February 1980.
   <http://www.brookslyn.com/print/Adelina1980/Adelina1980.php>
7. David Desser and Lester D. Friedman, *American Jewish Filmmakers*, 2nd edn (Chicago: University of Illinois Press, 2004), p. 145.
8. Crick, p. 108.
9. Mel Brooks, in Philip Fleishman, 'Interview with Mel Brooks', in *Maclean's Magazine*, 17 April 1978.
   <http://www.brookslyn.com/print/Maclean04-17-78/Maclean04-17-78.php>.
10. Richard Nelson-Jones, *Effective Thinking Skills* (London: Sage Publications, 2004) [1996], p. 18.
11. Crick, p. 111.
12. Georgette S. Fox, *Masters of Evil: A Study of the Archvillain in Film and Television* (San Bernadino: Borgo Press, 1998), p. 53.
13. Yacowar, p. 179.
14. Desser and Friedman, pp. 144-45.
15. Gloria Withalm, '"How Did You Find Us?" – "We Read the Script!": A Special Case of Self-Reference in the Movies', in *Semiotics of the Media: State of the Art, Projects, and Perspectives*, ed. by Winfried Nöth (Berlin: Walter de Gruyter, 1997), 255-268, p. 259.
16. Keyvan Sarkhosh, 'Metalepsis in Popular Comedy Film', in *Metalepsis in Popular Culture*, ed. by Karin Kukkonen and Sonja Klimek (Berlin: Walter de Gruyter Ltd., 2011), 171-95, p. 184.
17. Gerald Mast, *The Comic Mind: Comedy and the Movies*, 2nd edn (Chicago: University of Chicago Press, 1979), p. 312.
18. Yacowar, p. 184.
19. Molly Haskell, 'Hokey Hitchcock', in *New York Magazine*, 16 January 1978, 47-48, p. 47.
20. Roger Ebert, 'High Anxiety', in *The Chicago Sun-Times*, 1 January 1978.
    <http://www.rogerebert.com/reviews/high-anxiety-1978>
21. Jonathan Rosenbaum, 'High Anxiety', in *The Chicago Reader*, January 2000.
    <http://www.chicagoreader.com/chicago/high-anxiety/Film?oid=1063372>
22. James Plath, 'High Anxiety', in *Movie Metropolis*, 14 May 2010.
    <http://moviemet.com/review/high-anxiety-blu-ray-review>
23. Tom Becker, 'High Anxiety', in *DVD Verdict*, 17 May 2010.
    <http://www.dvdverdict.com/reviews/highanxietybluray.php>
24. Mel Brooks, in Carla Lalli Music, 'Mel Brooks on Omelettes, Coffee, and the Inimitable Appetite of Alfred Hitchcock', in *Bon Appetit*, 17 May 2013.
    <http://www.bonappetit.com/people/celebrities/article/mel-brooks-on-omelettes-coffee-and-the-inimitable-appetite-of-alfred-hitchcock>

# 7

# HISTORY OF THE WORLD: PART I (1981)

WITH *HISTORY OF THE WORLD: PART I*, Mel Brooks was to make a return to the kind of quick-fire sketch format that had first established his career as a writer for television many years earlier. The film marked a break from its tightly-plotted forerunner, its considerably looser structure proving much closer to the madcap genre-hopping of *Blazing Saddles* but with even an greater extent of narrative flexibility thanks to its episodic nature. However, whereas this unrestrictive approach was to aid the film in some ways, it would also hinder it in many others.

For the first time in several years, Brooks was to write the screenplay for his film without a collaborator, in addition to producing, directing and starring in it (in multiple roles). However, just as *High Anxiety* had not been a parody of any one specific film but rather a spoof of the entire Hitchcockian cinematic phenomenon, so too *History of the World: Part I* would turn out to be more than simply a send-up of the kind of large-canvas historical epic that had so preoccupied Hollywood throughout the fifties and sixties. Indeed, while Brooks uses the film to uncompromisingly parody the characteristics and stylistic conventions of the historical cinematic genre (especially the famous epics of classical antiquity, such as Mervyn LeRoy's *Quo Vadis*, 1951; William Wyler's *Ben-Hur*, 1959, and Stanley Kubrick's *Spartacus*, 1960), he generally chooses not to provide detailed commentary regarding the specific social, cultural or political dynamics of the historical environments that he explores, instead focusing upon one unifying narrative theme – that of the need for social justice in order to avoid the domination of the many by a privileged few. In advancing this position, he methodically and repeatedly rails against persecution of all kinds throughout the film – from religious oppression to plutocratic domination – in a manner which is arguably almost as forceful as had been the case when he had responded to racist bigotry in *Blazing Saddles* and personal discrimination in *Young Frankenstein*.

The film's title is also a subtle historical joke by Brooks. As historian Robert Lawson-Peebles has observed, *History of the World* was the name of an unfinished text by aristocratic Elizabethan explorer Sir Walter Raleigh (c.1554-1618) which was composed while Raleigh was imprisoned at the Tower of London on charges of treason. Spanning five volumes and a million words, Raleigh's epic work 'only reached as far as the second Macedonian War in 130BC', and – in spite of the unprecedented scope that its title suggested – ultimately remained incomplete at the time of his death.[1] Thus Brooks's own film, just like the tragically-curtailed scholarly masterpiece of Walter Raleigh, would only delineate a tiny fraction of the vast sweep of human cultural achievement; like his illustrious predecessor, though for rather different reasons, there would be no continuation beyond the self-imposed conclusion to Brooks's 'historical' account of human society and culture.

*History of the World: Part I* begins at the dawn of time, where we briefly witness the evolution of primitive human beings from *Homo Erectus* into *Homo Sapiens*, a transition which marks the beginning of our species as we know it. Then, briskly moving into the Stone Age, the leader of an ancient tribe (Sid Caesar) encounters difficulty harnessing the newly-discovered phenomenon of fire, before his fellow clan members eventually move on to revolutionary concepts such as marriage and early ceremonial burial. However, their unsophisticated existence soon becomes enlivened by the discovery of creative pursuits such as music and visual art, which in turn leads to the inevitable appearance of the first art critic (whose judgement turns out to be anything but affirmative).

Moving on to the Bronze Age, we join Moses (Mel Brooks) as

he receives the three stone tablets of the Fifteen Commandments from God (Brooks again) at the summit of Mount Sinai. Unfortunately for Moses, an ill-fated mishap with one of the tablets leads to the necessity for some quick thinking – the Jewish people are swiftly introduced to the (rather more familiar) concept of Ten Commandments instead. Staying with the Biblical theme, we then leap through several thousand years of history from the Old Testament to the New Testament, when the narrative picks up again in the Roman Empire of the early Common Era.

In Rome, cradle of modern civilisation, commerce is booming in a busy marketplace as soothsayers, entrepreneurs and even early plumbers ply their wares to a (largely) receptive public. However, it seems that not all Romans are prosperous. Stand-up philosopher Comicus (Mel Brooks) is in the process of trying to persuade an unemployment exchange clerk (Bea Arthur) of the importance of his craft when he is interrupted by his agent Swiftus Lazarus (Ron Carey), who brings good news – Comicus will be performing at Caesar's Palace later that day. Unlike its latter-day Las Vegas counterpart, this venue is the literal official residence of the reigning Caesar, Emperor Nero (Dom DeLuise) – and also soon to be the biggest gig of Comicus's career.

As Comicus and Swiftus are leaving the marketplace, they spot Josephus (Gregory Hines), a fast-talking Ethiopian man who – having remained unpurchased during a slave auction – has been sentenced to death at the Colosseum. Swiftus is impressed by Josephus's quick-witted attempts to evade his fate and resolves to sign him up with the talent agency, but they are interrupted when a commotion is caused by a nearby merchant savagely beating his horse. Miriam (Mary-Margaret Humes), one of the emperor's vestal virgins, attempts to spare the animal from his owner's brutal cruelty; when she is similarly attacked, Comicus steps in and knocks the vicious trader out cold. Swiftus recognises the horse as Miracle, once the fastest equine performer at the Circus Maximus but now reduced to a more humble station. Just as Josephus is on the verge of being taken into custody, the timely arrival of the Empress Nympho (Madeline Kahn) saves him from his lethal destiny – Miriam manages to persuade her to employ the ill-fated Ethiopian and add his talents to the royal staff. Comicus is clearly smitten by the beautiful Miriam, but knows that her ceremonial role makes any potential romantic relationship between them an impossibility.

Arriving at Caesar's Palace, victorious General Marcus Vindictus (Shecky Greene) regales the jaded Emperor Nero with tales of foreign battles before presenting him with an ornate bathing vessel and a seemingly-endless array of treasures plundered from Rome's foes. The flatulent Nero writhes in ecstasy within the bath as servants cover him with shining trinkets. While the loutish emperor's attention is diverted, Vindictus attempts to court the affections of Nympho but his attentions are playfully (yet firmly) rebuffed.

Next in the court's line-up of entertainments is a routine by Comicus. At first, his jokes go down favourably with Nero and his court, but things quickly go awry when the emperor takes umbrage after the stand-up philosopher mocks the overweight (given that the corpulent Nero is far from trim himself). Desperate to avoid causing offence, Comicus nonetheless manages to dig himself in even deeper ('The Roman Senate is the best legislature that money can buy!'), to the point that the emperor becomes affronted enough to order his execution. Worse still, Josephus – when serving Nero more wine – accidentally spills the contents of his amphora, soaking the emperor and thus resulting in his own death being ordered (once again). At Miriam's urging, Nympho tries to intercede on behalf of the two men; Nero thus proclaims that instead of being executed, Comicus and Josephus will fight each other to the death.

After a distinctly half-hearted battle, Comicus gains the upper-hand and pleads with Nero to spare his friend's life. The emperor will not be moved, however, and Comicus discovers that he is not capable of killing – even to save his own skin. Thus the two men resolve to fight back against Caesar's personal guard and, improbably enough, manage to make a getaway. Splitting up, Comicus only narrowly manages to escape a pursuing band of guards when Miriam pulls him into a hidden passageway.

Later, Nympho is inspecting a group of potential escorts for the evening orgy which have been selected by her personal assistant Competence (Dena Dietrich). They are all unaware that Miriam has secreted Comicus behind a drape, thus helping him evade the emperor's men. Shortly after, the palace guard arrives in the empress's chambers with the intention of searching the area, but are thwarted when Nympho objects to their presence.

The guard leader grows suspicious when he spots Josephus impersonating a eunuch, and decides to test the fugitive's impotence by watching his reaction when exotic dancer Caladonia (Diane Day) performs before him. But in spite of his best attempts at self-discipline, it quickly becomes apparent that the former slave is indeed no eunuch; with the guards once again in close pursuit, Josephus makes a break for it once more. Realising that he is heading for the Senate building, Miriam and Comicus set off in pursuit.

Following a brief reunion in the Senate cloakroom, Josephus and Comicus arrange a rendezvous with Miriam and Swiftus whereby they will all attempt to escape from Rome – and from Nero's clutches. Following a madcap chase through the streets, the foursome eventually encounter Miracle – the horse who had earlier been saved by Comicus. Together, they jump into the cart being drawn by Miracle and race out of the city into the Italian countryside. All appears to be going well until Josephus spots a crop of Roman Red ('wacky weedus') and calls a halt while he attempts to harvest it. His fellow fugitives watch in confusion as he rolls the freshly-picked leaves into a gigantic roll of papyrus, then lights it at the rear of their cart. The Ethiopian's plan soon becomes clear, though, when the smoke from the enormous joint has an immediate effect on the crew of the pursuing Roman chariots; instantly becoming mellowed out, they soon lose all co-ordination, allowing the fleeing friends to gain some extra ground.

Reaching a large body of water, Miracle comes to a halt as the escapees' getaway route seems to have been abruptly cut off. Before they can bemoan their bad luck, Moses appears – somewhat inexplicably – and creates a path through the river for them in the style of the parting of the Red Sea. (As they continue their escape, however, it becomes apparent that the ancient Jewish leader is in the process of being held up by a bandit, lifting up his legendary staff only because his wallet is being stolen.) Their route to freedom now clear once again, the fugitives head for a seaport where a ship bound for Judea is about to set sail.

Some time later, the group have arrived in Jerusalem – now free from Nero's grasp – and are looking for work in order to support themselves. Miriam spots a recruitment notice for a 'cashier, waiter and dishwasher' on the door of a restaurant, and she, Josephus and Comicus resolve to apply for the various posts. Swiftus, on the other hand, decides to head for Galilee in search of new opportunities. Comicus gains employment as the waiter, but his efforts are derided by the establishment's domineering maitre 'd (Fritz Feld). He wanders into a private engagement being held in one of the restaurant's anterooms and discovers Jesus Christ (John Hurt) and the twelve Apostles taking part in the Last Supper. Comicus's enquiries about their meal orders are met with angry dismissal, given that they are discussing the forthcoming prospect of Christ's betrayal. However, their gathering is further interrupted by the arrival of Leonardo Da Vinci (Art Metrano), about a millennium and a half earlier than anticipated, to paint a portrait of the supper. Leonardo arranges the room into a scene closely resembling his famous fresco, but with one unexpected addition – the grinning Comicus remains in the background, his circular serving tray forming a brightly shining halo around Christ's head.

Moving forward to medieval Europe, the action picks up again during the Spanish Inquisition. Grand Inquisitor of the Catholic Church, Tomas de Torquemada (Mel Brooks), is introduced in a grim monastic setting, giving a sombre warning to heretics and unbelievers to repent or die... before launching into a deeply anachronistic song-and-dance act which owes more than a little to Busby Berkeley. Having failed to persuade followers of Judaism to convert to Christianity through theological persuasion, Torquemada is now resorting to barbaric torture ('It's better to lose your skullcap than your skull') to force them to recant their religious beliefs. Aided in his persecution by an army of tap-dancing clergy and synchronised-swimming nuns, Torquemada sets to work on anyone he believes to hold views antithetical to the Christian faith. Jews are seen in various torment-inducing apparatus such as wooden stocks, spike-filled sarcophagi and a huge breaking wheel (which revolves in the manner of a giant fruit machine). Yet for all the agony-inducing suffering that he and his acolytes cause, victims and torturers alike eventually join in with the cavalcade of this deeply odd musical number as it reaches its big finish.

Centuries later, we find ourselves in France on the cusp of revolutionary fervour. The impoverished Madame Defarge (Cloris Leachman), a consumptive innkeeper, looks out on the streets of a

Paris mired in sharp social division – a city where grinding destitution rubs shoulders with incredible opulence. In a closed-door session within her tavern, it becomes clear that she intends to do something about this unwarranted social inequality; addressing a throng of disadvantaged peasants she calls for the death of King Louis XVI, the country's hard-hearted monarch, who continues to take no action to improve the lives of his underprivileged citizens.

Elsewhere, the foppish Count De Monet (Harvey Korman) and his companion Bearnaise (Andreas Voutsinas) are arriving at the royal residence of King Louis (Mel Brooks). Their appearance coincides with a live chess match (featuring various costumed courtiers in the role of the various game pieces) between the monarch and aristocrat Popinjay (Jonathan Cecil), where Louis is quite happily reworking the rules of the game to suit himself. De Monet astutely decides to avoid interrupting Louis, and instead relieves himself after his long journey with the assistance of the bucket-carrying Jacques (also Brooks), a nearby *Garcon de Pisse*. As he empties his bladder, De Monet cannot help but notice that the servant bears an uncanny resemblance to the king.

Once the chess game has been completed – albeit in the most unorthodox way possible – the lascivious Louis is approached by the striking young Mademoiselle Rimbaud (Pamela Stephenson), who begs his royal favour. Her father, Monsieur Rimbaud, had been imprisoned in the Bastille a decade previously for daring to speculate that the country's poor 'weren't so bad'. The king deviously agrees to his release, but only on the condition that Mademoiselle Rimbaud consents to sleep with him. The chaste young woman is scandalised by the frankness of his underhand deal, but decides that she must go against her deep religious convictions if she is to have any chance of saving her father's life.

Some time later, De Monet approaches the king with sobering news. Accounts have reached him of a growing threat of revolution, and – knowing that the aristocracy's survival depends upon a strong and stable monarchy – he pleads with Louis to leave Paris for his own safety. The monarch is puzzled, however; if he is to flee the palace, who will rule the country in his stead? De Monet suggests that Jacques, who will look identical with the right costume and make-up, should take the king's place on the throne. That way, the servant would be executed in the event of a peasant revolt whereas Louis will remain safe at another location.

In the royal chambers of the palace, Jacques is given a thorough makeover as De Monet's decoy scheme is relayed to him. The threat to his personal safety has barely had time to sink in when Mademoiselle Rimbaud arrives, resigned to being ravaged by the lustful monarch. Deeply puzzled by her presence, Jacques refuses to take advantage of the young woman and simply signs a royal pardon for her father there and then. She immediately heads for the Bastille and has Monsieur Rimbaud (Spike Milligan) released from prison, though his years of incarceration have had a deleterious effect on his mental health.

Soon after, De Monet's predictions prove true – violent revolution has gripped Paris at last. Mademoiselle Rimbaud races back to the palace and, still believing Jacques to be the real King Louis, implores him to get to safety before he can be guillotined. However, her supplication comes too late; a gang of angry peasants arrive in the royal chambers, led by Madame Defarge, and seize Jacques in the mistaken belief that he is the reigning monarch. The revolutionaries then take Jacques, Madame Rimbaud and her father to a guillotine at the heart of Paris, where a baying crowd call for their execution. Jacques tries valiantly to prove his innocence, but his attempts at justification fall on deaf ears. As he is being led towards his death, Madame Rimbaud suggests that only a miracle can save him now... when Miracle, the fastest horse in Rome, promptly comes to the rescue, pulling a chariot that carries none other than Josephus (who appears not to have aged a day since his last appearance). The executioners watch in stunned amazement as their prisoners jump down from the scaffold and race away from Paris to safety. Jacques reflects on his somewhat implausible stroke of luck as the four companions quite literally dash towards the end of the film.

Concluding the feature is a trailer for a promised (but never actually produced) sequel, including such improbable sights as 'Hitler on Ice' (a Third Reich-inspired skating show, where the Führer pirouettes athletically to the music of Émile Waldteufel's 'Les Patineurs'), a less than conventional Viking funeral (where the Vikings themselves, rather than their helmets, sport horns), and 'Jews in Space' (an intergalactic epic where a band of spacefaring Jews, in a ship shaped like a gigantic Star of David, work together to protect Hebrew culture from alien attack).

It seems ironic that what was to be Brooks's most adult film, in terms of its profanity and explicit sexual content, would ultimately seem – on the face of it – to also be his most self-indulgently immature. Hardly a scene is allowed to go by without reference to, or the appearance of, excrement, urine or semen, and unsubtle sexual puns are more prolific than in any previous Brooks movie (ranging from the vestal virgins' conveniently-placed 'no entry' signs to the squad of bottomless legionnaires drawn together for Nympho's selection as possible escorts). Yet beyond this deluge of bawdy and scatological humour, *History of the World: Part I* is a film which contains a great deal of anger and righteous resentment – towards social injustice, stolen freedoms and relentless but unnecessary cruelty throughout human history. David Desser and Lester D. Friedman observe that the film 'deflates several golden eras of Western culture, demonstrating that such ages were far less than golden for those not in power – and Jews never were in power',[2] and certainly Brooks appears determined to highlight the commonalities of human behaviour throughout the ages in order to emphasise the universal nature of the problems which face society in the here and now. It seems that as far as Brooks is concerned, there never was a Golden Age to begin with; throughout the various eras of history which are presented, we repeatedly witness the grand iconography of human achievement being systematically deflated, and the indifferent rich standing on the backs of the oppressed poor (quite literally, in the case of Count De Monet, who stamps vindictively upon a procession of peasants unfortunate enough to be caught under the red carpet rolled out to greet him at King Louis's palace). The seriousness of Brooks's social commentary, though naturally cloaked by the film's comic intentions, was nevertheless noted by journalists at the time of release; as Marc Kristal explained:

> Many of Brooks' plans had little to do with making people laugh. [Director Graeme] Clifford says of him : 'Mel is a very perceptive, thoughtful, sensitive, private man. The comedic aspect of his personality is just the public face. Behind that is a totally different individual.' To some degree, this is evident in his film comedies. Brooks describes his first film as a writer-director, *The Producers*, as being about 'the ego and the id, and launching oneself toward glory'; much of its humor derives from a satire of Nazism. *Blazing Saddles* dealt with racial hatred, albeit hilariously. And Brooks claims to have been motivated to make *History of the World, Part I* by the inequity at

Versailles.³

By using the grand sweep of history to make his point that social inequality has been common to all times and all cultures, Brooks ran a risk of making his film appear fragmented at a time when narrative cohesion appeared more crucial for his purposes than ever. There is also the point – which Robert Alan Crick raises – that as Brooks draws an epic arc running through all of human history from the Neolithic to the eighteenth century, it seems puzzling that he should choose to focus on such a select handful of time periods... and, even then, to concentrate on some eras much longer than on others. 'Where are Attila the Hun and Galileo and Joan of Arc and Columbus and Shakespeare?',⁴ Crick laments, and indeed even considering Brooks's strategy of introducing characters and concepts which are wildly out of their own time (often with hilarious results) to bridge the gap between modernity and the past, the effect of this sleight of hand eventually wears thin with overuse in ways that were rarely the case in earlier efforts such as *Blazing Saddles* or *Young Frankenstein*.

Maurice Yacowar opines that the film exhibited Brooks's 'characteristic energy and generosity of gag, [but] fell short of the qualities of rigour and coherence that distinguished his earlier works. The overall effect was of an artist so involved with the machinery of his budget (and how to spend it) that he skimped on the concentration and control. [...] The film is not so much a history of the world as a parody of various film types that have purported to represent man's past'.⁵ Brooks attempts to use familiar cinematic tropes and conceits as a kind of shorthand to suggest not historical realism but rather the kind of accounts of the past that the audience had come to recognise from famous cinematic historical tales across the decades. Thus the film's opening at the dawn of time features the famous booming notes of Richard Strauss's 'Also Sprach Zarathustra' (1896), in a manner that is instantly identifiable as a parody of Stanley Kubrick's legendary *2001: A Space Odyssey* (1968)... only for the profound prehistoric revelations of the early film to be rapidly debased into a communal bout of frenzied onanism. Likewise, much significance is placed on Comicus's big break as a stand-up philosopher at Caesar's Palace only for the audience to discover, in spite of assumptions to the contrary, that the building closely resembles the renowned Las Vegas casino of the same name rather than the expected architecture of classical antiquity. Deanne Schultz observes that 'the incongruities in *History of the World Part I* are intended to produce laughs, but they also reveal – and subvert – a sophisticated sense of historical chronology',[6] and certainly there is little doubt that Brooks carefully judges the degree and incidence of his deliberate anachronisms as much as he does the targets of his sharply satirical jibes. For instance, it seems pointless to quibble on points of historical accuracy – such as the fact that Emperor Tiberius, not Nero, reigned in Rome at the time of the Last Supper – in a film where Leonardo da Vinci turns up by appointment (fifteen centuries before the time of his birth) in order to paint the Last Supper. Certainly it is impossible not to admire Brooks's audacity in introducing Romans with ghetto-blasters listening to 'Funkytown' by Lipps Inc., or Josephus – when asked what part of Ethiopia he is from – immediately replying '125th Street'. As Jacques makes plain when he asks Mademoiselle Rimbaud, in pre-Revolutionary France, about her unusual-sounding name – 'Rimbaud? Is that French?' – this is not a film where precision of historical detail will ever be allowed to compete with a potential laugh. As Hannu Salmi has suggested, with the work of Mel Brooks 'there is never any doubt that all the anachronisms that appear are intentionally humorous. Films are always communicative events where the spectators arrive with a set of expectation formed by advertising and other information received beforehand. Spectators coming to see *The History of the World: Part I* are prepared to laugh from the start'.[7]

Because the audience had a good idea what to expect from Brooks's comic approach by this point in his career, he was able to play hard and fast with anachronistic terms and devices to comic effect – albeit with varying degrees of success. *Playboy* founder Hugh Hefner appears in a very brief cameo, effectively playing himself as a Roman entrepreneur (who has just invented the new breakthrough of 'the centrefold'), while Moses – arguably the greatest leader in Jewish history – is memorably reinvented by Brooks as a crotchety old patriarch muttering away to himself in Yiddish. ('Wow!', he exclaims – without much real enthusiasm – as God miraculously produces the three tablets of the Fifteen Commandments out of thin air.) Ron Carey's amiable Swiftus Lazarus is a parody of famous Hollywood talent agent Irving

'Swifty' Lazar (1907-93), just one of many showbiz allusions to crop up throughout the film. Likewise, Gregory Hines (appearing in his big screen debut) provides a memorably hip Josephus, a character who is so cool that he manages to transcend not only the conventions of the period in which he appears but later proves that he is able to confound the march of history itself. In a manner resembling the placid unflappability of *Blazing Saddles*'s Sheriff Bart, Josephus manages to overcome the twin impediments of racial discrimination and class-based oppression within the Roman Empire, providing the resourcefulness and improvisational talents necessary to make good an escape from Nero's court. Josephus is also able to lend a certain degree of malleability to his cultural identity when necessity calls: ironically foreshadowing the later cruelty meted out to innocent Jewish citizens during the Spanish Inquisition sequence, he desperately tries to convince his captors that he is actually Jewish in order to escape his execution, reckoning that only Christians are regularly thrown to lions at the Colosseum (and even asserting that none other than the illustrious 'Sammus Davis Jr.' will vouch for his heritage). But as only the ruling classes appear to be immune from the repression and unfairness that they administer, it eventually transpires that inventiveness – the ability to out-think the oppressor – can succeed where attempts to mollify established convention prove inadequate. Here, as Henry Jenkins has stated, Josephus's key role in the film is congruent with the wider exploration of involuntary personal subjugation which runs through much of Brooks's film-making:

> Brooks often couples issues of class and taste with those of ethnicity (in this case, Jewishness), race (often in terms of the blackness of some of his co-stars) and sexuality (persistent references to queer identities and desires). Brooks uses his 'low' humor and clownish status to speak about other forms of marginality and exclusion in American culture, a practice that made his films, especially those of the 1960s and 1970s, more pointed and topical than they might seem to contemporary viewers.[8]

As had been the case in so many of his earlier features, Brooks takes no prisoners when it comes to assailing ignorance, bigotry and greed. Yacowar correctly observes that 'behind the varying degrees of wit, corn, and offensiveness, lurks Brooks's familiar moral indignation. For Brooks still believes that the price of liberty is eternal belligerence. So even in the slave-fight from *Spartacus* and the *Birdman of Alcatraz* parodies, Brooks's subject is not just the film tradition and its idealising falsity, but the unrelieved history of human cruelty'.9 This fact is well established in the Roman Empire sequence when John Myhers's Senate Leader tables a motion to curtail spending on the opulent residences of senators in order to improve housing standards for the poor. 'How does the senate vote?' he asks, only to receive a seemingly-inevitable chorus of 'Fuck the poor!' in response. Thus the issue is promptly dropped and the inequitable status quo preserved. Similarly, Dom DeLuise's loutishly vulgarian Emperor Nero is insatiably gluttonous, farting and belching his way through endless palace entertainments while his courtiers cower in fear of falling from his favour. (Keen to maintain the leader's microscopic attention span, Marcus Vindictus is reduced to presenting the spoils of Roman military conquest as though they were a procession of prizes on a TV game-show.) Yet it is in the film's French Revolution sequence that Brooks lets loose his main fusillade against oppression, summed up in an opening scene where Cloris Leachman's Madame Defarge laments the near-total lack of individual freedoms for the citizens of France:

| | |
|---|---|
| MADAME DEFARGE: | We have no rights! We have no say! We have no dignity! We are so poor, we do not even have a language – just a stupid accent. |
| PEASANT: | She's right. She's right! We all talk like Maurice Chevalier! Aw-haw-haw! |

This juxtaposition of damning social criticism and arch self-awareness occurs right throughout the film, though for some reason the jagged edge of Brooks's analysis never seems to cut quite as deeply here as it had done in *Blazing Saddles*, or even *The Twelve Chairs*. In a society where the reigning monarch quite happily uses members of his poverty-stricken populace for target practice in place of clay pigeons, it is quite obvious that Brooks intends to leave no stone unturned in his quest to illuminate the restriction of personal freedoms by privileged minorities throughout history – no matter how comically exaggerated his metaphors have to be in order to make that point. But if state tyranny is in Brooks's sights for much of the film, organised religion certainly doesn't receive a free hand either. Reinventing

Tomas de Torquemada as an acrobatic song-and-dance man, complete with fervent mugging to camera, Brooks parodies one of the worst periods of religious excess history has ever witnessed by successively highlighting the many ways that the Inquisition's purpose and methods deviated from the tenets of the faith upon which the church was based. Desser and Friedman have made the point that:

> Brooks finds little comfort in the kind words and gentle messages of official Christianity. As a student of the Holocaust, he fully knows that few Christian leaders did anything to aid those suffering in concentration camps. As a student of Russian literature, he understands that anti-Semitism remains deeply embedded within Christian dogma. [...] Such emotions never fully disappear from Brooks's works, and he never misses an opportunity to spit in the face of organized Christian religion.[10]

Interestingly, of course, Brooks never targets individuals (such as Mademoiselle Rimbaud) for holding genuine religious convictions; his ire is exclusively reserved for those who hypocritically use religion as a means of advancing venal or otherwise dishonest ends. In the same way that he had derided *The Twelve Chairs*'s Father Fyodor for his covetous nature and disregard of his congregation, and disparages Reverend Johnson of *Blazing Saddles* for his singular lack of the very convictions of faith that he professes to preach, Brooks heaps scorn on Torquemada's claims to improve society by cleansing it of anyone unfortunate enough to hold a view that differs from his own – the very antithesis of a theology that is based upon tenets of peaceful coexistence and mutual understanding. Yacowar notes that 'the zany absurdity and self-reflexive nature of the film are, like the Spanish Inquisition number, a reminder both of Brooks's joy at the power of film and of his suspicion of its dulling, trivialising nature',[11] and certainly the Torquemada sequence provides an intriguing contrast between the gloomy, unerring brutality of the Dark Ages and the glossy professionalism of the brightly-lit Hollywood musical. The extent of Torquemada's savagery is by no means understated, but Brooks revels in the irony of presenting the Grand Inquisitor as a genial showman who orchestrates his blood-soaked barbarism with a song in his heart (and his hand firmly on the handle of a rack). Using a gigantic revolving Menorah in the swimming pool during the Inquisition sequence as a symbol of the oppressed Jewish faith, while a grinning Torquemada is flanked by tap-dancing monks and nuns attired in Esther Williams-style swimming costumes during the routine's conclusion, Brooks's contempt for religion's potential abuses as a state mechanism could not be made more obvious. Given the bold nature of this criticism's implementation, however, it is intriguing to note that even he wondered if the subject could possibly balance censure with humour in a manner which would please audiences; as he confided in an interview with Arthur Cooper:

> Mel Brooks was very, very nervous. Here he was, putting the final touches on his $11-million comedy, *History of the World – Part 1*, and he was worried that the film might offend. 'I don't know how audiences are going to like the Spanish Inquisition sequence', he is saying, seated in his Hollywood office behind a desk that might have been an aircraft carrier during World War II. 'I have three Jews, each on a wheel. Torquemada pulls the handle and the wheels spin around. If three rabbis come up, you win a lot of money. I mean it's very dangerous to put Jews on racks and have Catholics torture them, and get laughs'.[12]

Paradoxically, of course, it was to transpire that the film's release did not so much generate criticism for its treatment of religious subject matter as it did for the employment of its supporting characters in fleeting and largely undeveloped roles; the sequence featuring Torquemada and his victims is so brief, the audience has little time to sympathise with the plight of the individual Jewish prisoners or to gain more than a momentary appreciation of the Inquisition's violence and cruelty. This fed into a wider critique of the film's sketch-like structure by reviewers at the time, perhaps best typified by Roger Ebert's observation that there 'is nothing inherently funny about Jews, Catholics, nuns, blacks, and gays. They can all conceivably provide the makings of comedy, of course, but in *History of the World* Brooks doesn't have the patience to introduce a character and then create a comic situation about him. He introduces the character and expects us to laugh at the character himself'.[13] This view seems all the more compelling when considering Brooks's overarching intention to promote equality for all, illuminating unfairness so that it may be challenged and lambasting the erroneousness of unthinking prejudice. Thus the very conscious employment of Hollywood glamour to delineate the violence and gore of the Dark Ages was, in the view of some commentators, a strategy which proved to be rather too clever for its own good. Yacowar, for instance, argues that with the Spanish Inquisition sequence 'Brooks is practising what he preaches against: a spectacular entertainment industry that ignores the reality of human cruelty, and peddles palliative illusions about human goodness and success'.[14]

The Inquisition sequence directly follows the scenes which take place during the Last Supper, and here Brooks treats the central figure of Christianity with surprising respect and restraint. John Hurt, who here plays Jesus Christ, had famously appeared in the title role of David Lynch's biopic of John Merrick, *The Elephant Man* (1980), which Brooks had only recently produced. Hurt's portrayal is considerate and presented in a totally straight-faced way; he even brings some much-needed gravitas to the somewhat heavy-handed blasphemy gag, where Comicus repeatedly mutters 'Jesus!' only for the historical figure to reply 'Yes?' in a manner which rapidly outstays its welcome. The visual inventiveness of the recreation of Leonardo's *Last Supper* painting aside, the whole Judean-set coda to the Roman Empire sequence appears to have been singularly concocted in order to bring Comicus over to Jerusalem for a few gags at the expense of the Apostles – though in fairness to Brooks, they are often good gags (not least their expressions when, as Christ reveals his coming betrayal, Comicus asks if they all want to pay separately or have separate bills). It does, however, introduce a certain illogicality to proceedings, almost as though the Last Supper sequence had been added to the screenplay as an afterthought; when Josephus bemoans that it is the fate of Christians to be thrown to the lions by Nero, we later discover that Christ has yet to be crucified and resurrected, meaning that the Christian religion did not yet exist as an identifiable phenomenon by the Romans or anyone else. (Though not to labour the point, in a film where Comicus arrives in Caesar's court to the strains of 'Hooray for Hollywood' this kind of continuity criticism is somewhat surplus to requirements.)

What makes the inconsistency of *History of the World: Part I* so frustrating is the fact that when the material is entertaining, it is often very entertaining – but sadly, when it falls flat the effect is equally pronounced. To some extent, its variation in overall quality may owe something to the fractured nature of its narrative, which rarely allows characters to develop beyond anything other than ciphers and therefore limits the audience's emotional investment. Thus any dip in the amount of laughs deriving from the on-screen action seems all the more apparent, and emphasises the point that the film's overall methodology ultimately differs from that of Brooks's previous features. Beth Edith Bonnstetter makes the point that:

> *History of the World, Part I*, rather than one continuous narrative, is divided into five sketches of varying length, the longest being 'The Roman Empire' and 'The French Revolution'. [...] Like *Young Frankenstein*, *History of the World, Part I* is also a mosaic, but its mosaic has a great deal more satiric elements in it than parodic elements. To be sure, *History* also has parodic and carnivalesque elements, and a seeming emphasis on the grotesque. It too is a comedy. However, how the film operates rhetorically makes it more satiric than parodic. In other words, *History*'s 'grotesque' moments make a specific social critique, and it also contains ironic elements in its mosaic. The film maintains a hierarchical distance between critic (Brooks) and criticized (Caesar and King Louis XVI), and intertextuality and inversion is used differently in this film.[15]

Although *History of the World: Part I* contains much that is original, to its detriment some aspects of the film almost feel as though they are an attempt at gathering together a compilation of highlights cribbed from some of Brooks's earlier work. As mentioned earlier, thanks to Gregory Hines's assured performance Josephus is the very epitome of genre-transcendent cool in much the same vein as Cleavon Little's Bart had been in *Blazing Saddles*, and the character exhibits similar traits of ingenuity and likeability. Likewise, Fritz Feld revisits his Maitre d' role from *Silent Movie* without retreading similar ground, memorably officiating over the restaurant hosting the Last Supper, 'The Sign of the Fish'. But other similarities seem considerably more contrived. Harvey Korman's character Count De Monet must repeatedly correct the pronunciation of his name by others (it is usually misspoken as 'Count da Money'), as had been the case with Hedley Lamarr in *Blazing Saddles*... only this time, the joke is significantly overplayed. Josephus's comically elongated tongue at the sight of Diane Day's dancer Caladonia recalls some of that earlier film's exaggeratedly cartoon-like sight gags with less sophistication, while making its comeback from *Young Frankenstein* (though not for the last time) was the 'walk this way' joke. But on the occasions where Brooks signposts his humour as being deliberately corny, the gambit almost always works effectively. When Comicus starts his stand-up act with age-old chestnuts like 'I just got back from Venice, and boy, are my arms tired!', the audience knows exactly what to expect and appreciates it all the more. 'Sooth! Sooth! We give great sooth!' cries Charlie Callas's soothsayer, immediately turning occult mysticism into a sideshow attraction in one easy move. And occasionally some of the lines are so old and timeworn that they cannot help but raise a smile on account of their very familiarity:

> SENATOR #1: In pecuniam, sic transit gloria.
> SENATOR #2: I didn't know Gloria was sick!

The film also benefits from an array of characteristic Brooksian absurdity, not least in the way that he occasionally lays bare the nuts and bolts of film-making. This is perhaps best typified by the cleverly perceptive trick in the palace, where Jacques races along a corridor to discover that it is merely a painted backdrop with an uncannily accurate perspective – a well-realised visual conceit that has more than a hint of M.C. Escher about it. The authoritative tones of the legendary Orson Welles, acting as the narrator, often offer up a stentorian, commanding account of historical fact, only to be completely undermined by the cheerfully lewd on-screen action that the viewer is actually witnessing. And, of course, Josephus's effortless hopping forward through history from ancient Rome to the French Revolution ends the film on a high note – not only are we left to wonder exactly how Jacques even recognises the smooth-talking Ethiopian (having never met him prior to the point of their meeting), but when questioned about his apparent time-travelling abilities Josephus resolves the issue with the most elegant of non-explanations: 'Oh, don't be square, mon cher. Movies is magic!' As far as Brooks is concerned, that is all the clarification we need, and for some reason the honesty of Josephus's happily specious elucidation works more than adequately. And thus, as Crick has argued, the film's climax 'provides one of [Brooks's] all-time cleverest endings, brilliantly blasting all logic and, as in *Blazing Saddles*, celebrating film's unique capacity for anything-can-happen unpredictability. [...] It's all nonsense, and thus pure Mel Brooks: preposterous, inventive, totally off-the-wall'.16

Brooks provides many other moments of surrealism in his efforts to compel a head-on collision between (mock-)historical environments and the present day, among them the stoned, Lindy-hopping Roman legionnaires, Nero's request for a small lyre/ liar (who desperately protests 'the cheque is in the mail!'), and the grubby Madame Defarge knitting garments to the sound of a manual typewriter, later managing to accidentally deflate one of her own breasts with her knitting needle. It is in his razor-sharp attention to small detail that Brooks provides the film with its occasional flashes of inspired lunacy; the bizarrely poignant scenario of Monsieur Rimbaud 'freeing' his menagerie of dead birds, or the tongue-in-cheek appearance of Swiftus's hourglass wristwatch, linger in the mind much longer than any amount of double-entendres or near-the-knuckle explicitness. But as is so always the case in Brooks's movies, his rapier wit inevitably winds up being the real star of the show, ensuring that even the less successful sequences of the film benefit from a healthy supply of pithy one-liners. Occasionally this may simply be the wry recognition of the dramatic format being reflected by the dialogue ('But – dot dot dot – you don't understand!' blurts Jacques, upon being mistaken for King Louis), but at other times Brooks is able to completely subvert the seemingly-serious nature of a particular scene by using dialogic discourse to highlight a welcome vein of underlying absurdity:

> JACQUES: Last request! Last request!
> EXECUTIONER: What is it?
> JACQUES: Novocaine!
> EXECUTIONER: Wait a moment. [*Confers with colleague.*] There is no such thing known to medical science.
> JACQUES: I'll wait!

In multiple starring roles which require him to play characters as wide-ranging as a stand-up philosopher and *le Garcon de Pisse*, by way of a Grand Inquisitor and one of the greatest prophets of the Abrahamic religions, Brooks works hard to generate laughs in front of the camera as well as behind it. From the vainly self-interested King Louis to the all-powerful voice of God, it is difficult to claim that Brooks the screenwriter had in any way short-changed the professional range of Brooks the actor. Although many familiar faces were to make a welcome return appearance from earlier Brooks films – among them Harvey Korman, Dom DeLuise, Cloris Leachman and Madeline Kahn – in many ways *History of the World: Part I* benefits just as much from the brief eccentric turns from its minor supporting actors. These included pleasing cameos from the likes of Bea Arthur (the unemployment bureau clerk), Jackie Mason (a Jewish prisoner in the Spanish Inquisition sequence), Barry Levinson (the Roman column salesman) and Henny Youngman (the apothecary), amongst many others. Howard Morris's Roman court spokesman (simultaneously outrageously camp and politically savvy), Ron Carey's easy-going talent agent Swiftus, Mary-Margaret Humes's sweet-natured but quick-witted Miriam and most especially Spike Milligan's oddball Monsieur Rimbaud all give memorable performances in brief but noteworthy roles. Such a broad ensemble cast, with Brooks as its central anchor, may have proven to be a daunting prospect for any director, but there is a uniform reliability of performance quality evident throughout all of the film's various sequences. As Pamela Stephenson – the actress portraying Mademoiselle Rimbaud – was later to observe, the famously perfectionistic Brooks placed a high degree of importance on ensuring the most effective motivation of the film's actors:

> Mel would block the first scene and set up the shot, then disappear to change and be made up. As soon as he returned, the cameras would roll, and he would ping-pong between acting and observing the scene straight after on playback, then direct changes. Believing that the funniest takes occur when the actors are right on the edge of cracking up, Mel occasionally encouraged the actors to create skits that were nothing to do with the film. Then when we were boiling over with laughter, we'd return to the scripted scene and do it with heightened comic energy.[17]

Perhaps because of the fragmentary nature of the film's structure, it was imperative that Brooks chose recognisable character actors in key roles – as many sequences were to come and go quickly, employing familiar faces such as Sid Caesar's caveman chieftain and Andreas Voutsinas's supremely arch Bearnaise assisted in establishing these figures in distinctive ways even in spite of the brevity of their on-screen appearances. Naturally some characters fare better than others; Korman has far less time to craft Count De Monet into the kind of hiss-worthy villain he had conjured up for *Blazing Saddles* or *High Anxiety*, meaning that the character never quite has the opportunity to rise above the status of stock antagonist, while it is similarly a regret that Leachman's memorably grotty Madame Defarge (who lives, perhaps appropriately, on the *Rue de Merde*) has a similarly limited prospect of being fleshed out further than the sketchy character that Brooks presents us with. On the other hand, Dom DeLuise and Madeline Kahn use every second of their screen time to present the most dysfunctional of married couples: the podgy, sybaritic Nero and the cynical but wildly promiscuous Nympho. Both actors wring every ounce of entertainment value from these self-indulgent grotesques, clearly revelling in their larger-than-life nature while never concealing the privilege and abuse of power that the characters' attitudes represented.

In spite of the film's high public profile and a budget which was considerably enhanced in relation to earlier entries in Brooks's filmography, *History of the World: Part I* received a generally hostile reception with critics at the time of its release. The views of *New York Magazine*'s David Denby were largely representative of the majority of reviewers when he wrote that '*History of the World* is full of great beginnings followed by a quick collapse. The movie is a burlesque-show version of history. [...] Brooks's jokes fall below the level of satire; his movie is show-business blasphemy – funny, but not as bold as he thinks it is', adding that 'Brooks has made himself master of a kind of epic lowbrow surrealism – silly gags lavishly mounted, utterly gratuitous, and then ruthlessly thrown away'.[18] Even *The Chicago Sun-Times*'s Roger Ebert, often among the staunchest defenders of Brooks's earlier work, was deeply unimpressed: 'Brooks never seems to have a clear idea of the rationale of his movie, so there's no confident narrative impetus to carry it along. His "history" framework doesn't have an approach or point of view; it's basically just a laundry-line for whatever gags he can hang on it. What is this bizarre grab bag? Is it a parody of old Biblical, Roman, and French historical epics? Sometimes. Is it one-shot, comedy revue blackouts? Sometimes. Is it satire aimed at pompous targets? Sometimes. But most of the time it's basically just expensive sets sitting around waiting for Brooks to do something funny in front of them'.[19]

Although *History of the World: Part I* was a modest success at the box-office, having been released in the face of stiff competition thanks to various other prominent studio releases, Brooks later admitted that he had felt dissatisfied by the commercial performance of the film in cinemas:

> Well, summer product is summer product. I had a movie out last summer, *The History of the World Part I*. And I was a little disappointed. I mean, it did very well – whenever you do $20 million domestically in rentals, it's never anything to sneeze at. But we were up against very heavy summer fare: *Raiders of the Lost Ark*, *Superman II*. Blockbusters. There were a lot of kid-oriented pictures. Essentially, I think the summer audience is somewhere between eight and sixteen.[20]

In spite of its critical thrashing by reviewers in the summer of 1981, however, Brooks could still take comfort in the gradual revitalisation of the film's reputation amongst reviewers and the public which has come about in more recent years – thanks in no small part to repeated television screenings and subsequent home entertainment releases. Commentator Patrick Naugle claimed that the film's historical settings inoculated it from being visually dated by the fashions emanating from the time of its production, opining that 'though it was lambasted upon its original release, the fact of the matter is *History of the World: Part I* is a very funny movie. Critically drubbed for being scattershot and crude, the film has aged quite well and Brooks' combination of slapstick humor and witty one liners still elicit chuckles today. While the film retains some trappings of its time (the very early '80s), the setting and costumes make sure it never feels like a time capsule'.[21] Movie *Metropolis*'s James Plath has ventured a more muted analysis, noting that the film is 'nowhere near the comedy that Brooks is capable of producing. Maybe he was too close to the material to really make some hard decisions about the jokes that should stay and the jokes that should go. [...] By the time we get to the film's end and phony trailers like "Hitler on Ice" and "Jews in Space", you get the feeling that Brooks is still trying to find his way. This isn't one of his sure-handed efforts, but it passes, at least, for light entertainment'.[22] However, reviewers Frederic and Mary Ann Brussat were perhaps most perceptive of all in their observation that by attempting to satisfy public anticipation in a time of shifting cultural tastes, Brooks's efforts to cover too many bases at once could hardly be counted the worst of film-making sins:

> Along with Woody Allen, Mel Brooks has helped sustain the comedy genre in contemporary films. As Allen has turned more serious, Brooks has gotten more outrageous. He is the sole proprietor of vaudevillian yuks built around sexuality, scatology, and religion. His elemental energies are unleashed in spades with the release of *History of the World – Part I*. Brooks panders to the public's continual demand for the kind of bad taste humor that made burlesque popular in its heyday. [...] As in all movies by the ambitious Brooks, there are dull patches where the farce and the gags just don't work. But fans of this energetic comedian are sure to get plenty of belly shaking laughs out of this one.[23]

*History of the World: Part I* has, for many, become best-known as the film which introduced audiences to 'It's Good to be the King', an oft-repeated line that would evolve into a famous Brooksian stock phrase in later films (and indeed elsewhere in popular culture). The phrase succinctly exemplified King Louis's plutocratic self-interest but, when inherited by Jacques, we see it become something else: a realisation that power, like influence, is a mutable concept that is entirely dependent upon the perception of those who behold it. The film repeatedly offers examples of the malicious mishandling of authority by those in elevated positions, then shows us that the privileged few – who are either actively or unconsciously suppressing the liberty of others – have essentially become trapped themselves: by ennui, by ignorance, and indeed by the mass retribution of the very masses that they have subjugated. By contrast, we see in characters like Josephus, Comicus and Jacques a kind of iconoclastic emancipation, a freedom of thought and attitude which makes them stand apart from the despots who lord it over them. They may have been ground down by an uncaring establishment, but they have attained a degree of autonomy and resourcefulness which cannot be comprehended – much less achieved – by the tyrannical mind. In the creative liberty of the caveman chief's crudely-painted mural, Leonardo's portrait and even in the nonconformity of Josephus's tap-dancing, we see artistic invention used as a means of empowerment, refinement and escape – a form of unadulterated artistic freedom to which the autocrat (from Torquemada's rigidly-choreographed dance routine to the meticulously-planned leaps and loops of 'Hitler on Ice') cannot hope to aspire. Here, more than ever, we see Brooks endorsing creativity as the most potent of emancipating forces; the same kind of originality and inventiveness that had aided a talented, fast-talking kid from Brooklyn in rising to the pinnacle of the Hollywood hierarchy.

# REFERENCES

1. Robert Lawson-Peebles, 'The Many Faces of Sir Walter Ralegh', in *History Today*, Volume 48, Issue 3, 1998.
   <http://www.historytoday.com/robert-lawson-peebles/many-faces-sir-walter-ralegh>
2. David Desser and Lester D. Friedman, *American Jewish Filmmakers*, 2nd edn (Chicago: University of Illinois Press, 2004), p. 119.
3. Marc Kristal, 'Brooks' Bookshop', in *Saturday Review*, July 1983.
   <http://www.brookslyn.com/print/SaturdayReviewJul1983/SaturdayReviewJul1983.php>
4. Robert Alan Crick, *The Big Screen Comedies of Mel Brooks* (Jefferson: McFarland and Company, 2009) [2002], p.125.
5. Maurice Yacowar, *The Comic Art of Mel Brooks* (London: W.H. Allen, 1982), p. 188.
6. Deanne Schultz, *Filmography of World History* (Westport: Greenwood Press, 2007), p. xxiv.
7. Hannu Salmi, 'Introduction: The Mad History of the World', in *Historical Comedy on Screen: Subverting History with Humour*, ed. by Hannu Salmi (Bristol: Intellect, 2011), 7-30, pp. 17-19.
8. Henry Jenkins, 'Mel Brooks, Vulgar Modernism, and Comic Remediation', in *A Companion to Film Comedy*, ed. by Andrew Horton and Joanna E. Rapf (Chichester: John Wiley and Sons, 2013), 151-74, p. 154.
9. Yacowar, p. 193.
10. Desser and Friedman, p. 136.
11. Yacowar, p. 191.
12. Arthur Cooper, 'Blazing Anxieties: Mel Brooks is Just a Little Bit Crazy', in *Mademoiselle*, August 1981.
    <http://www.brookslyn.com/print/Mademoiselle-8-1981/Mademoiselle-8-1981.php>
13. Roger Ebert, '*History of the World: Part 1*', in The Chicago Sun-Times, 15 June 1981.
    <http://www.rogerebert.com/reviews/history-of-the-world-part-1-1981>
14. Yacowar, p. 190.
15. Beth Edith Bonnstetter, 'An Analytical Framework of Parody and Satire: Mel Brooks and His World' (unpublished doctoral thesis, The University of Minnesota, June 2008), p. 49.
16. Crick, p. 121.
17. Pamela Stephenson, *The Varnished Untruth* (London: Simon and Schuster, 2012), p. 82.
18. David Denby, 'The Decline and Fall of Mel Brooks', in *New York Magazine*, 22 June 1981, 48-50, p. 48.
19. Ebert, 1981.
20. Mel Brooks, in Michael Sragow, 'The Not-So-Flip Side of Mel Brooks: He's Serious About Producing', in *Rolling Stone*, 14 October 1982.
    <http://www.brookslyn.com/print/RollingStone10-14-82/RollingStone10-14-82.php>
21. Patrick Naugle, '*History of the World: Part I*', in *DVD Verdict*, 20 May 2010.
    <http://www.dvdverdict.com/reviews/historyworldpartibluray.php>
22. James Plath, '*History of the World Part 1*', in *Movie Metropolis*, 16 May 2010.
    <http://moviemet.com/review/history-world-part-1-blu-ray-review>
23. Frederic Brussat and Mary Ann Brussat, 'Mel Brooks' *History of the World: Part 1*', in *Spirituality & Practice*, 31 January 2004.
    <http://www.spiritualityandpractice.com/films/films.php?id=7810>

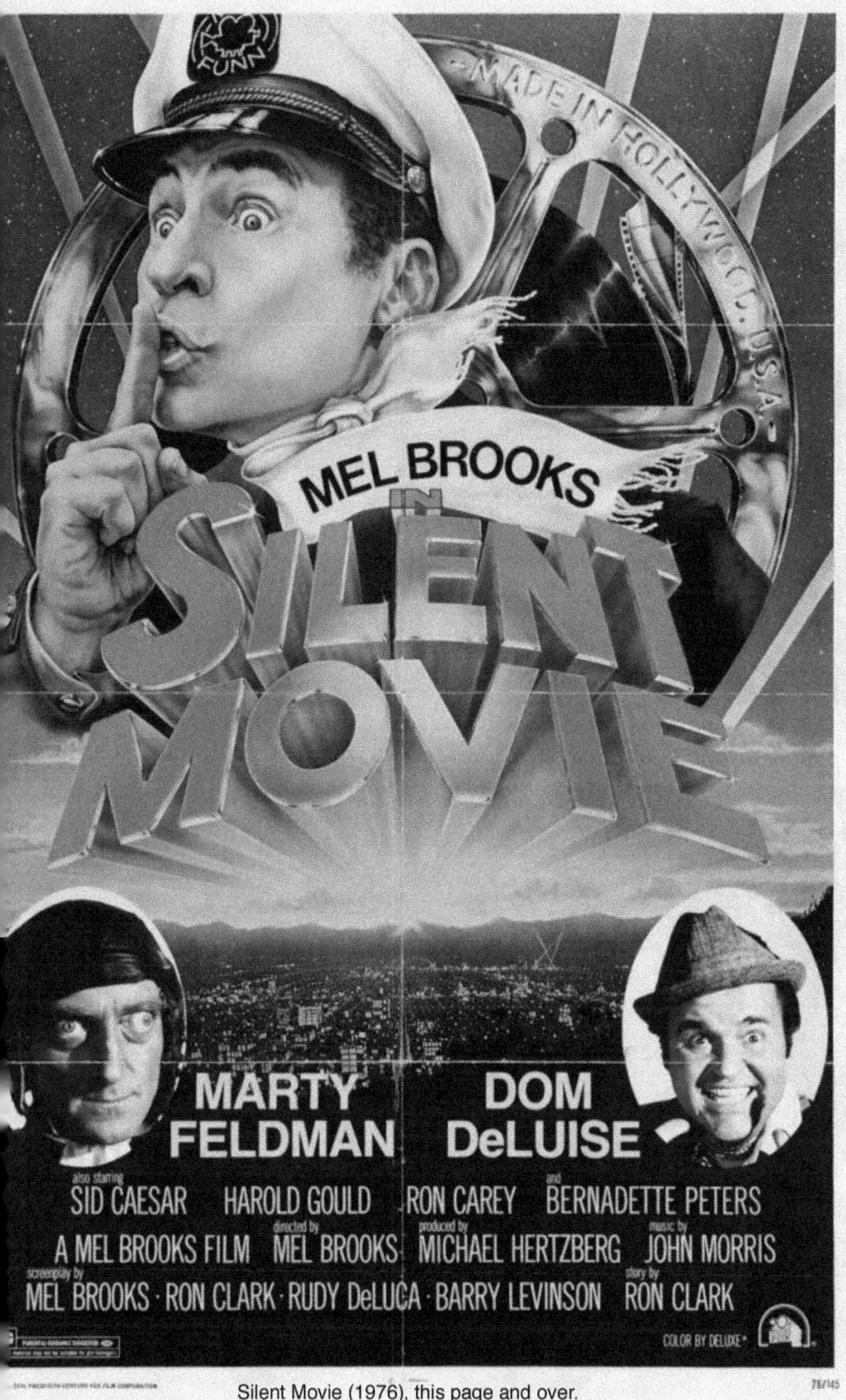

Silent Movie (1976), this page and over.

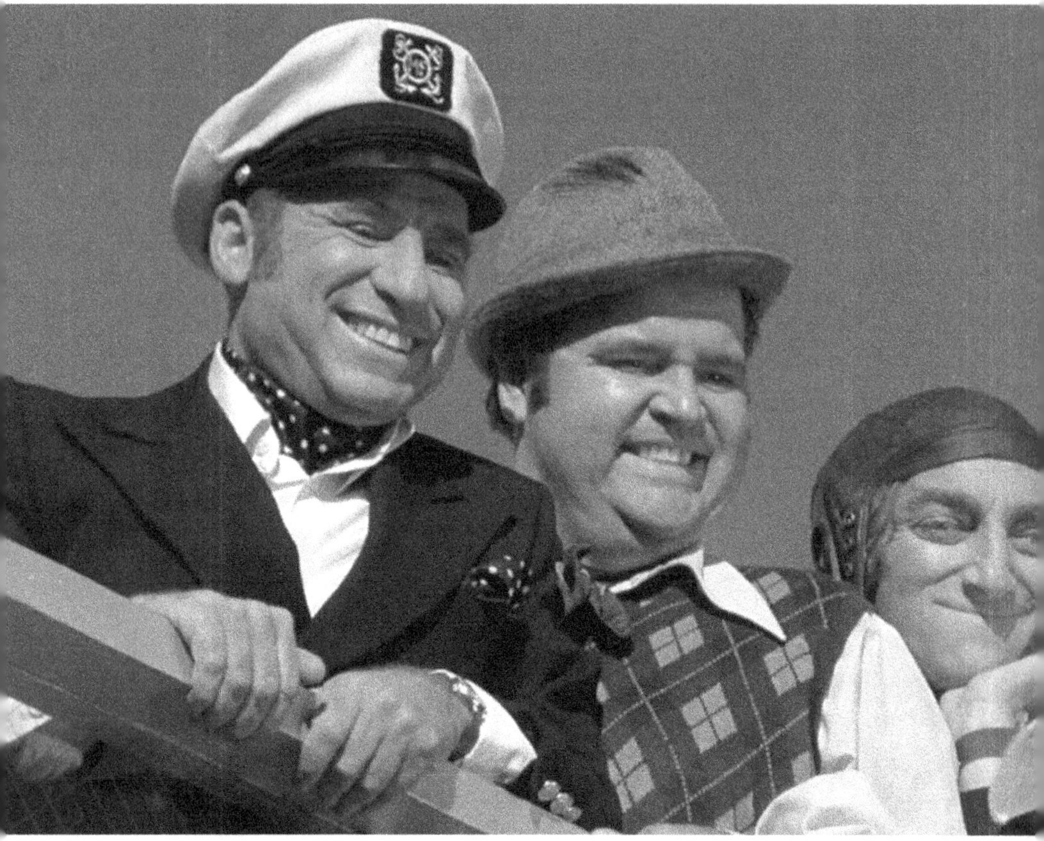

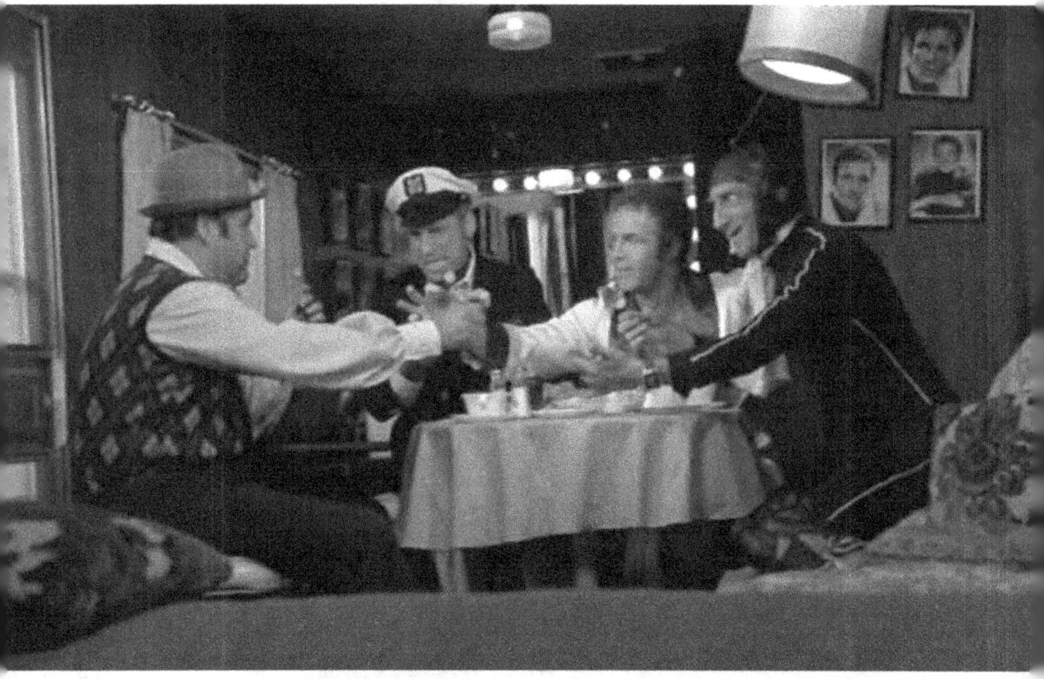

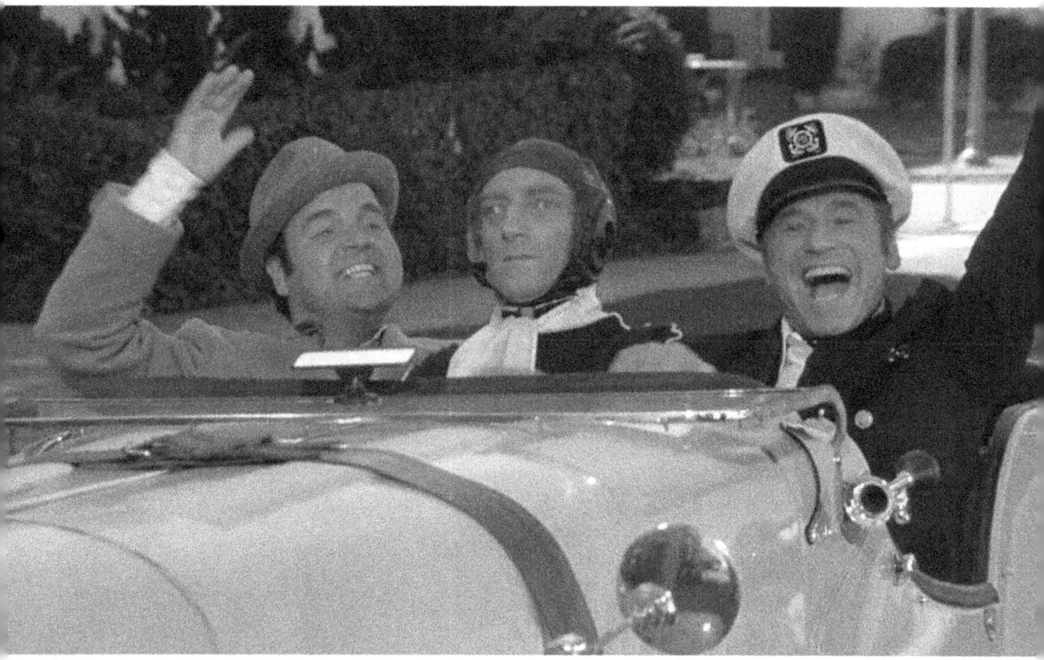

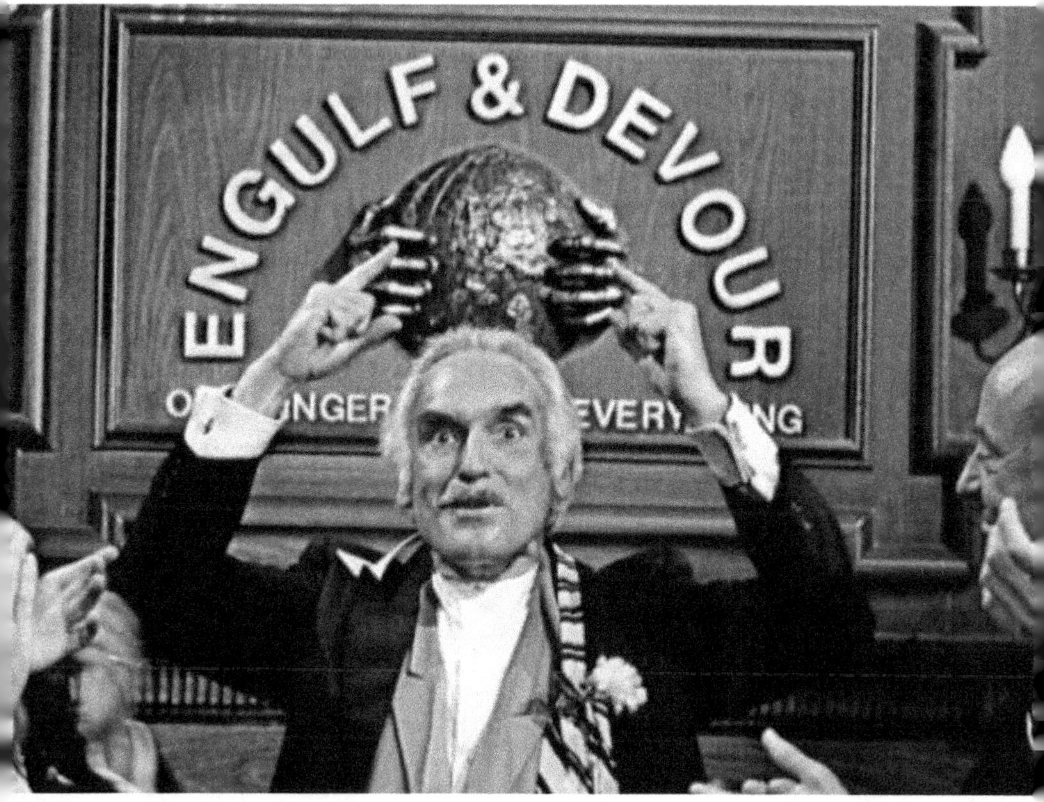
ENGULF & DEVOUR

This page and over from High Anxiety (1977)

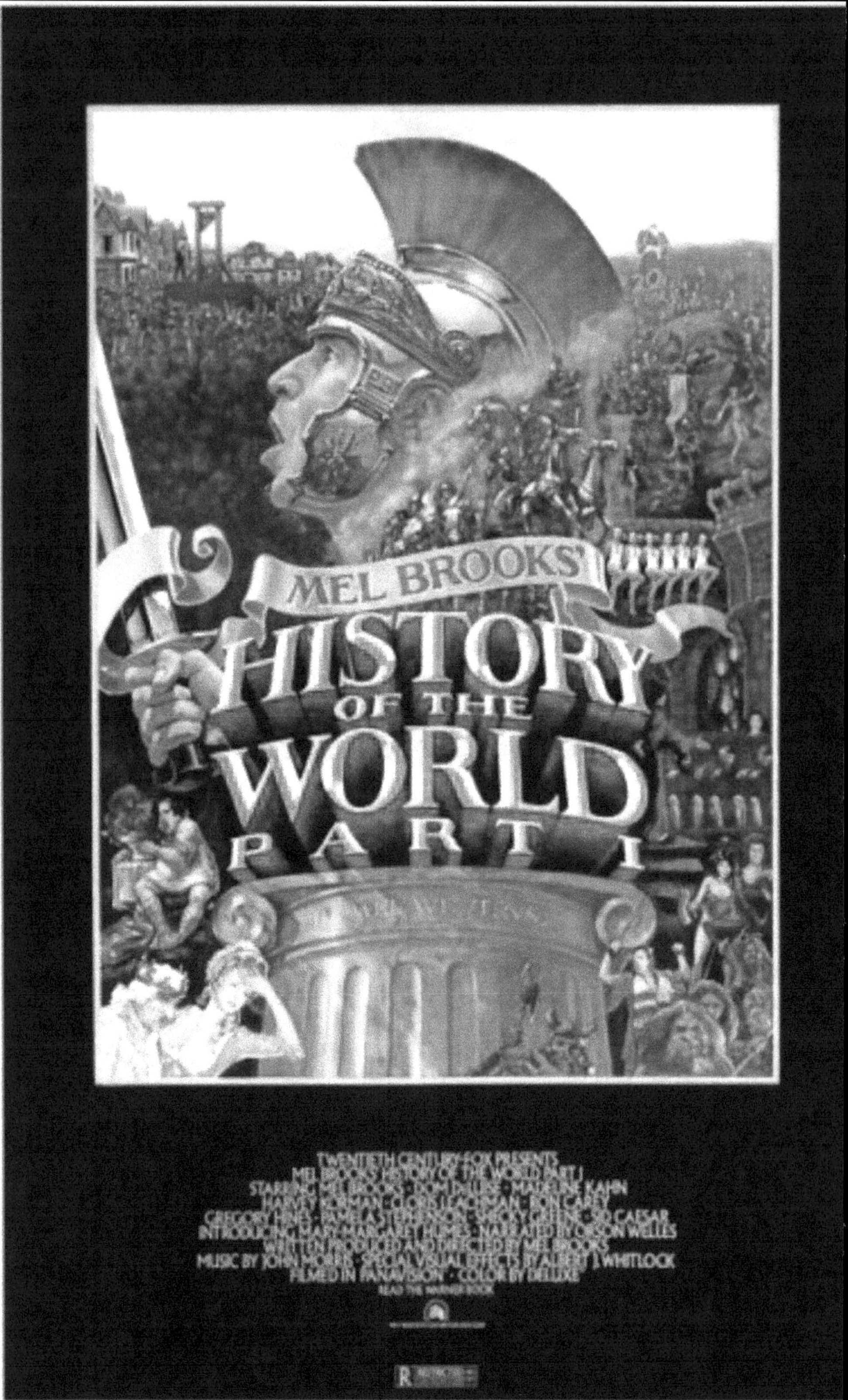

This page and over from
History of the World, Part One (1981)

# HISTORY OF THE WORLD PART I

# 8

# SPACEBALLS (1987)

MEL BROOKS HAD concluded *History of the World: Part I* with a coming attractions reel which featured 'Jews in Space', a jokingly-promised highlight of a sequel that would never be produced. Making good use of some nifty model-based special effects, and presenting an appealing theme song which proved so catchy that Brooks would later re-use the melody for *Robin Hood: Men in Tights*, few suspected that this seemingly-innocuous sketch had contained a hint for the tone and subject of Brooks's next directorial project: a science fiction spoof named *Spaceballs*.

Although Brooks had not directed a film in over half a decade since the release of *History of the World: Part I*, he had remained prominent in the public eye thanks to the work of his production company Brooksfilms and also his starring role in *To Be or Not to Be* (1983), an Alan Johnson-helmed remake of Ernst Lubitsch's 1942 comedy which focused upon a group of Warsaw-based actors who are forced to use their wits and performance talents in equal measure to outmanoeuvre Nazi troops occupying Poland during the Second World War. Brooks was not to contribute to the film as either writer or director, though he did act as its producer. Also, as if to further underscore his antipathy towards fascism (which had already been well established throughout so many of his earlier films), Brooks appeared in character as Adolf Hitler in a widely-released music video based upon the film, 'To Be or Not to Be (The Hitler Rap)', ridiculing the brutality and excesses of Nazi Germany during the totalitarian state's historical rise and fall. The track fared successfully in a number of countries, though not to the same extent as the 'It's Good to be the King' rap which had accompanied the release of *History of the World: Part I* (to which it bears considerable musical similarity) some years earlier.

Now back in the director's chair once again, Brooks was to turn his attention to a genre that, until now, had remained relatively undisturbed by his parodic efforts – that of the space opera. Science fiction had proven to be big business in cinemas throughout the 1980s, spurred on to no small degree by the phenomenal success of George Lucas's *Star Wars* trilogy, and it was from this ground-breaking series of films that Brooks would borrow the central narrative basis of *Spaceballs*, his tribute to some of the most prominent sci-fi franchises ever to have earned their entrance into mainstream popular culture. Working on the screenplay in collaboration with writing partners Thomas Meehan and Ronny Graham (both of whom had contributed to the script of *To Be or Not to Be*), Brooks was to produce a film which – with its aping of Lucas's classic Manichean battle between good and evil – was to further expound upon his preoccupation with the preservation of personal liberty in the face of governmental tyranny.

'Once upon a time-warp, in a galaxy very, very, very far away,' the audience is informed by way of a familiar-looking opening crawl, treachery is afoot in outer space. The government of a planet named Spaceball, having totally exhausted their world's atmosphere (though it is never quite explained how), is plotting to steal all of the breathable air from Druidia, a planet in a neighbouring star system. *Spaceball One*, a mammoth spaceship under the command of diminutive autocrat Dark Helmet (Rick Moranis), is already en-route to Druidia with sinister intentions. Dark Helmet's endlessly put-upon subordinate, Colonel Sandurz (George Wyner), explains their villainous plot: Princess Vespa (Daphne Zuniga), the daughter of Druidia's reigning monarch, is shortly to be married, and the Spaceballs plan to take her hostage during her honeymoon. This will force her father, King Roland (Dick Van Patten), to furnish the invaders with the entry code to the orbital shield that protects Druidia's atmosphere, allowing them to carry out their dastardly scheme.

Down on Druidia, however, Princess Vespa has other plans. In spite of her father's protestations that she must marry the soporific Prince Valium (J.M.J. Bullock), Vespa insists that she can't go through with a wedding to a virtual stranger that she doesn't love. Just as the ceremony is about to begin, Vespa races out of the temple with her unsuspecting Droid of Honour, Dot Matrix (Lorene Yarnell; voice of Joan Rivers) and takes off in her Mercedes shuttle (with the tellingly appropriate registration 'Spoil'd Rott'n I'). Roland calls on the services of mercenary Lone Starr (Bill Pullman), captain of a space-borne Winnebago named *Eagle 5*, and entreats him to track down his missing daughter. Fortunately for Lone Starr and his half-man, half-dog sidekick Barf (John Candy), the commission couldn't come at a more opportune time; space gangster Pizza the Hutt (voice of Dom DeLuise) has just called in an old loan which totals a million spacebucks, and he has demanded payment by the following day. Unabashedly taking advantage of King Roland's vast wealth, Lone Starr manages to persuade the harried monarch to pay him enough money to placate Pizza's extortionate demands, on the condition that he can retrieve the princess and get her back to safety on Druidia.

On Planet Spaceball, the government's President, Skroob (Mel Brooks), is obstinately attempting to persuade the mass media that there is no air supply crisis... while secretly resorting to the use of a secret stash of canned oxygen ('Perri-Air') for his own personal gratification. The population has been forced to live in enclosed habitation spheres, such is the deterioration of the planet's atmosphere, so Skroob is elated when he hears the news that *Spaceball One* has intercepted Princess Vespa's shuttle (thus moving forward his plans of a stolen supply of air). He sends an order to Dark Helmet warning that Vespa is to be taken hostage and thus not to be harmed. Their villainous plans are thwarted at the last minute, however, when Lone Starr jams their radar (quite literally, by striking a receiver dish with a gigantic jar of raspberry jam) and Barf rescues the princess from her shuttle while it is caught in the Spaceballs' tractor beam. Lone Starr is less than impressed by Vespa's imperious manner and ingratitude regarding her freedom from Spaceball incarceration, to say nothing of the fact that her insistence on saving her matched luggage has cost them vital time.

Dark Helmet is outraged when he discovers that the Mercedes shuttle is empty, but before he can take out his frustration on his hapless subordinates a radar operator discovers the *Eagle 5* on the scanner. Preventing any attempt by *Spaceball One* to attack the Winnebago, Lone Starr engages a concealed set of hyper-jets which allow his ship to retreat at faster-than-light speed. Exasperated, Dark Helmet ignores the objections of Sandurz and sends *Spaceball One* in pursuit at 'ludicrous speed' – a velocity so mindbogglingly fast that no-one has ever dared to see if the ship can hold together under the strain of it. Unfortunately for the Spaceballs, they wind up not just catching up with the Winnebago but tearing right past it as the traditional hyperspace effect of streaming star-fields rapidly weaves into a bizarre pattern of tartan ('They've gone to plaid!').

Lone Starr's jubilation at evading Dark Helmet and his cohorts is short lived, alas, when he discovers that the *Eagle 5* has run out of power as a result of the emergency escape ('I told you we should've put more than $5-worth in!'), forcing him to make a crash landing on a nearby desert planet. Barf suggests that they temporarily abandon the ship and try to find help – a task made all the more difficult due to the constant sniping between Vespa and Lone Starr, who are immediately repulsed by, and simultaneously attracted to, each other. Meanwhile, back on *Spaceball One*, Colonel Sandurz hits on an idea to pursue the escapees; Spaceball technology has advanced to such a stage that it is now possible to rent a movie while it is still in production. Cueing up an appropriate VHS videotape, they soon manage to track down Vespa's current location to the arid moon of Vega.

Lone Starr and Vespa manage to move beyond their mutual loathing to share an intimate night-time conversation around their camp fire in the desert, where the mercenary reveals that he is an orphan who was abandoned at a monastery in another galaxy – and, as the monks were part of a silent order, he has no idea of his family heritage. Vespa is moved by his story, but they are interrupted from any closer acquaintance thanks to the interjection of the matronly Dot Matrix and her deafening 'Virgin Alarm'. Setting off further into the desert, they soon succumb to the scorching heat of the day and fall down unconscious onto the blazing sands. Fortunately for them, a diminutive band of wandering desert-dwellers spot them from a distance and come to their aid. They bring the four bewildered travellers to their home, a huge concealed cavern that is hidden deep beneath the moon's surface. There, they meet Yogurt (Brooks again) – a legendary mystic who is revered throughout the galaxies. Yogurt claims to be a sage who is trained in the arts of the Schwartz, a strange supernatural power... but is also revealed to be a savvy entrepreneur who has branched out into a vast range of *Spaceballs* merchandise.

Lone Starr undergoes Schwartz training with Yogurt, and soon discovers that he has access to telekinetic abilities that he had never before suspected. Yogurt also interprets the strange glyphs on a medallion that was found with Lone Starr when he was abandoned as a child. Though the old mage can read the markings without difficulty, he explains to Lone Starr that their meaning will not be revealed until the correct time has arrived. The Spaceballs, in the meantime, are following President Skroob's orders to the letter and are quite literally combing the desert in their search for the princess. Dark Helmet senses the presence of the Schwartz and deduces that his old nemesis Yogurt is nearby. But reasoning that the pint-sized mystic is too strong to confront directly, Dark Helmet determines to extract Vespa from Yogurt's protection by more insidious means.

Later that night. Dark Helmet uses the power of the Schwartz to persuade Vespa that he is King Roland. Dot Matrix sees through his disguise, but too late – Sandurz takes the prisoners into custody aboard *Spaceball One*, leaving Lone Starr and Barf watching helplessly as the villains blast off into orbit. The two friends resolve to pursue the kidnappers and get the princess back to safety. Yogurt refuels the *Eagle 5* and leaves Lone Starr with two parting gifts – a mysterious fortune cookie, and his Schwartz ring. Lone Starr is touched by the gesture and wonders if they will ever meet again, to which Yogurt drolly replies that he's personally banking on a reunion in the sequel.

Dark Helmet transports the princess back to Planet Spaceball, where he has devised an inventive way of gaining leverage with King Roland. He introduces cleaver-wielding plastic surgeon Dr Philip Schlotkin (Sandy Helberg), 'the greatest nose-job man in the entire universe... and Beverly Hills'. Unless Roland surrenders the access code for Druidia's air-shield, Schlotkin will reverse Vespa's previous plastic surgery and restore her nose to its earlier, bulbous appearance. Alarmed at the thought of his daughter going back under the knife, Roland relents and provides the planetary access code to the Spaceballs. Ecstatic, Skroob orders *Spaceball One* to depart immediately – this time with him on board to personally oversee the culmination of their malign plan.

Lone Starr has managed to track down Vespa to a prison complex on Planet Spaceball. He and Barf infiltrate the base and release the princess and Dot Matrix, leading to a frantic escape (which only succeeds when the enemy troopers accidentally capture their stunt doubles by mistake, allowing them the diversion they need to get back to the *Eagle 5*). The Winnebago only just manages to catch up with *Spaceball One* as the enemy ship is reaching orbit around Druidia. While they wonder aloud how the Spaceballs intend to extract the atmosphere of the planet, *Spaceball One* transforms into a gigantic robotic maid holding a vacuum cleaner – *Mega-Maid*. It immediately begins to suck the air from the world below into the vacuum's dust-bag, the orbital shield now unlocked with King Roland's override code. The inhabitants on the ground begin to suffocate as breathing rapidly becomes impossible. However, with some quick thinking Lone Starr dons the Schwartz ring that was gifted to him by Yogurt, using his mental powers to reverse the airflow on *Mega-Maid*'s vacuum cleaner and return Druidia's atmosphere back to the planet.

Realising that Druidia cannot be safe so long as *Spaceball One* remains a threat, Lone Starr pilots the *Eagle 5* inside the huge ship and locates its self-destruct mechanism. He is intercepted by Dark Helmet and nearly defeated when he loses the Schwartz ring... until the spirit of Yogurt informs him that the real power lies within him – the costume jewellery was nothing more than a symbol. Newly energised by this realisation, Lone Starr outwits the accident-prone Dark Helmet and succeeds in initiating the ship's self-destruct sequence. Utter pandemonium breaks out aboard *Spaceball One* as the crew evacuate, leaving aboard only Skroob, Sandurz and Dark Helmet (all of whom have had their escape pods usurped by others). The enemy ship explodes into a massive fireball mere seconds after Lone Starr has piloted the *Eagle 5* to safety.

Returning the reluctant princess to the arms of her deeply dull royal fiancé, Lone Starr learns via a news broadcast that Pizza the Hutt has been found dead (having eaten himself to death).

Barf is overjoyed that he and Lone Starr will be able to keep King Roland's massive reward to themselves, but the *Eagle 5*'s captain seems strangely melancholic. After they depart Druidia, however, Barf cracks open Yogurt's fortune cookie and triggers a message from the old wizard himself. Yogurt not only reveals that Lone Starr's medallion proves him to be of royal lineage, meaning that he is eligible to marry Vespa, but also that he has hidden a canister of liquid Schwartz in the Winnebago's glove compartment. By using it, the ship can just make it back to King Roland's court in time to stop the marriage (once again) between Vespa and Prince Valium.

Back on Druidia, Vespa is smarting at Lone Starr's quick departure, though when Roland explains that her rescuer had refused the reward money – taking only a token amount to cover his expenses – she realises that the dashing outlaw must have had feelings for her all along. She is only just saved from marriage to Valium when Lone Starr arrives in the nick of time, revealing that he too is a prince. As Vespa and Lone Starr are wed by the court's increasingly irritable minister (Ronny Graham), heading off on honeymoon thereafter, we discover that Dark Helmet, Skroob and Sandurz have managed – against all odds – to survive the destruction of *Spaceball One*, and now appear to be stranded on *The Planet of the Apes*.

Brooks and co-screenwriters Graham and Meehan endeavour throughout the duration of *Spaceballs* to expend every effort in sending up just about every sci-fi cliché they can lay their hands on. Although the film is most obviously influenced by *Star Wars*, many other franchises affiliated to the genre are gleefully harangued along the way. With an estimated budget of $22,700,000,[1] the film was more than twice as expensive to produce as had been the case with *History of the World: Part I* (itself a high water-mark in the production values of Brooks's filmmaking at that point). But in taking the big-budget grandeur of *Star Wars* as the central basis of his spoof, Brooks was determined that his own production would look suitably credible in the view of cinemagoers; as Brian Lowry observed at the time of the film was being shot, 'this comedy stuff can be serious business, particularly in the dollar department. *Spaceballs* is a sprawling production, shot on three separate sound-stages. "This is a major motion picture," a Brooks aide says, eyeing the sets with admiration. "It never would have gotten made without Mel's name on it"'.2 Certainly there is no lack of visual flair throughout the film, to say nothing of the trademark Brooksian creative ingenuity. *Spaceballs* is a much more restrained affair than *History of the World: Part I*, the bawdy, adult-oriented humour of its predecessor making his sci-fi spoof appear greatly reined-in by comparison. Instead, the film offers a greater array of semantic cleverness, providing a wealth of verbal wit as it proceeds to prick the worst pretensions of science fiction cinema.

Perhaps the most regular criticism to be levelled against *Spaceballs* was the fact that it arguably came too late to make the maximum impact with audiences; it was to arrive in cinemas ten years after the landmark debut of *Star Wars* and four years after the conclusion of the cycle's original trilogy, *Return of the Jedi*, thus meaning that the pop culture relevance of Lucas's films – while still very strong amongst audiences – was no longer as immediately prominent. Wes Gehring makes the point that 'timeliness is integral to parody. For instance, the most consistent complaint against Mel Brooks' *Spaceballs* (1987) was that it appeared a full decade after the birth of the *Star Wars* (1977) phenomenon. Though still entertaining, it was not cutting-edge funny'.3 Certainly this fact was far from lost on Brooks and his creative team. Lowry notes that 'once Brooks, Meehan and Graham had decided to pen a space movie [...] they did have qualms about the four-year lapse since the opening of *Return of the Jedi*. "We were concerned that it might get too old, but we felt that the whole genre of big space films had become part of American popular culture. They *weren't* going to be forgotten", Meehan says'.4 Indeed, the ongoing interest of viewers and commentators towards the science fiction genre was in no danger of slowing down in the late eighties, with many sequels jostling with original features for box-office success. M. Keith Booker explains that *Spaceballs* operates by 'employing an unending stream of sight gags and puns that work only because Brooks can assume that his audience has extensive familiarity with the works being parodied',5 and certainly many of the film's jokes depend upon a working knowledge of the source material in order to leave a meaningful impression amongst audiences.

While Lone Starr is clearly an amalgam of Han Solo's roguishness and Luke Skywalker's mystic destiny, his wisecracking and laid-back nature centres him more in the guise of the former character than the latter. (His revelation of being born in 'the Ford Galaxy' is not only a sly reference to *Star Wars* actor Harrison Ford, but also the popular *Ford Galaxie 500* automobile – itself a comic throwback to the naming convention behind *The Producers*'s Carmen Ghia.) The nature of his motivating intentions, which are initially summed up by his avaricious line 'We're not just doing this for money – we're doing it for a *shitload* of money!', soon develop into rather more noble objectives as the film continues. His co-pilot Barf, on the other hand, replaces the unintelligible but fiercely loyal sidekick Chewbacca with an amiable, quick-thinking slob – a 'Mawg' rather than a Wookiee, the only commonality between the two is a tendency towards furriness: 'I'm a Mawg. Half man, half dog. I'm my own best friend!'. In the hands of then-rapidly rising star John Candy, who appeared in many popular comedies throughout the 1980s (not least Ron Howard's *Splash*, 1984, and John Hughes's *Planes, Trains and Automobiles*, 1987), Barf moves beyond a mere parody figure to become a truly distinctive creation; with his expressive Animatronic ears and highly mobile tail, to say nothing of his penchant for dog biscuits, he presents a truly appealing character who is always fun to spend time with.

Likewise, Princess Vespa is a rather more stereotypically haughty noblewoman than the *Star Wars* films' Princess Leia had ever been ('That's all we needed – a Druish princess!' moans Lone Starr ruefully, to which Barf replies 'Funny; she doesn't *look* Druish'). Her robotic handmaiden Dot Matrix – an allusion to an early type of computer printer – supplants the prissy protocol droid C3PO with a roller-skating automaton sporting always-perfect hair and a barbed tongue (courtesy of the waspish tones of Joan Rivers). 'The everlasting know-it-all' Yogurt is also an inspired creation, displacing the tortured syntax and off-kilter tones of Frank Oz's Yoda puppet with Brooks's trademark strongly accented Yiddish. Wandering around with slippers on his knees to bring the character down to the same height as his assistants, the Dinks (parodies of *Star Wars*'s chattering, desert-abiding Jawas), Yogurt's lair provides one of the film's standout scenes when he proudly reveals his hidden supply of branded *Spaceballs* products. 'Merchandising – where the real money from the movie is made!' Yogurt proclaims with infectious merriment (in response to Barf's all-too-innocent question 'Merchandising? What's that?'), promptly introducing us to such items as *Spaceballs*: The Flame Thrower – 'A Children's Toy' – and *Spaceballs*: The Breakfast Cereal (a wholesome snack which, we are reliably informed, contains '100% sugar'). Thereafter, the audience are treated to endless visual gags in this strain, often in unexpected places, ranging from '*Spaceballs*: The Placemat' to '*Spaceballs*: The Toilet Paper', though Lone Starr eventually resorts to using – of all things – a canister of '*Spaceballs*: The Shaving Foam' to subdue a guard when he is infiltrating *Mega-Maid*. The running mockery of highly conspicuous merchandising based upon the movie was, of course, a satire of the hugely lucrative, culturally ubiquitous spin-off products from the *Star Wars* trilogy – though, as Brooks was later to point out, *Spaceballs* would not give rise to its own range of branded commodities in reality, explaining that George Lucas 'certainly did [give approval for the production of *Spaceballs*], but he gave me one incredibly big restriction: no action figures. He said, "Yours are going to look like mine." I said OK'.[6] But even bereft of its own line of spin-off items, *Spaceballs* proved memorable enough in its playful skewering of the multimedia empire that was Lucasfilm – a company which had immortalised *Star Wars* not only in celluloid, but in everything from comic books to video games.

If Brooks enjoys the act of sending up the heroes of the *Star Wars* films, he clearly derives even more amusement when it comes to the villains. At the pinnacle of Planet Spaceball's governmental tree is President Skroob, a wily but ultimately inept political operator whose character suggests a hybrid of *Blazing Saddles*'s corrupt Governor Lepetomane and the debauched King Louis from *History of the World: Part I*. Robert Alan Crick observes that 'while an interplanetary politico, at heart [Skroob] is pure, or impure, Washington, D.C. – conning, philandering, mismanaging left and right. He's *Blazing Saddles*' penlight-dim Gov. Lepetomane turned Machiavellian conniver, a bureaucratic bumbler incapable of intelligent decision-making without top-level aid'.[7] (Crick's comment seems all the more perceptive when we note that the central government of Planet Spaceball seems to have an uncanny resemblance to Capitol Hill.) Clearly falling some way short of Ian McDiarmid's cunning intellectual powerhouse Emperor Palpatine from the *Star Wars* films – both in mental acuity and deadliness – Skroob presents an entertaining depiction of governmental overindulgence, combining moral dissolution with executive ineptitude to highly compelling effect. ('I can't make decisions! I'm a president!' he exclaims at one point.) Brooks seems to relish his dual role, which makes his shift from top billing to supporting act seem somewhat less conspicuous than it might have been. As he explained:

> *Spaceballs* is fathers and sons, of course, because it's me. And because it's a fairy tale with a princess and a guy who turns out to be a prince in the end and marries her, there's a love story. But it turned out to be mothers and daughters, too. So I got the whole family in that one. I got a lot of freaks, a lot of weirdoes who like to see little pert people with golden faces. I also played President Skroob, which is 'Brooks' backward. And I played just plain Yogurt, you know. I just played the two characters. [...] Well, I really didn't *just* want to be the bad guy. And President Skroob is really evil; he's really a bad guy. So I say, 'Oh, I'll play a good guy, too. I'll play this magical guy Yogurt. Just plain Yogurt'.[8]

Perhaps the most prominent of all the characters to hail from Planet Spaceball is the miniature overlord Dark Helmet – a neatly-observed performance by character actor Rick Moranis, who had shot to prominence during the eighties through impressive appearances in films such as *Ghostbusters* (Ivan Reitman, 1984) and *Little Shop of Horrors* (Frank Oz, 1986). A deliberate subversion of the tall, lumbering Darth Vader, a cybernetically-enhanced Sith Lord whose features are (as forever celebrated in pop culture) hidden behind a sinister breath mask, Dark Helmet is a short, bespectacled and often puerile individual who – as his name suggests – is never to be seen without his comically oversized head covering. Unlike Vader, whose survival depended upon the air supply provided by the breathing apparatus inside his mask, it is pointedly apparent that Dark Helmet's headgear is little more than a bizarre status symbol – indeed, he actually has *difficulty* breathing when inside its confines – though he does lapse into an ominously stentorian mode of intonation (knowingly similar to that of *Star Wars* stalwart James Earl Jones) whenever his helmet's visor is in place. At all other times, he speaks clearly and in a perfectly normal tone – a slight but nonetheless trenchant thumbing of the nose at Vader's laboured exhalations and famously disguised voice. A preening egotist, Dark Helmet is more often than not the victim of some cartoonish physical mishap or another, which helps to highlight his general ineffectiveness in comparison to the lethally ruthless Dark Lord of the *Star Wars* series. This includes him trapping his helmet in a sliding door, flying into a bank of computers after an emergency stop, colliding with the camera during an extreme close-up, numerous unfortunate pratfalls, and – perhaps most memorably – being walloped by Lone Starr when his face is exposed, the assault coming at the worst possible juncture (during the one point in the film when it would actually have made sense for him to have his visor down).

The offbeat crew of *Spaceball One* also parodies the seemingly endless parade of faceless, interchangeable Imperial officers from the *Star Wars* films, many of whom seem to exist only for Darth Vader to subject them to some unfortunate fate in punishment for issues which are beyond their control. Among the line-up of peculiar shipboard operatives are *Police Academy*'s Michael Winslow as a radar operator, Jim Jackman's cross-eyed Major Asshole, and (back on Planet Spaceball) Leslie Bevis as the supremely arch Commanderette Zircon. But the best lines belong to George Wyner's straight-faced Colonel Sandurz, the beleaguered commander of *Spaceball One* who appears to be named by Brooks as a tribute to Colonel Harland Sanders of Kentucky Fried Chicken, as we learn when Lone Starr and Princess Vespa flee from the Spaceballs' clutches:

| | |
|---|---|
| DARK HELMET: | What happened? Where are they? |
| SANDURZ: | I don't know, sir. They must have hyper-jets on that thing. |
| DARK HELMET: | And what have we got? A Cuisinart? |
| SANDURZ: | No, sir. |
| DARK HELMET: | Well, find them! Catch them! |
| SANDURZ: | Yes, sir! [*Into intercom*] Prepare ship for light speed! |
| DARK HELMET: | No, no – light speed is too slow. |
| SANDURZ: | Light speed too slow?! |
| DARK HELMET: | Yes. We're going to have to go right to... ludicrous speed! |
| SANDURZ: | [*Gasps*] Ludicrous speed? Sir, we've never gone that fast before! I don't know if the ship can take it. |
| DARK HELMET: | What's the matter, Colonel Sandurz? *Chicken?* |

Sandurz's interactions with Dark Helmet provide some of the finest entertainment value during the scenes set aboard *Spaceball One*. There is particular gratification to be found in Dark Helmet mistaking a coffee machine for a long-distance radar, and Sandurz immediately leading the rest of the crew in placating their pompous overlord – together, they collectively pretend that it had always been his intention to have a coffee *prior* to consulting the radar monitor. The whole sequence appears better suited to an office full of awkward colleagues trying to appease a pompous boss than on the command deck of a vast spaceship, the sheer incongruity making the scenario seem all the more pleasingly surreal.

Likewise, the employment of 'ludicrous speed' is just one way in which Brooks mocks the timeworn conventions common to many science fiction productions. 'We're going into... hyperactive,' Lone Starr announces as his ship jumps away at a speed which defies all known science, and sure enough we see the usual outlandish sci-fi velocities being ridiculed on *Spaceball One*'s command deck – from 'light speed' to 'ridiculous speed' and eventually the aforementioned 'ludicrous speed'. So extreme is the latter option that the familiar hyperspace effect of series such as *Star Trek* and *Star Wars* becomes displaced by an eccentric chequered pattern as Dark Helmet's ship races headlong into the void. The epic opening shot of *Spaceball One* as it thunders across the screen is quite manifestly a parody of the famous Star Destroyer reveal at the beginning of *Star Wars: A New Hope* (iterations on the 'We brake for nobody' bumper-sticker gag had already become a Brooksian staple, with appearances in *Silent Movie* and *History of the World: Part I*), while Brooks parodies the colossal capital ships of the *Star Wars* universe by ensuring that *Spaceball One* is so absurdly gigantic that it houses a three-ring circus and a zoo, amongst many other (equally implausible) things. At one point Skroob is out of breath upon reaching the ship's command centre, explaining that he had no choice but to run there – if he'd walked, the vessel's immense size would have meant that the film would have ended before he'd got to his destination.

Arguably *Spaceballs* is at its most astute when it is sending up the most trite generic chestnuts of the science fiction genre. A particularly long piece of exposition from Colonel Sandurz at the beginning of the film, setting up the convoluted plot, elicits Dark Helmet to ask the audience 'Everybody got that?', just to be on the safe side. Likewise, stereotypically long-winded sci-fi dialogue such as 'Prepare to go to lightspeed!' is derided beautifully by Dark Helmet; after several such banal utterances from Sandurz, he exasperatedly enquires 'What are you preparing? You're *always* preparing! Just go!' Yet perhaps surprisingly, Brooks often tends to avoid the most obvious *Star Wars*-specific truisms in favour of his own, rather less predictable creations. There are no whistling pedal-bins to be found here in place of reliable old R2D2, for instance, but instead we are presented by the band of Dinks – whose language only extends to the word 'Dink' – belting out the tune of the 'Colonel Bogey March', thus referencing Alec Guinness in the role of Colonel Nicholson in David Lean's *The Bridge on the River Kwai* (1957) who would later go on to become the *Star Wars* series's Obi-Wan Kenobi (and who is first introduced in a similar desert-based scene). That said, when Brooks *does* aim for the obvious targets he really goes for broke. Darth Vader's paternal revelation, perhaps the most pivotal scene in the entirety of *The Empire Strikes Back*, is subverted by Dark Helmet's shock disclosure at the film's conclusion: 'Before you die there is something you should know about us, Lone Starr. [...] I am your father's brother's nephew's cousin's former room-mate'. There is also a send-up of the harrowing *Death Star* trench run (the *Eagle 5* racing down the ear canal of *Mega-Maid* in vague tribute to Richard Fleischer's *Fantastic Voyage*, 1966), complete with a similar conveniently-placed destruction mechanism. The Vulcan Neck Pinch [sic] is given a name-check too, but this is but a mere sideshow to the film's main tribute to the crew of the *Starship Enterprise*. Faced with the prospect of matter transportation, otherwise known as 'beaming', Skroob is unconvinced by the technology but eventually relents with a reluctant 'What the hell – it works on *Star Trek*!' Sure enough, we are then introduced to Snotty – a Tam o' Shanter-wearing engineer with an exaggerated Scottish accent – who immediately launches into lines such as 'Lock one, lock two, lock three... Loch Lomond!' (After a transporter malfunction, it eventually transpires that Skroob was only in the next room and thus could have walked to his destination in less time than it took to beam him there.)

Key to the *Star Wars* phenomenon, of course, is the mystical Force – a mystical energy drawn on by Jedi Knights and Sith Lords alike. Using the 'Light Side' or 'Dark Side' of the Force denotes the user's affiliation to either good or evil, thus providing the film series with its strong Manichean message of right and wrong. And even in the world of *Spaceballs*, amidst Dark Helmet's smirking assertion that 'evil will always triumph because good is dumb', we eventually see virtue overcoming malignity – if more through luck than good judgement on some occasions. Supplanting the Force (even though Barf does give it a brief name-check) is the similarly incomprehensible power of the Schwartz – a capability which combines telepathic and telekinetic abilities along with the physical properties of a *Star Wars* lightsaber – hence the admiring observation of Dark Helmet that 'your Schwartz is as big as mine!' as he fights Lone Starr at the film's conclusion. Typical of Brooks, however, there is no unambiguous light and dark moral division where the Schwartz is concerned – instead, its significance is rather more oblique, and the consequences of any potential ethical alignment are ultimately left to the individual to discern:

> DARK HELMET: Yogurt has the Schwartz! It's far too powerful.
> SANDURZ: But sir, your ring! Don't you have the Schwartz too?
> DARK HELMET: Nah, he got the upside, I got the downside. See, there's two sides to every Schwartz.

By wielding the Schwartz, Lone Starr finds his eyes opened to new possibilities which his current existence as a lackadaisical drifter cannot offer. He is thus liberated not so much by discovering he has the capacity to tap into supernatural resources, but rather by having Yogurt challenging his expectations with regard to what is possible in his life. Similarly, the spoilt Vespa begins to look beyond the privileged confines of her cosseted existence when she realises that her personal own abilities – discovered during her flight from the Spaceballs – far exceed her own predictions. Finding a new sense of independence in her escape from Dark Helmet and his minions, the princess begins to realise that the path circumscribed by her royal birth need not define her life quite so completely as she had first anticipated. Thus when Lone Starr's noble bloodline is eventually revealed, both characters have already autonomously discovered their new potential for personal freedom, meaning that the royal marriage between them at the conclusion of the film is truly a match between equals.

Brooks draws attention to his main characters' capacity for individual liberty in opposition to a tyrannical regime which is in equal parts dangerous, excessive and incompetent. It comes as no surprise, then, that he uses this parallel to highlight a familiar theme that he had established throughout several of his previous films. As David Desser and Lester D. Friedman state, 'Brooks peppers the script with overtly Jewish elements and familiar motifs. Because this is a Mel Brooks movie, for example, Nazis hide just around the next asteroid. The soldiers form planet Spaceball dress like Third Reich refugees, with Colonel Sandurz clearly resembling a storm trooper. The Spaceballers [sic] also employ German phrases, answering "Jawohl" and addressing their leader as "Herr Helmet"'.[9] Thus Brooks's disdain towards the characteristic totalitarian disregard for civil liberties remains palpable even in a fantastical setting, which in no small part explains the relentless humiliation of Dark Helmet as well as Skroob's total lack of redeeming qualities. In a low-key manner, Brooks celebrates the capability of science fiction to present political commentary through allegorical means, which would certainly explain his ambition in spreading his satirical net as wide as he does. Brian L. Ott and Beth Bonnstetter have observed the ambitious scale of Brooks's extensive target range thus:

> *Spaceballs* is a 'send-up' of science-fiction films. Its most obvious and central gestures are to the original *Star Wars* trilogy, featuring characters such as Dark Helmet (Rick Moranis) instead of Darth Vader and Princess Vespa (Daphne Zuniga) in place of Princess Leia. However, it also incorporates intertextual references to other science-fiction texts such as *Fantastic Voyage*, *2001: A Space Odyssey*, *Planet of the Apes*, *Star Trek*, *Alien*, *The Hitch Hiker's Guide to the Galaxy*, and Franz Kafka's novel *The Metamorphosis*, as well as to a few non-science-fiction texts such as *Lawrence of Arabia*, *Ferris Bueller's Day Off*, and the Warner Brothers' cartoon *One Froggy Evening*.[10]

In addition to blending together aspects of various instantly-recognisable sci-fi franchises, Brooks would also use *Spaceballs* to build upon his now-customary propensity for poking fun at the process of film-making itself. Perhaps more than in any of his films since *Blazing Saddles*, Brooks shatters the fourth wall with much aplomb, hitting heights of absurdity that had been left largely undisturbed since his mid-seventies heyday. We are asked to accept, for instance, the notion that Sandurz manages to land the gargantuan *Spaceball One* in the desert – right next to Yogurt's lair – without anyone noticing or even suspecting this fact. 'Helmet! So, at last we meet for the first time, for the last time,' Lone Starr barks at his arch-nemesis, before momentarily pausing to check that he has enunciated the line properly. Dot Matrix exclaims 'I hate these movies!' while pinned down in the prison block, and Dark Helmet accidentally slashes one of the filming crew during the climactic Schwartz fight (before swiftly blaming the accident on Lone Starr). In the depths of the desert covering Vega's moon, Bart admiringly observes 'Nice dissolve!' as the desert night turns to scorching day, before later noting that Yogurt's lair 'looks like *The Temple of Doom*!' Similarly, Yogurt hopes that a reunion will soon be on the cards due to his aspiration that 'God willing, we'll all meet again in *Spaceballs II: The Search for More Money*'. And perhaps most prominent of all the film's surreal inter-genre crossovers involves the presence of the crew of the infamous mining vessel *Nostromo*, who appear in an otherwise-superfluous scene set in an interstellar gas station (where *Star Wars*'s famous *Millennium Falcon* is briefly seen being refuelled on a nearby platform). The *Nostromo* crew, who had featured in Ridley Scott's seminal sci-fi horror *Alien* (1979), are seen in uncharacteristically upbeat mood sharing a meal in the station's diner… until Executive Officer Kane (John Hurt, reprising his role from the original film) is wracked by agonising pain as an embryonic xenomorph bursts out of his chest. 'Oh, no! Not again!' he gasps wearily with his dying breath, recalling the iconic 'Last Supper' scene from the Scott film. The tiny alien then jumps onto the diner's bar and – complete with straw boater and spats – apes Warner Brothers' Michigan J. Frog as he launches into a rendition of 'Hello, Ma Baby' (1899). The scene was so inspired (and unexpected) that it won over many of even the film's more sceptical critics; Howard Hughes, for instance, comments: 'That thudding sound you can hear throughout the movie is joke after joke falling flat. In a rare moment of amusement, the heroes evade capture, but their stunt doubles do not, and an alien bursts from John Hurt's chest […] and performs a song-and-dance number'.[11]

From the sight of an expedition-equipped Dark Helmet – complete with oversized pith helmet, safari suit and saddle shoes – barking orders for troops to 'comb the desert' quite literally, using gigantic plastic hair-combs to rake over the sands, to Colonel Sandurz accidentally turning off the film by hitting the wrong button on a remote control, there is no doubting the sheer unrelenting energy of Brooks's creative resourcefulness and ingenuity. However, perhaps the most celebrated of all the film's forays into overt surrealism takes place in the 'Instant Video' scene – a concept which, even by Brooks's standards, challenges all narrative expectation. Searching for the fugitive Vespa, Sandurz suggests that the Spaceballs simply rent the video of the film and fast-forward to a point where they can determine the princess's location. When a sceptical Dark Helmet asks how this can be possible, Sandurz replies that Spaceball technology has now advanced to the point where a film can be rented out even while it is still in production. (The irony of VHS videotapes being at the bleeding edge of future science would not be lost on future audiences.) A technician heads over to a helpfully-located bank of rental videos, where – as Desser and Friedman note – 'with a postmodern wink at intertextuality, their video library contains Brooks's previous features'.[12] (Indeed, not only does the collection hold a copy of every Brooks movie from *The Producers* onwards but also an endless progression of *Rocky* and *Friday the 13th* sequels, riffing on the commercial success of both franchises on home entertainment formats.) Cueing up a copy of *Spaceballs*, the technician winds the tape forward to the exact point where Dark Helmet and Sandurz are watching the playback, causing them to look in confusion at themselves watching the very scene that is currently playing out:

| | |
|---|---|
| DARK HELMET: | What the hell am I looking at? When does *this* happen in the movie? |
| SANDURZ: | Now! You're looking at now. Everything that happens now is happening *now*. |
| DARK HELMET: | What happened to then? |
| SANDURZ: | We passed then. |
| DARK HELMET: | When? |
| SANDURZ: | Just now. We're at *now*, now. |
| DARK HELMET: | Go back to then! |
| SANDURZ: | When? |

| | |
|---|---|
| DARK HELMET: | Now. |
| SANDURZ: | Now? |
| DARK HELMET: | Now! |
| SANDURZ: | I can't. |
| DARK HELMET: | Why? |
| SANDURZ: | We missed it! |
| DARK HELMET: | When? |
| SANDURZ: | Just now. |
| DARK HELMET: | When will then be now? |
| SANDURZ: | Soon! |

Perhaps more explicitly than any other scene in the movie, and arguably just as striking as the sudden eruption of *Blazing Saddles*'s Old West into a modern-day film studio, Brooks engages with the fact that the characters in *Spaceballs* are not only aware of the fact that they are operating within a fictional construct, but also that they are quite willing – if the opportunity arises – to use this knowledge to their advantage. Just as we suddenly see a Spaceball-helmeted drummer in the command centre thumping out a dramatic beat (in lieu of a full orchestra) as *Spaceball One* transforms into *Mega-Maid*, or hear Lone Starr's self-aware question 'Did I miss something? When did we get to Disneyland?!' when he first encounters Yogurt's troupe of Dinks, this scene more than any other emphasises the fact that when the metafilmic boundaries are so perceptibly malleable, viewer expectation is thrown into near-total uncertainty. Quite literally, in Brooks's cinematic world anything goes, further expanding upon the carnivalesque freedom of creative expression he had so staunchly advocated over the past two decades. Keyvan Sarkhosh explains that:

> [In *Spaceballs*] we can find a different kind of metaleptic intrusion of the real world of a film's production and distribution. When Dark Helmet (Rick Moranis) wants to find out where Lone Starr (Bill Pullman) and Princess Vespa (Daphne Zuniga) are hiding, Colonel Sandurz (George Wyner) advises them to have a look into the video cassette of the film *Spaceballs*. 'How can there be a cassette of the movie? We're still making it!', Lord Helmet wonders. But Sandurz tells him about the newly invented 'instant cassettes': 'they're out in the stores before the movie is finished'. And actually, as the corporal (Mitchell Bock) has a look at a storage rack where the video releases of all the previous Mel Brooks films are neatly strung, he finally comes to the last *Spaceballs* cassette. The cassette is put into a VCR, and after a fast-forward we can see Dark Helmet, Sandurz and the corporal watching themselves in the monitor watching themselves

and so forth – a perfect *mise en abyme*. As [Jean-Marc Limoges] convincingly points out, the humour of that scene results from the absurd fact that in the end, the characters are not at all bothered by finding objects in their diegetic world which originate from the extradiegetic – and supposedly real – world of the film's distribution.13

Because the characters are all in on the joke, Brooks fully expects that the audience will be too, and thus he is able to get away with an array of illogicalities which would be strictly off-limits for any non-comedic science fiction film. But then, if historical fact was never allowed to get in the way of a laugh in *History of the World: Part I*, the laws of physics similarly stood little chance of impeding Brooks's action in *Spaceballs*. For one, nobody seems to have any difficulty breathing in the vacuum of space, nor do they freeze to death within seconds of stepping out of the confines of their space vehicles into the depths of the surrounding cosmos. And while there is a subtle subtext of promoting environmental responsibility in the sight of the barren surface of Planet Spaceball, totally devoid of air having squandered their world's atmosphere, there is also the question of why Skroob and his minions would bother hatching such an elaborate plan to steal oxygen from Druidia when they could conceivably have chosen to extract it from any nearby unpopulated planet instead (thus saving themselves a great deal of trouble as a result). Because these issues do not concern the characters, Brooks seems to indicate, the audience should not lose any sleep over them either. It is possible to take this strategy too far, however, and some commentators – such as Roz Kaveney – have argued that Brooks was guilty of doing just that: 'Most of the time, comic SF films are, like Mel Brooks' *Spaceballs* [...], parodies of other SF films. This is not a problem in and of itself, but often comic writers' dislike of pomposity and pretension mean that they never get over the idea that this material is intrinsically ludicrous and therefore automatically funny. While there is a lot of material in the George Lucas *Star Wars* films worthy of parody, *Spaceballs* is generally crude in its comic appropriations; a good parody of *Star Wars* would understand what is loopily magnificent in the franchise as well as what is hopelessly crass'.14

In an uncharacteristic move by Brooks, *Spaceballs* was a film which featured relatively few actors who had worked on his previous features – and those regulars who did make an appearance were relegated to relatively minor roles, such as Dom DeLuise as the voice of Pizza the Hutt, an unrecognisable Rudy DeLuca as the robotic Vinnie, Ronnie Graham as the Druidian Royal Court's increasingly irascible Minister in charge of Vespa's wedding, and of course Dick Van Patten as the kindly but ineffectual King Roland ('Find her, save her [...] and if it's at all possible... try to save the car'). Instead, Brooks was to draw upon new emerging talent as well as established comedy stars of the time, and made full use of the chemistry between such unlikely combinations as Rick Moranis's geek-with-attitude Dark Helmet and his straight-faced underling Colonel Sandurz, beautifully underplayed by George Wyner. Bill Pullman and Daphne Zuniga produce just enough sparks between the feuding-yet-smitten Lone Starr and Princess Vespa to keep their relationship interesting – Brooks offers up an hilarious array of deliberately cliché-ridden love scene dialogue ('I realise now that love is one luxury a princess cannot afford') as the pair cack-handedly try to determine each other's intentions around the desert campfire. Yet as is so often the case with Brooks's films, it is the quirkier performances that remain most noteworthy – Joan Rivers's brusquely witty voice-work as Dot Matrix, John Candy's endearing likeability as Barf, and of course Brooks himself in the dual role of the wise Yogurt and corrupt Skroob (once again, as in *Blazing Saddles*, playing characters who exist at polar opposite ends of a particular hierarchy of power).

*Spaceballs* greatly benefited from John Morris's exemplary pastiche of John Williams's orchestral space opera scores. From the *Jaws*-like atmospheric music in the opening shot of *Spaceball One* to the strikingly effective theme which accompanies the metamorphosis of the ship into *Mega-Maid* ('Ready, Kafka?'), Morris perfectly captures the alternating liveliness and splendour of Williams's *Star Wars* soundtracks, and this is efficiently counterbalanced by The Spinners's title track 'Spaceballs', an effervescent, fast-paced song which accompanies the self-destruct sequence near the conclusion of the film. There is also much to enjoy about the film's skilful use of modelwork (achieved by Lucas's favoured special effects company Industrial Light and Magic, no less), particularly on the design and movement of *Spaceball One* itself, which harks back to a golden age of practical effects techniques which predated the prevalence of computer effects imagery to which audiences have become more readily accustomed in recent years.

More than most Brooks films, *Spaceballs* presented an interesting dichotomy whereby the film was received unfavourably by most critics, but nonetheless went on to find considerable popularity with audiences. Alan Neff, for instance, has stated the opinion that 'Director/ writer Brooks didn't harangue us back when he made *Blazing Saddles* and *Young Frankenstein*. Whatever his faults then, he didn't dawdle if a joke died, he was already on to the next one. He kept the punches rolling. In *Spaceballs*, I started keeping a running tally of how many stupid sight gags and shticks he was going to make us endure. Even as a star, Brooks doesn't seem to be having much fun (sniffing around women's bazooms, for instance). I guess even he doesn't believe in his cornball vaudeville routines anymore'.[15] On the other side of the argument, Sarah Miles Bolam and Thomas J. Bolam have praised the film's overall effectiveness, asserting that 'Brooks uses his mostly old visual and verbal jokes to transport his audience to a *Star Wars* world. [...] As President Skroob, Mel Brooks plays himself with the zany flair for which he has become noted. He also takes a turn as the dwarfish Yoghurt [sic] who makes a living doling out sage advice to wandering spacemen and selling them T-shirts and other merchandise with "*Spaceballs*" written all over them. And he does a good job in all his other capacities, particularly with his energizing of easygoing Bill Pullman. His humor is less vulgar than usual – visual puns such as "comb the desert" and dialogue such as "I can't make decisions. I'm the President", are truly funny'.[16] Robert C. Ring has argued that the film plays an important role in the evolution of the *Star Wars* spoof, laying the groundwork for many other parodies of the phenomenon which would be developed in later years: '*Spaceballs* is the first non-short *Star Wars* parody, and while it may arguably be no longer *the* best, its consistent, innocent humor remains laudable. Nowadays we have *Family Guy* characters injecting their crude sensibilities into *Star Wars* [...] and we've got *Robot Chicken* taking basic aspects of the saga and running wild with them. Back in the '80s, we had bad guys incensed because their radars were jammed with strawberry jam or because they got caught playing with dolls. Choose your poison'.[17]

So why does *Spaceballs* retain the tendency to divide critics all these years after its initial release? Certainly the cult following which grew around the film has helped to prolong its lifespan beyond several other entries in Brooks's *oeuvre* from this mid-to-late point in his career, assuring that it remains a visible feature of his filmography thanks to its many releases on home entertainment formats. Even in recent years, *Spaceballs* has remained a cult favourite amongst many sci-fi fans, its scenes having been adapted into many a *YouTube* mashup. Ott and Bonnstetter have made the insightful point that the film's very inventiveness may be one reason for its mixed fortunes with the critical community at the time of its debut in cinemas:

> Popular critics, who are guided by standards of taste and judgment created in relation to one cultural paradigm (i.e., modernism), suddenly find themselves evaluating art that reflects a new or emerging cultural paradigm (i.e., postmodernism) and thus are often highly critical of it. Since modernism privileged high art over low art, it is hardly surprising that critics would be so judgmental of *Spaceballs*. It is, after all, a mere 'oddball' (or more accurately 'spoof') comedy. But as a postmodern text, *Spaceballs* deconstructs the very high = low-art distinction central to modernism. Moreover, even when it is not the producer's (or director's) intent to reflect the new cultural paradigm, formal elements that address the anxieties of the new paradigm often seep into the art.[18]

There is no doubting that the film's reception by the critical community of the late eighties was, by and large, fairly damning. Marc Weinberg of *Orange Coast Magazine* led the charge with his assessment that: 'Once considered to be Hollywood's comic genius, [Brooks] is now more akin to a fossil who is unable to change with the times. [...] For a parody to work best, the material being satirized has to be straightforward to begin with. However, part of the charm of *Star Wars* was that it was always played for fun, with its tongue placed firmly in cheek. Subsequently, Brooks is not only lampooning material that comes 10 years after the fact, but is also sharply off target. Who cares about a *Star Wars* satire?'[19] Similarly uncomplimentary in his assessment was *New York Magazine*'s David Denby, who noted that 'when Mel Brooks makes one of his movie parodies, something obsessive and unself-conscious has to be there in the original to get him going. In the case of *Spaceballs*, his takeoff on the *Star Wars* series, the original material was kid-stuff-jokey to begin with, so Brooks can't find a way to be wild, vicious, or even naughty. Which is perhaps another way of saying that the great man may be tired at last. *Spaceballs*, nearly a super-production in its own right, is very tame'.[20] *The Washington Post*'s Hal Hinson bemoaned the fact that 'Brooks seems to have run out of gas in his movie takeoffs. Watching this new one, you get the feeling that he's just going through the motions with his genre series – that as long as there are genres there will be Mel Brooks genre-parodies. And for no other reason than that they are there to do. [...] There's no inspiration left – no drive. After that first joke, which at least gets you tittering, I don't think there's another first-rate comic idea in the whole film. And most of what he comes up with is achingly unfunny'.[21] Even the usually-appreciative Roger Ebert of *The Chicago Sun-Times* was unconvinced of the film's merits, opining that 'I enjoyed a lot of the movie, but I kept thinking I was at a revival. The strangest thing about *Spaceballs* is that it should have been made several years ago, before our appetite for *Star Wars* satires had been completely exhausted. [...] With *Spaceballs*, he has made the kind of movie that didn't really need a Mel Brooks. In bits and pieces, one way or another, this movie already has been made over the last 10 years by countless other satirists'.[22]

The cacophony of disapproval from reviewers did nothing to dent the popularity of *Spaceballs* with the moviegoing public, however. The film's commercial performance would prove to MGM that their faith in Brooks's talents was well-placed, as *People Weekly*'s Margot Dougherty reported at the time: 'With *Spaceballs*, the king of cinematic slapstick completes two decades of feature filmmaking. As a visit to the set suggested, Brooks still gets a kick out of what he does. But the question of the moment was whether audiences still get a kick out of what he does. [...] *Spaceballs* grossed $20 million in its first two weeks. More gratifying to Brooks, the movie is earning him praise. "Extremely funny – buoyantly tasteless," said the *Wall Street Journal*. "Eight trillion on the laugh meter," crowed *Today*'s Gene Shalit. Chutzpah blazing, Mel Brooks is back in the saddle again'.[23] Just to underscore her point, the film would eventually go on to accumulate a total domestic gross of $38,119,483 at the box-office,[24] comfortably covering both its budget and marketing. But it has continued to sell convincingly on videotape, DVD and Blu-Ray as well as making numerous repeat appearances on television, thus gathering new generations of fans while – due to its basis in science fiction – even managing to attract admirers of cult movies who were not necessarily devotees of Brooks's other cinematic work. And due to the film's enduring success, more recent reviews have reappraised *Spaceballs* in a rather less mordant light. *Movie Gazette*'s Gary Panton, for instance, acknowledges Brooks's benign intentions towards his source text, naming the film 'one of the most memorable space spoofs there's ever been. [...] It's there to be enjoyed rather than thought about. After all, there's nothing remotely intelligent about the line of humour being followed here. If anything, Brooks is perhaps guilty of aiming too low too often, but there's no denying that this film is funny. What's more, it's clearly been made with a lot of affection for the material it's satirizing, and that's the sort of touch which makes it impossible to dislike'.[25] Yet it is commentator Michael Rubino who provides what is perhaps the most succinct explanation of why *Spaceballs* has remained so perennially popular amongst such a wide demographic of cineastes:

> Brooks, along with co-writers Thomas Meehan and Ronny Graham, not only packed the film with as many gags and laughs as *Airplane!*, they also infused it with heart. That's the secret that most modern parody films miss: the audience still has to care about the stories and the characters... even if your movie prominently features a man covered in pizza. *Spaceballs* gets just about everything right, from the Industrial Light and Magic-created special effects to the fourth-wall-breaking sight gags (that whole home video, 'now is now' sequence is brilliant). Even if you don't get the references, or appreciate the fact that John Hurt reprises his role from *Alien*, the film still has enough jokes for everyone. It may not be his best movie, but I would argue that it's his last great one.[26]

When *Spaceballs* concludes with Skroob and his associates careening down onto *The Planet of the Apes* in the battered remnants of *Mega-Maid*, inadvertently recreating that film's famous Statue of Liberty twist ending and leading one of that world's puzzled simian denizens to exclaim 'There goes the planet!', no doubt many in the audience were wondering whether Yogurt's tongue-in-cheek predictions of a sequel would indeed bear fruit. Although actor Rick Moranis has spoken in recent years of Brooks's ultimately-abortive intention to produce a *Spaceballs* sequel after the commercial success of the original, no such production was to be forthcoming.[27] However, in 2008 – some two decades after *Spaceballs* had first arrived in American cinemas – Brooks and Meehan unveiled an animated spin-off entitled *Spaceballs: The Animated Series*. Broadcast on the G4 Channel, the short-lived show lasted for only thirteen half-hour episodes and was not well received by the critical community. Commencing with a pilot episode which retold the story of the *Spaceballs* movie in a heavily truncated format, the series proceeded to have all of its subsequent episodes focused upon a parody of a particular pop-culture phenomenon. These ranged from film franchises (including the *James Bond* series and *Jurassic Park*), prominent video games (*Grand Theft Auto*), comic books (*Spider Man*) and popular television shows (*American Idol*), as well as the then-recent *Star Wars* prequel series (a conceit used to present Dark Helmet's origin story). Brooks, Daphne Zuniga and Joan Rivers all reprised their roles from the original film, though Bill Pullman was replaced by the voice of Rino Romano and Rick Moranis was succeeded in the role of Dark Helmet by the vocal talents of Dee Bradley Baker. The late John Candy's role was also recast, with Tino Insana in the part of Barf. The series was not widely broadcast outside of North America, and has thus far failed to secure the same cult following enjoyed by the original movie.

By providing his own distinctive twist on the classic tale of good versus evil, Brooks had again presented audiences with a heartfelt validation of individual liberty – entreating us to value autonomy of expression, cherish the liberation offered by romance, and protect ourselves against the creeping encroachment of political oppression. His dexterous toying with the manifold conventions of the sci-fi genre had much more in common with the affectionate mockery of *Young Frankenstein* and *High Anxiety* than it had with the full-scale demolition of the Western demonstrated by *Blazing Saddles*, meaning that Brooks makes no attempt to conceal his fondness for the dramatic and entertainment potential of strange and eccentric fantasy situations suggested by a science fiction environment. As Crick sagely observes, 'after all the comedic stretching and squeezing, is space cinema itself left any the worse for wear? No, because Lucas fan Brooks is only pillow fighting here [...] as his targets' continuing success (*Star Wars'* later "prequel" series; endless *Star Trek* spin-offs; still more *Alien* movies; a big-budget relaunch of *Planet of the Apes*) makes clear'.[28] While the film could not, in and of itself, claim to have anything close to the long-term cultural impact of these mammoth franchises, its uninterrupted success as a cult feature and continued goodwill amongst mainstream audiences and sci-fi fans alike towards its aimiably offbeat charm have made it one of the most popular features of Brooks's later career. And while there are many reasons for the lasting appeal of *Spaceballs* – the engaging performances, wacky line of surreal situations, and consistently witty dialogue – the basic fact remains that it is very difficult to dislike a film which appends the legendary *Star Wars* opening crawl with the line: 'If you can read this, you don't need glasses'.

# REFERENCES

1. Box-office data drawn from the Internet Movie Database. <http://www.imdb.com/title/tt0094012/business>
2. Brian Lowry, '*Spaceballs*: The Set Visit', in *Starlog*, Issue 119, June 1987, 44-48, p. 44.
3. Wes Gehring, *Parody as Film Genre: Never Give a Saga an Even Break* (Westport: Greenwood Press, 1999), p. 198.
4. Lowry, p. 46.
5. M. Keith Booker, *Alternate Americas: Science Fiction Film and American Culture* (Westport: Praeger, 2006), p. 21.
6. Mel Brooks, in Patrick Carone, 'Interview: Icon Mel Brooks: A chat with the genius who brought us dancing monsters, the Schwartz, and the perfect fart joke', in *Maxim Online*, 6 February 2013. <http://www.maxim.com/entertainment/interview-icon-mel-brooks>
7. Robert Alan Crick, *The Big Screen Comedies of Mel Brooks* (Jefferson: McFarland and Company, 2009) [2002], p. 164.
8. Mel Brooks, in Steve Heisler, 'Mel Brooks on how to play Hitler, and how he almost died making *Spaceballs*', in *The Onion A.V. Club*, 13 December 2012. <http://www.avclub.com/article/mel-brooks-on-how-to-play-hitler-and-how-he-almost-89843>
9. David Desser and Lester D. Friedman, *American Jewish Filmmakers*, 2nd edn (Chicago: University of Illinois Press, 2004), p. 151.
10. Brian L. Ott and Beth Bonnstetter, '"We're at Now, Now": *Spaceballs* as Parodic Tourism', in *Southern Communication Journal*, Vol. 72, No. 4, October-December 2007, 309-27, p. 313.
11. Howard Hughes, *Outer Limits: The Filmgoers' Guide to the Great Science-Fiction Films* (London: I.B. Tauris, 2014), p. 252.
12. Desser and Friedman, p. 151.
13. Keyvan Sarkhosh, 'Metalepsis in Popular Comedy Film', in *Metalepsis in Popular Culture*, ed. by Karin Kukkonen and Sonja Klimek (Berlin: Walter de Gruyter Ltd., 2011), 171-95, p. 180.
14. Roz Kaveney, *From Alien to the Matrix: Reading Science Fiction Film* (London: I.B. Tauris, 2005), p. 53.
15. Alan Neff, *Movies, Movie Stars and Me* (Bloomington: Authorhouse, 2013), p. 63.
16. Sarah Miles Bolam, and Thomas J. Bolam, *Fictional Presidential Films: A Comprehensive Filmography of Portrayals from 1930 to 2011* (Bloomington: Xlibris, 2011).pp. 147-48.
17. Robert C. Ring, *Sci-Fi Movie Freak* (Iola: Krause Publications, 2011), p. 143.
18. Ott and Bonnstetter, pp. 311-12.
19. Marc Weinberg, 'Failing Film Makers', in *Orange Coast Magazine*, July 1987, 189-191, p. 190.
20. David Denby, 'Death Trap', in *New York Magazine*, 13 July 1987, 54-55, p. 55.
21. Hal Hinson, '*Spaceballs*', in *The Washington Post*, 24 June 1987. <http://www.washingtonpost.com/wp-srv/style/longterm/movies/videos/spaceballspghinson_a0c94a.htm>
22. Roger Ebert, '*Spaceballs*', in *The Chicago Sun-Times*, 24 June 1987. <http://www.rogerebert.com/reviews/spaceballs-1987>
23. Margot Dougherty, 'May The Farce Be With Him: *Spaceballs* Rockets Mel Brooks Into Lunatic Orbit', in *People Weekly*, 20 July 1987. <http://www.brookslyn.com/print/PeopleWeekly07-20-87/PeopleWeekly07-20-87.php>
24. Box-office data drawn from Box Office Mojo.

<http://www.boxofficemojo.com/movies/?id=spaceballs.htm>
25. Gary Panton, '*Spaceballs*: Movie Review', in *Movie Gazette*, 6 April 2005.
<http://movie-gazette.com/1269>
26. Michael Rubino, '*Spaceballs: 25th Anniversary*, in *DVD Verdict*, 28 August 2012.
<http://www.dvdverdict.com/reviews/spaceballs25thbluray.php>
27. Nick Venable, 'Rick Moranis Talks The *Spaceballs* Sequel That Never Was', in *CinemaBlend*, 24 June 2013.
<http://www.cinemablend.com/new/Rick-Moranis-Talks-Spaceballs-Sequel-Never-Was-38212.html>
28. Crick, p. 155.

# 9

# LIFE STINKS (1991)

IN THE EARLY NINETIES, Mel Brooks made an unexpected creative detour in his filmic career with the production of *Life Stinks*, interrupting his filmography's unbroken cycle of genre spoofs for the first time since the production of *The Twelve Chairs* more than two decades previously. A satirical appraisal of social attitudes in contemporary America, the film was to share with *The Twelve Chairs* the theme of unexpectedly coming to terms with poverty, and the insidious manner in which monetary affluence can deleteriously affect an individual's view of the less economically fortunate. The film's profound cultural themes and comparatively measured narrative pace marked it out as a conspicuous change in direction for Brooks – a controversial artistic choice which provoked some degree of curiosity amongst commentators.

In stark contrast to the broad-stroke defence of liberty depicted in *Spaceballs'* interstellar battle of good and evil, *Life Stinks* was to take a rather more nuanced view of personal freedom, asking reflective questions about the way that money provides autonomy while also, paradoxically, its accrual may inadvertently restrict individual choice. Brooks would use the film to examine the nature of independence, expounding upon the manner in which wealth has the adverse ability of affecting those who wield it by blinding them to the plight of the poor, leading to a distorted view of the underprivileged which emasculates any political or grass-roots attempts at achieving social parity. It was a bold move by Brooks, providing perhaps his most prominent socio-cultural subtext since *Blazing Saddles*, but implemented via a more sober and thoughtful approach than had been the case in his earlier, strident vindication of interpersonal equality.

Goddard Bolt (Mel Brooks) is an immensely wealthy American property magnate; the owner of the influential Bolt Enterprises corporation, he is a man for whom an interest in the lives of others is a trifling issue in comparison to the maintenance and growth of his massive personal fortune. He (quite literally) steps on the fingers of his employees without the slightest concern for their wellbeing, and his business dealings are revealed to be even less humane when he ruthlessly presses ahead with extravagant property developments that will displace South American tribal natives and elderly Floridians with equal callousness. During a meeting with his attorneys (prominent legal advisers otherwise known as the 'Three Wise Men'), Bolt unveils his ultimate dream – the construction of a massive, ultra-modern complex named the Bolt Center, which he intends to build atop a large area of slum housing in Los Angeles. Bolt already owns half of the real estate in that region, and intends to spend billions purchasing the other half from the city authorities in order to clear out the slums and start work on his new development. It is obvious that he cares nothing for the hundreds of dispossessed people who will need to be forcibly removed from the derelict area, which serves as the closest thing they can call a home.

The intended ease of his plans is swiftly thwarted, however, when he discovers that his business rival Vance Crasswell (Jeffrey Tambor) has already bought up the remaining real estate, leaving Bolt at an impasse. Crasswell asks Bolt to relinquish the slums under his ownership, revealing that he had been born in an impoverished area nearby and claiming (not entirely convincingly) that he had always wanted to renovate the area for the benefit of its residents when he had the financial means to do so. Crasswell knows only too well that his competitor has no compassion whatever for the poor, and thus does not even attempt to appeal to the hard-nosed man's empathy. But as Bolt had been born into wealth, Crasswell taunts him that he could never begin to comprehend the hardships that the slums' denizens must face on a daily basis. The wily Crasswell thus uses Bolt's vanity to trick him into agreeing to a bet: if Bolt can survive for thirty days in the slums, he will relinquish his ownership of the real estate that he has just bought from the city. On the other hand, if Bolt is unable to make it through the whole month he must then hand over his half of the property to Crasswell.

Against the advice of his legal advisors, Bolt agrees to Crasswell's wager under three conditions: that he be electronically tagged to prove that he will not leave the slum area during the next thirty days, that he not reveal his true identity to anyone, and that he not take a single penny of cash with him during his time there. To ensure that he is not recognised, he shaves off his moustache, while Crasswell takes custody of his expensive toupee. Trusting his financial affairs into the hands of his lawyers with an official Power of Attorney, Bolt is then unceremoniously dropped off in the centre of the slum district in the sweltering heat of the summer sun, his only comfort being the knowledge that his electronic tag will be automatically deactivated when his month of self-imposed exile is over.

Bolt's problems begin in earnest that night when he is unable to secure even the most modest shelter because he is incapable of raising the necessary $2.50 for a bed at a flophouse. Trying an alleyway, he is soon besieged by vermin, and the staff of the local church show him no compassion – spiritual or otherwise. Eventually, he finds a doorway to sleep in, only to be accidentally tipped into a dumpster by a blissfully unaware waste disposal operative. Then, having finally stumbled across an empty cardboard box to sleep under, he is rudely awakened by the kindly-but-eccentric Sailor (Howard Morris) who is obliviously urinating next to him. Sailor (so called because 'I was nearly in the Navy') decides that Bolt must be named 'Pepto' on account of the fact that he has the word imprinted on his forehead, having spent the night sleeping against a Pepto-Bismol container. Though Bolt finds the encounter distinctly awkward, Sailor takes a shine to him when the down-on-his-luck tycoon offers him a monogrammed handkerchief to blow his nose on, lamenting that nobody gives anything away in this district.

As the day progresses, Bolt lurches from one indignity to another. He tries to appropriate some waste food from a fast food seller only to be hounded away, and even briefly contemplates stealing from a blind beggar before trying his luck as a windshield washer instead. His scheme soon turns awry, alas, when his fingers are trapped in the window of a fast-retreating car, meaning that he is still no further forward in his attempts to gather some much-needed money. And as for his desperate attempts to raise cash by street dancing, the least said the better. Just as Bolt is beginning to think that his lot can't get any worse, he is mugged in an alleyway by the intimidating Mean Victor (Brian Thompson) and his diminutive accomplice Yo (Raymond O'Connor), who rough him up and steal his expensive leather shoes. The assailants are driven off by Molly (Lesley Ann Warren), a feisty bag-lady who is incensed that her territory has been violated by strangers, but Bolt is astonished that someone would be willing to take his life just to purloin a pair of shoes. Molly is short-tempered and fiercely protective of her turf, a section of alleyway which contains all of her worldly possessions (a collection of useful refuse that she has salvaged from garbage cans and other places nearby). She takes pity on Bolt when it becomes apparent that his current situation has left him completely out of his depth, and furnishes him with an old pair of shoes that she has recovered.

Molly takes Bolt to the local homeless mission, where the ravenous millionaire tucks into a plate of the free stew that has been provided for service users living in the area. There, they meet Sailor and his similarly genial friend Fumes (Teddy Wilson) who engage them in conversation, but Bolt is puzzled by Molly's strangely nihilistic views on life when the other locals seem upbeat even in spite of their desperate circumstances. Later, they witness a wedding being conducted at a run-down church nearby. With no small amount of respect in his voice, Bolt openly admires the fact that a couple can find love even amidst the most mournful poverty, but Molly scoffs at their happiness. She reveals that her own husband had left her years beforehand, plunging her life into chaos as she had no way of tying up the financial mess that his sudden departure had caused. Though she had been a successful dancer prior to her marriage, she had given up her career upon meeting her husband and thus had no way of supporting herself after he had gone, eventually leading her into a nervous breakdown. At this point she has been living on the streets for eight years.

Bolt and Molly return to her living area, only to discover that all of her possessions have been doused in gasoline and set alight by a vengeful Victor and Yo. When a nearby homeowner asks if she should call the fire brigade, a disparaging bystander replies that there is no need, as from his viewpoint all that is on fire is a collection of old garbage. He has no idea that he is witnessing the destruction of the closest thing that Molly has to a home. However, not one to lick her wounds for long, Molly swears vengeance and rounds up Sailor and Fumes to help her extract justice from her enemies. She instructs Bolt to antagonise Victor and his motor-mouthed comrade, goading them into chasing after him – at which point he is to lead them to the door of a nearby Chinese restaurant. Bolt is bewildered at why Molly doesn't take legal action against them instead (oblivious to the sheer implausibility of suing them under the circumstances), but reluctantly goes along with her plan. Invading the enemies' den and kicking over a table as they are busily bagging up quantities of cocaine for sale, Bolt succeeds in suitably aggravating the pair and causing them to chase after him. But Molly's plan goes awry when Victor easily breaks down the restaurant's door after Bolt heads inside to safety, causing him to be punched repeatedly by Victor and cast onto the road outside. This sets off the proximity alert on Bolt's electronic tag, meaning that he is outside the territorial boundary agreed in Crasswell's bet. Thus he has no choice but to repeatedly head back for a beating by the increasingly perplexed Victor, keeping the tag within range, until Molly scalds both antagonists with the boiling hot contents of a waste container that she has taken from the restaurant's kitchens. As the burned villains flee from the scene, Molly reflects with admiration at what she believes to be an commendable display of bravery by Bolt... little realising the true reason for his apparent courage.

Back at Crasswell's office, his team of personal advisors notify him that with Bolt venturing out of bounds (due to their tracking of his tag) he was at risk of breaching the terms of the bet by mere seconds. Crasswell suggests that this should be reason enough to declare him the winner of the wager, until he is informed that Bolt's own lawyers will have a copy of the same data and thus will know that he was not outside the agreed area for the full half-minute necessary to void the agreement. Crasswell seems reflective when he is told of the circumstances of Bolt's predicament on the streets, but can barely contain his glee when one of the advisors reflects on the fact that with so much danger surrounding his old rival living rough, Bolt's very life may be in peril.

A storm sets in that night, causing a flood of rainwater in the storm drain where Bolt and his new acquaintances are sleeping in cardboard boxes. As their makeshift accommodation is swept away by the tide, they make their way to the mission, only to discover that it is mysteriously closed. Nobody suspects the truth of the situation, which is that Crasswell has deliberately had the building shut down knowing that it will make Bolt's situation all the more difficult. Eventually they head to a nearby demolition site, though Sailor's health takes a turn for the worse and he leaves during the night in search of medical aid. The next morning, Fumes panics at his friend's absence and leads a search for him. Shortly after, Bolt discovers Sailor's corpse on the sidewalk next to a restaurant, still clutching his monogrammed handkerchief as though it was a prized possession. The proprietor unfeelingly tells Bolt to remove the body at once, to avoid any damage to his trade. Paramedics arrive on the scene and unceremoniously bundle Sailor's remains into the back of their van, reasoning that they will take him straight to the morgue as he isn't significant enough to warrant the coroner's attention. Bolt watches the unemotional disposal of his friend's body in quiet contemplation. Some time later, Fumes manages to persuade the authorities to part with Sailor's cremated ashes, and he, Bolt and Molly bid the old eccentric an emotional farewell by scattering him in a storm drain (the closest they can manage to achieving his dream of a funeral at sea).

With only two days left until Bolt reaches the deadline of the bet, Crasswell is starting to panic. Frantic at the notion that he may lose his own craftily-conceived wager, he visits Bolt's attorneys and pleads with them to betray their employer in exchange for vast sums of money. Back in the slums, however, Bolt has been counting down the days and is euphoric that he has somehow managed to overcome the odds and survive the terms of Crasswell's bet. Stealing a bottle of champagne, he celebrates his victory with Molly, though she remains unaware of his true identity or even the reason for his blatant jubilation. But joy soon turns to fury when Bolt returns to his palatial mansion with Molly... only to discover Crasswell is there, hosting a black-tie dinner party. Now denying all knowledge of the bet, Crasswell reveals that Bolt's lawyers have used their Power of Attorney in order to declare their old employer *non compos mentis* – as far as the public are concerned, Bolt decided to live rough on the streets because of a mental breakdown, and thus all of his possessions and financial wealth now belong to his legal advisors. Even his very home now belongs to Crasswell, who has bought it from the attorneys. Affecting a dismissive attitude, Crasswell has the pair removed from the premises before anything further can be said about the real truth which lies behind the wager.

Now destitute for real, Bolt wanders the streets of the slum district frantically trying to devise a way of regaining what is rightfully his. He runs into a delusional homeless man (Rudy DeLuca) who swears that he is 'J. Paul Getty', and the pair get into a vicious fight over who is the richer of the two. Eventually the police intervene to break up the argument and, believing Bolt rather than the other man to be living out a fantasy, have him taken to hospital. Now suffering a full-fledged breakdown, Bolt mutters to himself continuously about the grim ramifications of his dishonest treatment at the hands of Crasswell. Believing the former mogul to be delusional, the doctor on duty (Marvin Braverman) mistakenly prescribes him large and repeated doses of a sedative which eventually leads to Bolt winding up in an Intensive Care Unit. Following corrective treatment, Molly comes to visit him at his bedside and pleads with the unconscious Bolt to pull through. After she declares a heartfelt proclamation of love for him, the one-time magnate stirs back into consciousness, seemingly alert and ready to act once more.

At a star-studded event, Crasswell is publicly unveiling his plans for 'Crasswell City' – the ostentatious new development which will be replacing the slum district in Los Angeles. With a flourish, he commences the demolition of the area, leading to a team of bulldozers thundering towards the buildings nearby and causing many homeless people to scramble for safety. Molly and Bolt, now discharged from hospital, meet with a fleeing Fumes who hastily explains the situation to them. Filled with a new determination, Bolt steals a loudhailer from one of the bulldozers and – with some help from Molly and Fumes – manages to persuade the displaced people of the area to stop their retreat and invade Crasswell's high society party instead. With a promise of good food and drink, the starving destitute locals pile into the nearby exhibition area, promptly causing total disarray. While the ensuing hubbub is causing a distraction, Bolt commandeers one of the bulldozers; Crasswell, recognising his old nemesis, decides to do likewise in an attempt to prevent him from causing further disruption. Following a battle between the demolition machines, Bolt eventually manages to catch his weaselly enemy in the claws of his bulldozer and – in full view of nearby television cameras – forces Crasswell to admit to his scheming, leading him to suddenly 'recall' that Bolt won the bet that they had earlier agreed upon.

With his competitor's perfidious plot now blown wide open, Bolt successfully sues Crasswell and wins back his fortune... in addition, as originally arranged, to the land rights of the slum district itself. But forever changed by his experiences on the streets, Bolt resolves to have the area renovated not for the benefit of the super-rich, but rather to aid the people who are currently living there. Zero-cost housing, a large public park and new facilities for medical care and counselling are all promised. In the film's epilogue, Bolt is seen marrying Molly at the modest church at the centre of the very district that he plans to modernise, surrounded by the friends and acquaintances he had made while living rough there. As the honeymooners drive off in a white Rolls Royce, bearing the personalised registration plate 'PEPTO', their car is angrily accosted by none other than 'J. Paul Getty', who swears that it has been stolen from him because he left his keys in the ignition.

Whether fairly or not, *Life Stinks* has acquired the reputation of being perhaps the most forgettable comedy of Mel Brooks's entire cinematic career. Largely this notoriety has been derived from the fact that the film was largely ignored by audiences at the time of its release, and has failed to make much of an impact in the years since. Robert Alan Crick acknowledges this very fact when he observes that, 'generally dismissed as the least successful of his post-1970s directorial efforts, Mel Brooks's *Life Stinks* has been struggling to pull free of the stigma of failure ever since it slid in and out of American theaters pretty much unnoticed during summer of 1991. Though a fair-sized hit overseas in the months that followed, at home *Life Stinks* caused barely a ripple'.[1] Indeed, the film was a rare example of Brooks facing both critical disdain *and* commercial disappointment – with a production budget of $13,000,000, it went on to accrue a domestic total gross of only $4,102,526.$[2] From a financial standpoint, the film's performance with US audiences was deeply unsuccessful, leading commentators of the time such as *Spy* Magazine's Celia Brady to note that 'Mel Brooks's *Life Stinks*, a.k.a. *Mel Sucks*, did $600,000 total business its second weekend. At 845 theaters, 6 shows per weekend, $5 per ticket, that's 24 people per viewing'.[3] But the reason for this apparent failure may have been reliant on a number of different contributory factors. *Life Stinks* was released alongside very strong box-office competition in the summer of 1991 (James Cameron's *Terminator 2: Judgment Day* and Kevin Reynolds's *Robin Hood: Prince of Thieves* most prominent among them), including many successful comedies (Ron Underwood's *City Slickers*, David Zucker's *The Naked Gun 2 1/2: The Smell of Fear*, Jim Abrahams's *Hot Shots!*). Perhaps most notably of all, the marked and unanticipated change in direction from what had by then become entrenched audience expectation of Brooks's cinematic output may not have helped the film's fortunes in American theatres.

One possible reason for *Life Stinks*'s descent into relative obscurity may lie in an uncharacteristic lack of assuredness in Brooks's handling of his movie's challenging subject matter. Working in collaboration with Rudy DeLuca and Steve Haberman on the screenplay, the film's central premise of a wealthy and powerful figure struggling to exist in straitened circumstances of poverty had been regularly revisited ever since Mark Twain's novel *The Prince and the Pauper* (1881) and its many subsequent adaptations, most notably in original scenarios posited in films such as Gregory LaCava's *My Man Godfrey* (1936), later remade by Henry Koster in 1957, and Preston Sturges's *Sullivan's Travels* (1942). Arguably, however, the proximity of *Life Stinks* to the then-fading age of high capitalism associated with the eighties means that the film also bears fruitful comparison to John Landis's well-received satires *Trading Places* (1983) and *Coming to America* (1988), which also saw the juxtaposition of affluence and deprivation cast against contemporary American urban settings to great effect. (Indeed, there is a pleasingly oblique reference to *Trading Places* when the delirious Bolt, hospitalised and convinced that his stocks are in peril, cries 'Dump my pork bellies!', recalling the earlier film's Randolph and Mortimer Duke.) Brooks faced an uphill struggle in employing such a scenario for comedic effect; as Crick succinctly notes, '*Life Stinks*' very premise is at odds with itself, really, [as it] demands Brooks somehow wear kid gloves and boxing gloves at the same time. Play the material too gently, nobody laughs; come on too strong, risk charges of blatant insensitivity'.[4] There is a palpable effort on the part of Brooks and his co-writers to allude to some of the major issues facing the homeless, not treating these problems superficially but likewise avoiding the temptation to dwell upon them overduly. Thus there are only occasional hints towards the substance abuse, sexual peril and health difficulties which blight the lives of so many homeless people, and though Brooks never lingers on any one issue for too long, the relative brevity accentuates rather than undermines the seriousness of these concerns because collectively they form a larger social patchwork which is considerably more difficult for the viewer to ignore. As Roger Ebert notes, 'this is a premise Brooks and his writers have borrowed from *Sullivan's Travels* [...] in which Joel McCrea plays a Hollywood director who went on the road as a bum. But the streets are a little meaner in 1991 than they were in 1939, and the affluent are stingier. It is sometimes all Brooks can do to make his movie seem like a comedy, when the desperation of the homeless is so evident in every scene'.[5] For all the film's company of amiable eccentrics and warm-hearted itinerant outcasts, there is no denying the overarching sense of urban decay and personal desperation that the film generates at times. Witnessing Molly's despondency as her meagre possessions are torched, only for a bystander to dismiss the event as merely the destruction of a collection of worthless old waste, is a genuinely affecting moment, as is the death of the ever-sociable Sailor who – as Bolt accurately states at his 'funeral' – may have been perpetually filthy, but whose 'heart was always good and clean'. In investing the film with both pathos and genuine social concern, Brooks was attempting to heighten awareness of the plight of dispossessed people not just on the Californian coast, but across America at large – though, of course, in seeking to address such contentious subject matter within the framework of a comedy the overall effectiveness of his efforts were often judged with some scepticism by commentators. William Brigham, for instance, has argued:

In Gregory LaCava's *My Man Godfrey* (1936), a disillusioned millionaire eschews his life of luxury and joins the 'real people' living in plywood and aluminum shanties along New York's East River. Two generations later, in *Life Stinks* (1991), Mel Brooks's millionaire protagonist wagers that he can survive on guts and instinct among a similar population on Los Angeles's skid row – the stakes being possession of a large chunk of prime Los Angeles real estate. In 55 years, the story line changed enough to reflect the shift in financial nexus from one coast to another, but remained constant enough to illustrate the seemingly unending plight of what Henry Miller called 'the dispossessed in America'. Even considering the differences in the solvency of the American economy during the Great Depression and what now precipitates the dilemma faced by millions of homeless people, and millions of housed but poor families, it is still clear that Hollywood is only superficially addressing (or not addressing at all) the elemental yet important causes of homelessness in America today: poverty, unemployment, and lack of adequate and affordable housing.[6]

Because of Brooks's perennial and heartfelt espousal of individual liberty, it seemed inevitable that he would lament the deleterious impact of homelessness on the potential life choices of anyone affected by such destitution; after all, when someone must by necessity expend all of their resourcefulness on finding shelter from the elements and grieving over the fact that they 'don't know where [their] next meal's comin' from', exploring their innate creative freedom is not necessarily at the top of their list of personal priorities. That said, while Brooks in no way demeans the immediacy or seriousness of the perils which regularly face those who are living on the streets, he also emphasises the sheer inventiveness that they must (by necessity) employ in their attempts to live another day. When we see Terrence Williams's street kid dancing with such skill and verve ('Hot two!') as a means of artistic expression conceived primarily to raise money from admiring bystanders, for instance, we become even more aware of his talents when the completely untrained Bolt tries his hand at the same routine and ends up seeing his efforts greeted not with appreciation but piteous contempt. Brooks also seems to take much satisfaction in developing the fanciful notions that the various street-dwellers concoct to stoke up their dwindling supply of hope, their inventiveness spurred on solely in an attempt to grasp some vestige of optimism from the grimness of their immediate situation. And yet with equal cogency we also see that the pre-bet Bolt, for all his billions, is unwittingly also trapped –

albeit in his case by unthinking prejudice and a worldview which is utterly driven by profit motive, thus rendering him almost as bereft of autonomy as those who have freer minds but no material resources.

At the heart of *Life Stinks* is the idea that freedom is an essentially mutable concept, and one which is sought by different people in different ways. Before Bolt makes his wager, we see clearly his disdain for anyone other than himself – a characteristic which could not be made more obvious than when he casually flicks a tiny figure of a homeless person casually off his scale model of the slum district prior to development as though it were a wayward insect. His time spent living on the streets makes him realise the extent to which his own freedoms have been largely predicated upon his vast wealth rather than his personal skills, a humbling realisation which changes his viewpoint drastically. Mindful that Molly had helped him survive during his time in the slums, he does not cast her aside when he believes that his fortunes have been restored but rather – realising that he truly loves her for who (and not what) she really is – invites her to share in his wealth. Only when Bolt is betrayed by Crasswell and realises that he now really does have nothing, can he finally understand the essentially ephemeral nature of his materialistic life – an apprehension which leads to his mental breakdown. Ultimately it takes Molly, pleading with him at his hospital bedside to pull through, to make him see the bigger picture: 'I know they're only moments. But that's all life is. Just a bunch of moments. Most of them are lousy. But once in a while, you steal a good one'. By emphasising the fact that while she may have no worldly possessions of note, she and Bolt still have each other (a bond that no money can buy), he finally rallies and eventually manages to successfully challenge Crasswell's treachery at the last minute. Yet tellingly, having realised the transient nature of affluence Bolt does not choose to give away his vast fortune to the less fortunate, but rather resolves to use his resources in a more responsible and supportive manner for the greater good of all. Thus in regaining his fortune, even with a fresh personal philosophy which has been forged by his more fully-rounded understanding of life, it is left to the audience's own opinion with regard to whether Bolt's new-found sense of altruism will extend beyond the renovation of the slum district into an area designed to better support the less fortunate. As Sylvia P. Flanagan argues, 'without his fortune, servants, limos and lawyers, [Bolt] stumbles his way through life at the bottom, begging for change, scrambling for shelter and running for his life. Bolt's philosophy is, "Money isn't the most important thing in life. But without it, life stinks"'.[7]

It is, perhaps, a more accurate notion to suggest that Brooks intends for the film to have a transformative effect on the audience's own views regarding the difficulties facing the lives of the homeless, mirroring Bolt's own personal conversion from cold-hearted corporate penny-pincher into an empathetic, socially-responsible individual. Edgar A. Levenson concisely surmises that 'maybe, as Mel Brooks put it, "life stinks" and recognizing that is a prerequisite for living successfully'[8] – a viewpoint which certainly embodies with some degree of accuracy Bolt's reflections following his breakdown. Yet a case may be made that his personal journey is ultimately shaped by the people who he meets along the way. Had he encountered relentless abuse and social deprivation rather than the generous, well-meaning individuals whom he stumbles upon in the slum, presumably his situation and subsequent outlook may have been different indeed. Even the narcotic-peddling Mean Victor and Yo, the nominal antagonists within the run-down district, are played largely for laughs – there is a definite aspect of cartoon violence as Victor repeatedly thumps Bolt, genuinely puzzled as to why the newcomer keeps coming back for yet another helping of hostility. The occasional lapse into physical humour may have been an attempt to lighten the mood of a film which otherwise contains an unusually intense series of dramatic scenarios for a Brooks film, but the effect appeared jarring in the eyes of many critics. Marjorie Baumgarten of *The Austin Chronicle*, for instance, bemoaned the fact that in her opinion the film appeared uneven and confused in the implementation of its social commentary, venturing that 'the problem with *Life Stinks* is that it's got its heart in the right place but not a whole lot else. The movie has an intrusively inauthentic feel to it. [...] The movie has its moments but it plays like a ball of confusion. *Life Stinks* seems to be Brooks' bid to be taken seriously and leave the fart jokes behind. And something about that stinks'.[9] While certainly there are times that the film stretches viewer credulity – consider for instance Lesley-

Ann Warren's suspiciously perfect white teeth, in spite of her character's eight years of sleeping rough, or hordes of homeless people swarming into a high-class demolition party which conveniently appears to have no private security protection – these lapses of plausibility appear all the more evident because of inevitable comparison to the outrageously larger-than-life settings regularly posited by most of Brooks's other films. But then, unlike so many earlier entries in the Brooksian canon, *Life Stinks* never breaks the fourth wall, and the only meandering into out-and-out fantasy occurs when the audience are treated to a brief dream-like sequence where Bolt and Molly engage in a touching dance number to the music of Cole Porter in a dingy warehouse filled with old recovered clothes.

*Life Stinks*'s occasional engagement with slapstick also seems striking – if ultimately a little jarring, given the film's heavyweight subject matter in contrast to Brooks's genre spoofs. As Jonathan Bernstein helpfully observed at the time of the film's release in 1991, *Life Stinks* 'is noteworthy [...] because it embodies not only this year's buzzword, redemption, but also next year's – Chaplinesque'.[10] Thus we encounter *The Three Stooges*-style slapping contest between Bolt and Rudy DeLuca's superlatively belligerent 'J. Paul Getty' over which man is the wealthier, are made immediately aware of the juxtaposition of grinding poverty and immense wealth from an opening sequence which shows Bolt's stretch limousine drenching a collection of homeless people in rainwater from a roadside puddle, and – in the ultimate ignominy – witness Bolt being manhandled as his very wheelchair is stolen from under him at the hospital where he is being treated for mental trauma. There is also a (somewhat contrived) battle between Bolt and Crasswell in control of roaring demolition vehicles, bringing to mind a *Godzilla* battle – complete with 'bleeding' hydraulics – as the villain of the piece gets his definitive comeuppance. Yet while it is difficult not to raise a smile at the desperate Bolt trying to strip his purloined mansion of tapestries and Rodin sculptures before a hall full of aghast socialites, waddling under the weight of a priceless painting ('My Van Gogh! Come on, Dr Gachet – we're leaving!'), these situations are strikingly few and far between in a film which contained arguably the greatest depth of characterisation since the height of Brooks's fame in the mid-seventies. Unlike so many of his later spoof movies, there is a real sense that he is making a determined attempt to present a full cast of real people with emotional needs and genuine concerns, rather than occasional lapses into caricature with comic ciphers who are designed specifically to drive the plot. But coming at such a late stage in his directorial career, this lurch in emphasis did not play well with critics such as *The New York Times*'s Janet Maslin, who found the change in direction largely unpersuasive: 'Stopped in his tracks by the essential grimness of his subject, Mr Brooks is no longer his customary wisecracking self. He becomes subdued, compassionate and – worst of all, given that this is Mel Brooks – polite. The film still occasionally finds time to be rude, but only in the most sophomoric way. [...] Only at rare moments does *Life Stinks* offer much in the way of surprise or grace'.[11]

Because of the greater prominence of satire within the film, given Brooks's heightened degree of social commentary, he does not pull his punches when it comes to apportioning the blame for the plight of homeless people and prevailing attitudes towards the difficulties which face them. The church is found wanting when, faced with Bolt's desperate pleas for basic shelter, the itinerant millionaire is sent packing with little regard to New Testament teachings on the moral obligations of providing care for the poor. (Once again Brooks draws a clear line between spiritual faith and organised religion, as Bolt's unsatisfactory experiences in the face of religious hypocrisy don't stop him from falling back on a traditional belief system to sustain him in his desperation: 'Thank you, God. I'm sorry I didn't believe in you when I was rich,' he prays as the duration of his bet finally expires.) The homeless mission may be a source of emergency shelter and nourishment for those who would otherwise go hungry, but its sudden closure as a result of Crasswell's scheming proves that it is just as susceptible to corruption as any other organisation. The medical profession is also not exempt from Brooks's censure: Bolt's experiences at the hospital are circumscribed by the casual neglect of overworked staff and the supercilious arrogance of Marvin Braverman's swaggering Dr Kahahn. A physician who is thoroughly lacking in concern for his patients, Kahahn's sole method of treatment appears to be repeated administration of 500mg of the antipsychotic drug Thorazine – a medication which proves rather too effective when he neglects to remember treating

Bolt and orders repeated injections, thus rapidly landing him in an Intensive Care Unit. ('How does a thing like this happen?' he wonders aloud upon news that Bolt has been overmedicated, automatically believing himself to be blameless for his condition – because, after all, he is in a position of seniority.) Yet for all his condescension and self-importance, there is no doubting the fact that Kahahn is operating under great pressure due to the sheer number of patients awaiting admission to a hospital ward; when he mordantly remarks that he feels as though he is the only doctor on duty at the hospital, Brooks lays emphasis on the hidden truth of the observation by making it seem as though this is actually the case (as every other member of medical staff that we see milling around are actually nurses, orderlies and other support personnel rather than medical doctors).

Foremost among the characters to fall within the sights of Brooks's satirical condemnation are, of course, the corporate executives and legal advisors with whom Bolt initially identifies and – as his ordeal plays out – eventually come to be responsible for his downfall. Jeffrey Tambor wrings every ounce of devious underhandedness out of the cunning Vance Crasswell's dissolute motivations; such is Tambor's quirky charisma as an actor, he is at his most entertaining as the villainous character's iniquitous plans reach their apex, Crasswell's sheer duplicity laid bare for all to see. Crasswell has even less concern for the homeless than Bolt initially does, though his grinding insincerity and lofty claims of being a 'poor kid made good' makes his supposedly benign – yet ultimately self-interested – intentions for the area seem all the more repellent. (Bolt blows open the truth of his rival's objective when he attacks the decorative archway of the new complex's development in half, inadvertently giving Crasswell City the more revealing name of 'Crass City'.) 'Where else but in America could a poor, deprived boy from this very same neighbourhood return one day to destroy it?' Crasswell asks without the merest hint of irony in his pre-demolition speech, and naturally enough the patriotic Brooks is quick to come to his country's defence: while it is true that the individual liberty afforded by the free market can bring about near-limitless possibilities for those with societal privilege and personal wealth, Brooks immediately draws attention to the fact that with rights also come responsibilities. 'This is America! Every person has a right to have a place to live!'

Bolt cries with passion, emphasising that the predicament of homelessness should not be stigmatised by those who are not willing to work towards a new and better resolution to society's problems. America is a nation which offers endless possibilities, Brooks argues, and any factor that unfairly limits an individual's potential – whether racial intolerance, as in *Blazing Saddles*, the damaging corporate excess shown in *Silent Movie*, or the reinforcement of unhelpful social attitudes as demonstrated in *Life Stinks* – needs to be challenged and overcome in order to ensure the greatest degree of freedom for all.

Although Brooks gives an atypically low-key performance as Bolt, arguably even more restrained than his thoughtful turn as Dr Thorndyke in *High Anxiety*, he is given excellent support by an eclectic cast of actors led by one-time Academy Award and Golden Globe nominee Lesley Ann Warren as the deeply unconventional but compassionate bag lady Molly. A trained ballet dancer, Warren provides an unexpected highlight of her character's onscreen relationship with Bolt via the Fred and Ginger-style dance routine that she and Brooks engage in through the dingy confines of a run-down warehouse (suddenly brightly lit as though it were the set of an old fifties musical). Though the actors' on-screen chemistry appears uneven at times, Brooks provides just enough character development to flesh out the budding romance between Bolt and Molly; highlighting the surprising areas of commonality which exist between them, the characters' growing attraction as well as their kindred spirit of independence aids them in overcoming their huge cultural differences. As Crick has stated, '*Life Stinks* closely recalls Brooks' early works, most of which aren't love stories per se, yet do spend some ninety minutes forging bonds between two people who at first seem to have nothing in common',[12] and certainly by ringing the similarities as well as the changes between Bolt and Molly – one voluntarily embracing hardship, the other impoverished through no fault of her own – Brooks succeeds in bringing a personal angle to broader social issues of personal adversity, helping to assuage any danger of overt preachiness.

As with so many Brooks films, some of the most enjoyable performances are enacted by the diverse range of supporting players which include Carmine Caridi's acerbically sharp-tongued flophouse owner, an easy-going turn from Teddy Wilson as the caring and dependable (if permanently inebriated) Fumes, and the ever-versatile Howard Morris as Sailor – notable for his entertainingly garbled accounts of life, such as his claims of being denied admission to the Navy because 'They said I had "pluralcy"'). Rudy DeLuca's brief but entertaining appearance as the frenzied 'J. Paul Getty' and the always-watchable Brian Thompson as the hulking Mean Victor (given able support by Raymond O'Connor's mildly hyperactive Yo) also help to ensure that even in spite of *Life Stinks*'s exploration of substantial social concerns, there are still plenty of compellingly oddball portrayals to aid in lightening the overall mood. Bolt's obsequious team of attorneys also provide excellent value for money, nominally led by Stuart Pankin's Pritchard – a legal advisor who effortlessly turns from slimy lackey to heartless snob after betraying Bolt as a result of no greater motivation than 'a shitload of money':

> BOLT: Ten years. You've been with me ten years! How could you turn on me? Where is your sense of loyalty, honesty, decency?
> PRITCHARD: Mr Bolt. We're lawyers!

Critical response to *Life Stinks* was overwhelmingly negative, with reviewers of the time highly sceptical of Brooks's departure from genre spoofery and his handling of controversial social issues within a narrative framework that was assumed to be, at heart, essentially played out as light entertainment. The criticism of *The Deseret News*'s Chris Hicks was largely representative: '*Life Stinks* is Mel Brooks' first film since 1987's *Spaceballs*, and though he is attempting to lace his brand of broad comedy with poignancy, it is still basically a vaudeville skit film. [...] Some of the shtick here is quite funny: A scattering-the-ashes scene, a take on both *Les Miserables* and Steve Martin's *The Jerk*, and a delightful musical number, an homage to the MGM musicals of old. Other bits are tiresome and weak, and the climactic battle of the earth-movers is particularly lame. Attempts at social commentary are equally uneven'.[13] Others, such as Hal Hinson of *The Washington Post*, were considerably more damning: 'The mood of the film is too crass to reach the level of fairy tale. The picture gives the impression that the filmmakers thought that homelessness was cute and that those ratty back streets and alleyways were filled with darling eccentrics. This is one of the unfunniest of subjects for comedy, and while there may be a graceful way of tackling it, Brooks and his compatriots haven't discovered it. [...] Brooks has never been as charmless onscreen as he is here; Bolt is a swine and we feel not the slightest trace of sympathy for him, even when it appears that he is truly down and out. When he's dumped into a trash bin and showered with garbage, we feel he deserves it. After all, Brooks has done the same to us'.[14] The *Chicago Sun-Times*'s Roger Ebert, on the other hand, swam against the critical tide by identifying an entirely different set of characteristics within the film, putting him at odds with a majority of his contemporaries:

> *Life Stinks* is a new direction in Brooks' directing career. The typical note in most of his earlier work was cheerful vulgarity, as he went for the laugh, no matter what. He has made some of the funniest movies I've ever seen, including *The Producers*, *Blazing Saddles* and *Young Frankenstein*. This is not one of them. It has its laughs, but it's a more thoughtful film, more softhearted toward its characters. It's warm and poignant. Brooks, as usual, is his own best asset. As an actor, he brings a certain heedless courage to his roles. His characters never seem to pause for thought; they're cocky, headstrong, confident. They charge ahead into the business at hand. There is a certain tension in *Life Stinks* between the bull-headed optimism of the Brooks character, and the hopeless reality of the streets, and that's what the movie is about.[15]

Perhaps on account of its relatively low profile in comparison with many of Brooks's earlier, rather more prestigious features, *Life Stinks* has not received the rehabilitation at the hands of more recent commentators that several other movies of his post-seventies filmography have been treated to. Patrick Naugle, for instance, found the film's situations contrived and stylistically tired: 'Mel, Mel, Mel... what happened? When did you lose your precious sense of what is funny? [...] It's not that you made a terrible movie – just a very outdated and boring one. The gags all seem tiered and strained, as if you and your co-writers were working on auto-pilot. There's one joke in particular that lingers in my mind. Your character is fighting with a homeless man about who's presumably richer. Then you slap each other. Over and over and over and over again. Slap, slap, slap. I'd like to think that you of all people would know the comedy rule of threes: anything over that number is generally not funny. And yet you break it over and over again in *Life Stinks*'.[16] Rather more unflattering – though the sentiment was by no means isolated – was the view of Jason Bovberg, who argued that the film marked a point in Brooks's directorial career where his comedic talents were noticeably on the wane: '*Life Stinks* actually attempts to find laughs while making an earnest statement about our society's down-and-out and mentally challenged urban populations. It's an idea that a younger Brooks might have pulled off with a certain audacity, but unfortunately, Brooks was officially a senior citizen when he made *Life Stinks*, and the snappier instincts of the man who made *Young Frankenstein* had been dulled. [...] The movie's message is driven home forcefully at the climax, and at that point any laughter that you might have enjoyed seems compromised. Brooks wants to have it both ways – a silly romp and a heartfelt message – but how can I feel for the homeless when I've been laughing at (not with) them for an hour? In the face of this confusion, *Life Stinks* just never gels'.[17]

If *The Twelve Chairs* can be considered Brooks's forgotten classic, it is probably fair to observe that *Life Stinks* is more a feature that has become lost in the mists of the public consciousness. Yet Brooks himself remains characteristically bullish about the film's legacy, noting that 'I get more letters for *Twelve Chairs* and *Life Stinks* than I get from any other movies, because people actually agree with the philosophy, or were moved, or they love the movie'.[18] Certainly there is no denying the sincerity of Brooks's intention to use his favoured art-form to advance serious social commentary, even though homelessness is a contentious subject which few would ever consider to be comedy gold waiting to be mined. And though the film contains arguably the least quotable dialogue of any Brooks feature (*Silent Movie* notwithstanding), it also presents some of his most scathing criticism of societal ills, containing more than a few moments of genuine anger directed at the injustice of a world that neglects its neediest citizens at the same time as attitudes towards them are driven by fear and ignorance. Yet most intriguingly of all, Brooks does not attempt to offer any glib solutions to this massively complex social problem, knowing too well that even to try to do so would be to appear to trivialise them. Although Bolt manages to escape a lifetime of destitution only because of his quick-thinking, ultimately allowing him to take back what is rightfully his, the audience knows that he is not advocating the notion that innovation and quick-thinking inevitably guarantee success – after all, the character had already amassed his fortune prior to (voluntarily) becoming homeless. Rather, if there is any hint of a moral message at the heart of *Life Stinks*, it is that those who are in a position to improve the lives of others should feel an ethical obligation to do so not because of material incentives, but because it is essentially the right thing to do. The reformed Bolt turns down a once-in-a-lifetime opportunity to cream revenue from the ultra-wealthy by scrapping his plans for the Bolt Center and instead developing the slum district into an area built with the benefit of low earners and non-earners in mind. In so doing, Brooks reinforces his defence of the need for personal autonomy in a free society by stating very clearly that a nation which does not provide the capacity for individual improvement across all of its citizens cannot claim to be truly egalitarian in nature. Because he so demonstrably admires the culture of freedom upon which America is based, *Life Stinks* strenuously argues that the United States is uniquely placed amongst the countries of the world to consider and implement the need for such parity, proving that the American Dream is not an impossible ideal to be scoffed at, but a blueprint for a future of greater fairness and diversity. And with this towering principle, he presents a constructive attitude which has the potential to unite rather than to divide, mirrored in Bolt's sudden realisation – in a moment of awareness that transcends his grim circumstances – that for every individual, where there's life there is also hope: 'It's good to be alive. There's so many things you can't do when you're dead'.

# REFERENCES

1. Robert Alan Crick, *The Big Screen Comedies of Mel Brooks* (Jefferson: McFarland and Company, 2009) [2002], p. 168.
2. Box-office data drawn from BoxOfficeMojo.com.
   <http://www.boxofficemojo.com/movies/?id=lifestinks.htm>
3. Celia Brady, 'Prognostication, Cantonese Style', in *Spy*, October 1991, p. 20.
4. Crick, p. 169.
5. Roger Ebert, '*Life Stinks*', in *The Chicago Sun-Times*, 26 July 1991.
6. William Brigham, 'Down and Out in Tinseltown: Hollywood Presents the Dispossessed', in *Beyond the Stars: Studies in American Popular Film: Volume 5: Themes and Ideologies in American Popular Film*, ed. by Paul Loukides and Linda K. Fuller (Bowling Green: Bowling Green State University Press, 1996), 165-86, p. 165.
7. Sylvia P. Flanagan, 'Movies to See: *Life Stinks*', in *Jet*, 5 August 1991, p. 56.
8. Edgar A. Levenson, 'Beyond Countertransference: Aspects of the Analyst's Desire', in *Contemporary Psychoanalysis*, Volume 30, Issue 4, 1994, 691-707, p. 706.
9. Marjorie Baumgarten, '*Life Stinks*', in *The Austin Chronicle*, 2 August 1991.
   <http://www.austinchronicle.com/calendar/film/1991-08-02/13960>
10. Jonathan Bernstein, 'Moving Images: Redemption Song' in *Spin*, December 1991, 99-100, p. 100.
11. Janet Maslin, 'Mel Brooks: From Riches to Rags to Humility', in *The New York Times*, 26 July 1991.
    <http://www.nytimes.com/movie/review?res=9D0CE0DB1430F935A15754C0A967958260>
12. Crick, p. 173.
13. Chris Hicks, 'Film Review: *Life Stinks*', in *The Deseret News*, 2 August 1991.
    <http://www.deseretnews.com/article/700001044/Life-Stinks.html>
14. Hal Hinson, '*Life Stinks*', in *The Washington Post*, 27 July 1991.
    <http://www.washingtonpost.com/wp-srv/style/longterm/movies/videos/lifestinkspg13hinson_a0a6ce.htm>
15. Ebert, 1991.
16. Patrick Naugle, '*Life Stinks*', in *DVD Verdict*, 18 February 2003.
    <http://www.dvdverdict.com/reviews/lifestinks.php>
17. Jason Bovberg, '*Life Stinks*', in *DVD Talk*, 18 February 2003.
    <http://www.dvdtalk.com/reviews/5452/life-stinks/>
18. Mel Brooks, in Steve Heisler, 'Mel Brooks on how to play Hitler, and how he almost died making *Spaceballs*', in *The Onion A.V. Club*, 13 December 2012.
    <http://www.avclub.com/article/mel-brooks-on-how-to-play-hitler-and-how-he-almost-89843>

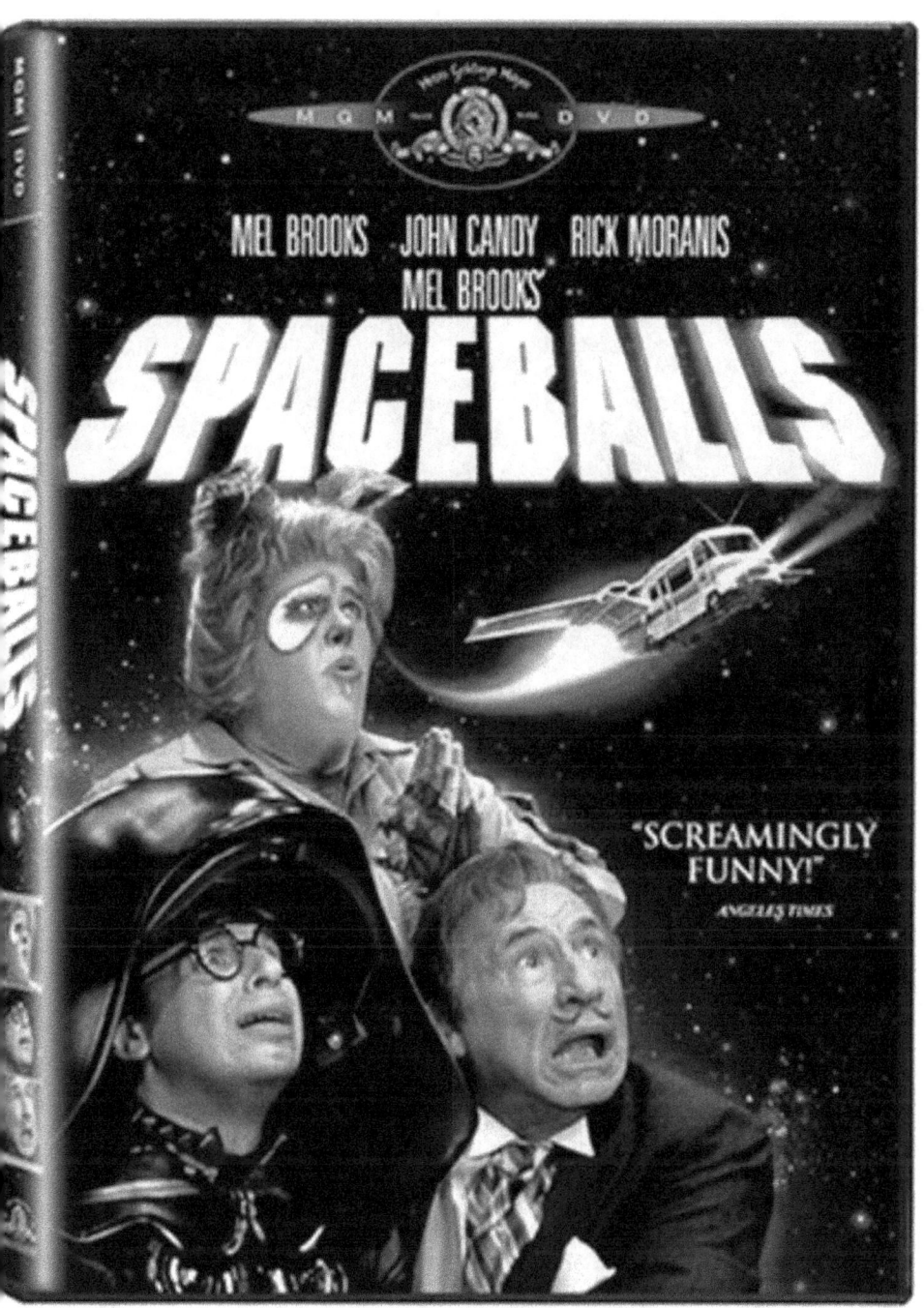

This page and over from Spaceballs (1985)

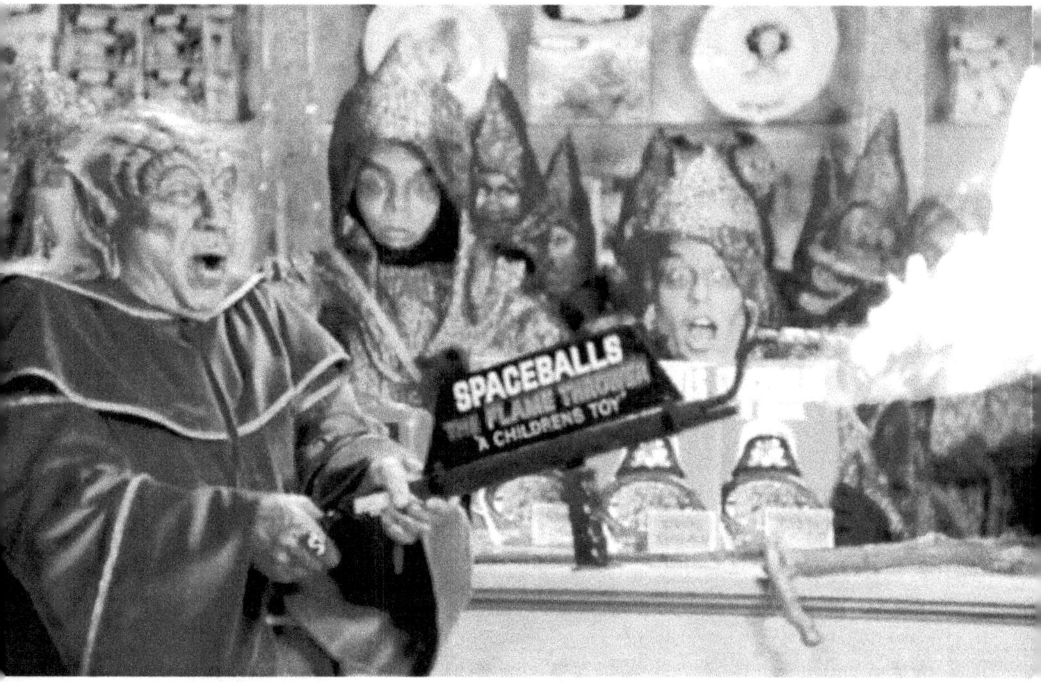
SPACEBALLS
THE FLAME
'A CHILDRENS TOY'

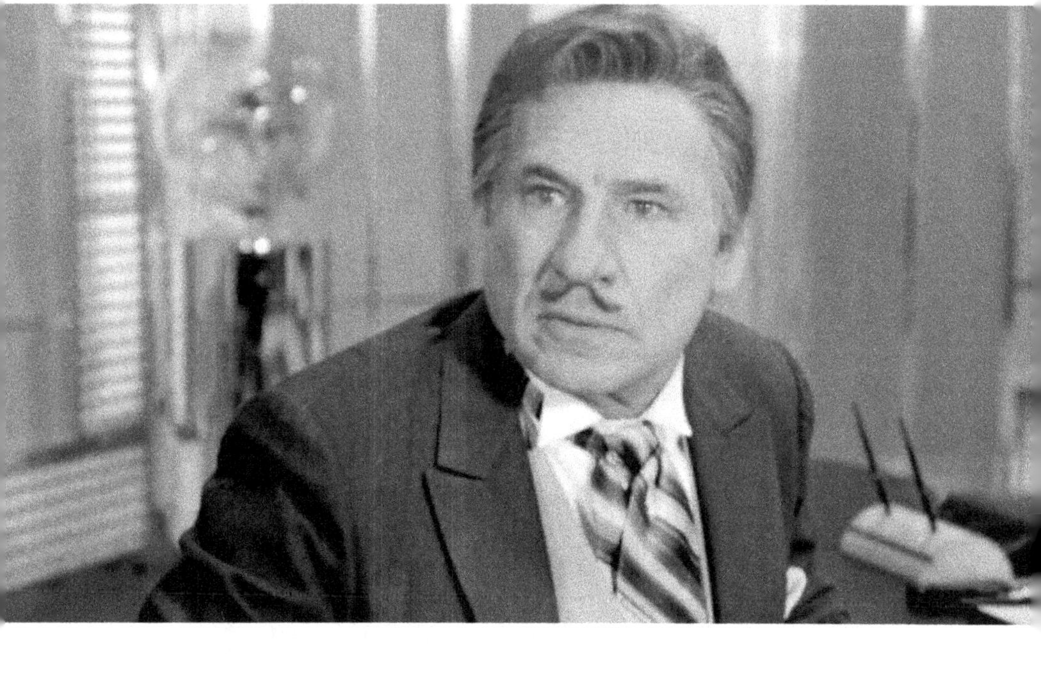

This page and over from Life Stinks (1991)

Robin Hood: Men In Tights (1993), this page and over.

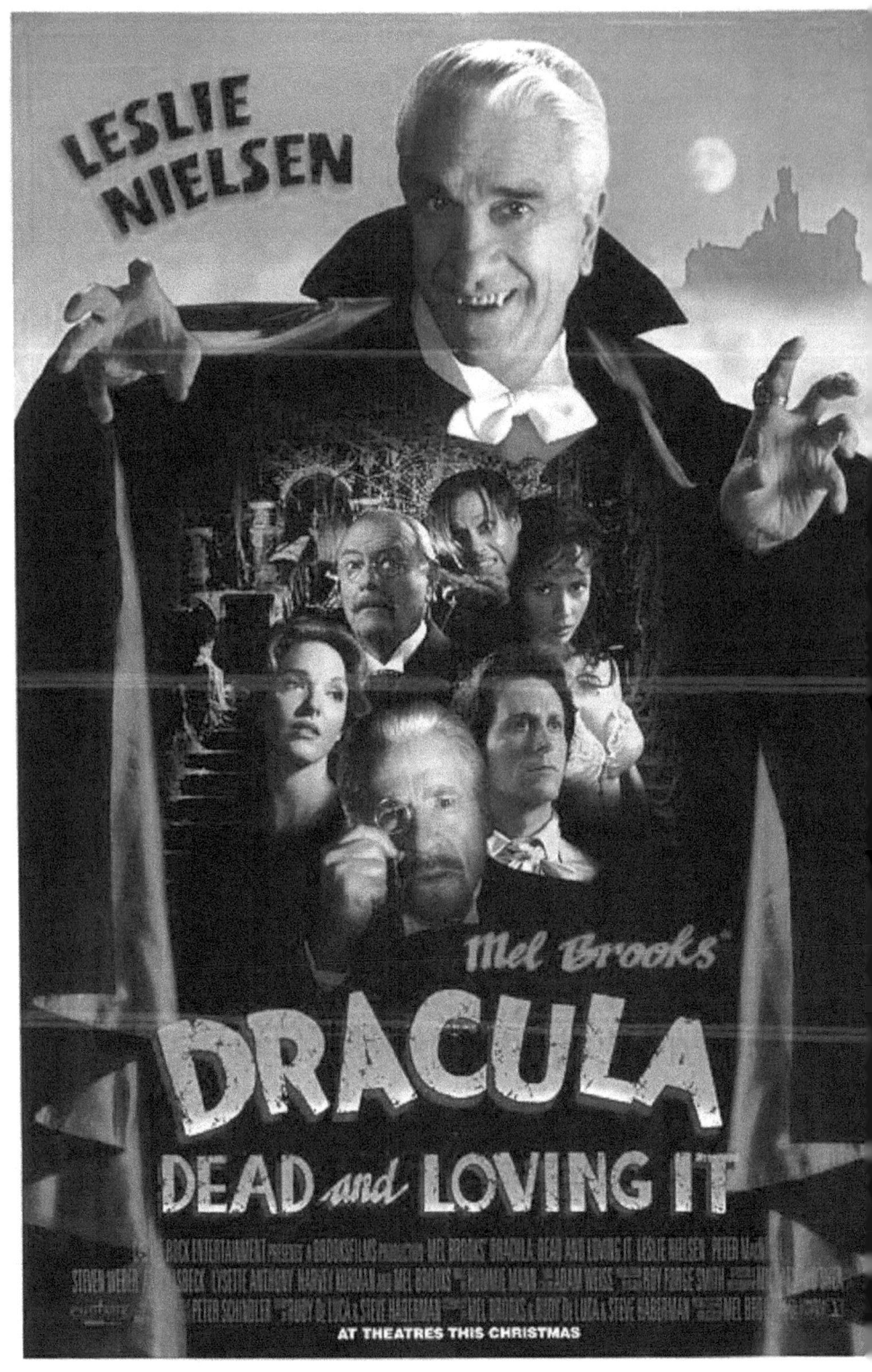

This page and over from Dracula, Dead and Loving It (1995)

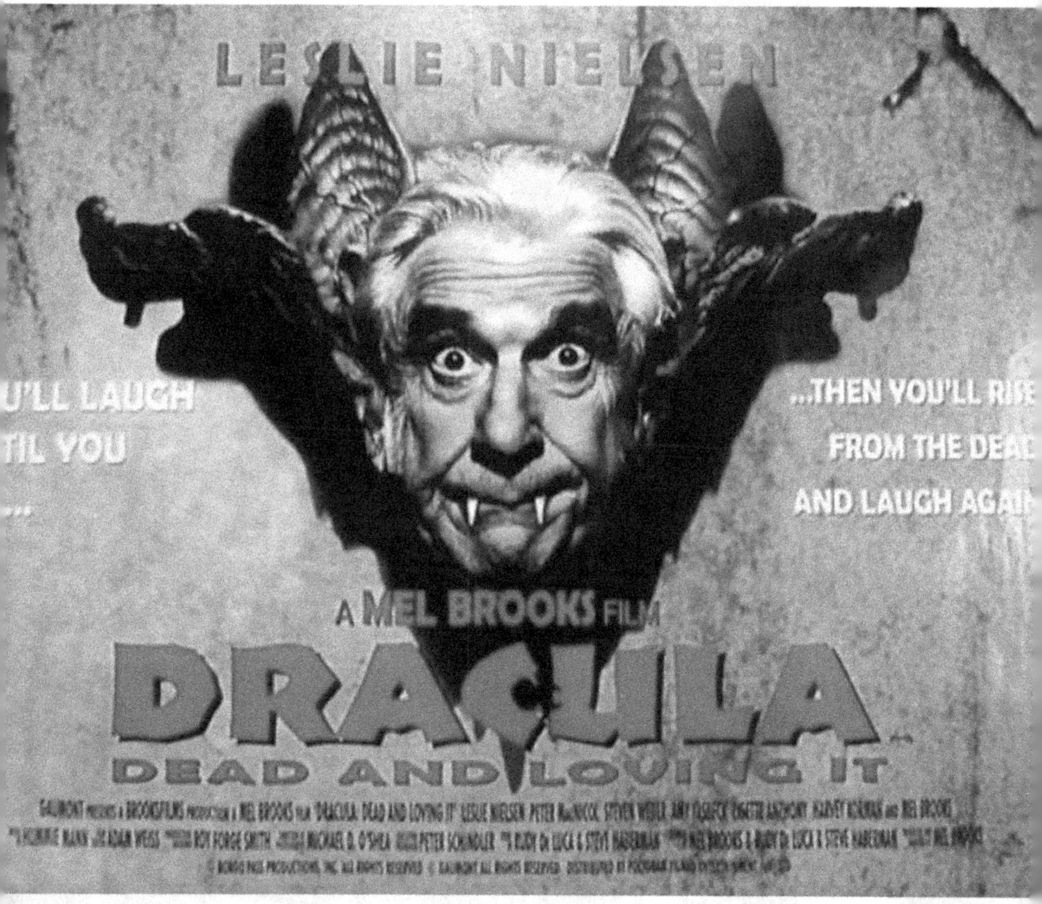
LESLIE NIELSEN
U'LL LAUGH
TIL YOU
...
...THEN YOU'LL RIS
FROM THE DEA
AND LAUGH AGAI
A MEL BROOKS FILM
DRACULA
DEAD AND LOVING IT

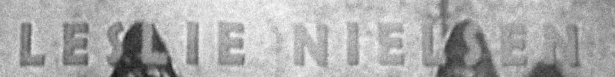

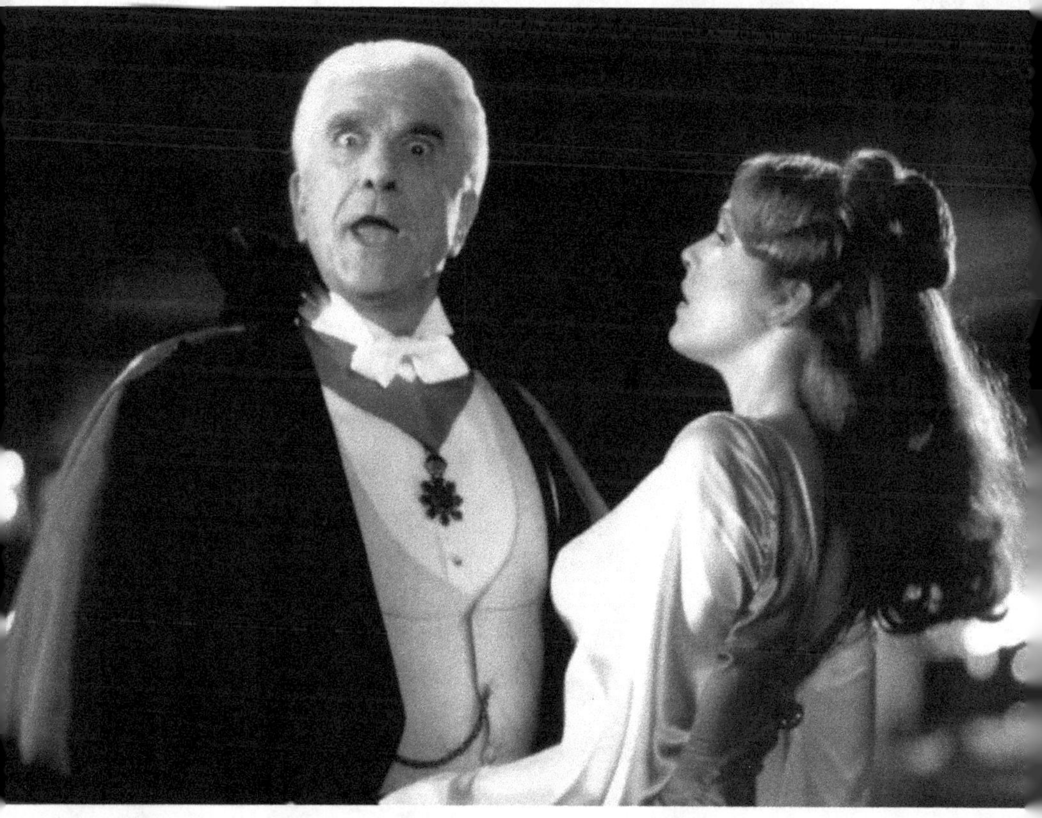

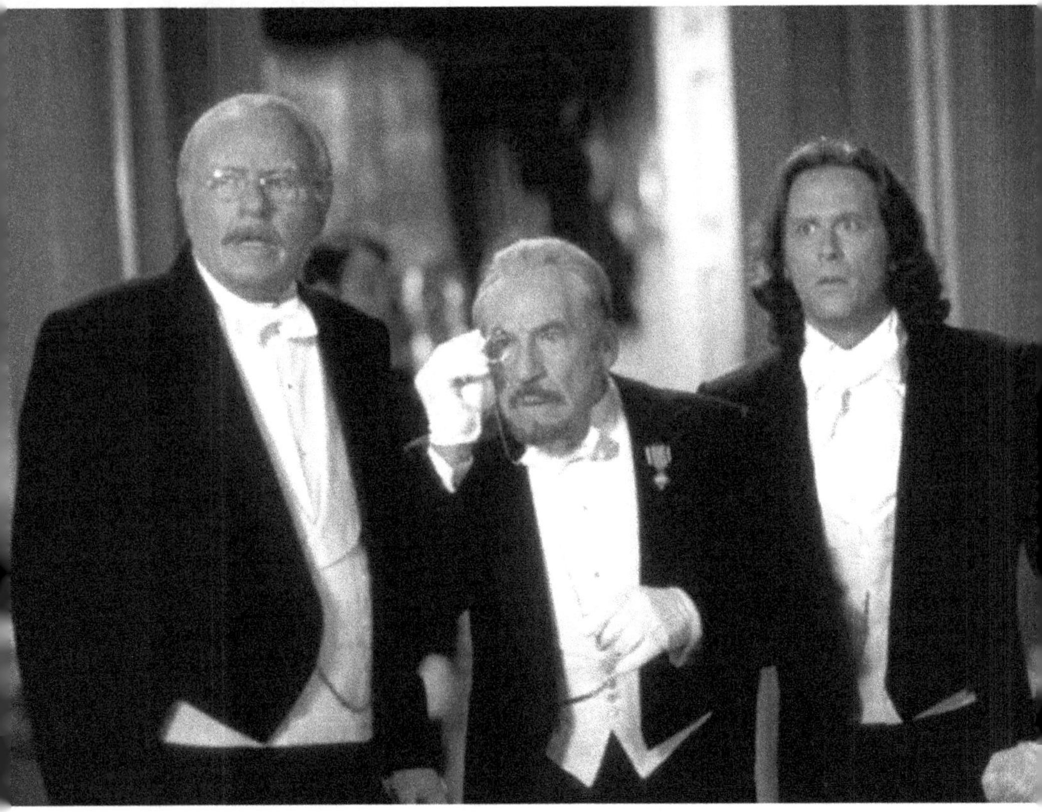

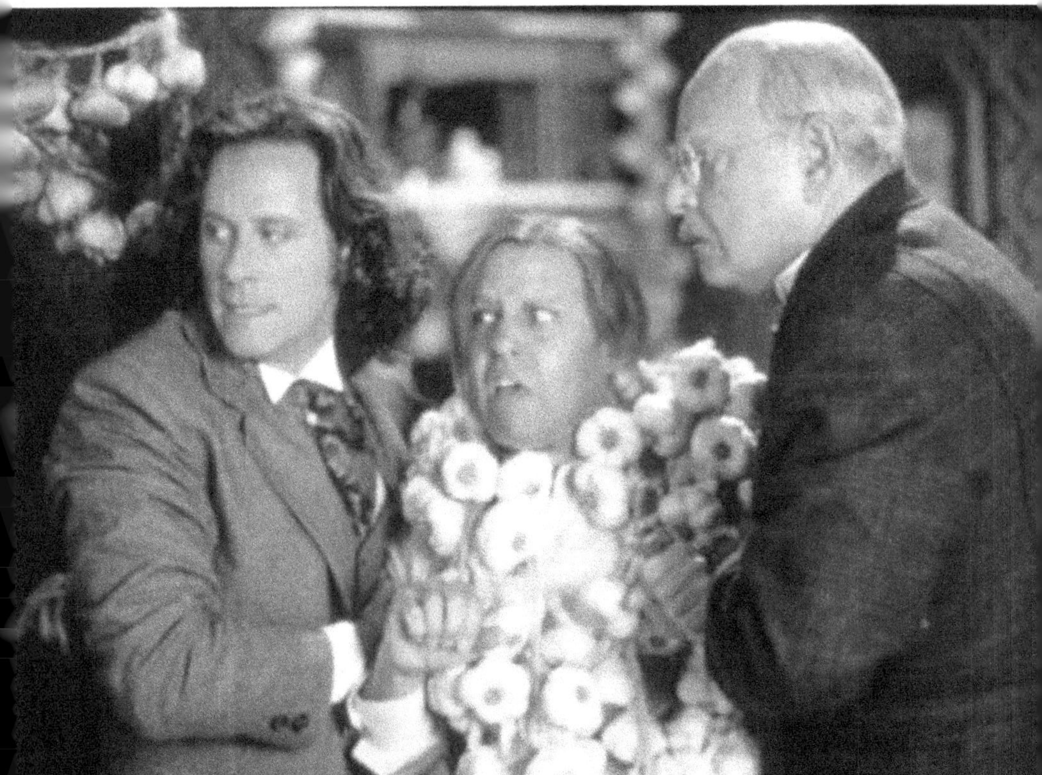

# 10

# ROBIN HOOD: MEN IN TIGHTS (1993)

FOLLOWING THE UNANTICIPATED SIDE-STEP of *Life Stinks*, Mel Brooks was to return to considerably more familiar ground with his next film of the nineties. *Robin Hood: Men in Tights* was to take a satirical side-swipe at the towering legend of Sherwood Forest's most celebrated defender, primarily using Kevin Reynold's enormously successful *Robin Hood: Prince of Thieves* (1991) as its basis. Brooks being Brooks, however, the film was to riff on just about every aspect of the Robin Hood mythology from its medieval origins through to Errol Flynn's iconic portrayal of the lead character in *The Adventures of Robin Hood* (Michael Curtiz and William Keighley, 1938).

*Robin Hood: Men in Tights* was also to prove an interesting phenomenon in Brooks's filmic career, in that it marked the first time that he had drawn upon his televisual work as the loose basis for a feature film. When *Things Were Rotten* had been a short-lived situation comedy co-created by Brooks, Norman Stiles and John Boni in 1975. The series was aired over thirteen episodes on ABC, and employed much characteristically surreal, quickfire Brooksian humour of the type which had proved so popular in the previous year's *Blazing Saddles* – this time shifting the action from the American Western Frontier to the England of the Dark Ages. What had worked so effectively in cinemas would soon reveal itself to be somewhat ahead of its time for contemporary television (in a manner similar to ABC's later *Police Squad!*, which eventually gave rise to the highly successful *Naked Gun* movies), meaning that the show would struggle for ratings and thus met with an early cancellation. Although the series' brevity has led to it becoming little more than a footnote in Brooks's career on television, its inspired sight gags and casual breaking of the fourth wall have led to some degree of cult longevity amongst his fans. Although only the basic premise would survive in *Robin Hood: Men in Tights* (along with an appearance by actor Dick Van Patten – the TV show's Friar Tuck, who portrayed a Christian Abbot in the later film), there was much about the series' distinctive style of humour which would make the transition from the small screen to cinemas. As Bob Leszczak has commented about the comic legacy of *When Things Were Rotten*:

> Sight gags, one-liners, slapstick, and humorous asides directed to the viewer were plentiful. The most memorable moments were those involving anachronisms, such as a reference to the *Galloping Gourmet*; the proposed cutting down of Sherwood Forest to build a housing complex; the Merry Men doing the Bunny Hop [...]; a working intercom system in the castle; a nurse asking a patient if he had medical insurance; and the destruction of the Rock of Gibraltar (to which Prince John added, "I've always wanted a piece of the rock," a line from those Prudential Insurance commercials). [...] The comedy came at you fast and furious. Critics loved it, but ratings weren't strong, and it quickly disappeared.[1]

Such was the global awareness of the Robin Hood legend that a spoof of the phenomenon allowed Brooks considerable latitude when it came to presenting modern social criticism within a period historical framework. If *Spaceballs* had offered up an archetypal conflict of good-versus-evil, satirising a mythos where very clear moral boundaries were portrayed and the antagonists' malevolent aims interrogated, the tale of the virtuous nobleman in exile who 'robs from the rich to give to the poor' provided even more fertile ground for Brooks to explore the victory of moral virtue over corrupt self-interest, extolling the virtues of personal freedom over the individual limitations imposed by despotic repression. The execution, unfortunately, proved only rarely to be as ambitious as the initial aim.

Following an opening sequence where a medieval English village is attacked by repeated volleys of flaming arrows ('Leave us alone, Mel Brooks!', the inhabitants cry), a group of forest-based Merry Men explain – by means of an energetic rap – that the Crusades are well underway. Prince John, ruling as Regent in the absence of his brother King Richard, is bleeding the nation dry with soaring taxation. In the town of Rottingham, the Sheriff is responsible for pressuring the citizens to relinquish an ever greater percentage of their income, presiding over unbridled intimidation and oppression in the pursuit of his aims. However, Robin Hood – the famous protector of civilians' rights and bulwark against despotism – can be of no aid to the people of Rottingham, on account of the fact that he is in the Holy Land fighting alongside Richard in the current Crusade... and, what is worse, he has just been captured by the Saracens.

Sure enough, we join Robin of Loxley (Cary Elwes) in Jerusalem's Khalil Prison where he is being interrogated – without much success – as the guards attempt to determine the location of King Richard. There, he meets Moorish prisoner Asneeze (Isaac Hayes), who has been imprisoned for jaywalking. Working together, they organise a jailbreak and manage to head for the coast. Robin proclaims that he intends to return to England, and Asneeze explains that his son Ahchoo (David Chappelle) is already there – as an exchange student. Robin promises to contact Ahchoo as soon as he gets back. He then dives into the sea and, improbably enough, swims all the way from the Middle East through the Mediterranean Sea, tracing the European coast until he finally makes landfall on English soil some weeks later.

All is not well in England's green and pleasant land, however. Robin hardly has time to take his bearings before he discovers Ahchoo, who is being brutally beaten by a squad of uniformed guards. Rescuing him, the pair head for Robin's ancestral home, Loxley Hall... just in time to witness the entire castle being rolled away on wheels by a cart (complete with 'wide load' sign). This, he is informed, is because the government is taking his estate into custody on account of unpaid back-taxes due while he was out of the country. In the exposed foundations of the hall he discovers Blinkin (Mark Blankfield), the family's servant, who – being blind – is thus far unaware that the Loxley residence has been impounded. Blinkin is delighted that his old employer has returned safely from the Crusades, but is the bearer of grim tidings – everyone in Robin's family has died in his absence, from his parents to his brothers, and even his pets. Blinkin does, however, pass on a mysterious locket – a posthumous gift from Robin's father which contains a key to a mysterious treasure.

Robin has barely had time to register this momentous news when a young boy (Corbin Allred) races out of the nearby woods, pursued by a band of armed swordsmen led by the Sheriff of Rottingham (Roger Rees). The Sheriff demands that Robin hand over the boy, who is wanted for poaching, but his command is refused. Instead, Robin reveals his identity to the Sheriff, who attempts to engage him in swordplay to punish his lack of cooperation. However, Robin uses the Sheriff's incompetence against him and sends the interloper into a humiliating retreat.

Elsewhere, the beautiful Maid Marian (Amy Yasbeck) is bewailing the fact that her one true love is yet to make himself known. Her maidservant Broomhilde (Megan Cavanagh) watches with a mixture of concern and tedium as Marian makes her romantic desires known – presumably not for the first time. But for the moment the noblewoman remains not only unbetrothed, but also sexually pure thanks to her bearing a heavily reinforced metal chastity belt. Meanwhile, the Sheriff is back at Rottingham Castle and reporting to England's Regent, Prince John (Richard Lewis). John is concerned to hear of Robin's return, not least given Loxley's faithful service to the country's rightful king and the fact that he now holds a grudge in response to what has happened to his family home. Panicking, the prince consults with Latrine (Tracey Ullman), a seer – and cook – who is resident in the castle tower. Latrine reveals that Robin is a formidable opponent who will stop at nothing to correct the injustice that has been dealt to his family. She agrees to concoct a potion which will render him completely unable to function normally, but only if John somehow manages to engineer a romance between her and the Sheriff, to whom she has become madly attracted.

In Sherwood Forest, Robin, Ahchoo and Blinkin are stopped at a bridge by Little John (Eric Allan Kramer), a huge, musclebound toll collector who demands a fee in exchange for crossing with their horse. ('But don't let my name fool you – in real life, I'm *very* big.') When revealing his noble status fails to ensure him safe passage, Robin is forced to fight Little John to gain access to the bridge – in spite of Ahchoo pointing out that the 'river' is a trickle of water mere inches across, meaning that they could cross it with a single step. In spite of this inconvenient fact,

Robin emerges triumphant and recruits Little John in his struggle against the Sheriff's cruelty. He also signs up his new friend's dagger-wielding sidekick, Will Scarlet O'Hara (Matthew Porretta), who explains his family name by clarifying: 'We're from Georgia'. Robin reveals that he intends to infiltrate Prince John's banquet at the castle that evening, and make known his challenge to the Regent's ruthless leadership.

Sure enough, the outlaw gatecrashes John's extravagant royal event, interrupting the Sheriff's unwanted advances on a deeply disinterested Maid Marian. Presenting the Prince with a wild boar killed in the nearby woods (thus committing a crime under the new laws), Robin informs him that if he will not cease his unfair taxation, there will be no alternative but for him to lead a rebellion against the government. The Sheriff challenges Robin to a duel, but quickly loses his nerve and calls for the castle guard instead. Just as the tide of the fight starts to turn against Robin, his fellow outlaws from Sherwood Forest unexpectedly rally to his aid. However, Robin and Marian are instantly attracted to each other, leading him to promise her that they will meet again.

Back in the safety of the forest once more, Robin is greeted by the sight of a large contingent of new recruits which have been drawn from villages across England. They (eventually) respond to his rallying cry, but elementary combat training soon reveals them to be far from ready to go into battle. Ahchoo sarcastically comments that they would be better to take combat dummies into action instead, which seems to give Robin an idea. At the castle, an increasingly concerned Sheriff reveals to Prince John their latest combat innovation – a 'stealth catapult' that is capable of destroying all in the path of the boulders that it launches. Sadly for the Sheriff, a mishap sees him hurled into the air instead – landing painfully (and with some alarm) in Latrine's tower.

Robin and his men make a new recruit of Rabbi Tuckman (Mel Brooks), a travelling circumcision salesman, who provides wisdom and counsel along with his cart's many barrels of sacramental wine. They are blissfully unaware that even as they speak, the Sheriff is entertaining Italian nobleman Don Giovanni (Dom DeLuise), who has travelled 'all the way from Jersey' with his associates Filthy Luca (Steve Tancora) and Dirty Ezio (Joe Dimmick). Together, they hatch a plan to lure Robin to an archery competition, where champion player Luca will beat him in the games prior to Ezio assassinating him. But from a nearby balcony, Marian overhears their murderous scheme and determines to alert Robin of the trap before it can be sprung.

Rousing Broomhilde, they sneak out of the castle and head for the forest. There, Marian pleads with Robin not to attend the following day's competition, but when he discovers that archery is involved – and that Don Giovanni's star competitor has an allegedly peerless talent – he immediately backpedals on his assurances. During a moonlit tryst, Robin declares his undying love for Marian, but she reveals that any liaison between them could only be chaste in nature on account of her seemingly-impenetrable chastity belt. Their misty-eyed rendezvous is interrupted by Broomhilde, who urges a swift return to the castle before their absence is noticed.

The next day, the Merry Men arrive at the Royal competition disguised as noblewomen, while Robin – also under a concealed identity – enters the archery contest in spite of his earlier, carefully-worded promise to Marian. He does not suspect that Dirty Ezio is situated at the Royal Folio Depository overlooking the games, readying a crossbow outfitted with a sniper scope. Sure enough, Robin strikes the target's bullseye and is immediately identified by the Sheriff... but seconds later, Ezio demonstrates his own prowess with the bow by splitting Robin's arrow in half. The crowd turn against Robin and start pelting him with rotten vegetables... until he remembers to check his copy of the script, and discovers that he is actually allowed a second attempt. The Sheriff becomes unnerved and signals to Ezio to fire his own shot... only for Blinkin to intercept the bolt in midair ('I heard that coming a mile away!'). Robin then fires a 'Patriot Arrow', which appears to have an inbuilt guidance system – one which comes in handy when Luca deliberately spoils his aim, as the arrow races around the playing field (inadvertently causing the world's first Mexican Wave) before destroying Luca's arrow as it tears into the bullseye. Exasperated, the Sheriff names Robin an enemy of the crown and orders him taken into custody. Desperately trying to avoid Robin's execution, Marian offers herself in marriage to the Sheriff in exchange for the outlaw's release. Robin pleads with her to change her mind, but the nefarious Sheriff is delighted by her unwilling (and unexpected) capitulation to his endless advances.

Later that day, a scaffold is erected to hang Robin while the hastily-arranged wedding of the Sheriff and Marian is set in motion. Before the town's Abbot (Dick Van Patten) can invite the couple to exchange vows, Ahchoo fires an arrow that releases Robin from his noose, freeing Marian from her forced matrimony. Chaos ensues as the Merry Men's recently-trained band of villagers enter the fray. The Sheriff takes advantage of the altercation to abscond with Marian, dragging her to the upper reaches of the castle ('He's gonna deflower her in the tower!'). Robin confronts the villain while he is attempting to remove Marian's chastity belt with a pneumatic drill, and they immediately engage in a surreal swordfight – a battle which includes duelling with shadow animals. During the clash, Robin's locket breaks open to reveal a key... which, incredibly enough, lands in the lock of Marian's chastity belt, where it fits perfectly. The Sheriff is mortally wounded (albeit accidentally) by Robin's blade, but is magically revived by Latrine on the condition that he agree to marry her. As she drags him from the room, it is immediately apparent that he is already regretting his hasty decision. Robin and Marian embrace, freed from the restrictions of her metal shackles, but their romantic encounter is interrupted – again – by Broomhilde, who insists that they get married before consummating their union.

Fortunately for the couple, Rabbi Tuckman is in town offering cut-price circumcisions ('half off'), and agrees to conduct the marriage ceremony. But yet again the matrimonial rites are disrupted, this time by the unexpected arrival of King Richard the Lionheart (Patrick Stewart) who has returned from the Crusades. Richard immediately strips John of his Regency, and – in response to his abuse of his royal powers – decrees that henceforth every toilet in the land shall be known as a 'John'. He then proceeds to knight Robin, restoring to him his family residence and lands, before allowing the wedding to proceed (once he has kissed the bride – a very heartfelt gesture indeed). The loving newlyweds canter off on horseback, facing a happy future with the country's rightful monarch restored and the Loxley family fortunes reinstated... though their wedding night hits a snag early on when Robin discovers that his key won't unlock Marian's chastity belt after all.

It is difficult to imagine a more determined shift in comic tone than that which Brooks achieved between *Life Stinks* and *Robin Hood: Men in Tights*. Whereas the previous film had been largely thoughtful and low-key, thus compromising Brooks's usual hit-rate of audience laughs, here he had returned to the kind of inspired lunacy that may not quite have reached the heady days of his mid-seventies features, but certainly recaptured the frenetic spirit of *History of the World: Part I* and *Spaceballs*. The end result is a great deal of fun and, in truth, *Robin Hood: Men in Tights* has suffered mainly from comparison to the very high quality of Brooks's early output than from any particularly severe flaws of its own.

The film benefits not only from the universal recognition of the Robin Hood legend, but also in the many shrewd ways that Brooks wryly lampoons particular aspects of Kevin Reynolds's blockbuster which had dominated cinemas – and the public consciousness – two years previously. (As Robert Alan Crick has observed, 'if his sci-fi parody *Spaceballs* had struggled into theaters too long after *Star Wars* for its own comic good, this time Brooks clearly struck while the iron was, if not hot, at least still warm'.[2]) Geraldine McEwan's witch Mortianna is mirrored in Tracy Ullman's knowingly repulsive character Latrine, while the suave Alan Rickman's supremely droll Sheriff of Nottingham is neatly spoofed by Roger Rees's tongue-tied, mishap-prone Sheriff of Rottingham. Michael Wincott's sinister Guy of Gisbourne from the Reynolds film (another traditional Robin Hood adversary) is supplanted by Richard Lewis's milquetoast Prince John, a character absent from *Robin Hood: Prince of Thieves* but who, strangely enough, has chosen here to establish his royal residence not in the capital London but in the geographically-obscure 'Rottingham' instead. Brooks piles on the allusions to the earlier film, from Morgan Freeman's Moorish wise man Azeem (introduced in the shared Jerusalem opening scenes) being split into the twin roles of Isaac Hayes and David Chappelle, to Cary Elwes's droll line that 'Unlike some other Robin Hoods, I can speak with an English accent!' – a none-too-subtle barb at Kevin Costner's highly variable attempts at a regional dialect during his own portrayal of the character. (Just in case there is the slightest chance that someone in the audience may be oblivious to his intentions, Brooks even provides Rabbi Tuckman with the awe-inspiringly unsubtle line: 'I've just come from Maid Marian, the lady whose heart you stole. You "Prince of Thieves", you!')

Yet Brooks broadens the target of his spoof beyond Reynolds's smash-hit film to encompass other characteristics of Robin Hood adaptations over the years; Elwes's Robin bears more visual resemblance to Errol Flynn's well-known portrayal than he ever does to Costner, whilst the main dynamics of the plotline – including the presentation of tyrannous Prince John as cosseted and ineffectual – has more in common with Disney's animated *Robin Hood* (Wolfgang Reitherman, 1973) than darker, earthier versions of the tale such as John Irvin's relatively muted *Robin Hood* (1991) which had starred Patrick Bergin in the title role. The overall effect is perfectly compatible with Brooks's established strategy for spoofing a specific and popular category of film, as Stephen Thomas Knight notes:

> Responding directly and often in detail to *Robin Hood: Prince of Thieves*, this is in the Brooks tradition of mocking an identifiable genre – as in his groundbreaking *Blazing Saddles* – and develops an idea that the young Brooks had written for [...] parodic series *When Things Were Rotten* on 1970s television. [...] In a roundabout and ironized way, the film subscribes to the hero's standing, including his masculinity: only he will unlock Marian's chastity belt, with however much difficulty. Within the farcical structure of the film the core image remains of the dashingly masculine, improbably theatrical hero who has intrigued audiences for six centuries; though small and often baffled, Cary Elwes is a perfectly formed Robin Hood who never quite loses his dignity.[3]

As Knight suggests, Elwes's dead-on-beam performance is one of the highlights of the film – his stoic, well-mannered Robin is every inch the gentlemanly hero, apologetically duelling with Little John over the stream (one of the legend's most recognisable situations) and constantly providing Prince John and the Sheriff with ample, almost polite admonition regarding his intention to seize back freedom for the people. He also has an almost entirely unruffled composure throughout; even during the obligatory swordfight with the Sheriff, fighting for the heart of his one true love, Robin's response to the opening 'En garde!' is merely a cool 'Thanks for the warning'. Naturally we expect his archery skills to be of unmatchable quality and his chivalry to be beyond reproach, because he is an amalgam of every Robin Hood we have come to recognise from the modern cultural tradition. Yet in the hands of Brooks and co-writers Evan Chandler and J. David

Shapiro, the character becomes an even more exaggerated parody of himself. With his guided missile-like arrows, unfathomable martial arts skills and the ability to swim all the way from the Holy Land to the south coast of England (presumably without even time to draw breath), we are presented with Robin Hood as superhero – a man whose very name causes his enemies to think twice about crossing him. Even when faced with news that would cause some to lapse into a nervous breakdown, the account of his decimated family and purloined estate barely leads Robin to the faintest quiver of his lip:

| | | |
|---|---|---|
| BLINKIN: | | This never would have happened if your father was alive. |
| ROBIN: | | He's dead?! |
| BLINKIN: | | Yes. |
| ROBIN: | | And my mother? |
| BLINKIN: | | She died of pneumonia whilst... oh. You were away. |
| ROBIN: | | My brothers? |
| BLINKIN: | | They were all killed by the plague. |
| ROBIN: | | My dog Pongo? |
| BLINKIN: | | Run over by a carriage. |
| ROBIN: | | My goldfish Goldie? |
| BLINKIN: | | Eaten by the cat. |
| ROBIN: | | My cat? |
| BLINKIN: | | Choked on the goldfish. Oh, it's good to be home, ain't it, Master Robin? |

From Robin's Winston Churchill-inspired speech to rally the villagers to his cause, to the carefully-constructed reveal of his ostentatious six-shooter bow and arrows, Brooks takes care to emphasise that his is a larger-than-life depiction of a figure that had already been embellished and exaggerated by the repeated retelling of the legend. He also ironically invokes Shakespearean grandeur with the paradoxical incorporation of famous lines such as 'my kingdom for a horse' and 'lend me your ears' (with predictable outcomes in both situations). In so doing, he seems more than aware that he is acknowledging the fact that Robin Hood's improbably heroic adventures were the stuff of popular mythology long before he decides to tip the whole narrative over into the territory of the unabashed (cod-)historical cinematic fable. While Brooks had already introduced us to fairytale castles and ermine-cloaked royalty on *Spaceballs'* Planet Druidia, here he takes a rather more Earth-bound approach to the subject of monarchy and the class system which is subordinated to it, puncturing the traditions of folklore with repeated references to the modern world. This, after all, is a kingdom where medieval castles sport illuminated 'EXIT' signs above doors, where a hangman's noose comes complete with a label indicating neck size, and torch sconces are operated by a simple clap as though they were modern electric lights. Knowing lines such as 'Grab your uniforms and equipment, and prepare for the training sequence!' and – even more blatantly – 'Prepare for the fight scene!' remind us of the fact that the characters are just as aware of the artifice of filmmaking as the audience is, and thus that the over-familiarity of the Robin Hood legend is as much a factor in the considerations of the film's heroes and villains as it is to cinemagoers. As Keyvan Sarkhosh explains:

> Even when they do not or cannot escape their diegetic confinement, film characters may well be aware of their fictional status as the beginning of *Robin Hood: Men in Tights* proves: some villagers complain that every time a Robin Hood film is made, their village is burnt down and then they shout: 'Leave us alone, Mel Brooks!' Of course, this is just a poor copy of a well-known metaleptic figure from literature: the independent existence of fictional characters and their rebellion against their creator as known most prominently from Flann O'Brien and Gilbert Sorentino. The example given from *Robin Hood: Men in Tights* refers to the god-like and even sadistic freedom of the creator – in cinema most often equated with the director – who at any time can interfere with the fictional world and change it according to his will.[4]

This conceit can, of course, sometimes be pushed to extremes – Robin's puzzlement at losing the archery match prompts him to retrieve his copy of the film's screenplay ('I'm not supposed to lose! Let me see the script') which in turn leads the villains to do likewise in order to corroborate his assertion that he is due a second shot. Brooks had played hard and fast with viewer expectation before, most notably with the eruption of *Blazing Saddles*'s climactic fight sequence out of its fictional historical setting into the real world of the modern day, but the introduction of the characters' awareness of the actual script seems like a rather laboured shorthand for the earlier film's anarchic destruction of the fourth wall – not least because the conceit had long been established as a popular pretence in the spoof movie genre. Yet Brooks shows all too clearly that by this point, the satirical edge of his comic apparatus had worn smooth with overuse in places, meaning that in *Robin Hood: Men in Tights* he employs certain strategies as much out of celebration of past glories than in anticipation of similar effectiveness. As Crick persuasively argues, many of the comedic tactics on display combine to make the film seem like a "best of" compilation patched together from many of Brooks's earlier features;[5] the 'walk this way' gag from *Young Frankenstein*, the camera collision from *High Anxiety*, the 'It's good to be the king' line from *History of the World: Part I*... all are dusted off and placed back on display in slightly different iterations. While many Brooks fans may well have enjoyed the self-referential nature of these familiar comic devices, the apparent dulling of his earlier, serrated wit came at an inopportune time given the stiff cinematic competition that *Robin Hood: Men in Tights* faced at the time of its release. David Desser and Lester D. Friedman explain that:

> A sense of having seen it all before was nevertheless pervasive among audiences as well as critics. The surreal musical numbers, the anachronisms, the bathroom humor, and a camera that tracks too close to the set and crashes through it had been done before and often by Brooks. [...] *Robin Hood: Men in Tights* was not only familiar from Brooks's canon but it was also not the only film parody released in 1993. Films like *Loaded Weapon 1* and *Hot Shots! Part Deux* made Brooks's film seem but one more addition to an increasingly familiar genre.[6]

If Brooks's vindication of creative freedom was rather more low-key than had been the case in films past, albeit surprisingly so, this was also to be the case with his espousal of civil liberties. In part this, too, may possibly stem from the highly recognisable subject matter with which he was dealing; the notion of a Prince John who ratchets up domestic taxation to increasingly untenable limits, and a Sheriff who withholds no cruelty in collecting these taxes from the helpless peasants in his political jurisdiction, had become so firmly grounded in public awareness that Brooks expends little time establishing the end result of their oppression – the cruelty, fear and threat of force which are employed to extract monies from people who cannot afford to pay them. Thus aside from brief scenes of malignity such as the brutal beating of Ahchoo by government militiamen (in candidly hoping that the attack is being filmed, Ahchoo's comment recalls the controversy of the Rodney King assault – and subsequent riots throughout Los Angeles – in the early 1990s), there is very little to explicitly suggest the menace or injustice of the corrupt Prince's actions, which leaves the character appearing more neurotic than intimidating. Even in the Sheriff's attempted sexual assault on Marian, a scene which had every potential to be truly horrific (consider by contrast the disturbing treatment Marian suffers in *Robin Hood: Prince of Thieves*), his repellent intent is undermined by his sheer ineptness and the absurdity of his actions – using a pneumatic drill, for instance, in a doomed attempt to remove her chastity belt. Crick correctly opines that 'neither Brooks nor his characters take Brooks' "right vs might" scenario seriously enough, resulting in heroes who seem apathetic and villains uninvolved',7 and certainly this does have the overall effect of making *Robin Hood: Men in Tights* appear to lack the earnestly-articulated ire and moral discontent of Brooks's earlier films, which so clearly expounded upon his exasperation at cruelty and social inequality wherever it was detected. Ahchoo may very well be as likeable and street-savvy as *Blazing Saddles*'s Sheriff Bart, but when he dons a pair of glasses in order to ape Malcolm X ('We didn't land on Sherwood Forest! Sherwood Forest landed on us!') the impact of his call for unity in opposing John's despotic rule seems infinitely less effective when we have such an indistinct sense of the peril that is facing him and the rest of the Merry Men. Whereas Bart was forced into facing danger and imminent death both from villains *and* the very people he was assigned to protect, the antagonists in *Robin Hood: Men in Tights* – with their kazoo-playing guards and moveable facial moles (an apparent tribute to Igor's constantly shifting hump in *Young Frankenstein*) – seem rather more difficult to consider credibly on account of their lack of demonstrable on-screen malice. And therefore, because the villains' cruelty is so imprecisely rendered (and indeed, it is difficult to take too seriously a royal usurper who must assure us that he isn't breaking wind in a jacuzzi), so too must Robin's heroism be cast in a correspondingly compromised light. As Tison Pugh and Angela Jane Weisl have posited, his grand intentions seem disproportionate to the feeble threat that he actually faces:

> Robin, as played by Cary Elwes, affirms his heroism by itemizing his martial objectives in a list that quickly degrades into ridiculousness: 'And tell them also that I vow to put an end to the injustice, right the

wrongs, end the tyranny, restore the throne, protect the forest, introduce folk dancing, demand a four-day work week, and affordable health care for Saxons and Normans'. The boy he has saved from attack merely agrees, 'Yes, yes, good, good', indicating his growing impatience with the hero's inflated ego.[8]

Just as the film's rendering of the conflict between good and evil is muddied by vagueness and ambiguity, so too does Brooks's hit-rate with the comedic content prove to be very inconsistent. His cultural references in particular vary widely from the current to the outmoded. Some, such the Monty Pythonesque Jerusalem dungeon, complete with its own Maitre d' (Brian George's startlingly affable Falafel), feel inspired in their inventiveness due to their skilful subversion of corresponding scenes in the Reynolds film. Others, including the visual reference to Chris Columbus's *Home Alone* (1990) – with Corbin Allred reproducing Macaulay Culkin's famous impersonation of Edvard Munch's *The Scream* ('It's getting dark, and I gotta go *Home Alone* now') – are pleasing but so heavily signposted that their overall impact is blunted. And then there is the intriguing inclusion of Dom DeLuise's comic Mafioso, Don Giovanni (perhaps named for the Mozart opera), who provides an entertaining impression of Marlon Brando – not just in his famous role as Don Vito Corleone in Francis Ford Coppola's *The Godfather* (1972), but also in other appearances such as Terry Malloy in Elia Kazan's *On the Waterfront* (1954). While DeLuise is always worth watching, the *Godfather* jokes (such as the cotton-wool-in-the-mouth gag) had already been fully explored in popular culture some time beforehand, leaving the scene appearing largely redundant. (Given the era, presumably the 'Jersey' that he is said to hail from is actually the island in the English Channel rather than the American State.) Equally variable in the effectiveness of their inclusion are the Don's oddball sidekicks. Joe Dimmick's Filthy Luca is an amusingly dimwitted version of the monosyllabic *Godfather* enforcer Luca Brazi, as played in the original by Lenny Montana (to further buttress the similarity, the Sheriff later calls the character 'Luca Pazzo' – literally, the Italian for 'Mad Luca'). Clint Eastwood lookalike Steve Tancora is likewise suitably inspired as the mute hitman Dirty Ezio (a take-off of Eastwood's hardman seventies detective *Dirty Harry*), who sets up a sniper-crossbow in the 'Royal Folio Depository' overlooking the archery match, thus lampooning the Dallas Book Depository where Lee Harvey Oswald assassinated President John F. Kennedy in 1963. But having spent time introducing these characters so elaborately, Brooks gives them comparatively little to do thereafter. Likewise, although the above cultural references refer to well-known phenomena, their essentially backward-looking nature robs the film of contemporary currency, suggesting that Brooks was more interested in maintaining a decent rate of gag generation than he was in using the Robin Hood mythos to drive home specific social criticism relevant to the time of production. Crick conjectures that 'so few of Brooks's [...] jabs are Sherwood-specific it's difficult to think of them as spoofing Robin Hood at all. [...] Either way, *Robin Hood: Men in Tights* isn't half so take-no-prisoners cheeky as its "The Legend Had It Coming" lobby posters promise, never so much explodes the Robin Hood myth as merely revisits it, tourist-like, smiling uncritically all the way'.9

While it is true that the film contains its fair share of repetitive gags – horses bearing mock vehicle signs including 'rent a wreck' and 'just married', or modern conveniences set in deliberately anachronistic settings such as 'Ye Olde Port-a-Privy' – it also presents a number of references to American products and social phenomena which would leave international audiences (and some later generations) scratching their heads. This included the Merry Men receiving their green tights in large plastic eggs (a spoof of L'eggs pantyhose, which were packaged in similar containers), Robin receiving 'the chop' at the archery competition (a custom at American university sports matches), and perhaps most prominently the appearance of the Lou Costello lookalike who cries 'Hey, Abbot!' at Dick Van Patten's senior clergyman – a homage to Costello's catchphrase during his many collaborations with Bud Abbott ('I hate that guy', the Abbot mutters darkly in response). But it is unfair to criticise the reuse of Brooks's sight gags *en masse*, as many of them do provide significant recycle value. The English coast having its own Hollywood-style sign, unexpected examples of anachronistic modernity (the castle's garage-like remote-controlled portcullis, for instance) and the random appearance of well-known commercial products (such as the Campbell's Soup tin on the head of a Sherwood combat dummy) all echo aspects of earlier Brooks features, as does the valet horse-parking service outside Castle Rottingham – where wheel immobilisers are fitted to the steeds after dismounting – which recalls the many equine jokes littering *Blazing Saddles*. Yet arguably the scenes which work best are those where the fourth wall is not so much breached as decimated, such as Robin accidentally skewering the lunch of a production crewman with his sword during the climactic fight with the Sheriff, and the Abbot unintentionally striking the camera overhead with his ceremonial staff. As Gloria Withalm explains, the inclusion of such self-aware sequences help to fit the film comfortably into Brooks's broader canon because of their correspondence with earlier entries in his filmography:

> The movies of Mel Brooks are full of self-referential and self-reflexive shots and scenes. In his *Robin Hood: Men in Tights* [...] he also lets us have a glimpse at film-making. After some twenty minutes the camera is slowly approaching a stained glass window high up in a fortress tower. With the next shot we are inside and watch Amy Yasbeck as Maid Marian taking a bath. Her soft singing is inter-rupted by the sound of shattering glass; cut; the shooting camera shows us a hole in the glass window and through the hole we see another camera slowly pulling back (obviously meant to be the one which made the establishing shot of this scene).[10]

There is most certainly an unabashedly self-referential aspect to, for instance, Ahchoo responding to scepticism about his appointment as the new Sheriff with the line 'Why not? It worked in *Blazing Saddles!*' Yet Brooks also uses the film's dimension of self-awareness to continue his unconventional exploration of Jewish cultural identity in a way that was perhaps more prominent than any of his films since *History of the World: Part I*, even assuming a cameo role as a Rabbi who provides the analogue to the Christian Friar Tuck in this eccentric, anything-goes take on the Robin Hood mythology. As Andrew B.R. Elliott explains, 'in place of the usual Friar Tuck scene, the director himself cameos as a maniacal "Rabbi Tuckman" who operates a mobile circumcision unit. Ignoring for one moment the bawdy and scatological humor, there is an interesting criticism of Jewish invisibility within the Middle Ages, an undertone which is perpetuated by running jokes about Judaism'.[11] Undoubtedly Brooks does not squander the opportunity that Elliott suggests, at times emphasising the generally hostile social environment that existed for followers of Judaism during the historical period that is being depicted (though not explicitly exploring, for instance, real incidents such as the widespread massacre of innocent followers of the Jewish faith following Richard the Lionheart's coronation – at this point a relatively recent historical event). Thus we see Prince John declaring Robin's stolen wild boar as 'Treyf' (a Yiddish term for food that is not Kosher), and ruminating that Latrine's attempt at a meal 'Looks like a Seder at Vincent Price's house' – referring to a traditional Passover meal – as he spits out an eyeball as though it were a ping-pong ball.

Just as had been the case with *High Anxiety*, where Brooks had occasionally extended the reach of his spoof beyond the principal target of Alfred Hitchcock's canon, *Robin Hood: Men in Tights* at times broadens its range of attack in order to satirise the exaggerated sensationalism and occasional absurdity of the modern action movie. In so doing, Brooks was tapping into a predominantly eighties zeitgeist where such features had reigned supreme at the box-office and, although the early nineties were to offer its own classics of the genre, there was a sense in many corners of the critical community that the new decade was ushering in a change of dramatic sensibility – a debate which Brooks acknowledges in the film through the unconventional depiction of his heroes and villains (and, of course, by sending up every training montage cliché). Because he closely emulates certain stylistic elements of *Robin Hood: Prince of Thieves* while simplifying the dynamics of the earlier film's narrative (complications such as Robin's familial relationship to Will Scarlet are completely dispensed with, for example), his attempt to correspond the Robin Hood legend to the framework of the contemporary action movie – with all its excesses and visual spectacle – appears especially pronounced. Katharine M. Morsberger and Robert E. Morsberger note that:

> [*Robin Hood: Men in Tights*] is such a close parody of the Costner film that, especially in the sequences with Roger Rees as the Sheriff of Rottingham (director Mel Brooks's response to Alan Rickman's over-the-top performance as the Sheriff) they tend to blur together in the memory. [...] Comedy can quickly shade off into satire and irony. *Robin Hood: Men in Tights* is a parody, true, but also, in diametric opposition to the 'action' film, its satire implies an admission that the heroic and simple martial solutions have failed. The icons of war are so exaggerated that they are rendered meaningless and ridiculous, suggesting that 'serious', 'action' films will ultimately have the same

effect.[12]

The film boasts many entertaining performances from a talented cast, most especially Cary Elwes's eloquent but prim Robin, Amy Yasbeck bringing a demure determination to Maid Marian, and David Chappelle (in his motion picture debut) providing a memorably hip Ahchoo, translating 1990s Californian cool to a rustic twelfth century setting. Mark Blankfield also provides stalwart support as Blinkin, even though the character's depiction in the screenplay manages to contain enough jokes at the expense of the visually impaired that the performance is virtually guaranteed to offend someone (whether he is viciously attacking a wooden support beam with his sword, mistakenly believing it to be an enemy soldier, or exploring the Braille edition of *Ye Olde Playboy* magazine). The film contains relatively few appearances by Brooksian regulars, though there are brief but pleasing performances by Dick Van Patten as the harried Abbot, Robert Ridgely (reprising from *Blazing Saddles* the executioner who enjoys his work just a little too much), and of course Brooks himself as the wise but Bris-obsessed Rabbi. Patrick Stewart also nicely sends up Sean Connery's King Richard the First, complete with heavy Scottish accent, at the film's climax.

As in so many films illustrating a clash between good and evil, the actors portraying the villains always seem to be enjoying themselves the most, and this is certainly the case with Roger Rees's saturnine, socially awkward Sheriff. With an appearance quite clearly modelled on the Alan Rickman portrayal, Rees relishes the delivery of his character's mangled dialogue, always delivering even the most garbled lines with perfectly measured dramatic tones. Though the audience becomes increasingly aware that the Sheriff is an essentially hopeless character – a failure as an antagonist, as a suitor, and as a strategist – there is never any indication that he ever begins to acknowledge this fact himself, and thus Rees continues to play him with an air of constantly frustrated cod-aristocratic aloofness throughout (bringing a touch of injured dignity even to lines such as 'A chastity belt?! That's going to chafe my willy!'). As Prince John, Richard Lewis sidesteps any attempt at conveying royal nobility and strives instead for the manner of an overanxious micro-manager. Though the character's increasingly desperate attempts to fend off Robin's popular rebellion seem all the more fruitless when they are being orchestrated by someone who appears so thoroughly neurotic ('I have a mole!?' he exclaims, panicked, when the Sheriff notes that the Regent's facial blemish seems to move location between scenes), and is far removed from John's general depiction in wider popular culture as a competent administrator and pitiless autocrat. Lewis enjoys some of his best lines during an unlikely conversation with Tracey Ullman's wizened seer (and occasional chef) Latrine, a noteworthy portrayal of both arch cunning and grotesque excess. Brandishing 'magic pills' which are quite obviously Polo Mints and lusting after the Sheriff even in spite of his empty bluster and doltish incompetence, the role gives Ullman's natural comic talents a real opportunity to shine. Even though Latrine's promised potion to neutralise Robin never actually appears, Ullman takes full advantage of the character's blunt candour to present a figure who is as sharp-talking as she is lecherous – even when entertaining royal company:

| | |
|---|---|
| PRINCE JOHN: | Such an unusual name: Latrine. How did your family come by it? |
| LATRINE: | We changed it in the ninth century. |
| PRINCE JOHN: | You mean you changed it *to* Latrine? |
| LATRINE: | Yeah. It used to be Shithouse. |

Beyond the acting performances, the film's musical variety presents similar entertainment. Hummie Mann provides *Robin Hood: Men in Tights* with a suitably cinematic score, maintaining both medieval whimsy and an energetic pace as and when required. The 'Men in Tights' song itself would no doubt have seemed familiar to many of Brooks's fans, given that it reuses the melody of the 'Jews in Space' sequence from *History of the World: Part I*, though it offers some welcome musical diversity when compared with Maid Marian's over-the-top, almost Disney-esque introductory ballad (an inspired vocal performance by Debbie James) or the admirably dexterous rap routines which bookend the film.

*Robin Hood: Men in Tights* marked a reversal of Brooks's cinematic commercial fortunes following the disappointing domestic returns from *Life Stinks*. Performing strongly amongst American audiences, with a budget estimated at $20,000,000[13] the film would eventually proceed to make a respectable domestic total gross of $35,739,755.[14] Not for the first occasion, however, Brooks's success at the box-office was not mirrored in the views of commentators at the time of the film's release. Owen Gleiberman of *Entertainment Weekly* was harshly critical of what he felt to be the movie's negligible relevance to current pop culture, opining that 'Brooks' humor now seems about as fresh as a Henny Youngman routine – it's not just ancient, it's Jurassic. Skewering both the timeless Errol Flynn *Adventures of Robin Hood* and the deadwood Kevin Costner blockbuster, Brooks has the Merry Men of Sherwood Forest swish it up in a mock-musical number, a joke that seems not so much politically incorrect as 20 years out of date. [...] As Robin Hood, Cary Elwes doesn't quite seem to realize he's starring in a comedy. It's sad to have to say it, but in *Men in Tights* Mel Brooks makes outrageousness itself seem desperate'.[15] In a similar vein, *The Washington Post*'s Rita Kempley questioned the wisdom of Brooks's choice of target for the film's spoofery: 'The real problem isn't that it's politically incorrect – a state of being truly worthy of a good skewering – but that it's about as funny as a butt-load of boils. For one thing, Brooks's target isn't worth the arrows. Released more than two years ago, the Kevin Costner movie was its own parody. Further, it lacked such spoof-worthy qualities as pomposity and memorability'.[16] Not all critical appraisals were entirely negative, although – as Vincent Canby demonstrated in *The New York Times* – even the more receptive reviews of the film were deeply qualified in their assessment of its perceived virtues:

> The movie takes a long time to get off the ground, and then it wobbles. It hits a couple of ecstatically funny high points, only to plummet into a bog of second-rate gags, emerging a long time later to engage the audience by the sheer, unstoppable force of the Brooks chutzpah. [...] What's missing is the kind of densely packed comic screenplay that helped to make *Young Frankenstein* and *High Anxiety* two of the most delectable movie parodies of the last 20 years. *Men in Tights* has the manner of something that wasn't argued over long enough. A few good gags are supplemented by dozens of others that still need to be worked on or tossed out entirely. Occasional lines are delightfully dizzy, but they are random shots. There's no comic momentum.[17]

In spite of the film's lack of impact amongst the critical community, its popularity both at home and abroad has led it to become – along with *Spaceballs* – one of the most successful of

Brooks's later comedies on home entertainment formats, ensuring that *Robin Hood: Men in Tights* has proven to be significantly more popular than the other entries in his filmography which hail from the 1990s. That said, its reputation amongst more recent reviewers has never been fully rehabilitated even in spite of its continued cult status. Leonard Norwitz was largely representative of this critical disposition when he commented that 'Mel Brooks' direction here is lazy and without a clue as to how to fill his frame. There is no excuse for a parody to look amateurish in the bargain. [...] The movie has its moments, but is not one of Brooks' better efforts'.18 A fuller consideration of the film's reputation amongst media critics has been given by Christopher Kulik, who echoed many of the concerns of earlier commentators in lamenting the effectiveness of Brooks's comedic aims in comparison to his features of the sixties and seventies:

> When *Robin Hood: Men In Tights* came out in 1993, Brooks' spoof cycle was drawing to a close, as this was his second-to-last project. The gifted jokester scored major successes with *The Producers*, *Blazing Saddles*, and *Young Frankenstein*; three of the greatest comedies ever made. For some reason, however, Brooks stumbled with many of his subsequent efforts; most have been dismissed as disappointments by fans and critics alike. This applies especially to *Robin Hood: Men In Tights*, a dull and silly blunder peppered with sporadic laughs. [...] The journey of Sherwood's hero is awfully familiar by now, and Brooks never really gives the narrative any amusing twists or engaging surprises. It's a shame too, because the immortal tale has the potential for a funny bashing, especially since there are many arguments regarding how much of the story is actual truth. The film is driven by reference rather than reverence; you can see what Brooks is making fun of with his jokes, yet they all lack freshness and spontaneity. Brooks simply seems to be running out of ideas, as the material is both negligible and forgettable.19

During the rap that concludes the film, the (by now almost expected) Brooksian tradition for mentioning ultimately-unproduced sequels continues with the line: 'Hope we meet again in *Robin Hood 2*'. In a manner similar to the unmade follow-ups to *History of the World: Part I* and *Spaceballs*, however, no continuation of the narrative was to be forthcoming – presumably more a result of the film's solid but unexceptional domestic box-office returns than the widespread hostility of reviewers. With *Robin Hood: Men in Tights*, Brooks had faced growing critical complaints over the extent of his ability to produce comedies which remained relevant to contemporary audiences – a naggingly persistent strain of critique which had gathered momentum since the late eighties, and which was exacerbated by his employment of overly-familiar techniques and comedic apparatus even when making an evident attempt to move with the times and adapt his satirical aims to impale targets which were more immediately current. Yet the intensity of his social criticism seemed strangely subdued given such prime subject matter, depicting one of Western culture's most immediately recognisable conflicts between the uprightness of a subjugated populace seeking social justice and a detached, morally repugnant tyranny which is solely concerned with greed and oppression. The factual basis of the Robin Hood mythos may well remain an issue of debate amongst historians, but the fictional accounts which have sprung up around the phenomenon over the centuries have provided fertile ground for allegorical explorations of personal and social liberation in the face of brutality and repression. Though Brooks's contribution to the Robin Hood cultural patchwork is often shamelessly entertaining, it ultimately presents only the most passive line of social analysis – disappointing given the full-throated nature of his earlier commentaries on emancipation and fairness. Given that the swashbuckling protagonist's singular claim to fame is 'stealing from the rich to give to the poor', the fact that the gallant righteousness of Elwes's incarnation of Robin Hood precludes him from doing anything more rebellious than poaching a single wild animal from royal land can only mean that the squandered potential for comic subversion must be considered something of a missed opportunity.

# REFERENCES

1. Bob Leszczak, *Single Season Sitcoms, 1948-1979: A Complete Guide* (Jefferson: McFarland, 2012), p. 200.
2. Robert Alan Crick, *The Big Screen Comedies of Mel Brooks* (Jefferson: McFarland and Company, 2009) [2002], p. 187.
3. Stephen Thomas Knight, *Robin Hood: A Mythic Biography* (Ithaca: Cornell University Press, 2003), p. 172.
4. Keyvan Sarkhosh, 'Metalepsis in Popular Comedy Film', in *Metalepsis in Popular Culture*, ed. by Karin Kukkonen and Sonja Klimek (Berlin: Walter de Gruyter Ltd., 2011), 171-95, p. 182.
5. Crick, p. 195.
6. David Desser and Lester D. Friedman, *American Jewish Filmmakers*, 2nd edn (Chicago: University of Illinois Press, 2004), p. 165.
7. Crick, p. 188.
8. Tison Pugh and Angela Jane Weisl, *Medievalisms: Making the Past in the Present* (Abingdon: Routledge, 2013), p. 78.
9. Crick, p. 194.
10. Gloria Withalm, '"How Did You Find Us?" – "We Read the Script!": A Special Case of Self-Reference in the Movies', in *Semiotics of the Media: State of the Art, Projects, and Perspectives*, ed. by Winfried Nöth (Berlin: Walter de Gruyter, 1997), pp. 255-268, p. 258.
11. Andrew B.R. Elliott, *Remaking the Middle Ages: The Methods of Cinema and History in Portraying the Medieval World* (Jefferson: McFarland, 2011), p. 136.
12. Katharine M. Morsberger and Robert E. Morsberger, 'Robin Hood on Film: Can We Ever Again "Make Them Like They Used To"?', in *Playing Robin Hood: The Legend as Performance in Five Centuries*, ed. by Lois Potter (Cranbury: Associated University Presses, 1998), 205-231, pp. 225-26.
13. Budgetary data drawn from the Internet Movie Database. <http://www.imdb.com/title/tt0107977/business?ref_=tt_ql_dt_4>
14. Box-office data drawn from BoxOfficeMojo.com. <http://www.boxofficemojo.com/movies/?id=robinhoodmenintights.htm>
15. Owen Gleiberman, 'So I Married an Axe Murderer; Robin Hood: Men in Tights', in *Entertainment Weekly*, 6 August 1993. <http://www.ew.com/ew/article/0,,20285249,00.html>
16. Rita Kempley, 'Robin Hood: Men in Tights', in *The Washington Post*, 28 July 1993. <http://www.washingtonpost.com/wp-srv/style/longterm/movies/videos/robinhoodmenintightspg13kempley_a0a39f.htm>
17. Vincent Canby, '*Robin Hood: Men in Tights*: Mel Brooks Aims His Comedic Barbs At Robin Hood et al.', in *The New York Times*, 28 July 1993. <http://www.nytimes.com/movie/review?res=9F0CE4DD1431F93BA15754C0A965958260>
18. Leonard Norwitz, 'LensViews: *Robin Hood Men in Tights*', in *DVD Beaver*, 15 May 2010. <http://www.dvdbeaver.com/film3/blu-ray_reviews51/robin_hood_men_in_tights_blu-ray.htm>
19. Christopher Kulik, '*Robin Hood: Men in Tights*', in *DVD Verdict*, 26 May 2010. <http://www.dvdverdict.com/reviews/menintightsbluray.php>

# 11

# DRACULA: DEAD AND LOVING IT (1995)

FOR HIS FINAL FILM of the 1990s, and what was to be the movie which would mark the conclusion of his directorial career, Mel Brooks made the bold and creatively precarious decision to return to a topic which had proven to be amongst his most successful – a spoof of cinematic horror. Some two decades after the huge box-office success of *Young Frankenstein*, he was to substitute the atmospheric monochrome of his earlier parody of the golden era of Universal horror movies in favour of the vibrant colours and mannered sets of the Hammer Films productions of the fifties and sixties. The result may well have been another fastidiously faithful recreation of a specific type and period of horror production, but it was one which – for a Brooks production – would often feel suspiciously light on either laughs or memorable dialogue.

Given the film's focus, namely Bram Stoker's perennially popular vampire Count Dracula, Brooks's directorial swan-song offered a unique opportunity to explore the concept and reality of personal freedom through a depiction of a character who endlessly manipulates and controls the thoughts, behaviour and feelings of others. Yet Brooks was to take his examination of liberation further still, juxtaposing Dracula's unconventional, licentious conduct with the strait-laced priggishness and rigidly-enforced morality of Victorian England in order to illuminate the way in which social mores inform the nature of independent action and attitudes.

In 1893, upright English solicitor Thomas Renfield (Peter MacNicol) has arrived in the sinister depths of rural Transylvania. His purpose: to consult with the infamous Count Dracula, with whom he has an appointment at the mysterious nobleman's mountaintop castle. On his journey, Renfield is baffled by the strange superstitions of the Transylvanian villagers who live near the ancient stronghold; they plead with him not to visit the Count, especially as the sun is going down. Renfield dismisses their strange beliefs as mere folklore, but not before the gypsy mystic Madame Ouspenskaya (Anne Bancroft) insists on giving him a Christian cross for protection.

Now thoroughly confused by the villagers' warnings, Renfield perseveres and makes the long trek up the mountain to the castle. There, he finds the medieval dwelling seemingly deserted, with cobwebs and rust in great abundance. However, upon venturing inside the building he soon discovers himself to be trapped, his only company appearing to be a debonair man in late middle-age who wears aristocratic clothing and appears to have a shadow with a mind of its own. Renfield's host identifies himself as Count Dracula (Leslie Nielsen), and also reveals the reason for the solicitor's presence – the Transylvanian intends to purchase Carfax Abbey, an estate in the United Kingdom, and Renfield has been summoned to legalise the transaction. The formalities progress smoothly, but Renfield becomes concerned during the signing of the necessary documents when he notices Dracula becoming unusually animated when the accident-prone solicitor accidentally cuts his finger.

During the night, Renfield's guest room is invaded by a pair of beautiful women who – inexplicably – decide to make an advance on him. The solicitor is even more puzzled when Dracula arrives, angrily dismisses the two strangers, and promptly hypnotises his guest. The count explains that from this moment onward, Renfield will be his willing slave... but in return, the beleaguered legal advisor will be able to harvest the lives of others. Not human beings, however – just insects, rodents and other small creatures. Dracula has chartered a berth on the *Demeter*, a ship which is bound for England, and warns Renfield that he must ensure his safety during the voyage due to the fact that he will be travelling inside a coffin. The journey to the British

Isles proves to be a difficult one due to a severe storm, but Dracula makes use of the distraction caused by the turbulence to feast upon the ship's crew.

At the Lyceum Theatre in London, noted sanatorium physician Dr Jack Seward (Harvey Korman) has arrived to join his daughter Mina (Amy Yasbeck), her friend Lucy Westenra (Lysette Anthony) and fiancé Jonathan Harker (Steven Weber) for an operatic performance. Seward reveals that he has been treating a difficult case – the sole survivor of the *Demeter*'s voyage to England, namely Renfield. They are interrupted by the unexpected appearance of Dracula, who introduces himself as the new owner of Carfax Abbey. As his estate borders the land of Seward's sanatorium, his declaration is met with a courteous but mildly suspicious welcome. Dracula seems to take a particular interest in Lucy, who warmly reciprocates his attraction.

That night, Lucy is undressing for bed as she looks forlornly through her window at Dracula's adjacent estate. Quietly wishing for the enigmatic aristocrat's company, Lucy soon receives more than she bargained for when the Count mystically transforms himself into a bat and flies across the fields which divide them. However, being oblivious to his transmutation Lucy closes her bedroom window and brings an abrupt (and painful) halt to his airborne advance. Then the arrival of Seward and Harker, who hear the collision and come to Lucy's aid, further compromises Dracula's dark intentions. But managing to evade detection, the Count has the last laugh as – back in human form again – he sinks his fangs into Lucy's neck, drinking her blood with great relish.

The next morning at the sanatorium, Seward invites Renfield (who is still being held in a locked room for his own safety) to join him for morning tea in order to ascertain his mental fitness. Renfield protests that he has returned to a state of complete mental stability following his earlier ordeal on the *Demeter*. His heartfelt protestations are soon proven false, however, when he begins to obsessively gobble every insect within reach, causing Seward to have him strait-jacketed. Elsewhere in the building, Mina pays a visit on Lucy only to discover her friend to be weak and feverish. Seward and Harker examine her, but as they can ascertain no sign of infection her condition appears inexplicable. Discovering two puncture marks on Lucy's neck, Seward is mystified and determines that he will contact Professor Abraham Van Helsing (Mel Brooks) - a noted expert on obscure diseases - in the hope that he can shed some light on the situation.

Van Helsing is summoned from his training hospital in London, and promptly arrives to examine Lucy. From the strange marks on her neck and the fact that she has evidently lost a great deal of blood, Van Helsing comes to the conclusion that she has been attacked by a vampire. Seward and Harker react with surprise at his findings, believing them to be nothing more than unscientific myths and legends, but the professor is adamant. He is certain not only that the assault on Lucy will be repeated, but that if she should die as a result of the vampire's blood-sucking onslaught then she will become one of their number herself.

Consulting a book on undead lore (which has conveniently arrived at the sanatorium that very day), Van Helsing discovers that garlic has an effect of repulsion on vampires. Thus Lucy is moved from her bedroom to a more easily guarded area downstairs, and the entire room draped with string upon string of garlic bulbs. Sure enough, Dracula attempts to gain entry through the room's window only to be driven back by the presence of the garlic. To this end, he frees Renfield from his secure room in the sanatorium and commands the increasingly damaged lawyer to clear Lucy's safe haven of every garland of garlic he can lay his hands on. Unfortunately for the hapless Renfield, he is quickly spotted by Lucy and taken back into confinement before he can ensure the Count's safety. Now forced to take alternative action, Dracula uses telepathy to convince Lucy to leave her room voluntarily. As soon as she has joined the vampire in the sanatorium gardens, he feasts upon her blood once more. But his actions are seen by Mina, who screams as she witnesses her friend being attacked by an unidentified figure. Seward, Harker and Van Helsing race to Lucy's side, only to discover that they have arrived too late. She is dead, her blood now completely drained by the vampire.

Following Lucy's funeral, Van Helsing, Seward and Harker are reflecting upon the mystery of the events which led up to her death. The professor strongly recommends that Lucy's body be staked through the heart in order to preclude any possibility of her rising as a vampire, but Seward angrily dismisses the suggestion as morbid superstition. Their argument is interrupted by an unexpected visitor – Dracula. Claiming to have only just learned of Lucy's demise, the Count has come to the sanatorium to offer his condolences. Van Helsing, who has an extensive knowledge of Transylvanian history, is all too aware of Dracula's bloodthirsty forebears and is immediately distrustful of the enigmatic newcomer. The pair take an instant dislike to each other, leading to a battle of wits where each attempts to trump the other by getting the last word in. Meanwhile, at the graveyard where Lucy has been interred a watchman (Clive Revill) is alarmed when he hears a voice emanating from the dead woman's crypt. He opens her casket, believing her to have been buried alive, only for Lucy to attack him by biting his neck. Baring her fangs, it is obvious that she has been reborn as a vampire.

Back at the sanatorium, Harker decides to head for the graveyard – much to Seward's derision – so that he can watch over Lucy's body in the fear that Van Helsing's grim theory of post-mortem reanimation is true. He is unaware that the professor himself is heading for the same cemetery, where he comes across the discarded body of the watchman with no small alarm. Harker arrives at the crypt and hears Lucy call him by name. He is astonished to see her, given that he had attended her funeral only hours earlier. Lucy offers Harker the chance to join her in the ranks of the undead, but Van Helsing interrupts her attack by appearing in the nick of time with a crucifix. Driving her back into the crypt, the professor rallies Harker to push home the advantage and stake Lucy through the heart, thus ending her vampiric nightmare. With the utmost reluctance, Harker does as Van Helsing asks, only to be completely drenched in gallon after gallon of fresh blood. ('There's so much blood!' the young doctor gasps, leading the nonchalant Van Helsing to explain: 'She just ate!')

While Lucy is finally laid to rest, Dracula has moved on to a different target – Mina. After some difficulty controlling her under the influence of hypnosis, Dracula eventually succeeds in spiriting Mina away from the safety of the sanatorium with the goal of making her his eternal bride. Bringing her unconscious body to Carfax Abbey while Seward and the others remain oblivious to her absence, the Count engages the semi-conscious Mina into a romantic dance before finally sinking his fangs into her neck.

In the morning, Harker pays a visit to Mina and discovers her to be unusually amorous. On account of her long-standing chaste relationship with her fiancé, he is appalled when she suddenly becomes tactile and affectionate – as is Seward, who stumbles upon the pair in an embrace and fears that he has interrupted a tryst between them (especially as they have 'only been engaged for five years'). Seward intends to have Harker ejected from his home for his supposed lustfulness, but is stopped by Van Helsing who discovers the true reason for Mina's out-of-character behaviour – a pair of familiar-looking puncture marks on her neck. Reasoning that the vampire who was responsible for Lucy's death is now intending to bring about Mina's downfall, an anxious Seward beseeches Van Helsing to find the responsible party and stop them before time runs out.

Some time later, the professor formulates a plan. Van Helsing persuades Seward – against the stuffy physician's better judgement – to hold a ball at the sanatorium. Dracula arrives, but is puzzled to find the still-disturbed Renfield at a high-class social gathering. Suspicious of his slave's presence there, the vampire quietly explains to Renfield that in the event of a disturbance they should rendezvous not at Carfax Abbey but rather at an abandoned chapel nearby. Dracula invites Mina to dance, but public admiration of their energetic waltz soon turns to horror when a huge mirror is unveiled overlooking the dancefloor, revealing that the Count has no reflection. Dracula is outraged at Van Helsing's trickery, which has exposed the vampire's true nature. Grabbing Mina, he smashes his way out of the ballroom window, leaving a confused Renfield in his wake.

A search of Carfax Abbey and the surrounding area shows no trace of Dracula. Van Helsing, now realising that Renfield is under the vampire's mental control, asks Seward to release the addled solicitor so that they can follow his trail and thus find the Count. This they do, and shortly after Renfield inadvertently leads Van Helsing and his associates all the way to the cliffside chapel where Dracula has moved his coffin. After a prolonged struggle with the vampire, Dracula appears to gain the upper hand – Van Helsing assails him with a large cross which is eventually destroyed, and Harker's attempts to stake the Count are also foiled. Just as it seems that Mina's fate has been sealed, dawn breaks outside the chapel. Knowing the lethal effect that daylight will have on the vampire, Van Helsing tears open the room's rusted shutters, leading Dracula's body to start smouldering. Desperately, he transforms into a bat and heads into the ceiling's buttresses for safety... only for Renfield to open a hatch in the roof, thus showering the Count with rays of sunlight and leading to his total incineration (and a decidedly unaristocratic cry of 'Renfield, you asshole!'). Mina is liberated from Dracula's malignant influence, and an overjoyed Harker sweeps her back to the safety of her family home. Renfield is distraught at the loss of his master; although Seward explains that the solicitor no longer needs to live under anyone's influence but his own, it becomes clear that he is now so weak-minded that he will happily substitute Dracula's manipulation over his actions for just about anyone else's. Van Helsing, his work now done, opens Dracula's coffin (where Renfield has secreted the vampire's ashes) and shouts an ancient Moldavian expression, thus succeeding in getting the 'definitive' last word over his rival. But not to be outdone, after the end credits have rolled Dracula's voice can be heard enunciating yet another phrase in Moldavian, proving that even the destruction of his undead form can't tame his competitive streak.

As had been the case with *Young Frankenstein*, Brooks does not target one specific adaptation of the *Dracula* legend but rather allows himself to borrow freely from the vampire's various cinematic outings of decades past. Thus we have an antagonist who has the costume and accent of Bela Lugosi's patrician Count (Tod Browning's *Dracula*, 1931), exhibits some of the charisma of Frank Langella's interpretation (John Badham's *Dracula*, 1979), and occasionally sports the outlandish hairdo of Gary Oldman's ancient vampire (Francis Ford Coppola's *Bram Stoker's Dracula*, 1992). While the film's copious dry ice and cobwebs could have been drawn from just about any past version of the tale, Brooks's take on the *Dracula* tale is arguably closest to the Browning film (itself an adaptation of the Hamilton Deane and John S. Balderston stage play of 1924) in terms of its characterisation and narrative structure. As Robert Alan Crick observes, 'perhaps the most surprising aspect of Brooks's film, in fact, is how utterly *un*surprising it is, following, if not Stoker's 1897 novel exactly, the familiar old Hamilton Deane/ John Balderston stage play and director Tod Browning's 1931 adaptation so faithfully, and with such oddly muted humor, it almost qualifies as a non-comic Browning remake, with bits and pieces of films like F.W. Murnau's *Nosferatu* (1922), Terence Fisher's *The Horror of Dracula* (1958), John Badham's *Dracula* (1979), and Francis Ford Coppola's *Bram Stoker's Dracula* (1992) thrown in'.[1]

Just as Browning's famous 1931 adaptation of *Dracula* had contained many deviations from Bram Stoker's 1897 novel – the changing role of Seward (originally Lucy's suitor, not her guardian), the absence of characters such as Quincey Morris and Arthur Holmwood, Renfield visiting Transylvania in place of Harker, and the markedly different finale – so too did Brooks's film diverge at times from the situations presented in the earlier movie. Renfield's first meeting with Dracula is quite dissimilar to the vampire's distinctive introduction in the Browning film, garlic is substituted for wolfsbane as the principal vampire-repellent, the use of a mirror to reveal the Count's true nature comes much earlier, and the prominent character of Nurse Briggs (played in the original by Joan Standing) does not appear in Brooks's version of the tale. However, what is perhaps more striking is the number of occasions where Brooks remains remarkably faithful to the classic thirties adaptation. Renfield's insect-devouring obsession, Van Helsing's gradual deduction of Dracula's schemes, the nature of Lucy's attraction to the Count... all bear more resemblance to the incidents of the Garrett Fort screenplay of 1931 than to Stoker's original text. As Andre Marc Strumer has reflected, Brooks's movie achieves its 'best accomplishments [in] bringing the book to the screen because it includes both elements from the book, as well as continuous homage to other film works, which have done the same thing. The film is the closest translation of the book to film of any comedic attempt to bring the story to the screen'.[2]

However, Brooks's attentive fidelity to the famous, seminal *Dracula* adaptation had some disadvantages when it came to the film's comedic content; Crick notes that in 'adhering so strongly to Browning, Brooks gives himself too little room to maneuver – a problem critic Leonard Maltin noted when he observed that the film "spends so much time retelling the familiar Transylvanian's story it forgets to be funny"'.[3] With *Young Frankenstein*'s alternative approach to the Mary Shelley mythos, Brooks crafted an archly self-aware addendum to the events of the classic Universal movies rather than a straight retread, but with *Dracula:*

*Dead and Loving It* he was instead to revisit the source material in a much more direct way. And while assuming the 1890s setting of the Stoker novel would not in itself prove limiting – lest we forget the extent of Brooks's cheerfully implausible convolutions presented within the nineteenth century milieu of *Blazing Saddles* – here he keeps the anachronisms to a bare minimum, lending the production a greater degree of historical accuracy but likewise restricting the extent of the uninhibited absurdity which had made *Young Frankenstein* such a successful comedy experience. As David J. Skal has opined:

> Mel Brooks, whose comedy *Young Frankenstein* (1974) fully earned its status as a classic, tried to work the magic again with *Dracula: Dead and Loving It* (1995), and missed the mark. This time, however, there was no attempt to re-create the black-and-white world of classic horror films, and by aiming darts at every Dracula variation from Lugosi to Lee to Langella to Oldman, Brooks ends up missing all targets. [...] Long stretches of the film don't feel satirical at all, but rather anemic re-creations of Hammer vampire films. The script appropriates huge hunks of dialogue from the 1931 film, raising questions about the precise dividing lines between homage, satire, and shoplifting.[4]

For a director who had become so synonymous with revelling in the sheer creative potential of film-making, this ostensibly unadventurous shift in gear seemed somewhat out of character. Indeed, rather than challenging restrictions on creative freedom, for once Brooks seemed to be self-imposing them. Yet as other commentators have pointed out, the dissimilarities in style and execution between *Young Frankenstein* and *Dracula: Dead and Loving It* do not entirely disguise the merits of the later film simply because they often compare unfavourably with those of its more illustrious predecessor. Bruce G. Hallenbeck, for instance, explains that '*Dracula: Dead and Loving It* may not be *Young Frankenstein*, but it was produced with just as much love of the genre. In fact, it was really made for the fans; mainstream audiences probably didn't get all the inside jokes. [...] Unlike *Young Frankenstein*, however, it's filmed in color, which gives it the rich look of Hammer's early *Dracula* films'.[5] Though much of the film's effectiveness may rest upon whether particular audience members remember the playful atmosphere of the Hammer movies with as much nostalgic fondness as the shadowy ambience of the Universal horror productions, the fact remains that Brooks's occasional foray into esoteric gags was arguably becoming less effective the more that time passed between the point of production and the cultural phenomena that he was spoofing. As Barbara Shulgasser commented: 'Although I enjoy Brooks' humor even when it falls a little flat, I see how its charm may elude younger viewers as so much of it refers to the Hollywood of yesteryear. [...] Brooks' enchantment with entertainments of the distant Studio Era past informs all of his movies, from *Blazing Saddles* to *Young Frankenstein*, *High Anxiety* and *Silent Movie*. But when so many of the jokes refer to old movie stars and the often hilarious conventions of movies from the 1930s and '40s, they fly over the heads of a major segment of today's movie-going population'.[6]

Certainly there is no shortage of abstruse references scattered throughout the film, both verbal and visual, some of which work more effectively than others. Anne Bancroft's gypsy mystic Madame Ouspenskaya is a rather oblique allusion to the actress Maria Ouspenskaya, famous for her appearances in the *Wolf Man* movies of the early 1940s. In the Transylvanian castle, the brides of Dracula roll along the floor with wheels under their dresses in an attempt to simulate the ethereal, floating-on-air movement of similar characters in previous adaptations. (When the Count admonishes his brides, he involuntarily causes their otherworldly choir to stop abruptly as the two women depart the room.) And perhaps most pleasingly, in true Hammer fashion the whole set wobbles slightly during the final confrontation as Harker and Seward try to break down a locked door in the chapel. Yet for all these evocations of *Dracula* films past, the film also contains an unusually high number of plot inconsistencies for a Brooks feature, the screenplay (a collaboration between Brooks, Rudy DeLuca and Steve Haberman) occasionally giving rise to some head-scratching discrepancies. Crick comments that 'this Harker never does visit Transylvania, either as solicitor nor anything else; Dracula's move to London, presumably to seek fresh victims, never gets explained; and while the Count at first focuses solely on Lucy, it's the previously all but ignored Mina he plans to make his bride'.[7] Taken together, it may be argued that these characteristics render the film rather less accomplished than many of Brooks's past features, but by that same token there is still no doubting the obvious affection which he holds for the horror movies of years past. Although *Dracula: Dead and Loving It* has received fairly harsh treatment by commentators since the time of its release, the overall quality of the production values – along with the sincerity of Brooks's creative intentions – has meant that critical condemnation has never been unanimous. Hallenbeck, for instance, has remarked that:

> All of the technical credits are first-rate and completely in tune with the subject matter; it's as if Brooks instructed everyone involved to study the classic vampire films, which he may very well have done. [...] Not especially well-received at the time of its release, *Dracula: Dead and Loving It* suffered by comparison to *Young Frankenstein* as far as most critics and audiences were concerned. But it has a charm all its own and makes other vampire parodies such as [Stan Dragoti's] *Love at First Bite* (1979) look even tackier than they were. In fact, it ranks with [Roman] Polanski's *The Fearless Vampire Killers* as one of the greatest vampire comedies ever made. Once again, Brooks' love for the material shows through; *Dracula: Dead and Loving It* is a valentine to the genre, not a stake through its heart.[8]

It is a criticism rarely levelled at Brooks that he did not push the envelope far enough in a cinematic presentation, but there is a definite sense of inertia present throughout *Dracula: Dead and Loving It* that seems particularly jarring when we consider the frenetic, rapid-fire lampoonery of its immediate predecessor. Though many critics had been unconvinced of the overall comedic hit-rate of *Robin Hood: Men in Tights*, there was no denying the pacy momentum of much of the previous film. However, while the perennial popularity of vampire lore appeared to offer a wide latitude for truly inspired spoofing (not least given the then-recent commercial success of films such as Tom Holland's *Fright Night*, 1985, Joel Schumacher's *The Lost Boys*, 1987, and Fran Rubel Kuzui's *Buffy the Vampire Slayer*, 1992), Brooks was rarely as subdued in his approach as he was here. The feature's strangely low-key tone led reviewers of the time to bemoan not only its dissimilarity to Brooks's earlier, much less reserved comedies, but also to question his reluctance to stray too far from the established tenets of the traditional *Dracula* movies of decades past. Desson Howe was particularly damning in his assessment that '*Dracula* is anemic and mediocre, with only one or two moments to remind you of the former, funnier Brooks. [...] You'd have more fun renting a few serious versions of the genre. One begins to wonder if, not unlike the premise in Brooks's *The Producers*, the filmmaker is intentionally creating a failure, so he can keep all his investment money'.[9]

The authentic but comparatively modest nature of Brooks's production did not go unnoticed by commentators, a fact which seemed all the more conspicuous given the big-budget nature of many vampire-centric horror films being produced in the late eighties and early nineties. James Craig Holte, for instance, notes that 'unlike Coppola's costly adaptation, Brooks's parody is low-key and small-scale. [...] The result is a film full of *Dracula* references and a summary of the century's film vampires; the movie is, however, for a Brooks film, curiously dead'.[10] So too, by alluding to the occasional campiness of the latter Hammer horror productions and the *grand guignol* of satires such as *The Famous Vampire Hunters* (Roman Polanski, 1967), Brooks appeared to consciously take measures that ensured the film would strike a stylistic note that was quite different from other similarly-themed features of the time. Yet as Joyce Jesionowski has observed, although *Dracula: Dead and Loving It* exhibited a preoccupation with matching the beats of audience expectation where earlier entries in the vampire subgenre of horror cinema were concerned, so too was it identifiably Brooksian in the presentation of its subject matter: 'The script, as written by Brooks, Rudy DeLuca, and Steve Haberman, follows Bram Stoker's classic closely enough for the credits to claim that the film has a legitimate link to the novel. But the adaptation is very much in the vein of Brooks's adaptations: it stays close enough to establish recognition, and then undercuts moments of high drama with absurd exaggeration and low comedy'.[11]

With a film which exhibits such an obvious concern with retaining faithfulness to – if not necessarily the original source text – at least the classic cinematic adaptations of *Dracula*, it is laudable that Brooks still continues his exploration of the concept of individual freedom through characteristically offbeat means. Though the Count's psychic control of the lawyer Renfield forms a major plot device (and also, through Peter MacNicol's mastery of physical comedy, brings about some effectively-realised humour into the bargain), it also inadvertently opens up a broader exploration of individuality and freedom within social frameworks. Because the bulk of the film is set in nineteenth century

England, Brooks extracts much wit from the buttoned-up mores of the upper-crust characters populating this genteel environment, and, as Crick has astutely remarked, 'it's Brooks's hilarious skewering of Victorian virtue that gets the biggest laughs'.[12] With the main cast's impressive command of English Received Pronunciation dialect, and well-judged lines such as Harker's 'Opera is astonishing. The music is fraught with love, hate, sensuality and unbridled passion. All the things in my life I've managed to suppress!', Brooks lets loose a stream of relentless mockery aimed at the starched-collars and stiff-upper-lip attitudes of Queen Victoria's Britain. From the prudish courtships and labyrinthine complexities of social etiquette to the aloof distance of the caring profession, perhaps made most explicit in Dr Seward's fixation on enemas as a panacea for all medical ills ('It'll give him a feeling of accomplishment,' he smiles as he prescribes yet another rectal procedure for a hapless patient), Brooks lavishes great attention on depicting an orderly but strangely joyless society where the inhibition – not celebration – of emotion is key to individual merit. In many ways this is played purely for laughs: such is Harker's stolid outlook on life, the best he can manage when rejecting the advances of the vampiric Lucy is a mannerly 'But Lucy – I'm engaged to Mina. And you're dead!' Likewise, when his old acquaintance continues her attempted seduction his response is equally reserved:

> LUCY: Jonathan, let me kiss you. Let me show you the deep, raw passion of unbridled sexual frenzy!
> HARKER: But Lucy! I'm British!

By contrasting Dracula's suave, sexually liberated persona with the repressed emotions of the Victorians, Brooks presents the audience with a greater understanding of the wily Transylvanian's intangible appeal to Lucy and Mina. The amoral vampire represents everything that is opposed to the cultural conventions of the time, which is precisely what makes him so alluring – and exciting – to his intended suitors. Yet here Brooks raises questions about the true nature of the Count's enslavement of Renfield, subtly enquiring with regard to just how much liberty the lawyer had enjoyed prior to his mental subjugation to his vampiric master. Under Dracula's control, Renfield quickly becomes a maniacal, insect-gorging lunatic, completely beholden to the Count's will. Indeed, he is shown to be so impressionable that the vampire's demise – which frees Mina from Dracula's influence entirely – has little to no effect on him, meaning that the hapless Renfield immediately looks for a substitute figure to dominate his thoughts and actions. Because the pre-hypnosis Renfield is so utterly enchained by the customary attitudes of his time, showing impeccable manners even in the most outlandish of situations (his initial reaction to being embraced in bed by Dracula's two beautiful brides is an indignant 'I'll have you know that's my knee you're straddling!'), coming under the direct control of a more dominant personality seems to be only a minor departure from his ordinary mental state. Whether this is a commentary on the bureaucratic mindset or the conformist imperative of prevailing Victorian social attitudes, Brooks leaves the distinct impression that Mina achieves liberation from Dracula's influence because she craves the very kind of personal freedom which Renfield appears content to abdicate.

Likewise, Brooks engages with the divide between scientific orthodoxy and the superstitions of folklore by pitching Van Helsing's free-thinking approach against Seward's much more conventional philosophy. Here he perforates the rigid propriety of Victorian precision and certainty by repeatedly proving Van Helsing's methodology (which appears little more than a collection of old folktales in the eyes of Seward and his assistant Harker) to be advantageous when mainstream science has failed. This may not seem particularly surprising when Seward's solution to the vampire problem is to suggest that everyone and anyone who may be affected should be given an enema – just as a precautionary measure. But the mildly ghoulish Van Helsing (consider the fate of his squeamish medical students) is equally at home consulting ancient lore as he is with reading up on the latest surgical techniques, and ultimately his revelation of Dracula's vampiric nature is built not upon his surgical brilliance but rather the arcane knowledge he gains from a dusty old tome on the subject which, implausibly enough, Seward has just had delivered in the mail ('Yes, we have *Nosferatu*! We have *Nosferatu* today!'). Yet even the intellectual giant Van Helsing is forced to question the sheer improbability of his notions, debating the situation with his colleagues as he weighs up the factors involved:

| | |
|---|---|
| HARKER: | Are you saying that Count Dracula is our vampire? |
| VAN HELSING: | Yes... and no. |
| HARKER: | Then what are you saying? |
| VAN HELSING: | I'm saying no. But... I'm leaning towards yes. |
| SEWARD: | You're saying yes? |
| VAN HELSING: | No. |
| SEWARD: | Then it's no? |
| VAN HELSING: | Not necessarily. |
| HARKER: | You sound dubious. |
| VAN HELSING: | No, I'm positive. |
| HARKER: | Of what? |
| VAN HELSING: | My theory! |
| HARKER: | And that would be? |
| VAN HELSING: | The theory of yes... or no. |

The inability of the Victorian characters to venture outside their rather unadventurous mode of thinking is the butt of many of Brooks's jokes, from Lucy and her housemaid Essie behaving a little too literally under the influence of Dracula's hypnosis to the look of incredulous disdain on Van Helsing's face when the ever-courteous Harker offers him back his blood-soaked handkerchief. Even Renfield, who is not a man of science *per sé*, cannot bring himself to overcome his sense of disbelief regarding the strange superstitions of rural Transylvania:

> MADAME OUSPENSKAYA: Please, my son. Take this cross.
> RENFIELD: Oh no, thank you.
> MADAME OUSPENSKAYA: Oh! Take the cross! Its holy love and spirit of goodness will shield you from the lurking danger.
> RENFIELD: No, no, no – really. No, thank you.
> MADAME OUSPENSKAYA: Dammit, *take the cross!*
> RENFIELD: Yes, of course.
> MADAME OUSPENSKAYA: That'll be fifteen kopecks.

If Dracula's opponents are a staidly conventional group, it seems only fair to observe that the Count himself is only variably traditional in his portrayal. The casting of Leslie Nielsen divided the critics of the time, some considering his quirky charm to be the perfect choice for a decidedly off-kilter Dracula, while others believed him to be inappropriate due to his lack of tangible menace. The one-time square-jawed dramatic actor was, by the mid-nineties, now better known for his deadpan performance as Detective Lieutenant Frank Drebin in the popular crime spoof *The Naked Gun: From the Files of Police Squad* (David Zucker, 1988) and its sequels as well as, to a lesser extent, his portrayal of Father Jedediah Mayii in *Reposessed* (Bob Logan, 1990), a clever if underrated parody of William Friedkin's *The Exorcist* (1973). Nielsen's straight-faced delivery of even the most unconventional lines led to him becoming a popular leading man in comedies throughout the latter decades of his life, with similar roles in features as diverse as *Spy Hard* (Rick Friedberg, 1996) and *2001: A Space Travesty* (Allan A. Goldstein, 2000), so Brooks's selecting him as the face of his urbane, charming but occasionally rather gormless Count Dracula certainly did not require a huge leap of logic. As Holte has suggested, Brooks required a slightly offbeat vampire due to the very familiarity of the character within the public consciousness: 'The vampire as both character and metaphor is undead and well in the popular culture. The depiction of Dracula, however, has changed. Modern readers and viewers are, like Stoker's "superstitious Transylvanian peasants", familiar with vampires and their ways. They are, after all, part of our culture now'.[13]

With his slyly-implemented Bela Lugosi accent and an outrageously bouffant wig-shaped hat in the style of Gary Oldman's peculiarly-styled hairstyle from the earlier Coppola adaptation, the versatile Nielsen faced the twin challenges of presenting a character who could convey comedy situations convincingly, but who could still occasionally present an air of intimidation and peril. However, in spite of his resourcefulness as a performer Nielsen perhaps inevitably succeeds better in articulating Dracula's injured pride than he does the character's sense of danger; 'Children of the night! What a mess they make,' he purrs smoothly, referring to the bats who inhabit his castle... before he slips on a pile of the mammals' guano and falls down a flight of stairs. There are many such well-played situations throughout the film, including the dapper Count rising from his coffin only to strike his head against an inconveniently-placed chandelier, the fact that his blood-sucking sounds suspiciously like someone drinking a milkshake through a straw, and the hapless vampire running on the spot in the manner of old Warner Brothers cartoons as he slowly combusts in sunlight during his "daymare" (thus foreshadowing his later demise). Yet Nielsen is less compelling in his assertion that Dracula's ancestor had maimed and tortured scores of innocent Transylvanians simply because 'They had it coming!', lacking any perceptible, below-the-surface sense of threat in the same way as the character appears to be simply going through the motions with his seduction of Lucy and Mina, rather than obsessively striving to ensure their ruination for his own perverse ends. Instead, Nielsen remains more impressive for his rubber-faced expressions (consider his priceless reaction when the Count's grandiose intimidation is interrupted by Harker unexpectedly poking him in the eyes) and his comic subversion of the already somewhat arch dialogue from the Browning adaptation: 'I never drink... wine,' he insists, in the manner of Lugosi, before then deciding 'Oh, what the hell'.

David Desser and Lester D. Friedman have suggested that 'where Brooks, perhaps arguably, mis-stepped was in rejecting his watchword and not siding with the underdog, of taking the part of the outsider. Although Nielsen's Dracula is certainly not a villain, neither is he quite a hero'.[14] Peculiarly, while neither the cunning Van Helsing or the virtuous Harker ever quite fit the mould of the film's champion, the character who made the greatest lasting impression on commentators was debatably none other than Peter MacNicol's frenzied, slightly tragic Renfield. Throwing himself into the role with total commitment, MacNicol excels in tracing the descent of the meek, decorous solicitor into a prat-falling, creepy-crawly-munching lunatic who is completely in thrall to Dracula's malevolent influence. As Barb Karg, Arjean Spaite and Rick Sutherland have rightly observed. *'Young Frankenstein* is a nearly impossible film to follow up given its cult status and the fact that to this day it remains terminally funny. But *Dead* has its moments, many of which are absolutely stolen by Peter MacNicol, who as Renfield pays perfect comedic homage to Dwight Frye's demented portrayal in the 1931 film. From his inability to move through the infamous spider web on Dracula's staircase to his maniacal bug swallowing and classic happy face drawn in the Count's ashes, MacNicol is a scream'.[15] Although the endless painful mishaps facing Renfield do admittedly start to become somewhat tiresome after a while, MacNicol's gift for physical comedy (witness his precision in arranging himself into an upside-down position in order to speak face-to-face with the bat-like Dracula) and the nicely understated tone of irony in his delivery (the ever-hungry Renfield's response to 'I smell a rat' is, of course, an excited 'Where?!') always make the studied goofiness of his performance entertaining, especially on the occasions where it is transcending the material which surrounds it.

The supporting cast are uniformly solid, foremost among them Brooks at his most restrained as Professor Van Helsing. With his laid-on-with-a-trowel Germanic accent and skilfully unassuming, scholarly demeanour, Brooks creates a no-nonsense vampire hunter whose inscrutable nature never quite overshadows the presence of his associates. Though he has many enjoyable exchanges with Harvey Korman's Seward (itself a note-perfect evocation of academic stuffiness from Korman), it is in his scenes with Steven Weber's dashing but often hopelessly impractical Harker that Brooks's Van Helsing really comes to life:

> HARKER: Now she's dead!
> VAN HELSING: No, she's not.
> HARKER: She's alive?
> VAN HELSING: She is Nosferatu.
> HARKER: She's Italian?!

Korman forges the austere, prudish Seward into an agreeable character, complete with patronly 'harrumphs' and disapproving glances galore, but Harker's striking good looks and visible awkwardness at anything even approaching genuine emotion means that Weber too is given plenty of opportunity to demonstrate his comic talents. ('Oh, this is... this is ghastly!' gasps Harker after being drenched by gallons of blood after staking Lucy. 'Yes, you're right,' a pokerfaced Van Helsing agrees. 'We should've put newspapers down.') While Korman provides stalwart support throughout, the most remarkable aspect of his character is almost certainly the sheer distance between the cartoonish villainy of his earlier appearances in Brooks's films and the guilelessness of this cultured gentleman doctor, neatly emphasising the acting range of a truly gifted comic performer.

Though Amy Yasbeck's Mina and Lysette Anthony's Lucy are both less evenly developed, both actresses give sound performances with Yasbeck in particular reprising the same degree of subtle wit and comedic timing that she had demonstrated in Brooks's previous film. Indeed, *Dracula: Dead and Loving It* was to feature a number of return appearances from *Robin Hood: Men in Tights* alumni, including Mark Blankfield, Megan

Cavanagh and Matthew Porretta in brief roles. (Though *Dracula: Dead and Loving It* was short on appearances by Brooks's cinematic regulars beyond Korman, it does feature minor cameos from the likes of Rudy DeLuca and Charlie Callas.) Also reprising his professional duties from the earlier movie was composer Hummie Mann, who once again brought a touch of class to proceedings with an original score which faithfully emulated the entertainingly lurid Hammer musical arrangements of years past.

Throughout his career, Brooks's films had never failed to split critical opinion, and with his final feature he would not buck this trend. Although many reviews of *Dracula: Dead and Loving It* were avowedly hostile, others identified particular aspects to admire which were often quite unexpected. Janet Maslin of *The New York Times*, for instance, felt that 'the title *Dracula: Dead and Loving It* is so perfect that it's almost a good-will ambassador for Mel Brooks's slight but amusing new parody. Mr Brooks may no longer be at the forefront of silly comedy, but he's still laying on the genre gags, horrible puns and enema references with dependable good cheer. [...] So even if this *Dracula* is thin-blooded, its better moments redeem a lot of dead air'.[16] Offering a contrary opinion, Hal Hinson of *The Washington Post* praised the film's star while criticising the quality of the screenplay: 'By now, Nielsen's patented comic delivery is polished to the point of infallibility. And at first, the sheer sight of him in his vampire regalia is enough to provoke a giggle. A comic is only as good as his material, though, and the stuff that Brooks and his collaborators – Rudy De Luca and Steve Haberman – have given their goofy star is several notches beyond painful. Filled with atrocious puns and corny sight gags, the movie looks cheap and has the feeling of having been cooked up on the spot'.[17] *Variety*'s reviewer sounded a note of caution over the film's overall effectiveness, opining that 'while *Dead and Loving It* earns a fair share of grins and giggles, it never really cuts loose and goes for the belly laughs. Compared with the recent glut of dumb, dumber and dumbest comedies, Brooks' pic seems positively understated. Indeed, there isn't much here that would have seemed out of place (or too tasteless) in comedy sketches for TV variety shows of the 1950s. And what little risqué humor there is seems mighty tame when compared with what often gets by on contemporary shows such as *Saturday Night Live*. As a result, unfortunately, *Dead and Loving It* is so mild, it comes perilously close to blandness'.[18] But on the other hand, Mick LaSalle of *The San Francisco Chronicle* guardedly defended Brooks's track record, remarking that the director had succeeded in fulfilling the particular artistic goal that he had set himself: 'Mark Twain observed that if you repeat the same story over and over, it becomes funny. Mel Brooks is doing something like that with movies. He makes the same kind of films with the same kinds of jokes, over and over, and at a certain point even the jokes that aren't funny work. [...] As for *Dracula: Dead and Loving It*, it's a modest attempt that succeeds. It has enough jokes to keep it moving and enough distinctly Brooksian gags to make it required viewing for his fans. But lacking the insane magic of *Robin Hood: Men in Tights* – or for that matter, Brooks' earlier horror parody, *Young Frankenstein* – it won't win any converts'.[19]

The scepticism of reviewers was ultimately to be mirrored in the film's performance at the American box-office; *Dracula: Dead and Loving It* was to accrue a domestic total gross of $10,772,144,[20] in spite of having cost an estimated budget of $30,000,000 to produce.[21] The movie's poor commercial return has subsequently led to it being labelled as one of Brooks's least successful ventures, and certainly it has been denied the longevity of other latter-day entries in the Brooksian canon such as *Spaceballs* and *Robin Hood: Men in Tights*. Yet the debate over the film's virtues and failings has continued amongst commentators even in more recent years. John J. Puccio of *Movie Metropolis*, for instance, has queried the exact reasons why the feature failed to match Brooks's earlier achievements: 'The question is why Mel Brooks's *Young Frankenstein* (1974) was so successful, so funny, so right on target, while the same director's *Dracula: Dead and Loving It* (1995) was so flat, so bloodless. Could it have been the script? The actors? The atmosphere? Or was Brooks just getting too old for this kind of thing? Maybe a little of each'.[22] Likewise, commentator Patrick Naugle has lamented the film's comparative failings in contrast to Brooks's mid-seventies work: 'The sad fact is that *Dracula: Dead and Loving It* is a truly unfunny movie. Are there a few light laughs? Yes, a few, and that's about it. The comedic high point of the film is watching Steven Weber [...] drive a stake through the heart of a vampire as blood explodes all around him. Har-har-har. If that sounds endlessly hysterical to you, then by all means snag yourself a copy of this movie. Me? I would much prefer Brooks's far better horror parody *Young Frankenstein*, a film that knew its sources and how to skewer them with both wit and love'.23 But not all retrospective opinion has been hostile. In 2013, *CriticWire*'s Matt Singer led the charge in attempting to persuade the public to reassess *Dracula: Dead and Loving It*'s disfavoured reputation:

> If I had to guess why *Dracula: Dead and Loving It* got so brutally panned, I'd point to the time in which it was released. In late 1995, beside the early works of guys like Quentin Tarantino and Kevin Smith, the movie looked about as cool as a shelf-worn bottle of Zima. Surrounded by comedies full of macho swagger and flights of profanity, Brooks' *Dracula* looked downright quaint; and it's certainly a long way from the edgy, boundary-pushing of *The Producers* and *Blazing Saddles*. In place of the bold racial humor and good taste demolishing jabs at Nazis and the Holocaust, *Dracula* goes for old fashioned screwball banter and cartoonish gore. At times, it might actually be closer to the tone of *Abbott and Costello Meet Frankenstein* than Brooks' own *Young Frankenstein*. [*Dracula: Dead and Loving It*] is deeply, almost defiantly old fashioned. It was shot mostly on sound stages, on plywood and plaster sets that look like leftovers from some forgotten Roger Corman quickie.24

As even the above, relatively positive appraisal suggests, there was a general sense amongst the critical community at the time of *Dracula: Dead and Loving It*'s production that Brooks's best years as a film director now lay behind him. In the fast-paced cultural environment of the mid-nineties, opinion was beginning to grow that, as Desser and Friedman have put it, 'circumstances and changing times had relegated the master of the parodic mode to being an also-ran'.25 Brooks would, of course, confound all expectation of his career's trajectory by reinventing himself as a monumentally successful Broadway producer only a few years later. But this perfectionistic artist, never one to take criticism of his work lying down, remained characteristically robust in his defence of *Dracula: Dead and Loving It*: 'There's a great quote: "Critics are like eunuchs at an orgy – they just don't get it". I ran into Roger Ebert. He didn't like *Dracula*. He made no bones about it – thumbs, pinkies, every digit that he had. And I said to him: "Listen, you, I made 21 movies. I'm very talented. I'll live in history. I have a body of work. You only have a body"'.26

*Dracula: Dead and Loving It* formed a strangely low-key conclusion to one of comedy cinema's most distinctive careers. With its affectionate recreation of cinematic horror from decades past, its subtle (and not-so-subtle) ribbing of genteel Victorian values and a script which features some of Brooks's most understated characterisation, the film was an unexpected climax to a filmography which had never failed to surprise. Yet although its engagement with freedom was largely subdued in comparison to almost all of his earlier features – the theme of escaping Dracula's sybaritic manipulations notwithstanding – Brooks still utilised the film to celebrate the need for individual empowerment, of transcending social expectation in order to achieve required aims. Thus by celebrating personal qualities and virtuous motivation, ensuring that the love between Harker and Mina overcomes the controlling schemes of the cold-hearted Dracula and that the methodical, benign brainpower of Van Helsing can ensnare a centuries-old vampire, Brooks's final film proved that its engagement with these recurrent themes of liberation could still prove compelling even when the film's reception with the critical community did not.

# REFERENCES

1. Robert Alan Crick, *The Big Screen Comedies of Mel Brooks* (Jefferson: McFarland and Company, 2009) [2002], p. 208.
2. Andre Marc Strumer, 'The Creatures of the Night: Vampires from Books to Films' (unpublished doctoral thesis, The University of Southern Mississippi, July 2008), p. 142.
3. Crick, p. 211.
4. David J. Skal, *Hollywood Gothic: The Tangled Web of Dracula from Novel to Stage to Screen*, rev. edn. (New York: Faber and Faber, 2004) [1990], p. 283.
5. Bruce G. Hallenbeck, *Comedy-Horror Films: A Chronological History, 1914-2008* (Jefferson: McFarland, 2009), p. 183.
6. Barbara Shulgasser, 'Brooks Gives *Dracula* a Little Bite', in *The San Francisco Chronicle*, 22 December 1995.
   <http://www.sfgate.com/news/article/Brooks-gives-Dracula-a-little-bite-3115591.php>
7. Crick, p. 210.
8. Hallenbeck, pp. 185-86.
9. Desson Howe, '*Dracula: Dead and Loving It*', in *The Washington Post*, 22 December 1995.
   <http://www.washingtonpost.com/wp-srv/style/longterm/movies/videos/draculadeadandlovingitpg13howe_b003a5.htm>
10. James Craig Holte, *Dracula in the Dark: The Dracula Film Adaptations* (Westport: Greenwood Press, 1997), p. 91.
11. Joyce Jesionowski, '*Dracula: Dead and Loving It*', in *The Encyclopedia of the Vampire: The Living Dead in Myth, Legend, and Popular Culture*, ed. by S.T. Joshi (Santa Barbara: Greenwood, 2011), 90-91, p. 90.
12. Crick, p. 217.
13. Holte, p. 120.
14. David Desser and Lester D. Friedman, *American Jewish Filmmakers*, 2nd edn (Chicago: University of Illinois Press, 2004), pp. 166-67.
15. Barb Karg, Arjean Spaite and Rick Sutherland, *The Everything Vampire Book* (Avon: Adams Media, 2009), p. 205.
16. Janet Maslin, 'Film Review: Giving New Fangs to an Old Vampire', in *The New York Times*, 22 December 1995.
    <http://www.nytimes.com/movie/review?res=9804E3DF1539F931A15751C1A963958260>
17. Hal Hinson, '*Dracula: Dead and Loving It*', in *The Washington Post*, 22 December 1995.
    <http://www.washingtonpost.com/wp-srv/style/longterm/movies/videos/draculadeadandlovingitpg13hinson_c03f0a.htm>
18. Anon., 'Review: *Dracula: Dead and Loving It*', in *Variety*, 17 December 1995.
    <http://variety.com/1995/film/reviews/dracula-dead-and-loving-it-1200444059/>
19. Mick LaSalle, 'Brooks Vamps on *Dracula*', in *The San Francisco Chronicle*, 22 December 1995.
    <http://www.sfgate.com/movies/article/FILM-REVIEW-Brooks-Vamps-on-Dracula-He-sucks-3017338.php>
20. Box-office data drawn from BoxOfficeMojo.com.
    <http://www.boxofficemojo.com/movies/?id=draculadeadandlovingit.htm>
21. Budgetary data drawn from the Internet Movie Database.

&lt;http://www.imdb.com/title/tt0112896/business?ref_=tt_ql_dt_4&gt;
22. John J. Puccio, 'Dracula: Dead and Loving It', in *Movie Metropolis*, 29 June 2004.
&lt;http://moviemet.com/review/dracula-dead-and-loving-it-dvd-review&gt;
23. Patrick Naugle, 'Dracula: Dead and Loving It', in *DVD Verdict*, 2 July 2004.
&lt;http://www.dvdverdict.com/reviews/draculadeadandlovingit.php&gt;
24. Matt Singer, 'Dracula: Dead and Loving It (and Loving It)', in *CriticWire*, 15 May 2013.
&lt;http://blogs.indiewire.com/criticwire/dracula-dead-and-loving-it-and-loving-it&gt;
25. Desser and Friedman, p. 166.
26. Mel Brooks, in Kate Meyers, 'Mel's Awefully Funny In Here', in *Entertainment Weekly*, 28 June 1996.
&lt;http://www.brookslyn.com/print/EntWeekly06-28-96/EntWeekly06-28-96.php&gt;

Mel Brooks
'It's good to be king!'

# CONCLUSION

IN OCTOBER, 2014, Mel Brooks received a singular tribute from the Twentieth-Century Fox Corporation when they named a street on their famous lot 'Mel Brooks Boulevard' in his honour.[1] It was no small achievement even for a man who had already received a star on the Hollywood Walk of Fame alongside a mass of industry accolades including Academy Awards, Golden Globes, Emmy Awards and Tony Awards over the course of a long and diverse career. With a number of his comedies considered culturally significant enough to be listed for conservation by the United States National Film Preservation Board due to their contribution to comedy cinema, and the rare distinction of a Life Achievement Award conferred by the American Film Institute in 2013, there is little doubt that amongst his peers as well as the general public Brooks had well and truly earned the mantle of a legendary entertainer.

Mel Brooks has long been lauded as the Renaissance Man of cinematic comedy, celebrated for the sheer ambition of his spoofery, his contribution to popularising bad taste humour, and his level of creative adaptability over the years. Yet the significance of his spirited defence of individual and social freedom has often been unfairly neglected. 'Mel Brooks's art is a varied body of comedy with distinctive emotional power, formal energy, and moral purpose,' Maurice Yacowar has asserted,[2] and indeed there is little doubt that behind the outrageousness of the comic situations he presents – and the eccentric characters who populate them – lies a creative power that is deeply concerned with the ethical and the empathetic. How can we truly be content with ourselves, Brooks has so often enquired through his films, if we seek to fulfil our goals at the expense of other people? If our freedom can only be achieved at the cost of the liberty of others, can we ever truly be independent individuals or are we actually as oppressed as those who are unwillingly (or unwittingly) propping up our fallacious illusion of liberation? As Brooks himself has explained, promoting the theme of principled consideration within and between societies has been a crucial element of his work:

> *Blazing Saddles*, with its black sheriff and racial jokes, is really a long sugar-coated tirade against bigotry. *The Producers* satirizes the horrors of Nazism. In *Young Frankenstein*, I'm saying that science has no morality in its quest for the truth. Insofar as I'm concerned, morality takes precedence over every form of progress. If you don't have it, what's the sense in living? *High Anxiety*, of course, is about the misuse of the public trust in psychiatry. My gripe in *Silent Movie* is the capitalist corporations which engulf smaller artistic organizations. I suppose one day we may have to succumb to the fact that Renault will own the Louvre. Often I will step out of the proscenium of the movie frame to talk directly to the audience because I like to surprise people. It wakes daddy up and stops kids from crunching the popcorn for ten seconds. It's an old trick from my favorite playwright, Bertholt Brecht.[3]

In spite of the larger-than-life nature of his approach to comedy, Brooks never trivialises his subject matter even when his satirical objectives are at their most frenetic. Thus in films such as *Blazing Saddles* and *Spaceballs* we see the corruption and indecisiveness of government in action, but by simultaneously making us aware of the sheer squandered potential of these political systems – bogged down by inertia or perverted by venal misdeeds rather than working for the common good of constituents – Brooks makes the dereliction and abuse of their leaders seem all the more frustrating. Likewise, he is uncompromising in his attacks on organised religion – whether in the form of the hypocritical Father Fyodor in *The Twelve Chairs* or the lethal oppressiveness of Grand Inquisitor Torquemada in *History of the World: Part I* – while simultaneously emphasising the comfort and fulfilment that individuals may find in spirituality (through characters such as Mademoiselle Rimbaud or Rabbi Tuckman). Because Brooks knows that human nature is complicated and intricate, he posits no easy solutions to the sociocultural quandaries that he presents; indeed, films such as *History of the World: Part I* suggest that covetousness and repression have been obstacles to overcome (or circumvent) throughout all of human history, thus underscoring the need to challenge them vigorously and continuously. Therefore, as Lawrence J. Epstein has suggested, 'perhaps Brooks's existence as a cult and peer favourite rather than a popular success may be due to his subject matter and his refusal to engage in the sort of simple and increasingly crude and physical comedy that is becoming popular. The internal struggle of Brooks's protagonists was about finding a self, but the struggle remained inside'.[4]

Brooks is determined that his audience know that liberty comes in many forms, and in so doing he emphasises his concern for the promotion of artistic freedom as well as individual independence within society, calling attention to the power of unfettered creativity in improving and enhancing the human condition. Whether in *The Producers'* Broadway scheming, the studio-saving cinematic inventiveness of *Silent Movie* or the Monster's unlikely transformation into a song-and-dance man in *Young Frankenstein*, Brooks repeatedly draws the correlation between creative freedom and social freedom, calling attention to the potential of artistic and philosophical self-determination to expand worldviews, improve individual conditions and bolster personal character. Yacowar posits that 'Mel Brooks's comedy is a full-scale dramatisation of the Freudian view of human nature. [...] There is a Freudian aspect in Brooks's central preoccupation with what his characters want'.[5] Naturally these psychological concerns are explored most explicitly in *High Anxiety*, but they are addressed throughout much of Brooks's filmography in revealing and rewarding ways. The desire to transcend the limits of an essentially joyless life, as in *The Producers*, *The Twelve Chairs* or *Life Stinks*; the need to correct social injustice, as in *Blazing Saddles*, *Silent Movie* or *Spaceballs*; or the imperative to circumvent or overcome tyranny, as in *History of the World: Part I* or *Robin Hood: Men in Tights*... through the use of all these dramatic situations, and more besides, Brooks encourages us all to live up to our full potential, in turn helping society to become all that it can be.

That Brooks achieves this not by way of intense existential drama but rather through outrageous comic situations populated by peculiar, oddball characters heightens the potency of his artistic objectives precisely because the sheer profundity of his philosophical intentions so often manages to fly beneath the audience's radar. Here, as Margot Dougherty has observed, Brooks does not seek merely to analyse the nature of human life, but to embrace it in all its chaos and unpredictability: 'For all his contradictions, one idea is central to Brooks. "Comedy," he says, "is the vanguard of life. It's the joyous point of it all for me. It's the opposite of death – a protest and scream against death. I scream to the heavens, "I'm alive! I'm alive! Listen, people are laughing! Listen!"'.6 Yet this *joie de vivre* in no way disguises Brooks's perfectionism and professional dedication, hallmarks of his work which are recognisable throughout his entire canon of films. As Yacowar notes, 'Brooks is so successful in his planning that his finished product seems spontaneous, but it is scrupulously planned. Close calculation and tight editing lie behind every Brooks film. [...] He's scrupulous about the length of time allowed each joke, as well as which to keep and which to cut'.7 Because Brooks takes his subject matter seriously, he also takes his comedy seriously – for him, humour is never regarded as a trivial issue. Every line of dialogue, situation and character motivation is regarded with care and consideration meaning that, as Jacoba Atlas remarks, every aspect of even the most anarchic Brooks comedy is painstakingly calculated: 'Superficially, Brooks' movies [...] seem less careful than carefree. But Brooks says he does not believe in chance: his films are the result of meticulous construction, especially in the scriptwriting stage. On the set, he is in complete control, often acting out the slightest inflection of voice or gesture. He can recall verbatim various scripting and editing sessions on all his films, and gives the impression that – at least while he's refining his gags and footage into the funniest possible whole – comedy is no laughing matter'.8

In spite of his long run of box-office success throughout the seventies and eighties, there is no doubting that the closing years of his cinematic career proved to be less successful with critics and the public at large. Adam Sternbergh astutely states that 'by the late nineties, Brooks's productivity had petered out; he hadn't had a hit since *Spaceballs* in 1987, and his previous two films, *Robin Hood: Men in Tights* and *Dracula: Dead and Loving It*, left even his most ardent fans worried that his skills had finally failed him'.9 The great survivor of cinematic comedy would have the last laugh, of course, by adapting *The Producers* into a hit Broadway stage musical soon after, not only reviving his fortunes amongst the critical community but also sealing his reputation for cross-media versatility which had already spanned television and audio productions in addition to his numerous films. James Robert Parish sums up Brooks's achievement by noting that 'in retrospect, it has proved to be an amazingly bumpy, zigzagging, and colorful life's journey for Melvin Kaminsky, a poor Jewish boy from Brooklyn, to emerge as Mel Brooks, the world-famous show-business personality. [...] If mere survival for decades in the highly competitive entertainment industry – a forum increasingly monopolized by the young – isn't enough of an accomplishment on its own, Brooks enjoyed the comeback of comebacks when he spearheaded the creation of the Broadway musical version of *The Producers* in 2001'.[10] But of course, Brooks's stage musical success did more than simply cement his legacy in the entertainment world as extending beyond the confines of a directorial career which was, in the view of many commentators, waning as it reached its conclusion. Rather, it marked his transcendence of analytical expectation by subverting commonly-held anticipation of his particular approach to comedy on film, thus adapting to changing tastes. As Alex Symons has ventured, 'it is evident that Brooks's latter films were judged against a set of critical expectations generated by broader trends in Hollywood film production. Following the rise of parody as a tradition of film-television hybrids, critics expected parody films to deliver eclectic or "innovative" combinations of texts from a variety of "popular" sources'.[11] Thus by choosing to adapt the satire of *The Producers* over the broader spoofery of his later features, crafting a musical which is specifically concerned with the staging of another musical, Brooks's distinctive but subtle metanarrative was to reach an entirely new audience: an approach which would establish itself as being just as successful in the eyes of reviewers as the more prominent metacinematic strategies of *Blazing Saddles* and *Silent Movie* which had already proven to be so influential to later film-makers.

Brooks's films were very much products of their time, meaning that their distinctive brand of bad taste humour – which today could not fail to be disparaged for content that conveys attitudes of casual sexism and homophobia, as well as contravening many other aspects of political correctness – is unlikely ever to be replicated in the light of modern sensibilities. Though making light of gender and sexual characteristics in such a way was not uncommon in the sixties and seventies, and Brooks was far from the worst offender when it came to this trend, the presence of such traits in his earlier work have not obscured his keen and overarching concern with equality and mutual understanding.

In spite of changing social attitudes, the energy and sheer inventiveness of Brooks's films have guaranteed that they continue to win favour with new audiences across generational boundaries. Yet Brooks's legacy remains an issue of contention amongst many commentators. Writing in the 1980s, for instance, Nick Smurthwaite and Paul Gelder note Brooks's significant influence within the entertainment industry at the time, stating that 'while many [...] comic actors, writers and directors have ridden on the new wave of American comedy with Mel Brooks, only Brooks has stayed firmly at the crest of the wave. While other directors have dabbled in spoofery, Brooks has made a career of it. His reputation is built on it. And his films have undeniably inspired a revival of spoofing'.[12] As the decade continued, and the popularity of the spoof comedy continued to grow as a result of commercially successful films such as *Airplane!* (1980), *Top Secret!* (1984) and *The Naked Gun: From the Files of Police Squad!* (1988), Brooks's part in the genre's rise was re-evaluated. Neil Sinyard conjectured that 'some critics have blamed Brooks for initiating some of the baser trends in modern American comedy. When did wit and screwball ingenuity disappear from Hollywood comedy to be replaced by bad taste and nastiness? [...] Yet it would be unfair to blame Brooks for [this emergent tendency]. In Brooks's movies vulgarity is often very funny; in so many of his rivals' movies it is just vulgar'.[13]

As Sinyard suggests, Brooks's skilfully (but shrewdly) ordered excess is central to his comic artistry. His films may be chaotic, true, but only because life is similarly erratic and disorderly. Yacowar makes the point that 'to Brooks, man is most adult, mature, noble, and wise when he is afrolic. Hence Brooks's magnificent wildness and vulgarity. And his characters are often most self-aware and fully humane at the instants they acknowledge that they are part of a fiction (i.e. when they admit that their lives are play)'.[14] Thus in order to truly embrace personal freedom, the characters must first liberate themselves from expectation, from mundanity, and from preconceived notions which tend them towards self-limitation. Brooks employs his characters and their relationships as a means of advancing positive and life-enhancing qualities in a manner universal enough to elicit widespread audience engagement. We are shown liberty and independence being brought about through friendship (*The Producers, The Twelve Chairs, Blazing Saddles, Young Frankenstein*), romance (*Silent Movie, High Anxiety, Spaceballs, Life Stinks, Robin Hood: Men in Tights*), and constructive challenges to an established way of thinking (*Young Frankenstein, High Anxiety, History of the World: Part I, Life Stinks, Dracula: Dead and Loving It*). Brooks uses the apparatus of the spoof comedy to promote these virtues in practical but unorthodox means, depicting characters who overcome prejudice, mundanity and hostility through ingenuity, resourcefulness and inventiveness. More than once, we see the arts and creativity used as a means of outwitting or thwarting forces of oppression, hailing the practical as well as holistic benefits of the humanities as a means of individual liberation. For Brooks, therefore, the creative impulse is not so much an indulgence as it is an essential part of what it means to be human.

Brooks is a film-maker who is not only unafraid of his critics, but who clearly feels that he has succeeded in spite of the general hostility of reviewers over the years rather than as a result of the praise of industry commentators. Because of his popularity with audiences, his directorial career weathered the storm of a deeply unreceptive critical community; as Brooks himself has said, 'I've outlived my bad reviews. Had I not done *Blazing Saddles*, let's face it, had I just done *The Producers* and *The Twelve Chairs*, they would not be the memorable cultist films that play around all the time in the small theatres on the edge of town. They would be gone'.[15] Yet the longevity of his career notwithstanding, Brooks has proven to be far from unaware that his films have suffered from the general treatment of the comedy genre at large over the years, meaning that they have been judged by their generic characteristics rather than their intrinsic value as a cinematic feature or a cultural artefact. Sinyard suggests that 'like a number of people within the industry [Brooks] feels that film comedy has always been undervalued in terms of critical praise and prestigious awards. It saddens him particularly on behalf of his collaborators. By all accounts, he tells them at the outset that he will personally expect superb work from them, but they must resign themselves to the fact that, in all probability, it will not get the recognition it deserves'.[16]

Brooks's evolution from writer to director to producer is one which was motivated by his own desire to ensure artistic freedom: as he has said, 'I direct a film to protect the writing. I produce a film to have total business control as well as creative control over the film's future. Little by little, in defense of the initial vision, I've learned to put on other hats'.[17] In so doing, he has secured the means to present a truly varied body of work which continues to prove influential even today – and not only amongst comedy film-makers. Symons posits the opinion that 'Brooks has made a significant [...] contribution to the historical development and transformation of production trends in the cultural industries through his adaptation strategies. [...] These numerous adaptations in different media together make Brooks a significant contributor to the modern-day integration of the cultural industries – in some respects, predating the work of modern multimedia artists'.[18] Brooks is a creative force who was considered, in his heyday, to be well ahead of his time, and even his later films arguably suffered most from comparison to a heavily-populated field of spoof features that had been influenced in no small part by his own early successes. Yet as many have noted, Brooks's heart always lay deep in the golden age of cinema, hence his loving *homages* to the era of the silver screen and his numerous tributes to the comedy giants of silent movies. He has declared a view that 'every contemporary movie has its antecedent in films of the twenties and thirties. Many romantic pictures can be correlated with *Gone with the Wind* and its romantic triangle. *Star Wars* was pure *Flash Gordon* a la Buster Crabbe. My movies relate to the Marx Brothers' comedies. More than any other comics, more than Chaplin or Keaton or Laurel and Hardy, the Marx Brothers blend of wit and zany physical comedy inspired me'.[19] Because his films celebrate the freewheeling spirit of these pioneering comic giants, while simultaneously making thought-provoking points about self-determination and urging that personal autonomy never be squandered or surrendered, it is perhaps of little surprise that he laments recent tendencies towards changes in modern commercial cinema which have reduced the number of stimulating and provocative ideas being presented in many modern features: 'You can't go too far if you're intelligent and your heart is in the right place. You can only go too far if you're stupid and you have nothing to say. [...] I'd like there to be just one sparkling, witty, wonderful screenplay like *The Philidephia Story* or *All About Eve* a season. There is nothing like that today. We're undernourished. There is malnutrition going on in our movie houses. There is too much sugar and not enough to chew on'.[20] Because Brooks – by his own admission – looks back with nostalgia and admiration to earlier films that often exhibited an abundance of emotional sensitivity and social concern, there is little doubt that in striving for similar principles his own canon demonstrated strong ethical values which belied the outrageous comic scenarios that surrounded them. With such impassioned pleas for personal development and collective responsibility being embedded within some of the richest comedy features ever committed to celluloid, Brooks proved that – with each of his films – things are only rarely as they seem at face value.

Mel Brooks is one of cinema's great contradictions: an anarchic perfectionist and a serious clown. He is a film-maker who repeatedly thumbed his nose at critical convention throughout his career, and yet openly admits his joy at witnessing favourable audience reactions: 'You feel a great sense of power when you see so many people responding to your work. That kind of laughter [...] is felt as love by a comedian. It bursts from the gut. It is absolutely without compromise. It's a vocal hug, a special sharing'.[21] Brooks is a unique talent, a true innovator of cinematic comedy whose influence on his chosen genre is incalculable. Yet it says much that, even at the very height of his powers and with a growing army of devoted fans, Brooks's sheer fastidiousness as an artist meant that he was never entirely content with the way that his comic vision was presented on screen:

> "Happy" is a five-letter word. Remotely satisfied would be the term. The image you have starts out pure in your mind, but it gets tattered and more than a bit soiled by the time you see it on screen. When you first put it down on paper, it's only a little soiled by those proverbial dirty hands. Acting it out, even by the greatest bunch of professionals – which my band certainly are – it becomes murky and slightly confused because they are adding their thoughts and impressions. In

directing, it starts to get cleaned up again, especially if it was the director who wrote the script. And then in editing there can be traces of impeccability. But it never – absolutely never – attains the purity and virginity of the original image you had in mind.[22]

Over the years, Brooks has prompted his audiences to question authority, revel in their personal liberty and expressiveness, and even explore the intangible nature of reality. But at heart, he wants us to laugh, to share in his merriment at the sheer potential presented by every human life and the sense of individual purpose that is brought about through love, friendship, altruism and compassion. And it is the positive, life-affirming attitude underpinning his work which truly marks Mel Brooks out as more than a comic mastermind, but also a film-maker who exhibits warmth and humanity even in the most outlandish of scenarios. In the eyes of his admirers, that is what elevates the best of his work to the level of comedy genius – and explains why, even today, audiences are loving it.

# REFERENCES

1. Aaron Couch, 'Mel Brooks Gets Street Named After Him: "People Are Going to Walk All Over Me"', in *The Hollywood Reporter Online*, 24 October 2014. <http://www.hollywoodreporter.com/news/mel-brooks-gets-street-named-743544>
2. Maurice Yacowar, *The Comic Art of Mel Brooks* (London: W.H. Allen, 1982), p. 201.
3. Mel Brooks, in Jerry Bauer, 'Mel Brooks: A Revealing Dialogue with the World's Funniest Man', in *Adelina Magazine*, February 1980. <http://www.brookslyn.com/print/Adelina1980/Adelina1980.php>
4. Lawrence J. Epstein, *The Haunted Smile: The Story of Jewish Comedians* (Oxford: PublicAffairs, 2001), p. 218.
5. Yacowar, p. 196.
6. Margot Dougherty, 'May The Farce Be With Him: *Spaceballs* Rockets Mel Brooks Into Lunatic Orbit', in *People Weekly*, 20 July 1987. <http://www.brookslyn.com/print/PeopleWeekly07-20-87/PeopleWeekly07-20-87.php>
7. Yacowar, p. 11.
8. Jacoba Atlas, 'New Hollywood: Mel Brooks Interview', in *Film Comment*, March-April 1975. <http://www.brookslyn.com/print/FilmComment1975/FilmComment1975.php>
9. Adam Sternbergh, 'History of The Producers: Part III', in *New York Magazine*, 12 December 2005. <http://nymag.com/nymetro/movies/features/15251/>
10. James Robert Parish, *It's Good to Be the King: The Seriously Funny Life of Mel Brooks* (Hoboken: John Wiley and Sons, 2007, pp. 283-84.
11. Alex Symons, *Mel Brooks in the Cultural Industries: Survival and Prolonged Adaptation* (Edinburgh: Edinburgh University Press, 2012), p. 113.
12. Nick Smurthwaite and Paul Gelder, *Mel Brooks and the Spoof Movie* (London: Proteus Books, 1982), p. 91.
13. Neil Sinyard, *The Films of Mel Brooks* (New York: Exeter Books, 1988), p. 93.
14. Yacowar, pp. 198-99.
15. Brooks, in Philip Fleishman, 'Interview with Mel Brooks', in *Maclean's Magazine*, 17 April 1978. <http://www.brookslyn.com/print/Maclean04-17-78/Maclean04-17-78.php>
16. Sinyard, p. 93.
17. Brooks, 'My Movies: The Collusion of Art and Money', in *The Movie Business Book*, 3rd edn, ed. by Jason E. Squire (Maidenhead: Open University Press, 2006), 39-48, p. 46.
18. Symons, pp. 1-2.
19. Brooks, in Bauer.
20. Brooks, in Anon., 'Still Blazing After All These Years', in *People Weekly*, 12 April 1999. <http://www.brookslyn.com/print/PeopleWeekly04-12-99/PeopleWeekly04-12-99.php>
21. Brooks, in Paul D. Zimmerman, 'The Mad Mad Mel Brooks', in *Newsweek*, 17 February 1975. <http://www.brookslyn.com/print/Newsweek02-15-1975/Newsweek02-17-1975.php>
22. Brooks, in Bauer.

# CHRONOLOGICAL FILMOGRAPHY

*THE PRODUCERS* (1968)

Production Companies: Embassy Pictures/ Springtime Productions/ U-M Productions/ Crossbow Productions.
Distributors: AVCO Embassy Pictures.
Running Time: 88 minutes.
USA Release Date: 18 March 1968.
Director: Mel Brooks.
Screenwriter: Mel Brooks.
Producer: Sidney Glazier.
Associate Producer: Jack Grossberg.
Original Score: John Morris.
Director of Photography: Joseph Coffey.
Film Editor: Ralph Rosenblum.
Casting: Alfa-Betty Olsen.
Production Design: Charles Rosen.
Set Decoration: James Dalton.
Costume Design: Gene Coffin.
Main Cast: Zero Mostel (Max Bialystock), Gene Wilder (Leo Bloom), Dick Shawn (Lorenzo 'LSD' Saint DuBois), Kenneth Mars (Franz Liebkind), Lee Meredith (Ulla), Christopher Hewett (Roger De Bris), Andreas Voutsinas (Carmen Ghia), Estelle Winwood ('Hold Me Touch Me'), Renee Taylor (Eva Braun), David Patch (Goebbels), Bill Hickey (The Drunk), Barney Martin (Göring), Shimen Ruskin (The Landlord), Frank Campanella (The Bartender), Josip Elic (Violinist), Madlyn Cates (Concierge), John Zoller (Drama Critic), Brutus Peck (Hot Dog Vendor), Anne Ives (Lady), Amelie Barleon (Lady), Elsie Kirk (Lady), Nell Harrison (Lady), Mary Love (Lady).

## THE TWELVE CHAIRS (1970)

Production Companies: Crossbow Productions/ The Twelve Chairs Company.
Distributors: Universal Marion Corporation.
Running Time: 94 minutes:
USA Release Date: 28 October 1970.
Director: Mel Brooks
Screenwriter: Mel Brooks, from a novel by Ilya Ilf and Yevgeni Petrov, translated by Elizabeth Hill and Doris Mudie.
Producer: Michael Hertzberg.
Executive Producer: Sidney Glazier.
Original Score: John Morris.
Cinematography: Dorde Nikolic.
Film Editor: Alan Heim.
Art Direction: Mile Nikolic.
Costume Design: Ruth Meyers.
Main Cast: Ron Moody (Vorobyaninov), Frank Langella (Ostap Bender), Dom DeLuise (Father Fyodor), Andreas Voutsinas (Nikolai Sestrin), Diana Coupland (Madam Bruns), David Lander (Engineer Bruns), Vlada Petric (Sevitsky), Elaine Garreau (Claudia Ivanovna), Robert Bernal (Curator), Will Stampe (Night Watchman), Bridget Brice (Young Woman), Nicholas Smith (Actor in Play), Rada Djuricin (Actress in Play), Branka Veselinovic (Natasha), Mladja Veselinovic (Peasant), Mel Brooks (Tikon).

## BLAZING SADDLES (1974)

Production Companies: Warner Brothers/ Crossbow Productions.
Distributors: Warner Brothers.
Running Time: 93 minutes.
USA Release Date: 7 February 1974.
Director: Mel Brooks.
Screenwriters: Mel Brooks, Norman Steinberg, Andrew Bergman, Richard Pryor and Alan Uger, from a story by Andrew Bergman.
Producer: Michael Hertzberg.
Original Score: John Morris.
Director of Photography: Joseph Biroc.
Film Editing: Danford Greene and John C. Howard.
Casting: Nessa Hyams.
Production Design: Peter Wooley.
Set Decoration: Morey Hoffman.
Main Cast: Cleavon Little (Bart), Gene Wilder (Jim, The 'Waco Kid'), Slim Pickens (Taggart), Harvey Korman (Hedley Lamarr), Madeline Kahn (Lili Von Shtupp), Mel Brooks (Governor William J. Lepetomane/ Indian Chief), Burton Gilliam (Lyle), Alex Karras (Mongo), David Huddleston (Olson Johnson), Liam Dunn (Reverend Johnson), John Hillerman (Howard Johnson), George Furth (Van Johnson), Claude Ennis Starrett Jr (Gabby Johnson), Carol Arthur (Harriett Johnson), Richard Collier (Dr Sam Johnson), Charles McGregor (Charlie), Robyn Hilton (Miss Stein), Don Megowan (Saloon Patron on Stage with Lili), Dom DeLuise (Buddy Bizarre), Count Basie (Himself).

# YOUNG FRANKENSTEIN (1974)

Production Companies: Gruskoff/ Venture Films/ Crossbow Productions/ Jouer Limited.
Distributor: Twentieth Century Fox Film Corporation.
Running Time: 106 minutes.
USA Release Date: 15 December 1974.
Director: Mel Brooks.
Screenwriters: Mel Brooks and Gene Wilder; based on characters in the novel *Frankenstein* by Mary Wollstonecraft Shelley.
Producer: Michael Gruskoff.
Original Score: John Morris.
Director of Photography: Gerald Hirschfeld.
Film Editor: John C. Howard.
Casting: Jane Feinberg and Mike Fenton.
Production Design: Dale Hennesy.
Set Decoration: Bob de Vestel.
Costume Design: Dorothy Jeakins.
Main Cast: Gene Wilder (Dr Frederick Frankenstein), Peter Boyle (The Monster), Marty Feldman (Igor), Madeline Kahn (Elizabeth), Cloris Leachman (Frau Blücher), Teri Garr (Inga), Kenneth Mars (Inspector Kemp), Richard Haydn (Herr Falkstein), Liam Dunn (Mr Hilltop), Danny Goldman (Medical Student), Oscar Beregi (Sadistic Jailor), Arthur Malet (Village Elder), Richard Roth (Inspector Kemp's Aide), Monte Landis (Gravedigger), Rusty Blitz (Gravedigger), Anne Beesley (Little Girl), Gene Hackman (Blind Man).

## SILENT MOVIE (1976)

Production Company: Crossbow Productions.
Distributor: Twentieth Century Fox Film Corporation.
Running Time: 87 minutes.
USA Release Date: 16 June 1976.
Director: Mel Brooks.
Screenwriters: Mel Brooks, Ron Clark, Rudy DeLuca and Barry Levinson, from a story by Ron Clark.
Producer: Michael Hertzberg.
Original Score: John Morris.
Director of Photography: Paul Lohmann.
Film Editors: Stanford C. Allen and John C. Howard.
Casting: Mary Goldberg
Production Design: Al Brenner.
Set Decoration: Rick Simpson.
Costume Design: Patricia Norris.
Main Cast: Mel Brooks (Mel Funn), Marty Feldman (Marty Eggs), Dom DeLuise (Dom Bell), Sid Caesar (Studio Chief), Harold Gould (Engulf), Ron Carey (Devour), Bernadette Peters (Vilma Kaplan), Carol Arthur (Pregnant Lady), Liam Dunn (News Vendor), Fritz Feld (Maitre d'), Chuck McCann (Studio Gate Guard), Valerie Curtin (Intensive Care Nurse), Yvonne Wilder (Studio Chief's Secretary), Harry Ritz (Man in Tailor Shop), Charlie Callas (Blind Man), Henny Youngman (Fly-in-Soup Man), Arnold Soboloff (Acupuncture Man), Patrick Campbell (Motel Bellhop), Eddie Ryder (British Officer), Al Hopson (Executive), Rudy DeLuca (Executive), Barry Levinson (Executive), Howard Hesseman (Executive), Lee Delano (Executive), Jack Riley (Executive), Inga Neilsen (Beautiful Blonde #1), Erica Hagen (Beautiful Blonde #2), Robert Lussier (Projectionist), Burt Reynolds (Himself), James Caan (Himself), Liza Minnelli (Herself), Anne Bancroft (Herself), Marcel Marceau (Himself), Paul Newman (Himself).

## HIGH ANXIETY (1977)

Production Companies: Twentieth Century Fox Film Corporation/ Crossbow Productions.
Distributor: Twentieth Century Fox Film Corporation.
Running Time: 94 minutes.
USA Release Date: 25 December 1977.
Director: Mel Brooks.
Screenwriters: Mel Brooks, Ron Clark, Rudy DeLuca and Barry Levinson.
Producer: Mel Brooks.
Original Score: John Morris.
Director of Photography: Paul Lohmann.
Film Editor: John C. Howard.
Production Design: Peter Wooley.
Set Decoration: Richard Kent and Anne MacCauley.
Costume Design: Patricia Norris.
Main Cast: Mel Brooks (Dr Richard H. Thorndyke), Madeline Kahn (Victoria Brisbane), Cloris Leachman (Nurse Diesel), Harvey Korman (Dr Charles Montague), Ron Carey (Brophy), Howard Morris (Professor Lilloman), Dick Van Patten (Dr Wentworth), Jack Riley (The Desk Clerk), Charlie Callas (Cocker Spaniel), Ron Clark (Zachary Cartwright), Rudy DeLuca (Killer), Barry Levinson (Bellboy), Lee Delano (Norton), Richard Stahl (Dr Baxter), Darrell Zwerling (Dr Eckhardt), Murphy Dunne (Piano Player), Al Hopson (Man Who is Shot), Bob Ridgely (Flasher), Albert J. Whitlock (Arthur Brisbane), Pearl Shear (Screaming Woman at Gate), Arnold Soboloff (Dr Colburn), Eddie Ryder (Doctor at Convention), Sandy Helberg (Airport Attendant), Frederic Franklyn (Man), Deborah Dawes (Stewardess), Bernie Kuby (Dr Wilson), Billy Sands (Customer), Ira Miller (Psychiatrist with Children), Jimmy Martinez (Waiter), Beatrice Colen (Maid), Robert Manuel (Policeman at Airport), Hunter Von Leer (Policeman at Airport), John Dennis (Orderly), Robin Menken (Cocktail Waitress), Frank Campanella (Bartender), Henry Kaiser (New Groom), Bullets Durgom (Man in Phone Booth), Joe Bellan (Male Attendant), Mitchell Bock (Bar Patron), Jay Burton (Patient), Bryan Englund (Orderly), Anne Macey (Screaming Woman), Alan U. Schwartz (Psychiatrist).

# HISTORY OF THE WORLD: PART I (1981)

Production Companies: Brooksfilms.
Distributor: Twentieth Century Fox Film Corporation.
Running Time: 92 minutes.
USA Release Date: 12 June 1981.
Director: Mel Brooks.
Screenwriter: Mel Brooks.
Producer: Mel Brooks.
Associate Producers: Stuart Cornfeld and Alan Johnson.
Original Score: John Morris.
Director of Photography: Woody Omens.
Film Editor: John C. Howard.
Casting: Jane Feinberg and Mike Fenton.
Production Design: Harold Michelson.
Art Direction: Norman Newberry.
Set Decoration: Antony Mondello.
Costume Design: Patricia Norris.
Main Cast: Mel Brooks (Moses/ Comicus/ Torquemada/ Jacques/ King Louis XVI), Dom DeLuise (Emperor Nero), Madeline Kahn (Empress Nympho), Harvey Korman (Count de Monet), Cloris Leachman (Madame Defarge), Ron Carey (Swiftus), Gregory Hines (Josephus), Pamela Stephenson (Mademoiselle Rimbaud), Shecky Greene (Marcus Vindictus), Sid Caesar (Chief Caveman), Mary-Margaret Humes (Miriam), Orson Welles (Narrator), Rudy DeLuca (Prehistoric Man/ Captain Mucus), Leigh French (Prehistoric Woman), Richard Karron (Prehistoric Man), Susette Carroll (Prehistoric Woman), Sammy Shore (Prehistoric Man), J.J. Barry (Prehistoric Man), Earl Finn (Prehistoric Man/ Disciple), Suzanne Kent (Prehistoric Woman), Michael Champion (Prehistoric Man), Howard Morris (Court Spokesman), Charlie Callas (Soothsayer), Dena Dietrich (Competence), Paul Mazursky (Roman Officer), Ron Clark (Stoned Soldier #1), Jack Riley (Stoned Soldier #2), Art Metrano (Leonardo DaVinci), Diane Day (Caladonia), Henny Youngman (Chemist), Hunter Von Leer (Lieutenant Bob), Fritz Feld (Maitre d'), Hugh Hefner (Entrepreneur), Pat McCormick (Plumbing Salesman), Barry Levinson (Column Salesman), Sid Gould (Barber-Bloodletter), Ronny Graham (Oedipus/ Jew #2), Jim Steck (Gladiator), John Myhers (Leader of Senate), Lee Delano (Wagon Driver), Robert B. Goldberg (Senator #1), Alan U. Schwartz (Senator #2), Jay Burton (Senator #3), Robert Zappy (Roman Citizen), Ira Miller (Roman Citizen), Milt Freedman (Roman Citizen), Johnny Silver (Small Liar), Charles Thomas Murphy (Auctioneer), Rod Haase (Roman Officer), Eileen Saki (Slave), John Hurt (Jesus), Henry Kaiser (Disciple), Zale Kessler (Disciple), Anthony Messina (Disciple), Howard Mann (Disciple), Sandy Helberg (Disciple), Mitchell Bock (Disciple), Gilbert Lee (Disciple), Molly Basler (Game Show Girl), Deborah Dawes (Game Show Girl), Christine Dickinson (Game Show Girl), Lisa Sohm (Vestal Virgin), Michele Drake (Vestal Virgin), Jeana Keough (Vestal Virgin), Lisa Welch (Vestal Virgin), Janis Schmitt (Vestal Virgin), Heidi Sorenson (Vestal Virgin), Karen Morton (Vestal Virgin), Kathy Collins (Vestal Virgin), Lori Sutton (Vestal Virgin), Lou Mulford (Vestal Virgin), Jackie Mason (Jew #1), Phil Leeds (Chief Monk), Jack Carter (Rat Vendor), Jan Murray (Nothing Vendor), Andreas Voutsinas (Bearnaise), Spike Milligan (Monsieur Rimbaud), John Hillerman (Rich Man), Sidney Lassick (Applecore Vendor), Jonathan Cecil (Poppinjay), Andrew Sachs (Gerard), Fiona Richmond (Queen), Nigel Hawthorne (Citizen Official), Bella Emberg (Baguette), Geoffrey Larder (Footman), George Lane Cooper (Executioner), Stephanie Marrian (Lady Marie), Royce Mills (Duke D'Honnefleur), Mike Cottrell (Tartuffe), Gerald Sladden (Le Fevre), John Ghavan (Marche), Rusty Goff (Le Muff).

## SPACEBALLS (1987)

Production Companies: Brooksfilms/ Metro-Goldwyn-Mayer.
Distributor: Metro-Goldwyn-Mayer.
Running Time: 96 minutes.
USA Release Date: 24 June 1987.
Director: Mel Brooks.
Screenwriters: Mel Brooks, Thomas Meehan and Ronny Graham.
Producer: Mel Brooks.
Co-Producer: Ezra Swerdlow.
Original Score: John Morris.
Director of Photography: Nick McLean.
Film Editor: Conrad Buff IV.
Casting: David Rubin and Bill Shepard.
Production Design: Terence Marsh.
Art Direction: Harold Michelson.
Set Decoration: John Franco Jr.
Costume Design: Donfeld.
Main Cast: Mel Brooks (President Skroob/ Yogurt), John Candy (Barf), Rick Moranis (Dark Helmet), Bill Pullman (Lone Starr), Daphne Zuniga (Princess Vespa), Dick Van Patten (King Roland), George Wyner (Colonel Sandurz), Michael Winslow (Radar Technician), Joan Rivers (Voice of Dot Matrix), Lorene Yarnell (Dot Matrix), John Hurt (Kane), Sal Viscuso (Radio Operator), Ronny Graham (Minister), J.M.J. Bullock (Prince Valium), Leslie Bevis (Commanderette Zircon), Jim Jackman (Major Asshole), Michael Pniewski (Laser Gunner), Sandy Helberg (Dr Schlotkin), Stephen Tobolowsky (Captain of the Guard), Jeff MacGregor (Snotty), Henry Kaiser (Magnetic Beam Operator), Denise Gallup (Charlene), Dian Gallup (Marlene), Gail Barle (Waitress), Dey Young (Waitress), Rhonda Shear (Woman in Diner), Robert Prescott (Sand Cruiser Driver), Jack Riley (TV Newsman), Tom Dreesen (Megamaid Guard), Rudy DeLuca (Vinnie), Tony Griffin (Prison Guard), Rick Ducommun (Prison Guard), Ken Olfson (Head Usher), Bryan O'Byrne (Organist), Wayne Wilson (Trucker in Cap), Ira Miller (Short Order Cook), Earl Finn (Guard with Captain), Mitchell Bock (Video Operator), Tommy Swerdlow (Troop Leader), Tim Russ (Trooper), Ed Gale (Dink), Antonio Hoyos (Dink), Felix Silla (Dink), Arturo Gil (Dink), Tony Cox (Dink), John Kennedy Hayden (Dink), Deanna Booher (Bearded Lady), Johnny Silver (Caddy), Brenda Strong (Nurse), Dom DeLuise (Voice of Pizza the Hutt).

## LIFE STINKS (1991)

Production Companies: Brooksfilms/ MGM-Pathé Communications Co.
Distributor: Metro-Goldwyn-Mayer.
Running Time: 92 minutes.
USA Release Date: 26 July 1991.
Director: Mel Brooks
Screenwriters: Mel Brooks, Rudy DeLuca and Steve Haberman, from a story by Mel Brooks, Ron Clark, Rudy DeLuca and Steve Haberman.
Producer: Mel Brooks.
Associate Producer: Kim Kurumada.
Executive Producer: Ezra Swerdlow.
Original Score: John Morris.
Director of Photography: Steven Poster.
Film Editors: Michael Mulconery, David Rawlins and Anthony Redman.
Casting: Bill Shepard and Todd Thaler.
Production Design: Peter Larkin.
Art Direction: Josan Russo.
Set Decoration: Marvin March.
Costume Design: Mary Malin.
Main Cast: Mel Brooks (Goddard Bolt), Lesley Ann Warren (Molly), Jeffrey Tambor (Vance Crasswell), Stuart Pankin (Pritchard), Howard Morris (Sailor), Rudy DeLuca (J. Paul Getty), Teddy Wilson (Fumes), Michael Ensign (Knowles), Matthew Faison (Stevens), Billy Barty (Willy), Brian Thompson (Mean Victor), Raymond O'Connor (Yo), Carmine Caridi (Flophouse Owner), Sammy Shore (Reverend at Wedding), Frank Roman (Spanish Interpreter), Marvin Braverman (Dr Kahahn), Robert Ridgely (Fergueson), John Welsh (Dodd), Stanley Brock (Store Owner), James Van Patten (Wheelchair Attendant), Michael Mike Pniewski (Male Nurse), Marianne Muellerleile (Head Nurse), Anne Betancourt (Nurse), Kathryn Skatula (Nurse), Robin Shepard (Nurse), Angela Gordon (Capacity Nurse), Mary Watson (Newscaster), Saida Pagan (Newscaster), Tamara Taylor (Newscaster), Henry Kaiser (Newscaster), Danny Wells (Mercedes Driver), Larry Cedar (Paramedic), Christopher Birt (Paramedic), Johnny Cocktails (Burrito-Eating Bum), Clifton Wells (Taco Stand Owner), Paul Brinegar (Old Bellboy), George Berkeley (Derelict Outside Flophouse), Anthony Messina (Policeman), David Correia (Policeman), Helene Winston (Society Patron), Terrence Williams (Boy Dancing in Doorway), Joan Crosby (Woman at Fire), Ira Miller (Man at Fire), James Mapp (Blind Man), Sam Menning (Old Wino), Ralph Ahn (Chinese Cook), Stu Gilliam (Desmond), Darrow Igus (Maynard), James Martinez (Dancing Vagrant at Party), Rose DuCaine (Dancing Dowager at Party), Ralph Mauro (Hors d'Oeuvres Vagrant at Party), Danny Dayton (Dirty Bum at Party), Christopher Weeks (Pompous Party Guest), S. Scott Bullock (Outraged Party Guest), Martin Charles Warner (Dirty-Faced Vagrant at Party), Anthony Thomas Mitchell (Nibbler Driver), Patrick Valenzuela (Street Person at Fight), Carmen Filpi (Pops), Casey King (Shopping Cart Chauffeur), Ronny Graham (Voice of Priest), Jere Laird (Stock Market Reporter).

## ROBIN HOOD: MEN IN TIGHTS (1993)

Production Companies: Brooksfilms, in association with Gaumont.
Distributor: Twentieth Century Fox Film Corporation.
Running Time: 104 minutes.
USA Release Date: 28 July 1993.
Director: Mel Brooks.
Screenwriters: Mel Brooks, Evan Chandler and J. David Shapiro, from a story by J. David Shapiro and Evan Chandler.
Producer: Mel Brooks.
Associate Producer: Evan Chandler.
Executive Producer: Peter Schindler.
Original Score: Hummie Mann.
Director of Photography: Michael D. O'Shea.
Film Editor: Stephen E. Rivkin.
Casting: Lindsay D. Chag and Bill Shepard.
Production Design: Roy Forge Smith.
Art Direction: Stephen Myles Berger.
Set Decoration: Ronald R. Reiss.
Costume Design: Dodie Shepard.
Main Cast: Cary Elwes (Robin Hood), Richard Lewis (Prince John), Roger Rees (Sheriff of Rottingham), Amy Yasbeck (Marian), Mark Blankfield (Blinkin), David Chappelle (Ahchoo), Isaac Hayes (Asneeze), Megan Cavanagh (Broomhilde), Eric Allan Kramer (Little John), Matthew Porretta (Will Scarlet O'Hara), Tracey Ullman (Latrine), Patrick Stewart (King Richard), Dom DeLuise (Don Giovanni), Dick Van Patten (The Abbot), Robert Ridgely (The Hangman), Mel Brooks (Rabbi Tuckman), Steve Tancora (Filthy Luca), Joe Dimmick (Dirty Ezio), Avery Schreiber (Tax Assessor), Chuck McCann (Villager), Brian George (Dungeon Maitre d'), Zitto Kazann (Head Saracen Guard), Richard Assad (Assistant Saracen Guard), Herman Poppe (Sheriff's Guard), Clive Revill (Fire Marshall), Joe Baker (Angry Villager), Carol Arthur (Complaining Villager), Kelly Jones (Buxom Lass), Clement Von Franckenstein (Royal Announcer), Corbin Allred (Young Lad), Chase Masterson (Giggling Court Lady), Don Lewis (Mime), Roger Owens (Peanut Vendor), Patrick Valenzuela (Lead Camel Jockey), Steffon (Sherwood Forest Rapper-Dancer), Dante Henderson (Sherwood Forest Rapper-Dancer), Bryant Baldwin (Sherwood Forest Rapper-Dancer), Diesko Boyland Jr. (Sherwood Forest Rapper-Dancer), Edgar Godineaux Jr. (Sherwood Forest Rapper-Dancer), Johnny Dean Harvey (Merry Men Dancer), Keith Diorio (Merry Men Dancer), Joseph R. McKee (Merry Men Dancer), Nathan Prevost (Merry Men Dancer), Don Hesser (Merry Men Dancer), Bill Bohl (Merry Men Dancer), Chris Childers (Merry Men Dancer), Raymond Del Barrio (Merry Men Dancer).

# DRACULA: DEAD AND LOVING IT (1995)

Production Companies: Brooksfilms/ Gaumont in association with Castle Rock Entertainment.
Distributor: Castle Rock Entertainment.
Running Time: 88 minutes.
USA Release Date: 22 December 1995.
Director: Mel Brooks.
Screenwriters: Mel Brooks, Rudy DeLuca and Steve Haberman, from a story by Rudy DeLuca and Steve Haberman; based on characters in the novel *Dracula* by Bram Stoker.
Producer: Mel Brooks.
Associate Producers: Leah Zappy and Robert Latham Brown.
Executive Producer: Peter Schindler.
Original Score: Hummie Mann.
Director of Photography: Michael D. O'Shea.
Film Editor: Adam Weiss.
Casting: Lindsay Chag and Bill Shepard.
Production Design: Roy Forge Smith.
Art Direction: Bruce Robert Hill.
Set Decoration: Jan Pascale.
Costume Design: Dodie Shepard.
Main Cast: Leslie Nielsen (Count Dracula), Peter MacNicol (Thomas Renfield), Steven Weber (Jonathan Harker), Amy Yasbeck (Mina Murray), Lysette Anthony (Lucy Westenra), Mel Brooks (Dr Abraham Van Helsing), Harvey Korman (Dr Jack Seward), Mark Blankfield (Martin), Megan Cavanagh (Essie), Clive Revill (Sykes), Chuck McCann (Innkeeper), Avery Schreiber (Peasant on Coach), Cherie Franklin (Peasant on Coach), Ezio Greggio (Coach Driver), Leslie Sachs (Usherette), Matthew Porretta (Handsome Lieutenant at Ball), Rudy DeLuca (Guard), Jennifer Crystal (Nurse), Darla Haun (Brunette Vampire), Karen Roe (Blonde Vampire), Charlie Callas (Man in Straitjacket), Phillip Connery (Ship Captain), Tony Griffin (Crewman), Casey King (Crewman), Nick Rempel (Crewman), Zale Kessler (Orchestra Leader), Barbaree Earl (Ballroom Guest), Maura Nielsen Kaplan (Ballroom Guest), Thea Nielsen (Ballroom Guest), Robin Shepard (Ballroom Guest), Elaine Ballace (Ballroom Guest), Maude Winchester (Ballroom Guest), Gregg Binkley (Woodbridge), Lisa Cordray (Hat Check Girl), Cindy Marshall-Day (Young Lover at Picnic), Benjamin Livingston (Young Lover at Picnic), Anne Bancroft (Madame Ouspenskaya).

# STATISTICAL DATA AND REPRESENTATIVE CRITICAL OPINION

*THE PRODUCERS* (1968)

USA Release Date: 18 March 1968.
Budget: $941,000.
USA Total Gross: $1,681,986.
Award Wins: Academy Award: Best Writing, Story and Screenplay Written Directly for the Screen (1969); Writers' Guild of America Award: Best Written American Original Screenplay (1969).
Award Nominations: Academy Award: Best Actor in a Supporting Role (1969); Golden Globe Awards: Best Motion Picture Actor, Musical/ Comedy (1969), Best Screenplay (1969); Writers' Guild of America Award: Best Written American Comedy (1969).

Representative Critical Opinion:

"Mel Brooks has turned a funny idea into a slapstick film, thanks to the performers, particularly Zero Mostel. [...] The film is unmatched in the scenes featuring Mostel and Wilder alone together, and several episodes with other actors are truly rare."
*Variety*, 31 December 1967.

"*The Producers* has many things going for it – notably a wild, ad-lib energy that explodes in a series of sight gags and punch lines. [...] Unfortunately, the film is burdened with the kind of plot that demands resolution, and here Brooks the writer has failed Brooks the director. *Springtime* is supposed to be like *Valley of the Dolls* – so excessively bad that it's hilarious. Instead it is just excessive. *Producers* ends in a whimper of sentimentality out of keeping with the low jinks that went before."
*Time Magazine,* 26 January 1968.

"*The Producers* [...] is a violently mixed bag. Some of it is shoddy and gross and cruel; the rest is funny in an entirely unexpected way. It has the episodic, revue quality of so much contemporary comedy – not building laughter, but stringing it together skit after skit, some vile, some boffo. It is less delicate than Lenny Bruce, less funny than *Doctor Strangelove*, but much funnier than *The Loved One* or *What's New, Pussycat?*"

Renata Adler, T*he New York Times*, 19 March 1968.

"This is one of the funniest movies ever made. To see it now is to understand that. To see it for the first time in 1968, when I did, was to witness audacity so liberating that not even *There's Something About Mary* rivals it. The movie was like a bomb going off inside the audience's sense of propriety. There is such rapacity in its heroes, such gleeful fraud, such greed, such lust, such a willingness to compromise every principle, that we cave in and go along."

Roger Ebert, *The Chicago Sun-Times*, 23 July 2000.

"Brooks's magnum opus is still a ferocious gale of bulldozing Jewish mockery, dominated by Zero Mostel's comb-over juggernaut. However familiar, it delivers like a shorted slot machine; memories of the tame and safely distant stage version will evaporate in the runway turbulence of Mostel's spittle-spray-in-your-eye performance."

Michael Atkinson, *The Village Voice*, 4 June 2002.

# THE TWELVE CHAIRS (1970)

USA Release Date: 28 October 1970.
Budget: Unavailable.
USA Total Gross: Unavailable.
Award Wins: National Board of Review Award: Best Supporting Actor (1971).
Award Nominations: Writers Guild of America Award: Best Comedy Adapted from Another Medium (1971).

Representative Critical Opinion:

"Most of the things that happen [...] are almost as joyless, and as joyless, as the Soviet Union the film purposefully depicts. This is, I think, because Mr Brooks's sense of humor is expressed almost entirely in varying degrees of rudeness and cruelty, unrelieved by any comic vision of mankind, of the Soviet Union, or even of his characters. [...] In *The Twelve Chairs* Mr Brooks wants to be lovable, and to stomp on your foot at the same time. I, for one, object."
Vincent Canby, *The New York Times*, 29 October 1970.

"*The Twelve Chairs* is the sort of movie that improves upon reflection. You go in expecting to laugh a lot, because you've seen *The Producers*. And you do laugh a lot – to the point, perhaps, that you miss what this new Brooks film is about. It's not going for the laughs alone. It has something to say about honor among thieves, and by the end of the film we can sense a bond between the two main characters that is even, amazingly, human."
Roger Ebert, *The Chicago Sun-Times*, 22 December 1970.

"[*The Twelve Chairs*] is Brooks' least-known film and the one most ripe for discovery. [...] The film's insanity comes from the characters' pursuit of the fortune within the chairs. But at the heart of the film is the friendship that develops. Brooks said they discover the real treasure is 'caring about people and being cared for'."
Donald Liebenson, *The Chicago Tribune*, 17 July 1997.

"[*The Twelve Chairs*] is probably the closest Brooks ever came to making a "normal" film. That may also be why it's largely ignored today — sandwiched between the classic *The Producers* and the brazenly outrageous *Blazing Saddles*. [...] The odd-couple friendship between Moody and Frank Langella works surprisingly well, but doesn't equal the Zero Mostel-Gene Wilder pairing of *The Producers*. Yet it gives the film a heart that's lacking in most of Brooks' work."
Ken Hanke, *Mountain XPress,* 26 July 2006.

"*The Twelve Chairs* has seemingly been forgotten about in recent years, which is unusual since it's by no means one of the weaker Brooks films. [...] It's a silly but entertaining lark, one that is actually a good deal more focused on its plot than many Brooks films. While Brooks' films grew increasingly episodic as his career progressed, *The Twelve Chairs* offers a story that rarely goes off on aimless tangents."
Clark Douglas, *DVD Verdict,* 21 December 2009.

## BLAZING SADDLES (1974)

USA Release Date: 7 February 1974.
Budget: $2,600,000.
USA Total Gross: $119,601,481.
Award Wins: Writers Guild of America Awards: Best Comedy Written Directly for the Screen (1975).
Award Nominations: Academy Awards: Best Actress in a Supporting Role, Best Film Editing, Best Music (Original Song) (1975); BAFTA Awards: Most Promising Newcomer to Leading Film Roles, Best Screenplay (1975).

Representative Critical Opinion:

"*Blazing Saddles*, which opened yesterday at the Sutton Theater, is every Western you've ever seen turned upside down and inside out, braced with a lot of low burlesque, which is fine. In retrospect, however, one remembers along with the good gags the film's desperate, bone-crushing efforts to be funny. One remembers exhaustion, perhaps because you kept wanting it to be funnier than it was. Much of the laughter Mr Brooks inspires is hopeful, before-the-gag laughter, which can be terribly tiring."
Vincent Canby, *The New York Times*, 8 February 1974.

"It is a pity that Brooks has brought in so many cooks to stretch out his own witty brew and somehow dilute and divert it in the process. But even if laughs weren't another of today's scarce commodities, the ones he does provide are hearty enough to please, his humor tartened by perception and marked by something more than irreverence – honesty. And that's just about the scarcest item around."
Judith Crist, *New York Magazine*, 25 February 1974.

"*Blazing Saddles*, a burlesque about a western town standing in the way of the railroad expansion and the black sheriff sent to discourage its citizens from deserting, is a limp, shapeless mess of a film [which] trades in a genuine respect for westerns' tropes for purile vulgarity and joy-buzzer showmanship (which wouldn't be so much of a crime, really, if most of the jokes didn't seem downright tame nowadays)."
Eric Henderson, *Slant Magazine*, 16 June 2004.

"No comic trope, however musty or studded with whiskers, is off limits, including bad puns, physical shtick, pie fights, goofy names and accents, song-and-dance numbers, Jewish Indians, or just having a bunch of cowpokes farting around the campfire. Some of the jokes drop like lead, but the film's anarchic spirit carries a lot of excitement, because Brooks' anything-goes philosophy means that no comedic possibilities go unconsidered."
Scott Tobias, *The Onion AV Club*, 28 June 2004.

"Thirty years on, we have trouble imagining any A-list studio, including Warner Brothers, having the gumption and guts to let Brooks, or anyone else, ring some of those bells today. But heaven knows they should. [...] In these times when sanctimony and sound-bite puritanism are treated as virtues, we need a *Blazing Saddles*, a wry, bold, good-hearted taboo-buster that deflates bigots (and their fear that others would monger), while simultaneously suggesting we unclench our sphincters and get over ourselves."
Mark Bourne, *DVD Journal*, 2004.

## YOUNG FRANKENSTEIN (1974)

USA Release Date: 15 December 1974.
Budget: $2,800,000.
USA Total Gross: $86,273,333.

Award Wins: Hugo Awards: Best Dramatic Presentation (1975); Academy of Science Fiction, Fantasy & Horror Films Golden Scroll Awards: Best Director, Best Supporting Actor, Best Horror Film, Best Make-Up, Best Set Decoration (1976); USA Golden Screen Award (1977).

Award Nominations: Academy Awards: Best Writing: Screenplay Adapted from Other Material, Best Sound (1975); Golden Globe Awards: Best Motion Picture Actress (Musical/ Comedy), Best Supporting Actress (Motion Picture) (1975); New York Film Critics Circle Awards: Best Supporting Actress (1974); Writers Guild of America Award: Best Comedy Adapted from Another Medium (1975).

Representative Critical Opinion:

"*Young Frankenstein* is as funny as we expect a Mel Brooks comedy to be, but it's more than that: It shows artistic growth and a more sure-handed control of the material by a director who once seemed willing to do literally anything for a laugh. It's more confident and less breathless. That's partly because the very genre he's satirizing gives him a strong narrative he can play against."
Roger Ebert, *The Chicago Sun-Times*, 16 December 1974.

"It would be misleading to describe *Young Frankenstein*, written by Mr Wilder and Mr Brooks, as astoundingly witty, but it's a great deal of low fun of the sort that Mr Brooks specializes in. Although it hasn't as many roof-raising boffs as *Blazing Saddles*, it is funnier over the long run because it is more disciplined. The anarchy is controlled. Mr Brooks sticks to the subject, recalling the clichés of horror films of the 1930s as lovingly as someone remembering the small sins of youth."
Vincent Canby, *The New York Times*, 16 December 1974.

"The movie works because it has the Mary Shelley story to lean on: we know that the monster will be created and will get loose. And Brooks makes a leap up as a director because, although the comedy doesn't build, he carries the story through. Some directors don't need a unifying story, but Brooks has always got lost without one. (He had a story in *The Twelve Chairs*, but he didn't have the jokes.) Staying with the story, Brooks even has a satisfying windup, which makes this just about the only comedy of recent years that doesn't collapse."
Pauline Kael, *The New Yorker*, 30 December 1974.

"It's hard to not start quoting the script from scene one to fadeout, but a lot of what goes on in the material still stays funny after all these years. Later Brooks films have not survived the test of time, but this one still holds up. Some jokes feel childish, and they are, but others include words that help show the characters are a little out of their element and a little immature. [...] The Library of Congress has *Young Frankenstein* on a small group of films selected for preservation and it's easy to understand why; it helps serve as an example of parody and satire that remains a comedy classic."
Ryan Keefer, *DVD Talk*, 7 October 2008.

"Remarkably, Brooks managed to create a perfect marriage between vintage visual splendor and his usual goofball humor. *Young Frankenstein* is widely regarded as one of Brooks' funniest films, and for good reason. There are dozens of laugh-out-loud scenes here, from the "roll in the hay" bit to the side-splitting scene with the old blind man (Gene Hackman, *Crimson Tide*) to the show-stopping dance number. Even so, the pacing of the humor here is a bit different than usual. Brooks sets aside his "everything but the kitchen sink" approach to comedy and offers laughs that are more carefully moderated. The jokes aren't fired off at rapid speed, but rather worked organically into Mary Shelley's source material."

Clark Douglas, *DVD Verdict*, 7 January 2009.

## SILENT MOVIE (1976)

USA Release Date: 16 June 1976.
Budget: $4,055,000.
USA Total Gross: $36,145,695.
Award Wins: National Board of Review Awards: Top Ten Films (1976).
Award Nominations: Golden Globe Awards: Best Motion Picture, Best Motion Picture Actor (Musical/ Comedy), Best Motion Picture Actor in a Supporting Role, Best Motion Picture Actress in a Supporting Role (1977); Writers Guild of America Awards: Best Comedy Written Directly for the Screen (1977).

Representative Critical Opinion:

"*Silent Movie* is funnier than *YoungFrankenstein* – that enormously popular, but essentially one-joke send-up – but that's not saying much. *Silent Movie* is so definitely not hilarious that I could tell you all the jokes in a few paragraphs, if pressed. [...] I wondered about the silent movie script Mel Funn carries with him throughout *Silent Movie*. If it were as terrific as he claimed, then its comedy would have been more natural, less forced, and, in the end, more satisfying than the real Brooks version."
Marie Brenner, *Texas Monthly*, September 1976.

"Mel Brooks will do anything for a laugh. Anything. He has no shame. He's an anarchist; his movies inhabit a universe in which everything is possible and the outrageous is probable, and *Silent Movie*, where Brooks has taken a considerably stylistic risk and pulled it off triumphantly, made me laugh a lot. [...] Everything's done amid an encyclopedia of sight gags, old and new, borrowed and with a fly in their soup. There are gags that don't work and stretches of up to a minute, I suppose, when we don't laugh -- but even then we're smiling because of Brooks's manic desire to entertain."
Roger Ebert, *The Chicago Sun-Times*, 30 June 1976.

"*Silent Movie* has the novelty of being a modern silent film going for it, but the thing that makes this film work is the story that it tells. [...] With the story being how it is and the lack of dialogue being a little bit of an obstacle, there are quite a few sight gags that you might have to sit through that are a little more prevalent here than in other Brooks films. But the film still kept moving, and the score (written by John Morris) helped to add to the overall enjoyment of things, not to mention the usual Brooks collaborators really doing their best like [Sid] Caesar and Charlie Callas."
Ryan Keefer, *DVD Verdict*, 1 May 2006.

"*Silent Movie* is a gentler, lighter comedy. While *Blazing Saddles* and *Young Frankenstein* stride across the land with seven-league boots, *Silent Movie* glides on tip-toe like Bugs Bunny in ballet slippers. Unlike Brooks's coarse and ribald anti-Western, in *Silent Movie* seldom is heard a discouraging word (or any other kind, in fact). Nor is its moviemaking anywhere near as impressive as his riff on Universal's classic monster. But this cheerful, scattershot bit of silliness is funny enough and ingratiating enough to not quite overstay its 87 minutes."
Mark Bourne, *DVD Journal*, 2006.

# HIGH ANXIETY (1977)

USA Release Date: 25 December 1977.
Budget: $4,015,000.
USA Total Gross: $31,063,038.
Award Wins: N/A.
Award Nominations: Golden Globe Awards: Best Motion Picture (Musical/ Comedy), Best Motion Picture Actor (Musical/ Comedy) (1978).

Representative Critical Opinion:

"Brooks seems to be standing still and possibly running backwards. His latest movie about other movies is a homage-cum-send-up of Alfred Hitchcock, and it is an exercise in redundancy. Hitchcock almost always has his tongue as well as a Maguffin in his cheek. How can you do a send-up, for instance, of *Psycho*, which is a black comedy? Brooks apes (apes is the right word) the shower scene from *Psycho*, and Hitchcock's style, which is really an attitude as well as technique, goes down the drain."
Richard Fuller, *Cincinnati Magazine*, April 1978.

"For subtlety *High Anxiety* isn't *Annie Hall*, but from a slapdash filmmaker who wants to be loved more than he wants to make a great film, it's an astonishingly good 95 minutes. In a time when the ABC honchos have decreed all comedy must feature blue-collar characters and be relentlessly stupid, this pleasant little entertainment looks disconcertingly like art."
Jesse Kornbluth, *Texas Monthly*, February 1978.

"Brooks has made a specialty of movie satires: *Blazing Saddles*, *Young Frankenstein*, and *Silent Movie*. But they took on well-chosen targets. It's one thing to kid the self-conscious seriousness of a Western or a horror movie. It's another to take on a director of such sophistication that half the audience won't even get the in-jokes the other half is laughing at."
Roger Ebert, *The Chicago Sun-Times*, 1 January 1978.

"Not everything one wants it to be, but Mel Brooks's parody of Hitchcock, in which he plays a psychiatrist, has enough high spirits to guide it over some of the rough and low spots. [...] If you can put up with his usual hit-or-miss attack, you might find yourself amused."
Jonathan Rosenbaum, *The Chicago Reader*, January 2000.

# HISTORY OF THE WORLD: PART I (1981)

USA Release Date: 12 June 1981.
Budget: $10,000,000.
USA Total Gross: $31,672,907.
USA Opening Weekend Revenue: $4,792,731.
Award Wins: N/A.
Award Nominations: N/A.

Representative Critical Opinion:

"*History of the World* is full of great beginnings followed by a quick collapse. The movie is a burlesque-show version of history – life in different epochs as a parade of fools, sadists, hucksters. Whether wearing a pelt, a toga, a cassock, or a ruffled shirt and frock coat, man is always the same low, dirty animal – a buffoon. Brooks's jokes fall below the level of satire; his movie is show-business blasphemy – funny, but not as bold as he thinks it is."
David Denby, *New York Magazine*, 22 June 1981.

"When a torture victim in *History of the World, Part I*'s extended "Spanish Inquisition" musical number – probably the best sequence Brooks ever wrote or directed, the centerpiece of the only underrated film in a predominately overrated catalog – kvetches about Torquemada's burly henchmen and mincing monks shoving a red hot poker up his ass, the punchline his companion sings about making his 'privates public for a game' ('Oy, the agony! Oy, the shame!') forms a pretty neat mission statement for Brooks's films."
Eric Henderson, *Slant Magazine*, 7 April 2006.

"Though it was lambasted upon its original release, the fact of the matter is *History of the World: Part I* is a very funny movie. Critically drubbed for being scattershot and crude, the film has aged quite well and Brooks's combination of slapstick humor and witty one liners still elicit chuckles today. While the film retains some trappings of its time (the very early '80s), the setting and costumes make sure it never feels like a time capsule. The film is stacked with hysterical moments – from King Louis XVI's naughty orgy to a revisionist take of The Last Supper – and Brooks is in fine form as writer, director and star."
Patrick Naugle, *DVD Verdict*, 20 May 2010.

## SPACEBALLS (1987)

USA Release Date: 24 June 1987.
Budget: $22,700,000.
USA Total Gross: $38,119,483.
USA Opening Weekend Revenue: $6,613,837.
Award Wins: N/A.
Award Nominations: N/A.

Representative Critical Opinion:

"A lot of the gags are pretty good. The *MillenniumFalcon*, for example, has been turned into an unkempt recreational vehicle, and its wookie [sic] copilot is now a dog-faced John Candy, who has trouble maneuvering his tail in tight places. Yoda has been transformed into Yogurt (Mel Brooks), the borscht-belt sage who has a profitable sideline in movie merchandising. And so forth. The crew flings itself energetically through space in search of laughs, but it will never penetrate the galaxy where *Blazing Saddles* and *Young Frankenstein* traced their giddy orbits."
Richard Schickel, *Time*, 13 July 1987.

"I keep wishing Brooks would satirize something current and tricky, like the John Hughes teenage films, instead of picking on old targets. With *Spaceballs*, he has made the kind of movie that didn't really need a Mel Brooks. In bits and pieces, one way or another, this movie already has been made over the last 10 years by countless other satirists. [...] How do you review a movie like this, anyway? I guess by saying whether you laughed or not. I did laugh, but not enough to recommend the film. I keep waiting for Mel Brooks to do something really great, instead of these machine-made satires, where three-quarters of the invention goes into the special-effects technology."
Roger Ebert, *The Chicago Sun-Times*, 24 June 1987.

"I really hesitate to say anything too negative about *Spaceballs*, as it is a film that is practically worshipped by some of Brooks's younger fans. However, for me it has always ranked as lesser Brooks. The story is a fairly predictable mash-up of *Star Wars* and a collection of other sci-fi flicks [...] but there's a real sense that Brooks has pretty much just run out of ideas and is repeating himself in the hopes that he can make the exact same thing work once again. It's a very obvious if sometimes amusing sci-fi spoof, throwing in expected references to popular movies of the previous two decades (*Planet of the Apes*, *Alien*, etc.) and tossing them into a story that's really nothing more than a thin excuse to set up a variety of gags. Some work, but an awful lot don't."
Clark Douglas, *DVD Verdict*, 21 December 2009.

## LIFE STINKS (1991)

USA Release Date: 26 July 1991.
Budget: $13,000,000.
USA Total Gross: $4,102,526.
USA Opening Weekend Revenue: $1,920,215.
Award Wins: N/A.
Award Nominations: N/A.

Representative Critical Opinion:

"Mel Brooks's new comedy, *Life Stinks*, is less downbeat than its title, but not by much. As the latest in a long line of movie millionaires (Mr Brooks's version is a billionaire, thanks to inflation) who regain their common sense by spending time with the common folk, Mr Brooks appears as Goddard Bolt, robber baron extraordinaire. He has a much surer sense of how to lampoon such a figure than of how to turn him into anyone nice. [...] Only at rare moments does *Life Stinks* offer much in the way of surprise or grace."
Janet Maslin, *The New York Times*, 26 July 1991.

"The problem with *Life Stinks* is that it's got its heart in the right place but not a whole lot else. The movie has an intrusively inauthentic feel to it. [...] The movie has its moments but it plays like a ball of confusion. *Life Stinks* seems to be Brooks's bid to be taken seriously and leave the fart jokes behind. And something about that stinks."
Marjorie Baumgarten, *The Austin Chronicle*, 2 August 1991.

"[*Life Stinks*] tries to play both sides of the political correctness coin. On one hand, Brooks tries to show the indignities heaped upon the homeless, and we see how difficult their lives can be. However, Brooks also wants to have fun at their expense, as we check out a long roster of wacky characters. The issues of the homeless are presented in a simplistic and caricatured manner that makes them neither amusing joke fodder nor realistic personalities. [...] Neither pointed social satire or rich character piece, *Life Stinks* stands as one of Mel Brooks' crummiest films."
Colin Jacobson, *DVD Movie Guide*, 15 January 2003.

## ROBIN HOOD: MEN IN TIGHTS (1993)

USA Release Date: 28 July 1993.
Budget: $20,000,000.
USA Total Gross: $35,739,755.
USA Opening Weekend Revenue: $6,841,830.
Award Wins: N/A.
Award Nominations: Young Artist Awards: Outstanding Family Motion Picture (Comedy) (1994).

Representative Critical Opinion:

"The movie takes a long time to get off the ground, and then it wobbles. It hits a couple of ecstatically funny high points, only to plummet into a bog of second-rate gags, emerging a long time later to engage the audience by the sheer, unstoppable force of the Brooks chutzpah. [...] What's missing is the kind of densely packed comic screenplay that helped to make *Young Frankenstein* and *High Anxiety* two of the most delectable movie parodies of the last 20 years. *Men in Tights* has the manner of something that wasn't argued over long enough. A few good gags are supplemented by dozens of others that still need to be worked on or tossed out entirely. Occasional lines are delightfully dizzy, but they are random shots. There's no comic momentum."
Vincent Canby, *The New York Times*, 28 July 1993.

"Most of the film's jokes, not to mention the casting of Elwes, are pointed at Michael Curtiz's Errol Flynn-vehicle *The Adventures of Robin Hood* and, to a lesser extent, 1991's *Robin Hood: Prince of Thieves*, allowing for a bevy of digs on folklore and genre stereotypes. The structure is loosened to Brooksian standards, and the gags are certainly broad, but *Men in Tights* rarely reaches the sublime lunacy and risqué attitude that characterized Brooks's best work."
Chris Cabin, *Slant Magazine*, 17 May 2010.

"It's a minor entry in Mel Brooks's filmography, though it does represent something of an upswing in his later period. It feels relaxed and confident, rather than desperate and eager-to-please. It has some good jokes, but it also recycles many old jokes and never really finds a rhythm, or a high point. At times it seems to have too much plot and too many characters and at other times, it doesn't seem to have enough."
Jeffrey M. Anderson, *Combustible Celluloid*, 27 May 2010.

## DRACULA: DEAD AND LOVING IT (1995)

USA Release Date: 22 December 1995.
Budget: $30,000,000.
USA Total Gross: $10,772,144.
USA Opening Weekend Revenue: $2,708,298.
Award Wins: N/A.
Award Nominations: N/A.

Representative Critical Opinion:

"The personality of Mel Brooks is what carries *Dracula: Dead and Loving It*, his latest satire, which opens today. Early in the picture, before he appears on screen, you can sense him behind the camera, shoveling piles of jokes, big and small, into the machinery. [...] Brooks has never asked to be taken seriously as an artist. He's never wanted respect, just laughs. A while ago that might have seemed lowbrow. But it's beginning to look generous – and very cool. As for *Dracula: Dead and Loving It*, it's a modest attempt that succeeds. It has enough jokes to keep it moving and enough distinctly Brooksian gags to make it required viewing for his fans. But lacking the insane magic of *Robin Hood: Men in Tights* – or for that matter, Brooks's earlier horror parody, *Young Frankenstein* – it won't win any converts."
Mick LaSalle, *The San Francisco Chronicle*, 22 December 1995.

"Mr Brooks may no longer be at the forefront of silly comedy, but he's still laying on the genre gags, horrible puns and enema references with dependable good cheer. So even if this *Dracula* is thin-blooded, its better moments redeem a lot of dead air. It's hard to resist a vampire film in which someone says: 'Yes, we have Nosferatu. We have Nosferatu today.'"
Janet Maslin, *The New York Times*, 22 December 1995.

Box office statistical data is drawn from:
Box Office Mojo (*www.boxofficemojo.com*),
the Internet Movie Database (*uk.imdb.com*)
and *Variety* (*www.variety.com*).

# RECOMMENDED FURTHER READING

*The Comic Art of Mel Brooks*
By Maurice Yacowar
Publisher: W.H. Allen (July, 1982)
ISBN-13: 978-0491029179
Publisher: Crescent Moon Publishing (Nov, 2015)
ISBN-13: 9781861715111
　　Perhaps the most comprehensive analytical work about Brooks's early-to-mid career in film, this book explains in great detail the dynamics of his complex comedic strategies in addition to the shared themes with his pre-directorial career in television. The book discusses in admirable depth the multifaceted socio-cultural influences which are evident throughout Brooks's canon.

*Mel Brooks and the Spoof Movie*
By Nick Smurthwaite and Paul Gelder
Publisher: Proteus (October, 1982)
ISBN-13: 978-0862760502
　　A brief, heavily illustrated account of Brooks's cinema from *The Producers* until the date of publication, fitting his work into the larger generic framework of the filmic spoof comedy.

*The Films of Mel Brooks*
By Neil Sinyard
Publisher: Bookthrift (March, 1988)
ISBN-13: 978-0671089610
　　A relatively short but nonetheless intriguing volume which focuses on Brooks's directorial career from the late sixties until the late eighties, and includes a useful exploration of the political subtext evident in his cinematic output.

*It's Good To Be the King: The Seriously Funny Life of Mel Brooks*
By James Robert Parish
Publisher: John Wiley & Sons (March 2008)
ISBN-13: 978-0470225264
　　Perhaps the most prominent biography of Brooks's life in the movies, this painstakingly-researched book describes the personal face of the man behind the camera and explores with panache the motivation which lay behind his artistic drive.

*The Big Screen Comedies of Mel Brooks*
By Robert Alan Crick
Publisher: Mcfarland & Co Inc (September, 2009)
ISBN-13: 978-0786443260
A detailed and informative account of all of Brooks's eleven films, in addition to a discussion of the Alan Johnson-helmed *To Be or Not to Be* (1983), with considerable information about each movie's production, the director's choice of performers, and the overall critical reception of his cinematic output.

*Mel Brooks in the Cultural Industries: Survival and Prolonged Adaptation*
By Alex Symons
Publisher: Edinburgh University Press (August, 2012)
ISBN-13: 978-0748649587
This book examines in great detail Brooks's versatility as a writer, director, actor, producer and cultural figure. Drawing upon all aspects of his career, it explains with incisive clarity the manner in which Brooks's work has adapted over the decades, crossing media platforms in order to accommodate changing cultural tastes.

# SELECT BIBLIOGRAPHY

Adler, Bill, and Jeffrey Feinman, *Mel Brooks: The Irreverent Funnyman* (Chicago: Playboy Press, 1976).
Adler, Renata, 'The Producers', in *The New York Times*, 19 March 1968.
<http://www.nytimes.com/movie/review?res=EE05E7DF173AE273BC4152DFB5668383679EDE>
Alleman, Richard, *New York: The Movie Lover's Guide: The Ultimate Insider Tour of Movie New York*, rev. edn. (New York: Random House, 2005).
Anderson, Jeffrey M., 'Forced Laughter', in *Combustible Celluloid*, 22 May 2005.
<http://www.combustiblecelluloid.com/classic/spaceballs.shtml>
—, 'Hysterical Accuracy', in *Combustible Celluloid*, 27 May 2010.
<http://www.combustiblecelluloid.com/classic/histworld.shtml>
—, 'Tense of Humor', in *Combustible Celluloid*, 11 June 2010.
<http://www.combustiblecelluloid.com/classic/highanx.shtml>
—, 'Zingers and Arrows', in *Combustible Celluloid*, 27 May 2010.
<http://www.combustiblecelluloid.com/archive/robinhoodmit.shtml>
Anon., 'Cinema: The Producers', in *Time Magazine*, 26 January 1968.
<http://www.time.com/time/magazine/article/0,9171,837773-2,00.html>
—, 'Review: *Dracula: Dead and Loving It*', in *Variety*, 17 December 1995.
<http://variety.com/1995/film/reviews/dracula-dead-and-loving-it-1200444059/>
—, 'Review: *The Producers*', in *Variety*, 31 December 1967.
<http://variety.com/1967/film/reviews/the-producers-4-1200421497/>
—, 'Still Blazing After All These Years', in *People Weekly*, 12 April 1999.
<http://www.brookslyn.com/print/PeopleWeekly04-12-99/PeopleWeekly04-12-99.php>
Ashkenazi, Ofer, 'Ridiculous Trauma: Comic Representations of the Nazi Past in Contemporary German Visual Culture', in *Cultural Critique*, No. 78, Spring 2011, pp. 88-118.
Atkinson, Michael, 'Flights of Clancy', in *The Village Voice*, 4 June 2002.
<http://www.villagevoice.com/2002-06-04/film/flights-of-clancy/>
Atlas, Jacoba, 'New Hollywood: Mel Brooks Interview', in *Film Comment*, March-April 1975.
<http://www.brookslyn.com/print/FilmComment1975/FilmComment1975.php>
Attardo, Salvatore, *Humorous Texts: A Semantic and Pragmatic Analysis* (Berlin: Walter de Gruyter, 2001).
Badley, Linda, R. Barton Palmer and Steven Jay Schneider, eds, *Traditions in World Cinema* (Edinburgh: Edinburgh University Press, 2006).
Bauer, Jerry, 'Mel Brooks: A Revealing Dialogue with the World's Funniest Man', in *Adelina Magazine*, February 1980.
<http://www.brookslyn.com/print/Adelina1980/Adelina1980.php>
Baumgarten, Marjorie, '*Life Stinks*', in *The Austin Chronicle*, 2 August 1991.

<http://www.austinchronicle.com/calendar/film/1991-08-02/139601/>
Becker, Tom, '*High Anxiety*', in *DVD Verdict*, 17 May 2010.
<http://www.dvdverdict.com/reviews/highanxietybluray.php>
Beier, Lars-Olav, 'Spiegel Interview with Mel Brooks: "With Comedy, We Can Rob Hitler of his Posthumous Power"', in *Spiegel Online International*, 16 March 2006.
<http://www.spiegel.de/international/spiegel/spiegel-interview-with-mel-brooks-with-comedy-we-can-rob-hitler-of-his-posthumous-power-a-406268.html>
Berliner, Todd, *Hollywood Incoherent: Narration in Seventies Cinema* (Austin: University of Texas Press, 2010).
Bernstein, Jonathan, 'Moving Images: Redemption Song', in *Spin*, December 1991, 99-100, p. 100.
Bianculli, David, 'Fresh Air: Mel Brooks – "I'm An EGOT; I Don't Need Any More"', on *National Public Radio*, 20 May 2013.
<http://www.npr.org/2013/12/27/256597762/mel-brooks-im-an-egot-i-dont-need-any-more>
Blake, Richard A., *Street Smart: The New York of Lumet, Allen, Scorsese, and Lee* (Lexington: The University Press of Kentucky, 2005).
Bolam, Sarah Miles, and Thomas J. Bolam, *Fictional Presidential Films: A Comprehensive Filmography of Portrayals from 1930 to 2011* (Bloomington: Xlibris, 2011).
Bonnstetter, Beth E., 'Mel Brooks Meets Kenneth Burke (and Mikhail Bakhtin): Comedy and Burlesque in Satiric Film', in *Journal of Film and Video*, Vol. 63, No. 1, Spring 2011, pp. 18-31.
—, 'An Analytical Framework of Parody and Satire: Mel Brooks and His World' (unpublished doctoral thesis, The University of Minnesota, June 2008).
Booker, M. Keith, *Alternate Americas: Science Fiction Film and American Culture* (Westport: Praeger, 2006).
Books, Andrew, 'The Comedic Genius of Mel Brooks: Laugh at Everything', on *LinkedIn Pulse*, 29 September 2014.
<https://www.linkedin.com/pulse/article/20140929150946-140254681-the-comedic-genius-of-mel-brooks-laugh-at-everything>
Bordwell, David, Janet Staiger and Kristin Thompson, *The Classical Hollywood Cinema: Film Style & Mode of Production to 1960* (London: Routledge, 1988) [1985].
Bourne, Mark, '*Blazing Saddles*: 30th Anniversary Special Edition', in *DVD Journal*, 2004.
<http://www.dvdjournal.com/reviews/b/blazingsaddles.shtml>
—, '*Silent Movie*', in *DVD Journal*, 2006.
<http://www.dvdjournal.com/quickreviews/s/silentmovie.q.shtml>
Bovberg, Jason, '*Life Stinks*', in *DVD Talk*, 18 February 2003.
<http://www.dvdtalk.com/reviews/5452/life-stinks/>
Bowen, Chuck, '*The Producers*', in *Slant Magazine*, 28 June 2013.
<http://www.slantmagazine.com/dvd/review/the-producers>
Boyd, David, and R. Barton Palmer, *After Hitchcock: Influence, Imitation, and Intertextuality* (Austin: University of Texas Press, 2006).
Brady, Celia, 'Prognostication, Cantonese Style', in *Spy*, October 1991, p. 20.
Brenner, Marie, 'Film: Easy Outing', in *Texas Monthly*, September 1976, pp. 60-64.
Brigham, William, 'Down and Out in Tinseltown: Hollywood Presents the Dispossessed', in *Beyond the Stars: Studies in American Popular Film: Volume 5: Themes and Ideologies in American Popular Film*, ed. by Paul Loukides and Linda K. Fuller (Bowling Green: Bowling Green State University Press, 1996), pp. 165-86.
Brooks, Mel, 'My Movies: The Collusion of Art and Money', in *The Movie Business Book*, 3rd edn, ed. by Jason E. Squire (Maidenhead: Open University Press, 2006), pp. 39-48.
Brussat, Frederic, and Mary Ann Brussat, 'Mel Brooks's *History of the World: Part 1*',

in *Spirituality & Practice*, 31 January 2004.
<http://www.spiritualityandpractice.com/films/films.php?id=7810>

Buhle, Paul, *From the Lower East Side to Hollywood: Jews in American Popular Culture* (London: Verso, 2004).

Cabin, Chris, 'Robin Hood: Men in Tights', in *Slant Magazine*, 17 May 2010.
<http://www.slantmagazine.com/dvd/review/robin-hood-men-in-tights/1728>

Caesar, Sid, with Eddy Friedfeld, *Caesar's Hours: My Life in Comedy, with Love and Laughter* (New York: Perseus, 2003), p. 137.

Canby, Vincent, 'Blazing Saddles', in *The New York Times*, 8 February 1974.
<http://www.nytimes.com/movie/review?res=EE05E7DF1730E261BC4053DFB466838F669EDE>

—, 'Robin Hood: Men in Tights: Mel Brooks Aims His Comedic Barbs at Robin Hood et al', in *The New York Times*, 28 July 1993.
<http://www.nytimes.com/movie/review?res=9F0CE4DD1431F93BA15754C0A965958260>

—, 'Screen: Mel Brooks on Prowl in Soviet '12 Chairs,' a Comedy, at Tower East', in *The New York Times*, 29 October 1970.
<http://www.nytimes.com/movie/review?res=9D04E4DC173BEE34BC4151DFB667838B669EDE>

—, 'Silent Movie with Golden Subtitles', in *The New York Times*, 1 July 1976.
<http://www.nytimes.com/movie/review?res=9E0CE6DA143FE334BC4953DFB166838D669EDE>

—, 'Young Frankenstein', in *The New York Times*, 16 December 1974,
<http://www.nytimes.com/movie/review?res=EE05E7DF173EAF2CA5494CC2B779988C6896>

Carlson, Alex, 'Top 8 Mel Brooks Movies of All-Time', in *Film Misery*, 1 June 2010.
<http://www.filmmisery.com/top-8-mel-brooks-movies-of-all-time/>

Carone, Patrick, 'Interview: Icon Mel Brooks: A chat with the genius who brought us dancing monsters, the Schwartz, and the perfect fart joke', in *Maxim Online*, 6 February 2013.
<http://www.maxim.com/entertainment/interview-icon-mel-brooks>

Carroll, Noël, 'Horror and Humor', in *The Journal of Aesthetics and Art Criticism*, Vol. 57, No. 2, Spring 1999, pp. 145-160.

Casper, Scott E., and Lucinda M. Long, *Moving Stories: Migration and the American West 1850-2000* (Reno: University of Nevada Press, 2001).

Conrich, Ian, 'Musical Performance and the Cult Film Experience', in *Film'sMusical Moments*, ed. by Ian Conrich and Estella Tincknell (Edinburgh: Edinburgh University Press, 2006), pp. 115-31.

—, and Estella Tincknell, eds., *Film's Musical Moments* (Edinburgh: Edinburgh University Press, 2006).

Cook, David A., *Lost Illusions: American Cinema in the Shadow of Watergate and Vietnam, 1970-1979* (Berkeley: University of California Press, 2002).

Cooper, Arthur, 'Blazing Anxieties: Mel Brooks is Just a Little Bit Crazy', in *Mademoiselle*, August 1981.
<http://www.brookslyn.com/print/Mademoiselle-8-1981/Mademoiselle-8-1981.php>

Couch, Aaron, 'Mel Brooks Gets Street Named After Him: "People Are Going to Walk All Over Me"', in *The Hollywood Reporter Online*, 24 October 2014.
<http://www.hollywoodreporter.com/news/mel-brooks-gets-street-named-743544>

Crick, Robert Alan, *The Big Screen Comedies of Mel Brooks* (Jefferson: McFarland and Company, 2009) [2002].

Crist, Judith, 'Too Many Cooks, Only One Brooks', in *New York Magazine*, 25 February 1974, pp. 52-53.

—, 'Vintage Brando', in *New York Magazine*, 2 November 1970, p. 61.

Cronke, David, '2,034 – and Still Ticking', in *The Los Angeles Times*, 27 May 1994.
<http://www.brookslyn.com/print/LATimes05-27-94/LATimes05-27-94.php>
Darrach, Brad, 'Mel Brooks', in *Playboy*, February 1975.
<http://www.brookslyn.com/print/PlayboyFeb1975/PlayboyFeb1975_part1.php>
Denby, David, 'Death Trap', in *New York Magazine*, 13 July 1987, pp. 54-55.
—, 'The Decline and Fall of Mel Brooks', in *New York Magazine*, 22 June 1981, pp. 48-50.
Desser, David, and Lester D. Friedman, *American Jewish Filmmakers*, 2nd edn (Chicago: University of Illinois Press, 2004).
DiMare, Philip C., ed., *Movies in American History: An Encyclopedia: Volume 1* (Santa Barbara: ABC-CLIO, 2011).
Dillon, Steven, *The Solaris Effect: Art and Artifice in Contemporary American Film* (Austin: University of Texas Press, 2006).
Dixon, Wheeler Winston, ed., *Film Genre 2000: New Critical Essays* (Albany: State University of New York Press, 2000).
Dougherty, Margot, 'May The Farce Be With Him: *Spaceballs* Rockets Mel Brooks Into Lunatic Orbit', in *People Weekly*, 20 July 1987.
<http://www.brookslyn.com/print/PeopleWeekly07-20-87/PeopleWeekly07-20-87.php>
Douglas, Clark, 'The Mel Brooks Collection', in *DVD Verdict*, 21 December 2009.
<http://www.dvdverdict.com/reviews/melbrooksbluray.php>
—, '*Young Frankenstein*', in *DVD Verdict*, 7 January 2009.
<http://www.dvdverdict.com/reviews/youngfrankensteinbluray.php>
Ebert, Roger, '*Blazing Saddles*', in *The Chicago Sun-Times*, 7 February 1974.
<http://www.rogerebert.com/reviews/blazing-saddles-1974>
—, 'Great Movie: *The Producers*', in *The Chicago Sun-Times*, 23 July 2000.
<http://www.rogerebert.com/reviews/great-movie-the-producers-1968>
—, '*High Anxiety*', in *The Chicago Sun-Times*, 1 January 1978.
<http://www.rogerebert.com/reviews/high-anxiety-1978>
—, '*History of the World: Part 1*', in *The Chicago Sun-Times*, 15 June 1981.
<http://www.rogerebert.com/reviews/history-of-the-world-part-1-1981>
—, '*Life Stinks*', in *The Chicago Sun-Times*, 26 July 1991.
<http://www.rogerebert.com/reviews/life-stinks-1991>
—, '*Silent Movie*', in *The Chicago Sun-Times*, 30 June 1976.
<http://www.rogerebert.com/reviews/silent-movie-1976>
—, '*Spaceballs*', in *The Chicago Sun-Times*, 24 June 1987.
<http://www.rogerebert.com/reviews/spaceballs-1987>
—, '*The Twelve Chairs*', in *The Chicago Sun-Times*, 22 December 1970.
<http://www.rogerebert.com/reviews/the-twelve-chairs-1970>
—, '*Young Frankenstein*', in *The Chicago Sun-Times*, 16 December 1974.
<http://www.rogerebert.com/reviews/young-frankenstein-1974>
Elliott, Andrew B.R., *Remaking the Middle Ages: The Methods of Cinema and History in Portraying the Medieval World* (Jefferson: McFarland, 2011), p. 136.
Elsaesser, Thomas, Alexander Horwath and Noel King, eds, *The Last Great American Picture Show: New Hollywood Cinema in the 1970s, Film Culture in Transition* series (Amsterdam: Amsterdam University Press, 2004).
Epstein, Lawrence J., *The Haunted Smile: The Story of Jewish Comedians* (Oxford: PublicAffairs, 2001).
Erens, Patricia, *The Jew in American Cinema* (Bloomington: Indiana University Press, 1984).
Fabe, Marilyn, *Closely Watched Films: An Introduction to the Art of Narrative Film Techniques* (Berkeley: University of California Press, 2004).
Fabrikant, Geraldine, 'A Funny Man Earns it the *2000 Year-Old*-Way', in *The New York Times Magazine*, 26 October 1997.

<http://www.brookslyn.com/print/NewYorkTimes10-26-97/NewYorkTimes10-26-97.php>

Faires, Robert, 'Robin Hood: Men in Tights', in *The Austin Chronicle*, 6 August 1993.
<http://www.austinchronicle.com/calendar/film/1993-08-06/139114/>

Felderstein, Kenny, *Happiness: The Forgotten Ingredient* (Bloomington: iUniverse, 2013).

Fermaglich, Kirsten, 'Mel Brooks's *The Producers*: Tracing American Jewish Culture Through Comedy, 1967-2007', in *American Studies*, Vol. 48, No. 4, Winter 2007, pp. 59-87.

Flanagan, Sylvia P., 'Movies to See: *Life Stinks*', in *Jet*, 5 August 1991, p. 56.

Fleishman, Philip, 'Interview with Mel Brooks', in *Maclean's Magazine*, 17 April 1978.
<http://www.brookslyn.com/print/Maclean04-17-78/Maclean04-17-78.php>

Fox, Georgette S., *Masters of Evil: A Study of the Archvillain in Film and Television* (San Bernadino: Borgo Press, 1998).

Friedman, Lester D., ed., *American Cinema of the 1970s: Themes and Variations* (New Brunswick: Rutgers University Press, 2007).

Fuller, Richard, 'Films', in *Cincinnati Magazine*, April 1978, pp.83-89.

Garner, Joe, *Made You Laugh!: The Funniest Moments in Radio, Television, Stand-Up, and Movie Comedy* (Kansas City: Andrews McMeel Publishing, 2004).

Gehring, Wes, *Parody as Film Genre: Never Give a Saga an Even Break* (Westport: Greenwood Press, 1999).

Gleiberman, Owen, 'So I Married an Axe Murderer; Robin Hood: Men in Tights', in *Entertainment Weekly*, 6 August 1993.
<http://www.ew.com/ew/article/0,,20285249,00.html>

Glut, Donald F., *The Frankenstein Archive: Essays on the Monster, the Myth, the Movies, and More* (Jefferson: McFarland, 2002).

Gold, Herbert, 'Funny is Money', in *The New York Times Magazine*, 30 March 1975.
<http://www.brookslyn.com/print/NewYorkTimes03-30-75/NewYorkTimes03-30-75.php>

Gillett, Philip, *Movie Greats: A Critical Study of Classic Cinema* (Oxford: Berg, 2008).

Goldman, Harry, *Kenneth Strickfaden: Dr Frankenstein's Electrician* (Jefferson: McFarland, 2005).

Grainge, Paul, ed., *Memory and Popular Film, Inside Popular Film series* (Manchester: Manchester University Press, 2003).

Grant, Barry Keith, ed., *American Cinema of the 1960s: Themes and Variations* (New Brunswick: Rutgers University Press, 2008).

Gubar, Susan, 'Racial Camp in *The Producers* and *Bamboozled*', in *Film Quarterly*, Vol. 60, No. 2, Winter 2006, pp. 26-37.

Hall, Sheldon, and Steve Neale, *Epics, Spectacles and Blockbusters: A Hollywood History* (Detroit: Wayne State University Press, 2010).

Hallenbeck, Bruce G., *Comedy-Horror Films: A Chronological History, 1914-2008* (Jefferson: McFarland, 2009).

Hanke, Ken, '*The Twelve Chairs*', in *Mountain XPress*, 26 July 2006.
<http://mountainx.com/movies/reviews/twelvechairs-php/>

Haskell, Molly, 'Hokey Hitchcock', in *New York Magazine*, 16 January 1978, pp. 47-48.

Hay, Peter, *Movie Anecdotes* (Oxford: Oxford University Press, 1990).

Heisler, Steve, 'Mel Brooks on how to play Hitler, and how he almost died making *Spaceballs*', in *The Onion A.V. Club*, 13 December 2012.
<http://www.avclub.com/article/mel-brooks-on-how-to-play-hitler-and-how-he-almost-89843>

Hellman, Roxanne, and Derek Hall, *Vampire Legends and Myths* (New York: The Rosen Publishing Group, 2012).

Henderson, Eric, '*Blazing Saddles*', in *Slant Magazine*, 16 June 2004.
<http://www.slantmagazine.com/film/review/blazing-saddles>

—, 'The Mel Brooks Collection', in *Slant Magazine*, 7 April 2006.
<http://www.slantmagazine.com/dvd/review/the-mel-brooks-collection>
Henderson, Felicia D., 'The Culture Behind Closed Doors: Issues of Gender and Race in the Writers' Room', in *Cinema Journal*, Vol. 50, No. 2, Winter 2011, pp. 145-52.
Hettrick, Scott, '*Spaceballs* Laserdisc Adds Little To Film', in *The Sun Sentinel*, 24 May 1996.
<http://articles.sun-sentinel.com/1996-05-24/entertainment/9605220414_1_brooks-spaceballs-young-frankenstein>
Hicks, Chris, 'Film Review: *Life Stinks*', in *The Deseret News*, 2 August 1991.
<http://www.deseretnews.com/article/700001044/Life-Stinks.html>
—, 'Film Review: *Robin Hood: Men in Tights*', in *The Deseret News*, 3 August 1993.
<http://www.deseretnews.com/article/700001551/Robin-Hood-Men-in-Tights.html>
Hillman, Jessica, *Echoes of the Holocaust on the American Musical Stage* (Jefferson: McFarland, 2012).
Hinson, Hal, '*Dracula: Dead and Loving It*', in *The Washington Post*, 22 December 1995.
<http://www.washingtonpost.com/wp-srv/style/longterm/movies/videos/draculadeadandlovingitpg13hinson_c03f0a.htm>
—, '*Life Stinks*', in *The Washington Post*, 27 July 1991.
<http://www.washingtonpost.com/wp-srv/style/longterm/movies/videos/lifestinkspg13hinson_a0a6ce.htm>
—, '*Spaceballs*', in *The Washington Post*, 24 June 1987.
<http://www.washingtonpost.com/wp-srv/style/longterm/movies/videos/spaceballspghinson_a0c94a.htm>
Holmlund, Chris, ed., *American Cinema of the 1990s: Themes and Variations* (New Brunswick: Rutgers University Press, 2008).
Holte, James Craig, *Dracula in the Dark: The Dracula Film Adaptations* (Westport: Greenwood Press, 1997).
Horton, Andrew, and Joanna E. Rapf, eds, *A Companion to Film Comedy* (Chichester: John Wiley and Sons, 2013).
Howe, Desson, '*Dracula: Dead and Loving It*', in *The Washington Post*, 22 December 1995.
<http://www.washingtonpost.com/wp-srv/style/longterm/movies/videos/draculadeadandlovingitpg13howe_b003a5.htm>
—, '*Robin Hood: Men in Tights*', in *The Washington Post*, 30 July 1993.
<http://www.washingtonpost.com/wp-srv/style/longterm/movies/videos/robinhoodmenintightspg13howe_a0afe4.htm>
Hughes, Howard, *Outer Limits: The Filmgoers' Guide to the Great Science-Fiction Films* (London: I.B. Tauris, 2014).
Izod, John, *Myth, Mind and the Screen: Understanding the Heroes of Our Time* (Cambridge: Cambridge University Press, 2001).
Jacobson, Colin, '*Life Stinks*', in *DVD Movie Guide*, 15 January 2003.
<http://www.dvdmg.com/lifestinks.shtml>
James, Roman, *Bigger Than Blockbusters: Movies That Defined America* (Westport: Greenwood Press, 2009).
Jameson, Fredric, *Postmodernism, or the Cultural Logic of Late Capitalism* (Durham: Duke University Press, 1997) [1991].
Jenkins, Henry, 'Mel Brooks, Vulgar Modernism, and Comic Remediation', in *A Companion to Film Comedy*, ed. by Andrew Horton and Joanna E. Rapf (Chichester: John Wiley and Sons, 2013), pp. 151-74.
Jesionowski, Joyce, '*Dracula: Dead and Loving It*', in *The Encyclopedia of the Vampire: The Living Dead in Myth, Legend, and Popular Culture*, ed. by S.T. Joshi (Santa

Barbara: Greenwood, 2011), pp. 90-91.
Johnson, Michael K., 'Migration, Masculinity, and Racial Identity in Taylor Gordon's *Born to Be'*, in *Moving Stories: Migration and the American West 1850-2000*, ed. by Scott E. Casper and Lucinda M. Long (Reno: University of Nevada Press, 2001), pp. 119-42.
Joshi, S.T., ed., *The Encyclopedia of the Vampire: The Living Dead in Myth, Legend, and Popular Culture* (Santa Barbara: Greenwood, 2011).
Kael, Pauline, 'A Magnetic Blur', in *The New Yorker*, 30 December 1974.
<http://www.newyorker.com/magazine/1974/12/30/a-magnetic-blur?currentPage=all>
—, 'Blazing Saddles', in *The New Yorker*, 18 February 1974, p. 100.
Karg, Barb, Arjean Spaite and Rick Sutherland, *The Everything Vampire Book* (Avon: Adams Media, 2009).
Kaveney, Roz, *From Alien to the Matrix: Reading Science Fiction Film* (London: I.B. Tauris, 2005).
Keefer, Ryan, 'The Mel Brooks Collection', in *DVD Verdict*, 1 May 2006.
<http://www.dvdverdict.com/reviews/melbrookscoll.php>
—, 'Young Frankenstein', in *DVD Talk*, 7 October 2008.
<http://www.dvdtalk.com/reviews/35133/young-frankenstein/>
Kempley, Rita, 'Robin Hood: Men in Tights', in *The Washington Post*, 28 July 1993.
<http://www.washingtonpost.com/wp-srv/style/longterm/movies/videos/robinhoodmenintightspg13kempley_a0a39f.htm>
King, Geoff, *Film Comedy* (London: Wallflower, 2002).
—, ed., *The Spectacle of the Real: From Hollywood to Reality TV and Beyond* (Portland: Intellect, 2005).
Knapp, Raymond, 'Music, Electricity, and the "Sweet Mystery of Life" in *Young Frankenstein'*, in *Changing Tunes: The Use of Pre-Existing Music in Film*, ed. by Phil Powrie and Robynn Stilwell (Aldershot: Ashgate Publishing, 2006), pp. 105-18.
Knight, Stephen, *Robin Hood: An Anthology of Scholarship and Criticism* (Cambridge: D.S. Brewer, 1999).
—, 'Robin Hood: Men in Tights: Fitting the Tradition Snugly', in *Robin Hood: An Anthology of Scholarship and Criticism*, ed. by Stephen Knight (Cambridge: D.S. Brewer, 1999), pp. 461-69.
—, *Robin Hood: A Mythic Biography* (Ithaca: Cornell University Press, 2003).
Kornbluth, Jesse, 'Review: Jung at Heart', in *Texas Monthly*, February 1978, pp. 99-100.
Kristal, Marc, 'Brooks's Bookshop', in *Saturday Review*, July 1983.
<http://www.brookslyn.com/print/SaturdayReviewJul1983/SaturdayReviewJul1983.php>
Kukkonen, Karin, and Sonja Klimek, eds, *Metalepsis in Popular Culture* (Berlin: Walter de Gruyter Ltd., 2011).
Kulik, Christopher, 'Robin Hood: Men in Tights', in *DVD Verdict*, 26 May 2010.
<http://www.dvdverdict.com/reviews/menintightsbluray.php>
LaSalle, Mick, 'Brooks Vamps on *Dracula'*, in *The San Francisco Chronicle*, 22 December 1995.
<http://www.sfgate.com/movies/article/FILM-REVIEW-Brooks-Vamps-on-Dracula-He-sucks-3017338.php>
Lane, Stewart F., *Jews on Broadway: An Historical Survey of Performers, Playwrights, Composers, Lyricists and Producers* (Jefferson: McFarland, 2011).
Langford, Barry, *Film Genre: Hollywood and Beyond* (Edinburgh: Edinburgh University Press, 2005).
Lavalley, Albert J., 'The Stage and Film Children of *Frankenstein*: A Survey', in *The Endurance of Frankenstein: Essays on Mary Shelley's Novel*, ed. by George Levine and U.C. Knoepflmacher (Berkeley: University of California Press, 1979), pp. 243-90.

Lawson-Peebles, Robert, 'The Many Faces of Sir Walter Ralegh', in *History Today*, Vol. 48, Issue 3, 1998.
<http://www.historytoday.com/robert-lawson-peebles/many-faces-sir-walter-ralegh>
Ledwon, Lenora P., 'Guilt, Greed, and Furniture: Using Mel Brooks's *The Twelve Chairs* to Teach Dying Declarations', in *California Law Review Circuit*, Vol. 3, No. 1, January 2012, pp. 72-79.
Leszczak, Bob, *Single Season Sitcoms, 1948-1979: A Complete Guide* (Jefferson: McFarland, 2012), p. 200.
Lev, Peter, *American Films of the 70s: Conflicting Visions* (Austin: University of Texas Press, 2000).
Levenson, Edgar A., 'Beyond Countertransference: Aspects of the Analyst's Desire', in *Contemporary Psychoanalysis*, Vol. 30, Issue 4, 1994, pp. 691-707.
Levine, George, and U.C. Knoepflmacher, eds, *The Endurance of Frankenstein: Essays on Mary Shelley's Novel* (Berkeley: University of California Press, 1979).
Liebenson, Donald, 'Rare Jewel: New Mel Brooks Package Unveils The Long-Lost Twelve Chairs', in *The Chicago Tribune*, 17 July 1997.
<http://articles.chicagotribune.com/1997-07-17/features/9707170364_1_vorobyaninov-twelve-chairs-jewels>
Lim, Dennis, *The Village Voice Film Guide: 50 Years of Movies from Classics to Cult Hits* (Hoboken: John Wiley and Sons, 2007).
Limon, John, *Stand-up Comedy in Theory, or, Abjection in America* (Durham: Duke University Press, 2000).
Loukides, Paul, and Linda K. Fuller, eds, *Beyond the Stars: Studies in American Popular Film: Volume 5: Themes and Ideologies in American Popular Film* (Bowling Green: Bowling Green State University Press, 1996).
Lowry, Brian, '*Spaceballs*: The Set Visit', in *Starlog*, Issue 119, June 1987, pp. 44-48.
Lowry, Katharine, 'Film: *Blazing Saddles*', in *Texas Monthly*, April 1974, pp. 36-37.
—, 'Film: Doin' the Monster Mashed', in *Texas Monthly*, March 1975, p. 40.
Maslin, Janet, 'Film Review: Giving New Fangs to an Old Vampire', in *The New York Times*, 22 December 1995.
<http://www.nytimes.com/movie/review?res=9804E3DF1539F931A15751C1A963958260>
—, 'Mel Brooks: From Riches to Rags to Humility', in *The New York Times*, 26 July 1991.
<http://www.nytimes.com/movie/review?res=9D0CE0DB1430F935A15754C0A967958260>
—, '*Spaceballs*: A Mel Brooks Comedy', in *The New York Times*, 24 June 1987.
<http://www.nytimes.com/movie/review?res=9B0DEED9163EF937A15755C0A961948260>
Massey, Anne, *Hollywood Beyond the Screen: Design and Material Culture* (Oxford: Berg, 2000).
Mast, Gerald, *The Comic Mind: Comedy and the Movies*, 2nd edn (Chicago: University of Chicago Press, 1979).
Mazur, Eric Michael, ed., *Encyclopedia of Religion and Film* (Santa Barbara: Greenwood Publishing, 2011).
McCaffrey, Donald W., and Christopher P. Jacobs, *Guide to the Silent Years of American Cinema* (Westport: Greenwood, 1999).
McNamara, Kevin R., ed., *The Cambridge Companion to the Literature of Los Angeles* (Cambridge: Cambridge University Press, 2010).
McNary, Dave, 'Mel Brooks Basks in the Glory of *Young Frankenstein* at the Academy', in *Variety Online*, 10 September 2014.
<http://variety.com/2014/scene/news/mel-brooks-young-frankenstein-academy-1201302418/>
McWeeny, Drew, 'If You Didn't Already Love Mel Brooks, This May Change Your Mind', in *HitFix*, 12 May 2014.

<http://www.hitfix.com/motion-captured/mel-brooks-discusses-blazing-saddles-brooksfilms-and-the-best-screening-ever/single-page>

Miller, Elizabeth, *A Dracula Handbook* (Bloomington: Xlibris, 2005).

Min, Eunjung, ed., *Reading the Homeless: The Media's Image of Homeless Culture* (Westport: Prager, 1999).

Mishra, Vijay, *The Gothic Sublime* (Albany: State University of New York Press, 1994).

Moore, Deborah Dash, and S. Ilan Troen, eds, *Divergent Jewish Cultures: Israel and America* (New Haven: Yale University Press, 2008).

Morey, Kathryn Anne, ed., *Bringing History to Life through Film: The Art of Cinematic Storytelling* (Lanham: Rowman and Littlefield, 2014).

Morsberger, Katharine M., and Robert E. Morsberger, 'Robin Hood on Film: Can We Ever Again "Make Them Like They Used To"?', in *Playing Robin Hood: The Legend as Performance in Five Centuries*, ed. by Lois Potter (Cranbury: Associated University Presses, 1998), pp. 205-231.

Murray, Noel, 'Dracula: Dead and Loving It', in *The Onion AV Club*, 25 October 2006.
<http://www.avclub.com/article/dracula-dead-and-loving-it-22348>

Music, Carla Lalli, 'Mel Brooks on Omelettes, Coffee, and the Inimitable Appetite of Alfred Hitchcock', in *Bon Appetit*, 17 May 2013.
<http://www.bonappetit.com/people/celebrities/article/mel-brooks-on-omelettes-coffee-and-the-inimitable-appetite-of-alfred-hitchcock>

Meyers, Kate, 'Mel's Awfully Funny In Here', in *Entertainment Weekly*, 28 June 1996.
<http://www.brookslyn.com/print/EntWeekly06-28-96/EntWeekly06-28-96.php>

Naugle, Patrick, 'Dracula: Dead and Loving It', in *DVD Verdict*, 2 July 2004.
<http://www.dvdverdict.com/reviews/draculadeadandlovingit.php>

—, 'History of the World: Part I', in *DVD Verdict*, 20 May 2010.
<http://www.dvdverdict.com/reviews/historyworldpartibluray.php>

—, 'Life Stinks', in *DVD Verdict*, 18 February 2003.
<http://www.dvdverdict.com/reviews/lifestinks.php>

Nelson-Jones, Richard, *Effective Thinking Skills* (London: Sage Publications, 2004) [1996].

Nilsen, Don L.F., 'Humorous Contemporary Jewish-American Authors', in *MELUS*, Vol. 21, No. 4, Winter 1996, pp. 71-101.

Norwitz, Leonard, 'LensViews: Robin Hood Men in Tights', in *DVD Beaver*, 15 May 2010.
<http://www.dvdbeaver.com/film3/blu-ray_reviews51/robin_hood_men_in_tights_blu-ray.htm>

Nöth, Winfried, ed., *Semiotics of the Media: State of the Art, Projects, and Perspectives* (Berlin: Walter de Gruyter, 1997).

Oring, Elliott, 'Risky Business: Political Jokes under Repressive Regimes', in *Western Folklore*, Vol. 63, No. 3, Summer 2004, pp. 209-36.

Ott, Brian L., and Beth Bonnstetter, '"We're at Now, Now": Spaceballs as Parodic Tourism', in *Southern Communication Journal*, Vol. 72, No. 4, October-December 2007, pp. 309-27.

Panton, Gary, '*Spaceballs*: Movie Review', in *Movie Gazette*, 6 April 2005.
<http://movie-gazette.com/1269>

Parish, James Robert, *It's Good to Be the King: The Seriously Funny Life of Mel Brooks* (Hoboken: John Wiley and Sons, 2007).

Picart, Caroline Joan S., *Remaking the Frankenstein Myth on Film: Between Laughter and Horror* (Albany: State University of New York Press, 2003).

Plath, James, '*High Anxiety*', in *Movie Metropolis*, 14 May 2010.
<http://moviemet.com/review/high-anxiety-blu-ray-review>

—, 'History of the World Part 1', in *Movie Metropolis*, 16 May 2010.
<http://moviemet.com/review/history-world-part-1-blu-ray-review>

Potter, Lois, ed., *Playing Robin Hood: The Legend as Performance in Five Centuries*

(Cranbury: Associated University Presses, 1998).

Powrie, Phil, and Robynn Stilwell, eds, *Changing Tunes: The Use of Pre-Existing Music in Film* (Aldershot: Ashgate Publishing, 2006).

Prince, Stephen, ed., *American Cinema of the 1980s: Themes and Variations* (New Brunswick: Rutgers University Press, 2007).

Puccio, John J., '*Dracula: Dead and Loving It*', in *Movie Metropolis*, 29 June 2004.
<http://moviemet.com/review/dracula-dead-and-loving-it-dvd-review>

—, '*The Twelve Chairs*', in *Movie Metropolis*, 1 January 2000.
<http://moviemet.com/review/twelve-chairs-dvd-review>

Pugh, Tison, and Angela Jane Weisl, *Medievalisms: Making the Past in the Present* (Abingdon: Routledge, 2013), p. 78.

Rabin, Nathan, '*The Mel Brooks Collection*', in *The Onion AV Club*, 11 April 2006.
<http://www.avclub.com/review/the-mel-brooks-collection-9121>

—, '*The Producers*', in *The Onion AV Club*, 13 December 2002.
<http://www.avclub.com/review/the-producers-12196>

Rhodes, Chip, 'Hollywood Fictions', in *The Cambridge Companion to the Literature of Los Angeles*, ed. by Kevin R. McNamara (Cambridge: Cambridge University Press, 2010), 135-44, p. 135.

Ring, Robert C., *Sci-Fi Movie Freak* (Iola: Krause Publications, 2011).

Robbins, Fred, 'What Makes Mel Brooks Run?' in *Show*, 17 September 1970, pp. 12-15.

Roberts, Graham, and Heather Wallis, *Key Film Texts* (London: Arnold, 2002).

Rollins, Peter C., and John E. O'Connor, eds, *Hollywood's West: The American Frontier in Film, Television and History* (Lexington: The University Press of Kentucky, 2005).

Roman, James, *Bigger Than Blockbusters: The Movies that Defined America* (Westport: Greenwood Press, 2009).

Rosenbaum, Jonathan, '*High Anxiety*', in *The Chicago Reader*, January 2000.
<http://www.chicagoreader.com/chicago/high-anxiety/Film?oid=1063372>

—, *Movies as Politics* (Berkeley: University of California Press, 1997).

Rubino, Michael, '*Spaceballs*: 25th Anniversary', in *DVD Verdict*, 28 August 2012.
<http://www.dvdverdict.com/reviews/spaceballs25thbluray.php>

Rugg, Rebecca Ann, *What It Used to Be: Nostalgia and the State of the Broadway Musical*, in *Theater*, Vol. 32, No. 2, Summer 2002, pp. 44-55.

Rushing, Janice Hocker, 'The Rhetoric of the American Western Myth', in *Communication Monographs*, Issue 50, 1983, pp. 14-32.

Salmi, Hannu, ed., *Historical Comedy on Screen: Subverting History with Humour* (Bristol: Intellect, 2011).

—, 'Introduction: The Mad History of the World', in *Historical Comedy on Screen: Subverting History with Humour*, ed. by Hannu Salmi (Bristol: Intellect, 2011), pp. 7-30.

Sanders, Steven M., ed., *The Philosophy of Science Fiction Film* (Lexington: The University Press of Kentucky, 2008).

Sarkhosh, Keyvan, 'Metalepsis in Popular Comedy Film', in *Metalepsis in Popular Culture*, ed. by Karin Kukkonen and Sonja Klimek (Berlin: Walter de Gruyter Ltd., 2011), pp. 171-95.

Scheer, Laurie, *Creative Careers in Hollywood* (New York: Allworth Press, 2002).

Schickel, Richard, 'Cinema: Hi-Ho, Mel', in *Time Magazine*, 4 March 1974.
<http://content.time.com/time/magazine/article/0,9171,944788,00.html>

—, 'Cinema: Lost in Space', in *Time Magazine*, 13 July 1987.
<http://content.time.com/time/magazine/article/0,9171,964962,00.html>

—, 'Critic's Roundup', in *Life*, 18 December 1970, pp. 6-7.

Scholl, Jaye, 'Will It Play in Peoria?: Mel Brooks Gets Ready for His Wall Street Debut', in *Barron's*, 15 January 1990.
<http://www.brookslyn.com/print/Barrons1990/Barrons1990.php>

Schor, Esther, 'Frankenstein and Film', in *The Cambridge Companion to Mary Shelley*, ed. by Esther Schor (Cambridge: Cambridge University Press, 2003), pp. 63-83.

—, ed., *The Cambridge Companion to Mary Shelley* (Cambridge: Cambridge University Press, 2003).

Schmidt, Steve, '2,037 – and Counting', in *The Los Angeles Times*, 25 May 1997.
<http://www.brookslyn.com/print/LATimes05-25-97/LATimes05-25-97.php>

Schultz, Deanne, *Filmography of World History* (Westport: Greenwood Press, 2007).

Shaffer, Alan Kennedy, '*The Producers*', in *Movies in American History: An Encyclopedia: Volume 1*, ed. by Philip C. DiMare (Santa Barbara: ABC-CLIO, 2011), 400-02, p. 401.

Shulgasser, Barbara, 'Brooks Gives *Dracula* a Little Bite', in *The San Francisco Chronicle*, 22 December 1995.
<http://www.sfgate.com/news/article/Brooks-gives-Dracula-a-little-bite-3115591.php>

Shute, Nancy, 'Mel Brooks: His Humor Brings Down Hitler, and the House', in *U.S. News and World Report*, 20-27 August 2001, p. 71.

Siegel, Larry, 'Interview: Mel Brooks', in *Playboy*, October 1966.
<http://www.brookslyn.com/print/PlayboyOct1966/PlayboyOct1966.php>

Simon, John, 'Movies: Unbabbling Brooks', in *New York Magazine*, 19 July 1976, pp. 84-88.

Singer, Matt, '*Dracula: Dead and Loving It* (and Loving It)', in *CriticWire*, 15 May 2013.
<http://blogs.indiewire.com/criticwire/dracula-dead-and-loving-it-and-loving-it>

Sitney, P. Adams, *Visionary Film: The American Avant-Garde, 1943-2000* (Oxford: Oxford University Press, 2002).

Slifkin, Irv, '*The Producers*', in *VideoHound's Groovy Movies: Far-out Films of the Psychedelic Era*, ed. by Irv Slifkin (Canton: Invisible Ink Press, 2004), pp. 378-80.

—, ed., *VideoHound's Groovy Movies: Far-out Films of the Psychedelic Era* (Canton: Invisible Ink Press, 2004).

Sinyard, Neil, *The Films of Mel Brooks* (New York: Exeter Books, 1988).

Skal, David J., *Hollywood Gothic: The Tangled Web of Dracula from Novel to Stage to Screen*, rev. edn. (New York: Faber and Faber, 2004) [1990].

Smurthwaite, Nick, and Paul Gelder, *Mel Brooks and the Spoof Movie* (London: Proteus Books, 1982).

Sollors, Werner, *Beyond Ethnicity: Consent and Descent in American Culture* (Oxford: Oxford University Press, 1986).

Squire, Jason E., ed., *The Movie Business Book*, 3rd edn (Maidenhead: Open University Press, 2006).

Sragow, Michael, 'The Not-So-Flip Side of Mel Brooks: He's Serious About Producing', in *Rolling Stone*, 14 October 1982.
<http://www.brookslyn.com/print/RollingStone10-14-82/RollingStone10-14-82.php>

Stam, Robert, and Alessandra Raengo, eds, *A Companion to Literature and Film* (Oxford: Blackwell, 2004).

Stauth, Cameron, 'Illuminations: Mel and Me', in *American Film*, April 1990.
<http://www.brookslyn.com/print/AmericanFilm1990/AmericanFilm1990.php>

Stein, Erica, '"A Hell of a Place": The Everyday as Revisionist Content in Contemporary Westerns', in *Mediascape: UCLA's Journal of Cinema and Media Studies*, No. 3, Fall 2009.
<http://www.tft.ucla.edu/mediascape/fall09_western.html>

Stephenson, Pamela, *The Varnished Untruth* (London: Simon and Schuster, 2012).

Sternbergh, Adam, 'History of *The Producers*: Part III', in *New York Magazine*, 12 December 2005.
<http://nymag.com/nymetro/movies/features/15251/>

Stone, Emily, *Did Jew Know?: A Handy Primer on the Customs, Culture & Practice of the Chosen People* (San Francisco: Chronicle Books, 2014).

Stone, Judith, 'The Shtick of Shticks', in *New York Magazine*, 6 October 1997. <http://www.brookslyn.com/print/NewYork10-06-97/NewYork10-06-97.php>

Strumer, Andre Marc, 'The Creatures of the Night: Vampires from Books to Films' (unpublished doctoral thesis, The University of Southern Mississippi, July 2008).

Susman, Gary, 'Mel Brooks on *Blazing Saddles* at 40, Richard Pryor's Genius, and Keeping His Edge at 87', in *Moviefone*, 20 May 2014. <http://news.moviefone.com/2014/05/20/mel-brooks-blazing-saddles-richard-pryor/>

Symons, Alex, 'An Audience for Mel Brooks's *The Producers*: The Avant-Garde of the Masses', in *Journal of Popular Film and Television*, Vol. 34, No. 1, 2006, pp. 24-32.

—, *Mel Brooks in the Cultural Industries: Survival and Prolonged Adaptation* (Edinburgh: Edinburgh University Press, 2012).

—, 'The Prolonged Celebrity of Mel Brooks: Adapting to Survive in the Multimedia Marketplace, 1961-2004', in *Celebrity Studies*, Vol. 2, Issue 3, 2011, pp. 335-52.

Tiffin, George, *All the Best Lines: An Informal History of the Movies in Quotes, Notes and Anecdotes* (London: Head of Zeus, 2013).

Tobias, Scott, '*Blazing Saddles*', in *The Onion AV Club*, 28 June 2004. <http://www.avclub.com/review/blazing-saddles-11389>

—, '*Spaceballs*', in *The Onion AV Club*, 8 July 2009. <http://www.avclub.com/review/spaceballs-30101>

Troen, S. Ilan, 'The Construction of a Secular Jewish Identity: European and American Influences in Irsaeli Education', in *Divergent Jewish Cultures: Israel and America*, ed. by Deborah Dash Moore and S. Ilan Troen (New Haven: Yale University Press, 2008), pp. 27-52.

Tueth, Michael V., *Reeling with Laughter: American Film Comedies – From Anarchy to Mockumentary* (Plymouth: Scarecrow Press, 2012).

Turner, Matthew R., 'Cowboys and Comedy: The Simultaneous Deconstruction and Reinforcement of Generic Conventions in the Western Parody', in *Film & History: An Interdisciplinary Journal of Film and Television Studies*, Vol. 33, No. 2, 2003, pp. 48-54.

Turner, Matthew R., 'Cowboys and Comedy: The Simultaneous Deconstruction and Reinforcement of Generic Conventions in the Western Parody', in *Hollywood's West: The American Frontier in Film, Television and History*, ed. by Peter C. Rollins and John E. O'Connor (Lexington: The University Press of Kentucky, 2005), pp. 218-38.

Tynan, Kenneth, 'Profiles: Frolics and Detours of a Short Hebrew Man', in *The New Yorker*, 30 October 1978, p. 46.

Ulin, David, 'Banterweight Champs', in *The Los Angeles Times*, 27 February 1998. <http://www.brookslyn.com/print/LATimes02-27-98/LATimes02-27-98.php>

Vacche, Angela Dalle, *Film, Art, New Media: Museum Without Walls?* (New York: Palgrave Macmillan, 2012).

Venable, Nick, 'Rick Moranis Talks The *Spaceballs* Sequel That Never Was', in *CinemaBlend*, 24 June 2013. <http://www.cinemablend.com/new/Rick-Moranis-Talks-Spaceballs-Sequel-Never-Was-38212.html>

Weinberg, Marc, 'Failing Film Makers', in *Orange Coast Magazine*, July 1987, pp. 189-191.

Weinstock, Jeffrey Andrew, *The Ashgate Encyclopedia of Literary and Cinematic Monsters* (Farnham: Ashgate Publishing, 2014).

White, Timothy, '*Producers* Producer: The Man Behind a Classic', in *Billboard*, 26 April 1997, p. 1; pp. 86-88.

Whitfield, Stephen J., 'The Distinctiveness of American Jewish Humor', in *Modern Judaism*, Vol. 6, No. 3, October 1986, pp. 245-60.

Wickline, Dan, 'Mel Brooks Is The Six Fingered Man... Someone Call Inigo Montoya', in *Bleeding Cool*, 9 September 2014.
<http://www.bleedingcool.com/2014/09/09/mel-brooks-is-the-six-fingered-man-someone-call-inigo-montoya/>

Willis, John, 'The Producers', in *Screen World 1968*, ed. by John Willis (New York: Biblo and Tannen Publishers, 1983), p. 86.

—, ed., *Screen World 1968* (New York: Biblo and Tannen Publishers, 1983).

Wilstein, Matt, 'Mel Brooks: I would Never Get Away with Using "N-Word" on Screen Today', in *Mediaite*, 14 May 2014.
<http://www.mediaite.com/tv/mel-brooks-i-would-never-get-away-with-using-n-word-on-screen-today/>

Wise, Damon, 'The Making of *The Producers*', in *The Guardian*, 16 August 2008.
<http://www.theguardian.com/film/2008/aug/16/comedy.theproducers>

Withalm, Gloria, '"How Did You Find Us?" – "We Read the Script!": A Special Case of Self-Reference in the Movies', in *Semiotics of the Media: State of the Art, Projects, and Perspectives*, ed. by Winfried Nöth (Berlin: Walter de Gruyter, 1997), pp. 255-268.

Yacowar, Maurice, *The Comic Art of Mel Brooks* (London: W.H. Allen, 1982).

Zimmerman, Paul D., 'The Mad Mad Mel Brooks', in *Newsweek*, 17 February 1975.
<http://www.brookslyn.com/print/Newsweek02-15-1975/Newsweek02-17-1975.php>

Zimmerman, Steve, *Food in the Movies*, 2nd edn (Jefferson: McFarland, 2010).

About the Author

Dr Thomas Christie has a life-long fascination with films
and the people who make them. A member of the Royal Society of
Literature and the Society of Authors, he holds an M.A. in Humanities
with British Cinema History from the Open University of Milton Keynes,
and a Ph.D. in Scottish Literature awarded by the University of Stirling.

Thomas Christie is the author of *Liv Tyler, Star in Ascendance:
Her First Decade in Film* (2007), *The Cinema of Richard Linklater* (2008),
*John Hughes and Eighties Cinema* (2009), *Ferris Bueller's Day Off: Pocket
Movie Guide* (2010) and *The Christmas Movie Book* (2011), all of which are
published by Crescent Moon Publishing. A study of Mel Brooks
is forthcoming.

For more information about Tom and his books, visit his website
at www.tomchristiebooks.co.uk.

Thomas A. Christie

# JOHN HUGHES
# & EIGHTIES CINEMA
## Teenage Hopes & American Dreams

**John Hughes** (1950-2009) is one of the best-loved figures in 1980s American filmmaking, and considered by many to be among the finest and most celebrated comedy writers of his generation. His memorable motion pictures are insightful, humanistic, culturally aware, and paint a vibrant picture of the United States in a decade of rapid social and political change.

Bibliography, notes, illustrations   372pp.
ISBN 9781861713896 Pbk   ISBN 9781861713988 Hbk
Also available: *Ferris Bueller's Day Off: Pocket Movie Guide*

# Arseny Tarkovsky

### Selected Poems

**Arseny Tarkovsky** is the neglected Russian poet, father of the acclaimed film director Andrei Tarkovsky. This new book gathers together many of Tarkovsky's most lyrical and heartfelt poems, in Virginia Rounding's new, clear translations. Many of Tarkovsky's poems appeared in his son's films, such as *Mirror*, *Stalker*, *Nostalghia* and *The Sacrifice*. There is an introduction by Rounding, and a bibliography of both Arseny and Andrei Tarkovsky.

Illustrated. Bibliography and notes.
ISBN 9781816171114 Pbk   ISBN 9781861712660 Hbk

# Beauties, Beasts, and Enchantment

## CLASSIC FRENCH FAIRY TALES

*Translated and with an Introduction*
by Jack Zipes

A collection of 36 classic French fairy tales translated by renowned writer Jack Zipes. *Cinderella, Beauty and the Beast, Sleeping Beauty* and *Little Red Riding Hood* are among the classic fairy tales in this amazing book.
Includes illustrations from fairy tale collections.
Jack Zipes has written and published widely on fairy tales.

'Terrific... a succulent array of 17th and 18th century 'salon' fairy tales'
- *The New York Times Book Review*

'These tales are adventurous, thrilling in a way fairy tales are meant to be... The translation from the French is modern, happily free of archaic and hyperbolic language... a fine and sophisticated collection' - *New York Tribune*

'Enjoyable to read... a unique collection of French regional folklore' - *Library Journal*

'Charming stories accompanied by attractive pen-and-ink drawings' - *Chattanooga Times*

Introduction and illustrations   612pp.   ISBN 9781861712510 Pbk   ISBN 9781861713193 Hbk

# CRESCENT MOON PUBLISHING

web: www.crmoon.com e-mail: cresmopub@yahoo.co.uk

## ARTS, PAINTING, SCULPTURE

The Art of Andy Goldsworthy
Andy Goldsworthy: Touching Nature
Andy Goldsworthy in Close-Up
Andy Goldsworthy: Pocket Guide
Andy Goldsworthy In America
Land Art: A Complete Guide
The Art of Richard Long
Richard Long: Pocket Guide
Land Art In the UK
Land Art in Close-Up
Land Art In the U.S.A.
Land Art: Pocket Guide
Installation Art in Close-Up
Minimal Art and Artists In the 1960s and After
Colourfield Painting
Land Art DVD, TV documentary
Andy Goldsworthy DVD, TV documentary
The Erotic Object: Sexuality in Sculpture From Prehistory to the Present Day
Sex in Art: Pornography and Pleasure in Painting and Sculpture
Postwar Art
Sacred Gardens: The Garden in Myth, Religion and Art
Glorification: Religious Abstraction in Renaissance and 20th Century Art
Early Netherlandish Painting
Leonardo da Vinci
Piero della Francesca
Giovanni Bellini
Fra Angelico: Art and Religion in the Renaissance
Mark Rothko: The Art of Transcendence
Frank Stella: American Abstract Artist
Jasper Johns
Brice Marden
Alison Wilding: The Embrace of Sculpture
Vincent van Gogh: Visionary Landscapes
Eric Gill: Nuptials of God
Constantin Brancusi: Sculpting the Essence of Things
Max Beckmann
Caravaggio
Gustave Moreau
Egon Schiele: Sex and Death In Purple Stockings
Delizioso Fotografico Fervore: Works In Process 1
Sacro Cuore: Works In Process 2
The Light Eternal: J.M.W. Turner
The Madonna Glorified: Karen Arthurs

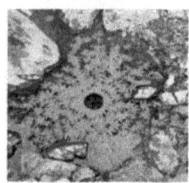

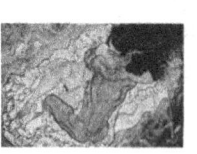

## LITERATURE

J.R.R. Tolkien: The Books, The Films, The Whole Cultural Phenomenon
J.R.R. Tolkien: Pocket Guide
Tolkien's Heroic Quest
The *Earthsea* Books of Ursula Le Guin
Beauties, Beasts and Enchantment: Classic French Fairy Tales
German Popular Stories by the Brothers Grimm
Philip Pullman and *His Dark Materials*
Sexing Hardy: Thomas Hardy and Feminism
Thomas Hardy's *Tess of the d'Urbervilles*
Thomas Hardy's *Jude the Obscure*
Thomas Hardy: The Tragic Novels
Love and Tragedy: Thomas Hardy
The Poetry of Landscape in Hardy
Wessex Revisited: Thomas Hardy and John Cowper Powys
Wolfgang Iser: Essays and Interviews
Petrarch, Dante and the Troubadours
Maurice Sendak and the Art of Children's Book Illustration
Andrea Dworkin
Cixous, Irigaray, Kristeva: The *Jouissance* of French Feminism
Julia Kristeva: Art, Love, Melancholy, Philosophy, Semiotics and Psychoanalysis
Hélene Cixous I Love You: The *Jouissance* of Writing
Luce Irigaray: Lips, Kissing, and the Politics of Sexual Difference
Peter Redgrove: Here Comes the Flood
Peter Redgrove: Sex-Magic-Poetry-Cornwall
Lawrence Durrell: Between Love and Death, East and West
Love, Culture & Poetry: Lawrence Durrell
Cavafy: Anatomy of a Soul
German Romantic Poetry: Goethe, Novalis, Heine, Hölderlin
Feminism and Shakespeare
Shakespeare: Love, Poetry & Magic
The Passion of D.H. Lawrence
D.H. Lawrence: Symbolic Landscapes
D.H. Lawrence: Infinite Sensual Violence
Rimbaud: Arthur Rimbaud and the Magic of Poetry
The Ecstasies of John Cowper Powys
Sensualism and Mythology: The Wessex Novels of John Cowper Powys
Amorous Life: John Cowper Powys and the Manifestation of Affectivity (H.W. Fawkner)
Postmodern Powys: New Essays on John Cowper Powys (Joe Boulter)
Rethinking Powys: Critical Essays on John Cowper Powys
Paul Bowles & Bernardo Bertolucci
Rainer Maria Rilke
Joseph Conrad: *Heart of Darkness*
In the Dim Void: Samuel Beckett
Samuel Beckett Goes into the Silence
André Gide: Fiction and Fervour
Jackie Collins and the Blockbuster Novel
Blinded By Her Light: The Love-Poetry of Robert Graves
The Passion of Colours: Travels In Mediterranean Lands
Poetic Forms

## POETRY

Ursula Le Guin: Walking In Cornwall
Peter Redgrove: Here Comes The Flood
Peter Redgrove: Sex-Magic-Poetry-Cornwall
Dante: Selections From the Vita Nuova
Petrarch, Dante and the Troubadours
William Shakespeare: Sonnets
William Shakespeare: Complete Poems
Blinded By Her Light: The Love-Poetry of Robert Graves
Emily Dickinson: Selected Poems
Emily Brontë: Poems
Thomas Hardy: Selected Poems
Percy Bysshe Shelley: Poems
John Keats: Selected Poems
Joh n Keats: Poems of 1820
D.H. Lawrence: Selected Poems
Edmund Spenser: Poems
Edmund Spenser: Amoretti
John Donne: Poems
Henry Vaughan: Poems
Sir Thomas Wyatt: Poems
Robert Herrick: Selected Poems
Rilke: Space, Essence and Angels in the Poetry of Rainer Maria Rilke
Rainer Maria Rilke: Selected Poems
Friedrich Hölderlin: Selected Poems
Arseny Tarkovsky: Selected Poems
Arthur Rimbaud: Selected Poems
Arthur Rimbaud: A Season in Hell
Arthur Rimbaud and the Magic of Poetry
Novalis: Hymns To the Night
German Romantic Poetry
Paul Verlaine: Selected Poems
Elizaethan Sonnet Cycles
D.J. Enright: By-Blows
Jeremy Reed: Brigitte's Blue Heart
Jeremy Reed: Claudia Schiffer's Red Shoes
Gorgeous Little Orpheus
Radiance: New Poems
Crescent Moon Book of Nature Poetry
Crescent Moon Book of Love Poetry
Crescent Moon Book of Mystical Poetry
Crescent Moon Book of Elizabethan Love Poetry
Crescent Moon Book of Metaphysical Poetry
Crescent Moon Book of Romantic Poetry
Pagan America: New American Poetry

## MEDIA, CINEMA, FEMINISM and CULTURAL STUDIES

J.R.R. Tolkien: The Books, The Films, The Whole Cultural Phenomenon
J.R.R. Tolkien: Pocket Guide
The *Lord of the Rings* Movies: Pocket Guide
The Cinema of Hayao Miyazaki
Hayao Miyazaki: *Princess Mononoke*: Pocket Movie Guide
Hayao Miyazaki: *Spirited Away*: Pocket Movie Guide
Tim Burton : Hallowe'en For Hollywood
Ken Russell
Ken Russell: *Tommy*: Pocket Movie Guide
The Ghost Dance: The Origins of Religion
The Peyote Cult
Cixous, Irigaray, Kristeva: The *Jouissance* of French Feminism
Julia Kristeva: Art, Love, Melancholy, Philosophy, Semiotics and Psychoanalysis
Luce Irigaray: Lips, Kissing, and the Politics of Sexual Difference
Hélene Cixous I Love You: The *Jouissance* of Writing
Andrea Dworkin
'Cosmo Woman': The World of Women's Magazines
Women in Pop Music
HomeGround: The Kate Bush Anthology
Discovering the Goddess (Geoffrey Ashe)
The Poetry of Cinema
The Sacred Cinema of Andrei Tarkovsky
Andrei Tarkovsky: Pocket Guide
Andrei Tarkovsky: *Mirror*: Pocket Movie Guide
Andrei Tarkovsky: *The Sacrifice*: Pocket Movie Guide
Walerian Borowczyk: Cinema of Erotic Dreams
Jean-Luc Godard: The Passion of Cinema
Jean-Luc Godard: *Hail Mary*: Pocket Movie Guide
Jean-Luc Godard: *Contempt*: Pocket Movie Guide
Jean-Luc Godard: *Pierrot le Fou*: Pocket Movie Guide
John Hughes and Eighties Cinema
*Ferris Bueller's Day Off*: Pocket Movie Guide
Jean-Luc Godard: Pocket Guide
The Cinema of Richard Linklater
Liv Tyler: Star In Ascendance
*Blade Runner* and the Films of Philip K. Dick
Paul Bowles and Bernardo Bertolucci
Media Hell: Radio, TV and the Press
An Open Letter to the BBC
Detonation Britain: Nuclear War in the UK
Feminism and Shakespeare
Wild Zones: Pornography, Art and Feminism
Sex in Art: Pornography and Pleasure in Painting and Sculpture
Sexing Hardy: Thomas Hardy and Feminism

*The Light Eternal* is a model monograph, an exemplary job. The subject matter of the book is beautifully organised and dead on beam. (Lawrence Durrell)
It is amazing for me to see my work treated with such passion and respect. (Andrea Dworkin)

### CRESCENT MOON PUBLISHING
P.O. Box 1312, Maidstone, Kent, ME14 5XU, Great Britain. www.crmoon.com

cresmopub@yahoo.co.uk   www.crescentmoon.org.uk

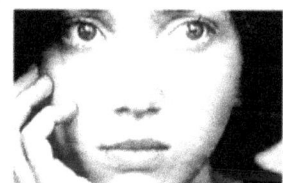
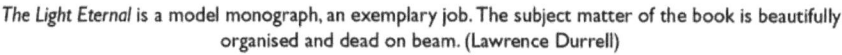

www.ingramcontent.com/pod-product-compliance
Lightning Source LLC
Chambersburg PA
CBHW070604170426
43200CB00012B/2582